CW00797227

Dante's Bones

Dante's Bones

How a *Poet*

Invented

Italy

Guy P. Raffa

THE BELKNAP PRESS OF HARVARD UNIVERSITY PRESS

Cambridge, Massachusetts

London, England

2020

Library of Congress Cataloging-in-Publication Data

Names: Raffa, Guy P., author.
Title: Dante's bones : how a poet invented Italy / Guy P. Raffa.
Description: Cambridge, Massachusetts : The Belknap Press of Harvard
University Press, 2020. | Includes bibliographical references and index.
Identifiers: LCCN 2019049287 | ISBN 9780674980839 (cloth)
Subjects: LCSH: Dante Alighieri, 1265–1321—Relics. | Dante Alighieri, 1265–1321—Death
and burial. | Dante Alighieri, 1265–1321—Tomb. | National characteristics, Italian.
Classification: LCC PQ4355.6 .R34 2020 | DDC 851/.1—dc23
LC record available at https://lccn.loc.gov/2019049287

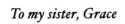

To my sister, Grace

Contents

Author's Note

In Dante's journey through Hell, he encounters a monster so amazing that he fears inciting disbelief in his readers (and shame for himself) should he tell what he sees: Geryon, whose honest human face is attached to a colorful serpentine trunk with leonine paws and a scorpion's tail, swimming up from the circle of fraud through the heavy, dark, infernal air.

Dante, being Dante, swears on the verses of his poem that this truly happened.

A mere scholar, I can only promise this: to the best of my knowledge, all the events in this book are true. The characters, for better and worse, are real people purported to have said and done what is recorded in the following pages.

Nonetheless I'm frightfully aware that, for certain episodes, even the best available sources of information are vague, incomplete, obscure, or blatantly contradictory—sometimes all at once. I aim, above all, to clear a path through the shadowed wood of Dante's graveyard history, but not necessarily a straight one: strange twists and knotty complications are an essential feature of the story, and they deserve respect. Does my reconstruction of this history at times veer toward conjecture, no matter how well informed or well intentioned? Guilty as charged. If and when new discoveries provide greater understanding, no one will be more pleased than I to join Dante's Virgil in proclaiming, "Let no falsehood deceive the truth!"

Dante's Bones

— Prologue —

A DISCOVERY OF BONES

We live in an age when miracles are no longer admissible, and when any approach to the marvellous immediately excites suspicion.

—HENRY CLARK BARLOW

Soon after Florence hosted national celebrations of Dante's six hundredth birthday in 1865, Ravenna planned for its own festivities by playing its strongest card: Dante was buried there. Florence claimed the glory of being his native city, but Ravenna boasted of having provided a welcoming home for the poet in his final years precisely because Florence had sentenced its gifted son to a life of exile. Dante had died in Ravenna, so it was only right for the city that had given him refuge in life to keep watch over his dead bones. This simple truth gave Ravenna a way to commemorate the poet's milestone birthday—and by extension his life—available to no other place in Italy. The city therefore prepared to celebrate Dante's entrance into the world by renovating the area around the most tangible sign of his earthly exit: his gravesite.

The poet's marble tomb, a plain affair for such a great man, was set in the back of the mortuary chapel—a modest neoclassical structure topped by a small dome—built by Camillo Morigia in 1780–1782. Over eight decades later, Dante's humble abode needed a fresh coat of paint and other touch-ups in addition to several repairs. Hemmed in by the cloister of the old Franciscan convent, the Church of Saint Francis, and the freestanding Braccioforte chapel, the poet's mausoleum also needed more room to breathe. Authorities in Ravenna first thought to create this space by demolishing Braccioforte, the imposing quadrangular structure standing less than thirty feet away from the sepulcher. However, further investigation into the area's architectural history resulted in a modified plan.

The Braccioforte chapel turned out to have ancient origins worthy of its name. Two good friends, the legend went, once secretly arranged for a loan in the sacred space, back then decorated with an image of Jesus (one arm extended) flanked by Saints Peter and Paul. The lender called on the "strong and terrible arm of the Savior" to serve as guarantor of the loan, with Peter and Paul as witnesses. But the borrower, after quadrupling the money in business, traveled to Constantinople and, not wanting to return to Ravenna, missed the deadline for repaying the loan. This default caused the lender to accuse God's holy image of neglecting its duty. With your "strong arm," he rebuked the Lord, "can you not compel even one man?" His assertiveness paid off handsomely, for God appeared in the wayward borrower's dream, the Lord's "strong arm"—*bracchium forte*—leading him back to Ravenna to satisfy his debt, and then some. The borrower added one hundred gold coins to the original sum, after which the two friends wept and kissed and "went in peace." From that day forward the chapel had been called *Braccioforte*.[1]

Filippo Lanciani, chief of the Corps of Civil Engineers in Ravenna, and Romolo Conti, the head municipal engineer, directed the renovations. Lanciani, who had held his post since 1860, was known for exercising caution when working around ancient buildings and monuments, urging "patience" and "abnegation" above all: "patience in seeking in each vestige, in each ruin, the preexisting forms; abnegation in rejecting one's own ideas and accepting the very modest task of the restorer and imitator."[2] As soon as Lanciani learned of architectural remnants around Braccioforte dating to the fourth or fifth century CE, he wisely decided not to remove the chapel completely from the scene. But he broke with his conservative philosophy by having workers tear down all but the thick corner pillars from the building's sides. The chapel was thus converted into a portico with four graceful arches where the solid walls had once stood. At the same time, Lanciani sought more precise information on the history of Braccioforte by ordering excavations of the original front wall, just off the main entrance to the chapel.[3]

Even skeptical observers could be pardoned for thinking some higher power lent a strong hand, if not an entire arm, to these operations. The catalyst for what would be called a miracle was precisely an arm, but this *braccio* was neither divine nor human. The Italian word also refers to inanimate limbs, such as the arm or lever of a tool or device. In this case, the influential arm was the handle of a mechanical pump used to remove excess water from the work site around the old wall of the Braccioforte chapel.

The twenty-seventh day of May fell on a Saturday in 1865. Dante, who tells us in the *Divine Comedy* that he is a Gemini, was probably born at the end of May—perhaps on that very day—six hundred years earlier.[4] With Ravenna's Dante festivities only weeks away, this Saturday was just another workday. But there was nothing normal about it. The original front—or southern—wall of Braccioforte abutted the Rasponi chapel (formerly the Fantuzzi chapel) off the left-hand side of the Church of Saint Francis. A piece of this wall jutted out from a corner of the Rasponi chapel, rising some five feet above the original floor of the Braccioforte chapel. Engineers Lanciani and Conti searched around the remains of this wall for clues to the chapel's origins.

Pio di Luigi Feletti, a master stone mason, led the work crew that morning. Fedele Spada, another master mason, also took part in the excavations, and Angelo Dradi helped with the manual labor. Giovanni Battista Lorenzatti, a city official, oversaw the work and reported back to the engineers. Maneuvering in the tight corner where the two chapels met, the masons used water to clean the stone surfaces and wash away dust and debris created by the pounding, scraping, and chipping of bricks and mortar. Before long, water collecting in the excavated area around the base of the wall began to impede progress by turning the site into a muddy ditch. Pio Feletti brought in the pump to drain the standing water so work could proceed. But the pump's handle was too long for the area's narrow confines. Blocking this mechanical arm were bricks on the outside of the Braccioforte wall—bricks used to cover the doorway that once allowed passage between the chapel and the cemetery. What happened next can be reconstructed from information recorded in official and personal documents of the time supplemented by likely if imagined details.[5]

It was still early in the day, not yet ten o'clock, when Lorenzatti, the city official on the scene, ordered head mason Feletti to create space for the pump handle by removing several obstructing bricks. Feletti swung his pickax at the wall, the first blows echoing in the enclosed area with the sharp ringing of metal on stone and mortar. After he dislodged a brick with the pointed edge of his tool, his next strike produced a different sound altogether, more of a hollow thud than a high-pitched clang. Perplexed, he alternately used his hands and the pickax to remove loosened bricks until a wood board came into view. He then saw what looked like an entire box or chest. The mason, growing more excited by the moment, tried to lift out the box when suddenly its outermost plank snapped off, releasing the contents. The split second it took for the objects to fall into the muddy water at Feletti's feet was enough for him to guess what they were: human bones.

Even before Feletti had time to formulate the question—"Whose bones?"—the board that broke off spelled out an answer like a sign from above: *Dantis ossa*. Those two words, followed by a string of other Latin words and a few numbers, were etched in dark letters on the plank. Even Angelo Dradi, who rushed over to help Feletti as soon as the bones tumbled out, could make sense of them, and he, like the majority of Italians in 1865, could not read Italian, much less Latin.[6] Dradi grasped the significance of the discovery because the "little temple" within sight of Braccioforte announced its function with two Latin words chiseled over its entrance, one of which exactly matched letters on the board: *Sepulchrum Dantis*. The young workman, like everyone else in Ravenna, knew what that meant: inside the building was "Dante's tomb." Putting two and two together, he quickly made the connection between *Dantis ossa* and the bones that had spilled out of the box in the wall. These bones belonged to Dante. At least that was what the writing on the board said.

Dante's mausoleum, in any case, was nearby and dry, so it was there that Feletti and Dradi, under the supervision of city official Lorenzatti, brought the bones and the broken chest that had held them. Scooping bones and wood out of the wall and the mud, they made several trips back and forth before all the pieces had been gathered inside the small temple.

The next few minutes passed in a whir of frenzied activity. Lorenzatti ran to Filippo Lanciani's office, just two hundred yards away, urging him to hurry to the site. The engineer arrived there just before—or just after—the arrival of his colleague Romolo Conti (each claimed to have been the first engineer on the scene). They were soon joined by Mayor Gioacchino Rasponi, members of Ravenna's city council, and not one but three notaries public. Local authorities took no chances: a box of bones with an indication they belonged to Dante was more than enough to convince officials that everything surrounding the unexpected find had to be carefully documented and authenticated. Discovery of the mortal remains of the man so many nineteenth-century Italians considered the father and prophet of Italy (not to mention its greatest poet) was a matter of national interest—if the bones really were Dante's, that is. The first step toward ascertaining this was to have scientific experts examine them. Mayor Rasponi promptly sent for Giovanni Puglioli, Ravenna's chief surgeon and medical officer. Dr. Puglioli joined Claudio

Bertozzi, Ravenna's second surgeon, who was already on hand to conduct the examination.

Doctors Puglioli and Bertozzi made a careful inventory of the bones and noted their condition. As would be expected of bones from a corpse that had decomposed above ground in an enclosed space with little or no air (such as a stone tomb), they showed a dark reddish color. But they were in very good shape overall, maintaining solidity even at their ends or joints. Properly arranged, the bones formed most of a single human skeleton, a male, including nearly all the major parts. The mandible—or lower jawbone—was missing, as were a calf bone (fibula), a vertebra (the atlas, or first cervical vertebra), a rib, two forearm bones (ulnae), the tailbone (coccyx), an ankle bone (astragalus), and many small bones of the hands and feet. No teeth were found. Still, considering the 206 bones and their distribution in a human adult, the doctors were justified in confirming the skeleton's near completeness.[7] To measure the full body, they placed the bones in their anatomically correct order, running a brass wire through the vertebrae. The length of one meter fifty-five centimeters, with the addition of another ten to twelve centimeters to account for missing cartilage and other soft parts, suggested a height of between 5 feet 5 inches and 5 feet 6 inches. This measurement was consistent with Boccaccio's description of Dante as a fourteenth-century man of "medium height."[8] Engineer Lanciani made sure to tell his father, in a letter written the day after the discovery, that while helping the doctors measure the skeleton, he had the honor of holding "Dante's head" in his hands.[9] Presumably he was not the only one.

As the doctors examined and collected data on the bones, other authorities turned their attention to the simple pine boards that, crudely nailed together, formed the box in which the bones had been found. Worn by time and humidity, the wood chest was in worse shape than its mortal contents.[10] To call it a coffin would be a stretch. At only two and a half feet in length and less than a foot each in width and height, the box was plainly not intended to hold anything remotely resembling the prone, complete skeleton of an adult human. Nor was it the work of a professional carpenter, as one side measured about an inch shorter than the other.[11] The bones may have been carefully arranged within the box before Feletti's pickax sent them flying, but even the image of a neat pile elicited an uneasy suspicion of violation. One or more persons had evidently disturbed Dante's peace to handle his mortal remains, the most intimate material left behind by the world's greatest explorer of life beyond the grave.

While events unfolded inside the mausoleum, news of the discovery spread swiftly through the city, filling ordinary citizens with joy and curiosity. A crowd soon amassed outside the building in which the bones were being guarded. Primo Uccellini, a librarian at Ravenna's Classense Library and witness to the scene, observed that everyone wished "to see them, to kiss them, to adore them."[12] People on both sides of the door anxiously awaited each new piece of information.

City officials paid close attention to the board that fell at Feletti's feet along with several bones. Written on the wood in black ink and tastefully adorned with lilies, the full inscription raised intriguing questions about these remains said to belong to Dante:

DANTIS OSSA
Denuper revisa die 3 Junij
1677

The writer left no doubt about what mattered most: the capital letters appeared at least three times larger than the other letters and numbers. The rest of the note announced that "DANTE'S BONES" had been "seen (or viewed) again" on June 3, 1677. But why had anyone looked at them even once (much less again) in the seventeenth century? And who was this person who claimed to have seen Dante's bones and thought to record his viewing on the inside of the bottom of the box?[13]

Another discovery, made soon after the bones and wood box had been brought from the Braccioforte excavation site into Dante's mausoleum, answered this last question. It also raised new ones. In the midst of the feverish activity, someone noticed writing on another board. Slightly larger in size than the inscription dated June 3, 1677, but in matching penmanship was another Latin note written in dark ink. The author, thankfully, this time gave his name:

DANTIS OSSA
a me Fr[at]e Antonio Santi hic posita
Ano 1677. Die 18 Octobris

Again leading with "DANTE'S BONES" in large capital letters, this inscription said that the bones had been "placed here [*hic posita*] by me, Brother Antonio Santi" on the "18th day of October in the year 1677." We have our man: Antonio Santi, whose fraternal title (*Frate,* or "Brother") signaled membership

P.1. Inscriptions by Brother Antonio Santi on the box of bones found on May 27, 1865
(Corrado Ricci, *L'ultimo rifugio di Dante Alighieri* [Milan: Hoepli, 1891], after page 352)

in a religious order. With the former convent of the Brothers of Saint Francis located right next door to Dante's mausoleum, it was not hard to guess which order that was.

But besides having been a Franciscan friar, who exactly was this Brother Antonio Santi? And why had he placed Dante's bones "here," wherever that may be? In the box? In the wall where Feletti accidentally found them? In some other location altogether? Whatever his meaning, Brother Santi wrote this second note on the outside of the cover so that whoever came upon the box would know right away the precise date on which he had placed Dante's bones "here." And if, as seemed almost certain, Antonio Santi had also written the first inscription some four and a half months earlier, what was the connection between his viewing of the bones (again) on June 3 and his placing of them "here" on October 18, 1677? Most crucially, what was Brother Santi doing with Dante's bones in the first place? If these bones were authentic, then why, when, and how had they been removed from Dante's tomb—and by whom—sometime before June 3, 1677?

While local historians and other scholars began consulting Ravenna's archives and libraries for answers to these and other questions, city officials and medical experts kept their eyes on the physical evidence. Once gathered inside the neoclassical mausoleum housing Dante's tomb, the bones were arranged on a cloth-covered table. After Doctors Puglioli and Bertozzi completed their examination, they placed the bones back in the same wood box, its boards now reattached, in which they had been found.[14] This dilapidated "coffin" bearing Brother Santi's inscriptions was then set within a new pine chest equipped with a lock. Tied crosswise with a white cord, the outer box was marked with the coat of arms of the Commune of Ravenna, a pine tree flanked by two standing lions, in four seals of red wax. For good measure, the city's symbol was stamped four more times in black ink surrounded by the words "Comunità di Ravenna." Mayor Rasponi locked the chest and personally deposited the key in a secure location at city hall. At five o'clock on May 27 the official report of the day's events was read aloud and signed by the participants and other witnesses, from the officials, doctors, and engineers down to mason Pio Feletti and his assistant, Angelo Dradi, who wrote an *x*. The three notaries public affixed their signatures to authenticate the historic document.

The locked double box of bones shared the same small room as Dante's original tomb, an ancient sepulcher partially lodged in the back wall of the "little temple." The doctors believed the bones to be consistent with the skeletal remains of a man who had died centuries earlier at a relatively advanced age (Dante lived to age fifty-six). But the awkward discrepancy between the presumed identity of these remains and the epitaph inscribed on the face of the marble sarcophagus—"here I, Dante, am confined" (*hic claudor Dantes*)— could not help but worry authorities and other observers. There was only one good way to confirm (or disprove) the conclusion that the bones discovered that morning were Dante's: look inside the original tomb.

Four days later, at a meeting of May 31, Ravenna's city council granted permission to do just that. Dante's tomb was scheduled to be opened, in the presence of a National Commission already en route to the city, on June 7, 1865. The great hope, of course, was that it would be found empty. No one wanted to confront a second body with claims to authenticity. Multiple skeletons and skulls of the same venerated person had been a notoriously problematic (if at times profitable) occurrence in the history of relics: inventories at one point in time gave Mary Magdalene six bodies and Saint

Gregory the Great two bodies and four heads.[15] One body of Dante would do just fine.

—

Henry Clark Barlow, a distinguished Dantophile from England who attended the festivities in Florence and Ravenna, remarked that news of the alleged discovery of Dante's bones so close in time to celebrations of the poet's six hundredth birthday was met with derisive humor. People joked that "the bones of Beatrice would soon follow their example." Barlow, writing in 1865, attributed this cynicism to the fact that "we live in an age when miracles are no longer admissible."[16] For others, the timing hardly seemed arbitrary. The appearance of Dante's bones during this formative period of Italian nationhood was a sign pointing to the fulfillment of his prophecy of a free and united Italy. Viewed in this light, the discovery marked the achievement of the Risorgimento and inspired Italians to complete unification by adding Venice, Rome, and other "unredeemed" lands to Italy's map.

It would indeed seem miraculous if Dante's one and only body had been discovered during celebrations of his six hundredth birthday and the recently created Italian nation that he was said to have envisioned. And it would be hard to imagine a more fitting culmination to these festivities than the return of the poet's bones to the tomb in which they had been buried over five centuries earlier.

— Introduction —

DANTE'S GHOST

In Latin, it was the verb *humare,* to bury, which gave the primary and proper meaning to the noun *humanitas,* human civilization.

—GIAMBATTISTA VICO

Timing was not the only "miraculous" part of the discovery of bones believed to be Dante's. The hidden location of the wood box extracted by Pio Feletti's pickax gave people even more reason to suspect the intervention of mysterious forces. Corrado Ricci, the foremost authority on the history of the poet's tomb and remains at the time, repeated a story he had heard from many living witnesses in the late nineteenth century. The anecdote, which Ricci reported as follows, was viewed in retrospect as a prophetic sign of Feletti's discovery of Dante's bones.

The sacristan of Ravenna's Braccioforte chapel recounted to fellow citizens a dream that had frightened him while he slept among the ancient tombs in the chapel. He often spent the night there, falling into a deep, heavy slumber after imbibing large quantities of alcohol. One of those nights, sometime before 1865, he saw in his dream a male figure, dressed all in red, materialize in a corner of the building and then stroll around the chapel and the neighboring cemetery before approaching the inebriated dreamer. When the sacristan asked who he was, the crimson apparition answered, "I am Dante!"[1] It was as if the master of the afterlife had risen from his tomb to wander the area around his gravesite.

Local residents with whom the sacristan shared his dream of Dante's ghost understandably dismissed it as a silly if entertaining story. Employed by the Confraternity of Mercy (a local charity organization), the sacristan was fittingly called *Grillo.* Italian for "cricket," this nickname implied not only a pro-

pensity to chatter like the chirping insect but also, less charitably, a reputation for flights of fancy.[2] It is small wonder that the man, sleeping off his
inebriation in a mortuary chapel beside a cemetery and Dante's tomb, said
he saw the poet's ghost in his dream. Even if nineteenth-century Italians
thought the sacristan was telling the truth, they were less likely than their
ancestors (and perhaps their descendants post-Freud) to find deep meaning
in such a dream.

People in Dante's day, conversely, frequently interpreted dreams as prophecies. They took the words and actions of their imagined figures as signs
explaining or pointing to future events. The poet himself, a learned man of
the late Middle Ages, put ample faith in prophetic dreams, one of which had
great bearing on his life. The night after he first received the greeting of
Beatrice—the young Florentine woman who would become his beloved yet unattainable muse—eighteen-year-old Dante had a dream revealing a "marvelous vision": a lordly man, enveloped within a fire-colored cloud, joyously
carried Beatrice as she slept, her naked body covered only by a blood-red
cloth; holding Dante's burning heart in his hand, the man woke Beatrice and
forced her to eat it, after which, weeping bitterly, he gathered her in his arms
and rose to Heaven. The meaning of this disturbing vision, Dante told readers
of his *New Life* (*Vita nuova*), was not seen by anyone at the time, though later
it was "perfectly clear to the simplest." Anyone could see in hindsight that
the dream was prophetic, a sign foretelling Beatrice's untimely death seven
years later in 1290 (at age twenty-four) and her ascension to God's celestial
kingdom.[3]

As happened for Dante's dream of Beatrice, later events cast the sacristan's
dream of Dante in a whole new light. While telling of his encounter with the
poet's ghost—as he frequently did—this "cricket" would point excitedly to a
corner of the Braccioforte chapel where a former doorway to the cemetery
had been sealed with bricks. That was the spot where he saw Dante's spirit,
clad in red, enter the chapel. Miracles aside, responses to the dream changed
from mocking condescension to reverent awe after Pio Feletti discovered a
box of bones hidden behind those same bricks. People marveled even more
at the sacristan's story because they knew it was not some tall tale he had
made up after the fact to appear clever or prophetic: the man had died a few
days before Feletti's pickax dislodged the bones—precisely where Dante's
ghost had appeared—on May 27, 1865.

Right after recounting the sacristan's dream, Corrado Ricci reminds
readers that this was not the first time the poet's ghost starred in a dream

with a message about hidden treasure—at least not if Giovanni Boccaccio's fourteenth-century word (or that of his sources) could be trusted. Dante's first biographer, Boccaccio (1313–1375) provided a wealth of information about Dante's life and times, much of it based on direct testimony from people who had known the poet in Florence and the cities in which he had lived in exile. But Boccaccio was also an extraordinarily inventive storyteller—a talent on full display in his prose masterpiece, the *Decameron*—whose engagement with Dante's life and works over many years shaped his own literary agenda. Numerous claims and episodes in Boccaccio's biography of Dante therefore merit a healthy dose of skepticism, this dream included. As it is, Boccaccio's account of Jacopo's encounter with his father's ghost eerily complements the sacristan's dream over five hundred years later, one pointing to the remaining pieces of the poet's body of work, the other to the discovery of remains purported to be his dead body.[4]

Boccaccio, who visited Ravenna in 1346, only twenty-five years after Dante's death, claims to have been told of the dream by Piero Giardino, a disciple and close friend of the poet during his final years.[5] This dream reveals information not about Dante's bones but about the final cantos of the *Divine Comedy*. At the time of Dante's death in 1321, according to Boccaccio, he had not yet sent the last thirteen cantos of *Paradiso* to Cangrande della Scala, his former benefactor in Verona. Dante dedicated the *Paradiso* to Cangrande and customarily sent batches of cantos to him upon their completion. After a fruitless search for the missing pages in Ravenna, the poet's sons, Pietro and Jacopo, reluctantly concluded that their father had not finished the work before his death. On the advice of friends, they decided they would do their best to compose the final cantos themselves when, mercifully, Dante appeared to Jacopo in a "marvelous vision" that saved him from "his foolish presumption." He also showed his son where to find the missing portion of the "divina *Comedia*."[6]

The first person known to attach the label "divine" to the title of the poem (Dante simply called it his "Comedy"), Boccaccio reports that Jacopo showed up at Piero Giardino's house late one night during the ninth month after the poet's death. He arrived just before dawn. Jacopo told Piero that just a short while earlier, he had seen his father in his sleep. Dante wore bright white garments, his face aglow with an otherworldly light. Jacopo asked him if he were alive, to which Dante replied yes, "but in the true life, not in ours." Still dreaming, Jacopo asked his father if he had managed to finish his poem before passing to this "true life," and, if he had, where were those last thirteen cantos? "Yes! I finished it," Dante reassured his son. Jacopo imagined that Dante then took him by the hand and led him to the poet's former bedroom. "Here is what you have looked for for so long," Dante said, while touching a spot on the wall. With these words, the ghost disappeared, and Jacopo snapped awake. Understandably agitated, he immediately sought out Piero Giardino so they could go to the indicated place and learn whether he had been visited by "a true spirit or false delusion."[7]

People in the Middle Ages believed that early-morning dreams were especially good at revealing the truth, and this one proved no exception.[8] When Jacopo brought Piero to his father's bedroom, they found a mat affixed to the wall at the very spot touched by Dante in the dream. After gently removing the mat, they saw a recess they had not known about. Reaching inside the opening, they grasped a bunch of written pages. Fragile and discolored from the humidity, the parchment was on the point of total ruin. As the men removed mold and mildew from the pages, Dante's unmistakable verses came into view. The final thirteen cantos all accounted for, Jacopo diligently copied them for Cangrande and then joined them with the rest of the poem, which Dante's son affectionately and proudly called his "sorella," his sister. Now totaling one hundred cantos, "the work of so many years" was finally complete. Jacopo had the original manuscript of the full *Divine Comedy*.[9]

Giannozzo Manetti (1396–1459), a Florentine humanist, drew freely from the Italian biographies of Dante by Boccaccio and Leonardo Bruni (1370–1444) in writing a Latin life of the poet in 1440. He views Jacopo's dream as evidence that Dante put the finishing touches on the "divine poem" (*divino poemate*) soon before he died. The poet, in Manetti's telling, had hidden several sheets containing the final cantos of the *Paradiso* somewhere in his house, waiting for the proper moment in which to add them to the other cantos and thereby bring the magnificent poem to completion. Because Dante did not live long enough to see this moment, it took a miraculous encounter with his ghost in the afterlife—the kind of extraordinary meeting the living poet imagined having with the dead—for the *Divine Comedy* to achieve its final form of one hundred cantos. The "shade of the deceased poet" speaks from beyond the grave, leading his son to the hidden location of the final cantos.[10]

Today we have only manuscript copies of the poem—and copies of copies—the earliest ones dating to the 1330s, a decade after Dante's death.[11] The original pages of the *Divine Comedy*, the verses written by Dante himself—or perhaps in later years dictated by the poet to his sons—did not survive or have otherwise been lost to posterity. This is true of Dante's other texts as well. So far as we know, no copy of any of the poet's works written in his own hand graces a library, museum, or private collection anywhere in the world. What happened, then, to those moldy pages with the final thirteen cantos (if the dream is to be believed) and to the first specimens of the other eighty-seven cantos of the poem? Were they destroyed by order of some high-ranking church official offended by Dante's theology or political philosophy or by his assignment of a particular bishop, cardinal, or pope to an undesirable room in the afterlife? Did Dante's original manuscript perish in one of those fires that often consumed libraries and archives in earlier times—as happened, for instance, during the sack of Ravenna in 1512? Did Dante's sons, aware of their father's enemies and feeling the heat, entrust his personal copy of the *Divine Comedy* to the Franciscan friars in Ravenna? Did they think it would be safe on consecrated property, only to have it pass into oblivion with the passing of time? Did the manuscript somehow wind up in the Vatican Library, where it patiently awaits the arrival of a real-life Robert Langdon to track it down or (more likely) stumble upon it by chance? The plain truth is, we will probably never know the fate of Dante's original pages.[12] The fate of his body is another story.

Jacopo Alighieri dreamed that his father, dead less than a year, came to reveal the place where he had hidden the final portion of his *Divine Comedy,* the heart and soul of his body of work. Over five centuries later, a humble sacristan saw Dante's ghost by a bricked-over doorway that was later shown to conceal bones said to belong to the poet. Both dreams pointed to precious objects hidden within walls—the wall in Dante's bedroom holding the finale to his epic poem of the spiritual afterlife, the wall of Braccioforte hiding alleged pieces of his physical afterlife. The equivalence of Dante's body with his poem follows a tradition going back at least as far as the late Middle Ages. A life of Ovid, probably composed in the thirteenth century, tells a story about the discovery of the Roman poet's tomb. The sarcophagus held not Ovid's bones but a small ivory casket containing a book "unconsumed by the ages." The poet's work—everlasting, pristine—stood for his corruptible body.[13]

Dante's Bones draws inspiration and information from the treasure revealed in Jacopo's dream, his father's *Divine Comedy,* but its primary subject is the treasure apparently revealed in the sacristan's dream.[14] It offers a novel perspective on the poet's "afterlife" by narrating and analyzing the graveyard history of the man who wrote the book on life beyond the grave. My book tells the true story of individuals burying, stealing, hiding, finding, examining, worshiping, and fighting over the remains of the Florentine poet from the Middle Ages who has become a first-name global icon. Actors in the drama of Dante's physical afterlife run the gamut from Lorenzo de' Medici, Michelangelo, and Pope Leo X to the Franciscan friar who hid the bones, the stone mason who accidentally discovered them, and the opportunistic sculptor who accomplished what Florentine princes, popes, and politicians could not: allow Dante's native city to claim a precious relic of the poet it had banished.

My research has benefited immensely from previous explorations of Dante's graveyard history, most of them dating to the nineteenth and early twentieth centuries. In addition to official reports by Ravenna and other cities, organizations, and individuals, I have drawn on eyewitness accounts and scholarly studies by Romolo Conti, Filippo Lanciani, Henry Clark Barlow, Corrado Ricci, Santi Muratori, and others.[15] Serendipity, a powerful force in the history of Dante's bones, has also smiled on my efforts to tell it: I came upon the valuable reports of engineer Lanciani, an active participant in the events of May and June 1865, by chance while browsing old Italian newspapers in the New York Public Library in search of something else. Scholarly research often takes the form of detective work, a hunt for evidence to solve a problem or validate a theory, but this inquiry into the vicissitudes of Dante's bones—many of them straining credulity—has even more closely resembled a criminal investigation. Such procedures, as the late Umberto Eco demonstrated in his theoretical and creative work over many decades, frequently benefit from intuition and even pure luck, and I have welcomed both in gathering and interpreting the pieces of Dante's skeletal history.[16]

Dante's bones and his tomb in Ravenna have attracted the attention of a host of celebrities over the centuries, literary luminaries above all. Besides Boccaccio, famous writers who have dipped their pens in Dante's sepulchral well include Vittorio Alfieri, Giacomo Leopardi, Lord Byron, Ugo Foscolo, Dora D'Istria, Henry Wadsworth Longfellow, and Gabriele D'Annunzio. Accounts by lesser-known names in popular venues—newspapers, magazines, pamphlets, guidebooks, programs—and personal communications (letters, journals) have also yielded precious information on the poet's graveyard history. Dante is far from the only major figure whose dead body has taken on a life of its own, and I am grateful for that morbid fact. A rich substratum of cultural history exploring the fate of famous corpses has informed my research. *Dante's Bones* profits from the physical afterlives of eminent names ranging from the apostle Peter, Thomas Becket, Francis of Assisi, Catherine of Siena, Michelangelo Buonarroti, and William Shakespeare to Galileo Galilei, René Descartes, Ugo Foscolo, Abraham Lincoln, Benito Mussolini, and Eva Perón.[17]

Francis of Assisi may be Italy's patron saint, but Dante Alighieri is as deserving as anyone to that title in the secular realm. His claim to this honor is twofold: widely recognized as the nation's prophet and father, he also created the world's most influential and enduring vision of the spiritual afterlife. It follows that Dante, who cast himself in the leading role for his poetic journey through Hell, Purgatory, and Heaven, would hold a sacred place within the collective Italian imagination. And like many saints, he has enjoyed a lively skeletal history conducive to the production, dissemination, and reverence of relics. Experts in the history and meaning of such cherished objects have helped me appreciate how the treatment of Dante's dead body has been conditioned by the way bodies of saints were venerated during the Middle Ages and early-modern period. Worshiped like the relics of a holy man, Dante's secular bones have been honored with ritual "translation" (both real and imagined), the hagiographic term for the removal and relocation of hallowed remains. Parts of his body, along with objects that came into contact with it, have circulated—as relics are wont to do—as gifts, commodities, and stolen goods. Just as believers looked upon pieces of the "true cross" and other traces of the life and death of Jesus and the saints as sacred treasures deserving opulent reliquaries—treasures in themselves—so Dante's admirers have designed ornate cases and urns to hold and display fragments of the poet's coffin and other mementos of his physical afterlife.[18]

In the *New Science,* an exploration of the origins and development of human society, the eighteenth-century philosopher Giambattista Vico observed that burial in the earth (*humare*) gives meaning and a name—*humanitas*—to humanity, thus marking one of the universal institutions of civilization. The literary scholar Robert Harrison has extrapolated from Vico's insight to show, with examples stretching from ancient gravesites to the Vietnam Veterans Memorial, that "humans bury not simply to achieve closure and effect a separation from the dead but also and above all to humanize the ground on which they build their worlds and found their histories."[19] Relics and funeral monuments bring the deceased to life, and in the case of honored ancestors, they encourage each generation to reflect on and study anew their achievements and legacies.

No one wrote more deeply and movingly on the meaning of tombs than Ugo Foscolo. The exiled Italian patriot composed his elegiac poem "Of

Tombs" ("Dei sepolcri") in response to a distressing consequence of the Edict of Saint-Cloud, a sensible Napoleonic reform (enacted in Italy in 1806) aimed at reducing the risk of infectious diseases by restricting the burial of corpses to cemeteries outside city limits. The legislation therefore banned the interment of famous individuals in marked graves within a city's churches. The nation that can lay claim to the tombs of its greatest names is a "beautiful and holy land," Foscolo believed, not least because these monuments have the power to spur other strong-minded individuals to pursue noble deeds. Like so many visitors before and after, he felt his spirits rise upon seeing the final resting place of such illustrious Italians as Machiavelli, Michelangelo, and Galileo—all interred in splendid sepulchers within the Florentine Church of Santa Croce. Yet a majestic tomb holding Dante's remains was precisely what a visitor to Florence would *not* find. The poet Giacomo Leopardi, writing in 1818 on Florentine plans to build a monumental but empty tomb for Dante, imagined this visitor's shock upon learning that the poet's bones still lay in exile. Worse still, Leopardi protested to Dante's native city, until that time "not a single monument was raised / within your walls to him whose greatness, Florence, / means the whole world honors you."[20]

Dante well understood the primal, civilizational function of burial and the purpose of marked gravesites to honor the dead and inspire the living. He shows this best in *Purgatorio,* the most intensely human part of his *Divine Comedy.* The Mountain of Purgatory, unlike Hell and Paradise, is a temporal realm, a place in which saved souls, still attached to their earthly lives, purify themselves to attain eternal life in Heaven. Purgatory, as Dante imagined it, celebrates reciprocity of the living and the dead through their prayerful care for one another.[21] The poet honors the tradition of proper burials by showcasing two dramatic examples of their absence or violation. The protagonists are souls in the Ante-Purgatory, the lower part of the mountain, where individuals who delayed their turn to God until the end of their lives must wait before they begin their penitential trials in Purgatory proper.

Here Dante stages an encounter with Manfred, the warrior son of Emperor Frederick II. Killed in battle at Benevento in southern Italy (1266), Manfred tells how, though denied burial in sacred ground because he had been excommunicated, he was honored with a monument built of stones laid by enemy soldiers as they walked past his grave at the edge of the battlefield. But Manfred was refused even this makeshift tomb when Pope Clement IV had his bones disinterred and cast outside the borders of the Kingdom of

Sicily. The penitent soul asks Dante to tell his daughter Constance of his salvation so she can offer prayers to help him advance more quickly.[22]

The body of another slain soldier suffered an even crueler fate. Buonconte da Montefeltro fought as a cavalryman with the Ghibellines of Arezzo against the Guelphs of Florence at the Battle of Campaldino on June 11, 1289.[23] Dante, who claimed to have been in the middle of the action as a Florentine *feditore,* or "striker" (a horseman in the center of the front line), asks his foe what drove him from the battlefield. Everyone presumes Buonconte was killed that day, but no one knows what happened to his dead body. Having been struck in the throat, the shade explains, he fled on foot, coloring the field red with blood. He finally arrived at the bank of the Archiano River, close to where it flows into the larger Arno. There, he recalls, "I lost vision and speech, and I died with the name of Mary; there I fell, and there my body was left, alone." But he did not remain there long. Cheated of the man's soul, an evil angel wreaked havoc on the corpse by summoning a storm that washed it into the raging waters. Covered by silt and debris, Buonconte's body was never found.[24]

Dante's portrayal of Manfred's and Buonconte's postmortem abuse—and the salvation they attain despite such offense—deftly performs the memorializing function of a funeral monument for the untombed soldiers. But the poem does this not just for them. "Dante is the greatest poet of the dead," declared the Florentine writer and editor Giovanni Papini in his influential volume *Dante vivo* (Dante alive) from 1933, before adding that "the dead of Dante resemble the living in almost every way." The poet indisputably brings the dead to life in his *Divine Comedy.* A contemporary Dante scholar observes that the poem contains "perhaps the greatest number and variety of eidolopoeia [dead speakers] in all of literature." Sherry Roush counts seventy-five speaking souls in addition to Virgil and Beatrice, and her list excludes speakers whose identity is not historically or individually confirmed, such as Matelda in the Terrestrial Paradise and the blessed rulers that together form a speaking eagle in the sphere of Jupiter.[25]

Dante's life-restoring poetry means for Papini that "nowhere is there the evil smell of the cemetery or the corpse in decay." Although all the people Dante meets in his journey through the afterlife are already dead (with the exception of traitors to guests), "there is no charnel-house, no ossuary, no verminous destruction of the body, no uncovering of tombs."[26] This is true enough for Purgatory and Paradise, and the poet's verses breathe life into even the most wretched of the damned. But Hell nonetheless carries the stench of death and decay emanating from rotting, broken shade-bodies. The reek grows so strong that Virgil and Dante must pause to adjust to it before proceeding to the lower circles.[27] From worm-eaten cowards, dismembered hotheads, and blood-boiled murderers to half-buried simonists, dissected sowers of discord, and festering falsifiers—all the way down to traitors cryogenically preserved in the frozen ninth circle—there are cadavers galore in Dante's Hell. Encased in the ice, Lucifer fills the largest tomb with the lower half of his gigantic body. The circle of heresy, moreover, is a literal graveyard, a horrid place where those who believe "the soul dies with the body" sorely wish that were true: instead, their wretched shade-bodies broil eternally in red-hot sepulchers.[28]

The *Divine Comedy* itself—not just the infernal realm it describes—unfolds as a vast cemetery for an astonishing assortment of lives from biblical, classical, and medieval literature and history: prophets, poets, philosophers, theologians, warriors, saints, lovers, political rulers, and religious leaders but also Florentine friends—a gluttonous bon vivant, a lethargic musician, a nun forcibly removed from her convent—and other people from all walks of life caught Dante's imagination.[29] Like a memorial park in verse, the poem keeps these individuals alive for later generations by confirming their bodily death. The Roman orator Cicero called on the legend of Alexander the Great at Achilles's tomb to illustrate the memorializing function of poetry. Alexander was right to recognize the Greek hero's good fortune in having Homer relate his valiant actions, Cicero believed, "for had the *Iliad* never existed, the same mound which covered Achilles' bones would also have overwhelmed his memory."[30]

Set in the afterlife, the *Divine Comedy* doubles down on literature's power to remember and therefore resurrect the dead. For many if not most of its historical characters, the poem is the surest—sometimes only—sign that they ever lived at all. Even for a famous figure like Francesca da Rimini, the Dante scholar Teodolinda Barolini reminds us, the poet "*is* the historian of record: in effect he saved Francesca from oblivion, giving her a voice and a name."[31] Endowing spirits with the ability to see future arrivals, Dante goes so far as to reserve plots in his poetic graveyard for several prominent figures—Popes Boniface VIII and Clement V among the simonists, Emperor Henry VII in the Celestial Rose—still alive at the time of the journey (1300).[32] The *Divine Comedy* is filled with marked graves remembering, through the poet's eyes, who these souls were in life. For better or worse, they are not forgotten.

Dante's popularity has ebbed and flowed since his death, with its driest periods occurring in the seventeenth and eighteenth centuries, but he has never been forgotten. Even Voltaire's dismissive claim in 1726 that "no one reads Dante any more in Europe" had the unintended consequence of expanding readership of the *Divine Comedy* by sparking debates "that resuscitated the poem once and for all."[33] The trials of his dead body have only helped to perpetuate his fame. Yet Dante's graveyard history amounts to more than a conventional reminder of human mortality or an extended memorial to a supreme poet. The restless bones of one of the world's most influential travelers—in art as in life—also bear witness to historic changes in Italy and beyond. Dante's remains, far from producing a fixed impression of the poet, have inspired worshipers of all stripes to fashion him in their own image.

This book puts flesh on Dante's bones by showing how claims to them have often been motivated by political, religious, or artistic claims to his legitimating authority. The poet has grown in stature as the relevant portion of his dead body has diminished in size from a skeleton to individual bones and fragments, finally to dust. An object of civic rivalry between Florence and Ravenna in the fourteenth through eighteenth centuries, Dante stood as a patriotic symbol for Italy during the Risorgimento and became a forceful proponent of Italian nationalism and expansionism during the late nineteenth and early twentieth centuries before attaining the global fame he enjoys today. Overlapping rather than exclusive, these roles involve and influence each other. The following pages also show how Dante's physical afterlife informs and reveals his apotheosis, his evolution from Italy's ancestral father and political prophet to the nation's secular saint and, in two global conflicts, its god of war—a less celebrated reason to revere him as a divine poet. But this life of Dante's bones begins, naturally, with his death and burial in Ravenna in 1321.

One

Bones of Contention and Nationhood

Death and Burial in Ravenna

In the month of September in the year of Christ 1321 . . . he rendered up
to his Creator his toil-worn spirit, which I have no doubt was received
into the arms of his most noble Beatrice.

—GIOVANNI BOCCACCIO

Quartan malaria, with its dreaded recurrence of chills and high fever
every fourth day, claimed an untold number of lives in Italy during the Middle
Ages. So familiar were its ominous signs that a fourteenth-century Italian
poet seeking to fill readers with bone-quaking fear need only conjure the
image of a man who "in a shivering-fit of quartan fever, / so ill his nails have
lost all color, / trembles all over at the sight of shade."[1] Dante identified with
malaria victims, whose suffering he had seen with his own eyes, to convey his
deathly fright at having to fly to a lower circle of Hell on the back of Geryon,
a monster with an honest-looking human face fronting a serpentine body
with leonine paws and a scorpion's tail. The writer of those words now experienced firsthand the sweats, chills, and aches of the debilitating illness.
He had contracted malaria for real, and it was a literal death sentence.

Although early chroniclers and biographers say precious little about
Dante's final days, their accounts, supplemented by contextual documentation, allow for a plausible representation of his illness, death, and burial. As
he languished in his damp bed, the poet would have been consoled by the
presence of loving family members and friends. Pietro and Jacopo, as sons of
an exile, were forced by law to leave Florence when they turned fourteen (between 1311 and 1314). They were by their father's side as he lay dying in
Ravenna in 1321. (If documents suggesting Dante fathered a third son are re-
liable, this eldest child—Giovanni Alighieri—had probably been dead for
over ten years.) Although we have no evidence that Gemma Donati lived with

her husband in exile, they may have finally been reunited in Ravenna. Her presence at Dante's deathbed cannot be ruled out. Their daughter, Antonia, certainly joined her father and brothers in Ravenna, where she later entered the convent of Santo Stefano degli Ulivi. She took the name of Beatrice. So Antonia—Sister Beatrice—also may have bid Dante a tender farewell as he passed to the other world.[2]

Dante's years in Ravenna were enriched by the company of devoted admirers and disciples, a number of whom were surely among those keeping vigil during his final hours. His closest friends were professional men— lawyers, notaries, physicians—in the city ruled by Guido Novello da Polenta. They revered Dante as a font of wisdom and paragon of moral integrity. The formidable intellect and outstanding verbal skills that distinguished Dante throughout his adult life made him a leading light among the best and brightest minds in Ravenna. They sought to learn from the master's experience in the public sphere and the knowledge on display in his treatises on philosophy (*Convivio*), language (*De vulgari eloquentia*), and political theory (*Monarchia*). They also knew him as the greatest poet of the time, the author of brilliant lyric compositions (many collected and glossed in the *Vita nuova*) and, above all, the epic verses of the *Divine Comedy*. Intellectual and creative energy flowed in both directions. Dante, according to Boccaccio, "trained many scholars in poetry, especially in the vernacular," showing them "how to compose in rhyme."[3] At the same time, Dante benefited from having well-educated interlocutors at hand in Ravenna as he completed his *Paradiso*.

Some of these dear friends were, like Dante, Tuscan natives who now called Ravenna home. Boccaccio identifies Dino Perini, a younger notary and lawyer, as "a fellow citizen and wise man" who confirmed the story of the discovery of the first seven cantos of the *Divine Comedy* in 1306, four years after Dante had been condemned to exile from Florence. Dino, claiming to be "a very close friend and colleague of Dante," told Boccaccio he had discovered a notebook with the cantos (in the poet's hand) while retrieving other documents from a box that Gemma Donati had moved to a safe place before political enemies ransacked their house in 1302. When the notebook was returned to Dante in Lunigiana (the northwestern tip of Tuscany), where he was a guest of Marquis Moroello Malaspina in 1306–1307, he resolved "to carry on with the work just as [he'd] originally planned to do."[4] Fiduccio dei Milotti was a physician and philosopher originally from Certaldo (Boccaccio's hometown on the outskirts of Florence) with professional and business ties to Bologna, Ravenna, and other cities in Romagna. The father-in-law of

Giovanni da Polenta (Guido Novello's brother), Fiduccio was an "intimate friend" of Dante. Corrado Ricci imagines that he accompanied Dante on walks in the pine forest outside Ravenna and that, "as a doctor and a friend, he must have tended to him in his final hours."[5]

Dante also had close friends among the native residents of Ravenna by the end of his life. Piero Giardino was a notary whom Boccaccio possibly met during a visit to Ravenna in 1346. He probably died during the plague of 1348. A "worthy gentleman," Piero was "one of the most intimate friends and servants whom Dante had in Ravenna." He was the friend who, in Boccaccio's account, told of having accompanied Jacopo Alighieri to recover the missing cantos that Dante had revealed to his son in a dream. Piero was also Boccaccio's source for the poet's age at his death, having affirmed that Dante, "lying on his deathbed, told him he was more than fifty-six years old and had been since the preceding May."[6] Dante was also close friends with another notary from Ravenna. Meneghino Mezzani became one of the poet's most fervent promoters, writing out, in his own hand, the complete text of the *Divine Comedy*. This manuscript of the poem, dated 1363, contains marginal comments by Mezzani and others, as well as canto summaries by Mezzani that imitate Dante's *terza rima* rhyme scheme. To the delight of me and my students, the prized object is housed today in the Harry Ransom Center, a hundred yards or so from my office on the campus of the University of Texas at Austin.[7] Dino Perini, Fiduccio dei Milotti, Piero Giardino, Meneghino Mezzani—it is reasonable to imagine that these and other friends joined family members in comforting their beloved Dante in those final hours and in consoling one another after his death.

Dante lived his final two decades in exile from Florence because he was a victim of the local and papal politics that roiled Tuscan cities. The factions of his day were the Black Guelphs and the White Guelphs—color-coded labels imported from Pistoia in 1301—headed by, respectively, the aristocrat Corso Donati and the banker Vieri de' Cerchi. Dante climbed the ladder of Florentine governance as a White Guelph, reaching its highest rung when he was elected to the city's six-member Council of Priors for a two-month term beginning on June 15, 1300. His triumph could not have come at a worse time. "All my woes and all my misfortunes," he reflected in a letter, "had their cause and origin in my ill-omened election to the priorate."[8]

Dante's opposition to Pope Boniface VIII's campaign to annex Tuscan lands led to troubles the following year. Boniface sent the French prince Charles of Valois to Florence ostensibly as a peacemaker but really as a mili-

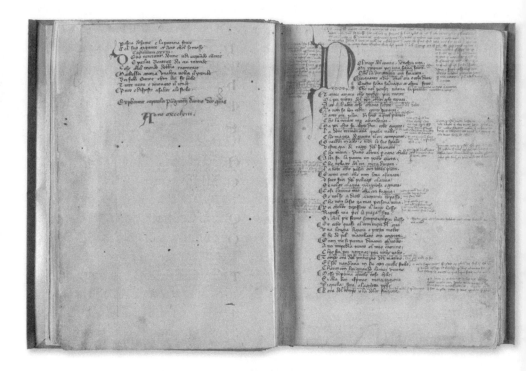

1.1. HRC 45: Dante's *Divine Comedy* in Meneghino Mezzani's hand (1363), summary of *Purgatorio* 33 (left) and text of *Inferno* 1.1–43 (right) (Harry Ransom Center, University of Texas at Austin)

tary occupier allowing propapal Black Guelphs to overthrow the White Guelph government. Dante was one of three Florentines dispatched to meet with Boniface, who flatly rejected their appeal to negotiate. The poet was still in Rome or on his way back to Florence when Charles entered the city on November 1, 1301. Black Guelph mobs soon unleashed a wave of terror against their White Guelph neighbors. Chief Magistrate Cante de' Gabrielli issued two proclamations naming Dante among those accused of committing various crimes while in office. Because Dante failed to present himself to answer the initial charges, the second proclamation, dated March 10, 1302, sentenced him to death by fire should he "at any time come within the power of the commune."[9] The poet never set foot again in Florence.

Dante traveled widely after his banishment—"almost like a beggar through virtually all the regions to which this tongue of ours extends," he wrote—with stays in over fifteen Italian cities (several more than once) before he arrived in Ravenna.[10] In exile he gravitated toward the proimperial politics of Ghibelline cities, culminating in his support of Henry VII of Luxemburg's campaign to pacify Italy and reclaim Rome as the center of the empire as well as the church. Appalled by Florentine hostility toward Henry, Dante urged him to attack the recalcitrant city. But Henry's siege in 1312 ended in failure, and his death a year later quashed the poet's hopes for an imperial counterweight to papal overreach.

As a political exile, Dante was excluded from a Florentine pardon in 1311, but another amnesty in 1315 would have allowed him to return. Unwilling to comply with terms of the offer—admission of guilt and payment of a fine—Dante was again sentenced to death, this time by beheading rather than fire, the penalty now also applying to his sons Pietro and Jacopo. An additional provision stated that anyone had permission "to harm them in property and person, freely and with impunity."[11] Dante's refusal reflected not only his great pride but also better living conditions. He was now residing in Verona as a guest of the Ghibelline ruler Cangrande della Scala. Having cut ties with his native city, he declared himself "Florentine by birth, not by disposition."[12] Dante had learned how bread outside Florence "tastes of salt," but by 1316 he could say that such bread "will surely not be lacking."[13]

Moving to Ravenna under the patronage of Guido Novello da Polenta in 1318—perhaps as late as 1320—improved life even more for the Alighieri family by providing a measure of stability and independence. Da Polenta connections enabled Dante's daughter, Antonia, to enter the convent of Santo Stefano degli Ulivi and his son Pietro to obtain rectorates of two churches that financially benefited the entire family. The poet had his own house in Ravenna, the city in which he found the resources, inspiration, and ambiance conducive to writing the final cantos of the *Divine Comedy*. Ravenna was located only three miles inland, its vast pine forest (*pineta*) stretching some twenty miles along the shoreline between the Adriatic and the city. Its inhabitants—estimated at seven to ten thousand—lived in a metropolis boasting splendid monuments to its illustrious past as capital of the Western Roman Empire and the Ostrogothic Kingdom before reaching its height of glory with the reestablishment of the empire in Italy under Justinian, whom Dante celebrates in canto 6 of the *Paradiso*. Ravenna dazzled residents and visitors with the Byzantine architecture and art for which it is famous today. The Basilicas of San Vitale and Sant'Apollinare in Classe, both consecrated during Justinian's reign, fired Dante's imagination with their gorgeous mosaics depicting Byzantine rulers and church leaders as well as biblical characters and symbols.[14]

No longer a center of political and ecclesiastic power, Ravenna retained an aura of its past grandeur that appealed to Dante at this late stage of his life. Boccaccio grasped this nostalgic essence of the city, remarking that it "is like one great sepulcher of most holy bodies," a land "bathed with the precious blood of many a martyr" and packed with "the bodies of many mighty emperors and others most illustrious both for their ancestors and for their own virtuous deeds." Five centuries later, the Irish writer Oscar Wilde likewise imagined Ravenna, a "poet's city," as "like Proserpine, with poppy-laden head, / guarding the holy ashes of the dead." The city's "lone tombs where rest the Great of Time" inspire "hearts to dream of things sublime." Ravenna's deep invocation of the past—what the Dante scholar Giuseppe Mazzotta calls its "posthumous" nature and "dreamy immobility"—meshed perfectly with the medieval poet's vision of the afterlife as a conversation between the living and the dead. Ravenna gave Dante a safe and comfortable home in which to display, share, and refine his considerable literary and intellectual talents. The renowned poet's presence, in turn, brought honor to the city and its ruler.[15]

Dante also contributed to Ravenna's welfare by participating in diplomatic negotiations, one of which cut short his life. With Ravenna on the brink of war with the Republic of Venice, its powerful neighbor on Italy's northern Adriatic coast, Guido Novello sent Dante on a diplomatic mission to the Serenissima, hoping that the "eloquence and reputation of the poet might avert impending ruin from him" and bring the conflict to a peaceful resolution. Venetian records show that the city was indeed preparing for military operations against Ravenna in August 1321, with negotiations to end the crisis beginning soon thereafter.[16]

The casus belli was Ravenna's capture of Venetian vessels and its killing of a captain and several crewmen (with others injured in the attack). Seeking revenge for the unjustified aggression, Venice called on Forlì to join in waging war as soon as possible against their common enemy and enlisted the support or at least neutrality of Rimini. Grasping the seriousness of this threat to Ravenna, Guido dispatched Dante and other ambassadors to Venice at the end of August. Covering about eighty miles, the three-day journey over land took the travelers through the pine forest outside Ravenna and over the thin strip of land between the lagunas of Comacchio and the Adriatic (day one), then past the magnificent Benedictine abbey at Pomposa and across the Po delta to Loreo (day two), and finally to Chioggia and by boat across the laguna to Venice (day three).[17]

The diplomatic mission, though unsuccessful, was not the abject failure that chronicler Filippo Villani laid at the feet of Venice. Lacking "knowledge of eloquence," Villani wrote, the Venetians were "so scared by the wonderful power of persuasion that report assigned to the poet that, for fear of being moved from their arrogant purpose, they refused his repeated request for permission to expound his embassy to them." It appears, rather, that Venice expected the Ravennese ambassadors to offer more concrete proposals for a peaceful resolution, which another diplomatic team in fact did on October 20, just over a month after Dante's death. Even less credible is Villani's account of Dante's return journey to Ravenna. Again hyping the poet's oratorical prowess, he accused the Venetians of not granting Dante passage aboard one of their ships because they feared he would convince the admiral of the fleet, holding in his hands "the whole power of peace and war," to "turn the way he wanted." More likely, Dante took the land route back to Ravenna, as most travelers did at the time, because it was preferable to enduring an arduous voyage of up to twenty days in the rough waters of the Adriatic. Maybe, as Giannozzo Manetti supposed, Dante returned by land to avoid the dangers of voyaging on seas under Venetian control, but that was the better option in any case.[18]

The land route between Venice and Ravenna posed risks of its own, more so during the time of year when Dante traveled. With the first rains of the season wetting the marshlands, parched after the hot summer months, conditions were ripe for contracting malaria. The rivers, canals, swamps, and lagunas of the region have always made it a fertile haven for mosquito-borne illnesses. Dante was only the most famous among countless victims of the area's malarial mosquitoes. Malaria drove the Benedictines from Pomposa Abbey in 1640 and took the life of Anita Garibaldi in Mandriole (just outside Ravenna) in 1849. The area's ecosystem, with a boost from global warming, was likewise receptive to an outbreak of the Chikungunya fever (transmitted by the tiger mosquito) that claimed over two hundred victims in and around Ravenna in August 2007.[19] It matters little in the end whether the poet fell ill during the journey to Venice or was infected while passing through marshlands on the way back to Ravenna. Either way, the final leg of the return trip was the last time Dante saw the pine wood on which he modeled his Terrestrial Paradise—"the divine forest, thick and lush"—at the summit of the Mountain of Purgatory. By the time Dante returned to Ravenna in early September, the recurring bouts of fever had so weakened him that he died within days.[20]

As Dante lay dying, wrote Boccaccio, he "received every sacrament of the Church humbly and devoutly, and reconciled himself with God by contrition for everything that, being but a man, he had done against his pleasure." Following medieval Christian practice, a priest would have administered last rites—confession, communion, and extreme unction—to the dying man at home. Bringing consecrated oil and hosts, he would have heard Dante's last confession, absolved him of sins, administered last communion—food for passage to the afterlife (viaticum)—and anointed his body. The poet's earthly life ended "in the month of September in the year of Christ 1321, on the day on which the exaltation of the holy cross is celebrated by the Church," meaning on September 14. Based on this passage and other sources, scholars commonly date Dante's death to the night of September 13–14, 1321. Boccaccio gave his illustrious forebearer an appropriately literary farewell, writing about his death, "he rendered up to his Creator his toil-worn spirit, which I have no doubt was received into the arms of his most noble Beatrice, with whom, in the sight of Him who is the supreme Good, the miseries of this present life left behind, he now lives most joyously in that life the happiness of which has no end."[21]

Mourners typically carried the dead body to the church for recitation of the office of the dead and a requiem mass before proceeding to the cemetery for burial.[22] Dante's funeral probably conformed to this late-medieval Christian model but with a few differences in keeping with the poet's exalted status. Piero Giardino, the friend who said he had been at Dante's deathbed, was probably also Boccaccio's source for information on the funeral. Guido Novello da Polenta, who had felt "the greatest grief" at Dante's death, placed his body, "adorned with poetic insignia, upon a funeral bier, and had it borne on the shoulders of his most distinguished citizens to the place of the Minor Friars in Ravenna, with such honor as he deemed worthy of such a corpse." Carlo Wostry (1865–1943), a talented artist from Trieste, depicted Dante's funeral procession for the six hundredth anniversary of his death. After the procession, which was accompanied by "public lamentations," Guido had Dante's body "placed in a stone chest, in which he still lies." He then returned to the poet's house, where, following Ravennese custom, he "delivered an ornate and long discourse both in commendation of the profound knowledge and virtue of the deceased, and in consolation to his friends, whom he had left in bitterest grief."[23]

1.2. Carlo Wostry, *I funerali di Dante,* ink and watercolor on paper, 1921 (Museo Dantesco /
Istituzione Biblioteca Classense)

Chronicler Giovanni Villani reiterated the high tribute paid to Dante on
his death, noting that he was interred close to the main church "with great
honor, in the attire of a poet and of a great philosopher." One of Dante's earliest commentators (1333) went much further, opining that "he received the
sort of singular honors not given since the death of Octavian Caesar." Observing that Dante "still lies" in the simple stone tomb (*arca lapidea*) several
decades after his death, Boccaccio reported that this was not inevitable.
On the contrary, Guido Novello had promised—"if his estate and his life
endured"—to honor the poet "with such an excellent tomb that if never another merit of his had made him memorable to those to come, this tomb
would have accomplished it." Manetti described Dante's original tomb in far
more generous terms, calling it "a splendid and imposing tomb built of finely
hewn square stones," but the fact remains that over a century after his death,
Dante's bones lay in the same plain sarcophagus in which they had been
placed in 1321.[24]

The sort of political conflict that had vexed Dante in life was likewise responsible for Guido's failure to provide the "excellent tomb" he had said

would keep the poet's memory alive for future generations. The noble ruler's good intentions came to naught when, during a stay in Bologna soon after Dante's burial, political enemies (led by a cousin) staged a coup back in Ravenna and Guido was never again able to return to the city. As if intuiting that a physical structure worthy of holding Dante's bones would be a long time coming (if at all), Boccaccio therefore took it upon himself to build—with words, not stone—the magnificent tomb that Guido had promised, a "monument to Dante," as one scholar labels the younger writer's work as editor, biographer, apologist, and commentator on behalf of his illustrious predecessor. "Not indeed a material tomb," Boccaccio commented on his verbal homage to the poet, it "is nonetheless—as that was to have been—a perpetual preserver of his memory."[25]

But if words are building blocks, Dante is ultimately his own best tomb maker. Stone—even marble—can seem a flimsy medium in which to memorialize a man whose monumental house of the afterlife immortalizes himself and his characters in verse. Giuseppe Verdi, the renowned composer of opera, drove home this point when asked to contribute to a fund for the construction of a new mausoleum for Dante in the 1890s, a project that never materialized. "Sir!" Verdi indignantly responded, *"put right this unseemly situation,* you say? But what situation? *Unseemly* because I haven't sent in my offering for the monument to Dante? Dante raised by and for himself a monument so great—and so high—that no one can reach it. Let's not lower it with displays that place him on the same level as so many others, even the most mediocre. To that name I don't dare raise hymns: I bow my head and worship in silence." In *Italian Hours,* a collection of astute commentary on Italian locales and monuments, the novelist Henry James expressed similar reverence for Dante at the expense of any monument built to honor him. Underwhelmed by the poet's tomb in Ravenna—a sight "anything but Dantesque"—James decided that in this case the physical structure mattered little. "Fortunately of all poets he least needs a monument," the novelist reflected, "as he was preeminently an architect in diction and built himself his temple of fame in verses more solid than Cyclopean block."[26] This was undeniably fortunate, for while Dante's sepulchral home would take various forms over the years, the monumental tomb promised by Guido Novello da Polenta and later proposed by others, including the great Michelangelo, would not be one of them.

2

A Marked Grave

Here I, Dante, am confined, an exile from my native shores,
Born of Florence, a mother of little love.

—EPITAPH INSCRIBED ON DANTE'S TOMB

Aware of Guido Novello's determination to provide a handsome sepulcher for Dante's bones, the best poets of the Romagna region composed verses—short Latin poems—in honor of the deceased, all hoping their submission would be chosen as an epitaph for the tomb. Of course, Guido's fall and exile scuttled plans both for the building of Dante's "excellent tomb" and for the inscription of the winning words on it. Boccaccio claimed to have examined the entries himself and selected the composition of Giovanni del Virgilio, a scholar-poet from Bologna, as the one most fit to adorn Dante's tomb.[1] If these words were inscribed on or close to Dante's original sarcophagus (not a new tomb), this only occurred many years later, and they did not remain there long.

Del Virgilio—so named because of his devotion to Virgil (his real name was Giovanni di Antonio)—had exchanged Latin poems with Dante in 1319–1321.[2] These compositions give valuable insight into the poet's mind-set in those final years. In the first poem, an epistle or carmen in the style of Horace, del Virgilio declared his admiration and affection for Dante, whom he called his "master." He fully recognized Dante's literary talent but chided the poet for writing his *Divine Comedy* in the vernacular—the "language of the marketplace"—and on themes that appealed to common, uneducated folk. "Don't wastefully cast your pearls before boars," he scolded Dante. If the poet instead wrote a Latin epic on the "great labors of men" and other worthy topics of immediate interest, del Virgilio would gladly crown him poet laureate in Bologna, a center of protohumanistic studies and literature.[3]

Responding with a full-blown Latin eclogue, Dante showed himself the true heir to Virgil by reviving a genre that had received only sporadic, unremarkable attention in the centuries since the Roman poet had written his ten eclogues in the first century BCE. He would joyfully receive the laurel crown, not in dangerous Bologna but back home in Florence, not for a Latin epic poem but for his Italian *Comedy* upon completion of the *Paradiso,* ten cantos of which he proposed to send to del Virgilio.

Not to be outdone, del Virgilio wrote an eclogue of his own, employing— as Dante had done—pastoral ciphers for historical personages: Tityrus for Dante, Mopsus for del Virgilio, and Meliboeus for Dino Perini, Dante's fellow Florentine exile and friend in Ravenna. Praising the poet as a second Virgil, del Virgilio agreed it would be wonderful if he were crowned in Florence. But recalling how Dante had been torn from his native land—"a mark of shame for the ungrateful city"—he repeated his offer to honor the poet in Bologna. Yet he knew that Guido Novello (Iollas in the poem) would never allow Dante to leave the safe confines of Ravenna.

In Dante's second eclogue, probably the last piece of poetry he ever wrote, he introduced Alphesiboeus. A shepherd who employs magic and witchcraft in Virgil's eighth eclogue, this character was a stand-in for Fiducio dei Milotti, the physician from Certaldo who, like Dino Perini and Guido Novello, was with the poet in Ravenna at the end of his life. Fiducio pleaded with Dante not to leave Ravenna for Bologna, abode of Polyphemus, the Cyclops in Homer's epic who slaughtered Ulysses's men. This murderous figure was most likely a mask for Fulcieri da Calboli, a ferocious enemy of Florentine exiles. Dante was well acquainted with Fulcieri's reputation for cruelty: elected *podestà* of Florence in 1303, he had hunted down White Guelphs and delivered them to their enemies for execution, thus "depriving many of life and himself of honor," as the poet puts it in the *Purgatorio.* With Fulcieri about to take over as Bologna's Captain of the People in 1321, Dante's fear of entering the "Cyclops's den" was fully justified.[4]

In the Latin verses Giovanni del Virgilio wrote for Dante's tomb, he naturally sang the poet's praises as author of the *Divine Comedy,* a theological epic "most pleasing to the common people" for its vernacular language. But he also celebrated Dante's pastoral muse, noting that the Latin eclogues were the final poems he wrote before "Atropos, alas, broke off the joyous work." Most striking, del Virgilio highlighted—as he had done in his own eclogue—the stark opposition between Florence and Ravenna, the cities, respectively, of

Dante's birth and death. "Ungrateful Florence bore him the bitter fruit of exile, a cruel homeland to her own poet," the epitaph lamented, while "pious Ravenna rejoices in having gathered him into the bosom of Guido Novello, her eminent ruler."[5]

Other admirers marked Dante's death in 1321 not with Latin verses to adorn his tomb but with lyrics in the vernacular tongue the poet had championed. Dante's unsurpassed status as a vernacular poet—recognized by del Virgilio in Latin—was itself a fitting theme for several Italian compositions. Giovanni Quirini, a Venetian merchant and poet, wrote a sonnet in which he grieved over the death of "our Italian father and poet, / who had within him an almost divine radiance." Dante himself had honored Cino da Pistoia, an esteemed jurist and prolific poet, as an exemplary love poet and had addressed a letter to him when both were in exile. Cino had shared Dante's high hopes for the imperial campaign of Henry VII of Luxemburg. He was probably in Siena, where he taught law, when he heard the news of his friend's death, prompting him to write a thirty-nine-line canzone. Dante's demise was a devastating blow for love's followers, for fortune had robbed the world of the "sweet tongue" that pleased everyone who heard it.[6]

Giovanni Quirini and Cino da Pistoia also joined Giovanni del Virgilio in inaugurating the practice of exalting Ravenna at Florence's expense. "The world weeps for glorious Dante," wrote Quirini, "but you, Ravenna, who had him in life / and now have him in death, are celebrated even more." The love Dante inspired was truly remarkable if it could rouse a Venetian to heap praise on Ravenna, his city's mortal enemy. Mirroring del Virgilio's opposition of "ungrateful Florence" and "pious Ravenna," Cino set the two cities against each other. Florence, "stripped now of hope" because its separation from Dante had become permanent, could wallow in its grief and misery. He goaded the poet's native city that "wise Ravenna heartily rejoices in preserving your treasure, / for which she deserves great praise."[7]

Not everyone was moved to glorify Dante at his death or soon thereafter. Cecco d'Ascoli (1269–1327), for one, did not share his colleague Giovanni del Virgilio's admiration for the poet. A lector in astrology at the *studium,* or university, of Bologna, Cecco launched a full-scale attack on several of the *Divine Comedy*'s major premises. In *L'Acerba,* a long Italian poem presenting a scientific—largely astrological—explanation of the universe, Cecco dismissed Dante's embrace of Beatrice, a flesh-and-blood woman, as his intellectual and spiritual guide. Declaring that attributing intellect to women was like "looking for Mary in the streets of Ravenna," Cecco considered Dante's view of Beatrice, as the author of a recent study of Dante and Cecco writes, scandalously "absurd" and "an exercise in futility."[8] Cecco also took issue with Dante's idea of fortune as a female angelic minister compelled by "necessity" to redistribute worldly goods swiftly and frequently. This "necessity," for Cecco, marked Dante as a sinner for empowering determinism at the expense of free will. A victim of tragic historical irony, Cecco was himself accused of heresy by the Inquisition for favoring deterministic necessity—created by astral influences—over free will and divine providence. He was burned at the stake, along with *L'Acerba* and one of his Latin treatises on astrology, in Florence on September 16, 1327.[9]

Others found Dante's work sinful, even heretical, for a different reason. A poet whose theology and political philosophy imposed clear limits on papal powers and whose popular Italian epic consigned several powerful pontiffs to eternal pain in Hell was bound to incur the wrath of those who advocated the church's right to temporal as well as spiritual supremacy. The primary cause of such consternation was not the poet's *Divine Comedy* but his *Monarchia,* the Latin treatise he wrote sometime between 1314 and 1318. Dante's work of theologically informed political philosophy contained his mature reflection on the relationship between political and religious rule, specifically between the emperor and the pope and their proper jurisdictions.

This, in a nutshell, was the vexed issue at the heart of Dante's moral vision and several major events in his life—an issue that has shown various faces over the centuries, including the divine right of kings espoused by King James I of England and the wall of separation between church and state raised by Thomas Jefferson. The relationship between religion and politics clearly continues to shape and reflect societal organization around the world today, as seen in the articles published in a scholarly journal entirely devoted to the subject.[10] Dante's three-fold argument holds that the world is best served by a universal monarch, the Roman people legitimately acquired the power of this office, and the emperor receives authority to exercise this power directly from God, not from the pope. This last point, not surprisingly, was the one that stuck in the craw of the papacy and its apologists for the church's temporal claims.

Still, Dante's controversial position would not have triggered such a vehement response from church officials had it not been adopted by proimperial forces within a few years of his death. When Ludwig IV of Bavaria, crowned king of the Germans in 1314, sought ten years later to consolidate power in

Italy, his conflict with Pope John XXII intensified, with each declaring the other a heretic and John excommunicating his nemesis on March 23, 1324. Within four years, in January 1328, Ludwig was crowned emperor in Rome, not by John (whose court was in Avignon) but by one of the pope's enemies, Sciarra della Colonna. That spring Ludwig accused John of lèse majesté, punishable by death, and arranged the election of an antipope, Nicholas V, who gave a veneer of legitimacy to the emperor's rule by recrowning him on May 22, 1328. Within months, however, Ludwig and his officials created a violent backlash by persecuting their enemies. Angry Romans ran Ludwig and his entourage out of the city on August 4, 1328, John's legate returned, parliament declared null and void the emperor's edicts, and Nicholas renounced his claim. Papal control was restored.[11]

During this tumultuous period, Ludwig's closest advisers, notably Marsilio da Padova, a formidable political theorist and theologian, mined Dante's *Monarchia* for arguments supporting the king's claim to the imperial throne and supreme authority in temporal affairs. This high-profile endorsement immediately put Dante on the papal radar, and not in a good way. Guido Vernani, a learned Dominican friar from Rimini who taught in Bologna, was so distraught by the poet's argument for the emperor's political supremacy, given directly by God, that he wrote an entire, albeit brief, point-by-point rebuttal. Vernani addressed his *Refutation of the "Monarchia" Composed by Dante* to Graziolo de' Bambaglioli, chancellor of the commune of Bologna and author of the earliest Latin commentary on the *Divine Comedy* (*Inferno* only). Written in 1324, Graziolo's commentary praised Dante as a great and wise poet, even when making controversial statements, such as the damnation of Popes Nicholas III, Boniface VIII, and Clement V for the sin of simony or ecclesiastic corruption.[12]

Vernani, by contrast, condemned Dante as one of the devil's "own vessels" for his thinking on imperial and papal authority. Without deigning to name the target of his ire in the text, he left no doubt as to its identity: "a certain individual, who wrote many fantastic things in poetry, a palaverous sophist, pleasing through his eloquence with its hollow words; one who, using his poetical phantasms and fictions and, in the words of Philosophy as she consoled Boethius, bringing whores onto the stage with their sweet, siren songs, fraudulently seduces not only sick minds, but even zealous ones, to the destruction of salutary truth." Smearing his adversary as a purveyor of falsehood, one whose "hollow words" and "sweet, siren songs" spread like fake news to corrupt minds, Vernani followed Boethius in pitting virtuous philosophy against meretricious poetry, with Dante dangerously aligned with the latter. But consistent with the treatise's title, the preacher's chief complaint was with Dante's philosophy, not his poetry, in particular with his claim for the emperor's universal political sovereignty. Vernani vigorously disagreed. For him, not the emperor but the pope, "the universal vicar of Jesus Christ," was "the prince of the world," the one "in whom, if all men obeyed according to the law of the Gospels handed down by Christ, there would exist the most perfect monarchy in the world." The pope reigned supreme in both earthly and spiritual matters. To believe otherwise, as Dante and Marsilio da Padova did, was not just absurd. It was diabolical.[13]

Dante's *Monarchia*, according to Boccaccio, paid a heavy price for espousing such controversial ideas, and its author's bones nearly did as well. The treatise, "scarcely known before," gained such notoriety after Ludwig's court had embraced its proimperial arguments that Bertrando del Poggetto (Bertrand du Pouget)—cardinal legate to his uncle, Pope John XXII—decided to take action following the emperor's return to Germany and the dispersion of his followers.[14] In the *Paradiso*, Dante condemned John, elected pope in 1316, for his abuse of the papacy for personal enrichment—he was reported to have issued baseless excommunications so he could extort money to rescind them. The poet had the apostle Peter, Christ's first vicar on earth, angrily accuse the reprobate French pontiff of being one of the "ravenous wolves in shepherds' clothing" preparing to drink the blood of his martyred predecessors.[15]

In 1329, around the time Guido Vernani published his refutation of Dante's work, John's nephew returned the favor. Declaring that the *Monarchia* contained heretical ideas, Bertrando forbade anyone from studying it. Just to be sure, he "seized the book and condemned it publicly to the flames" in Bologna. But for the intervention of two power brokers, the cardinal also would have made good on his threat to carry out what Dante's sentence of exile said would have happened if he had been caught in Florentine territory: whereas the proclamation of March 10, 1302, promised to have Dante burned alive, Bertrando now sought, only eight years after Dante's death, "to burn the bones of the author," an act that would bring "eternal infamy and shame" to the poet's memory.[16]

Later apologists for papal political supremacy evidently felt much as Guido Vernani and Cardinal Bertrando del Poggetto did about the *Monarchia*, for Dante's Latin treatise—not his vernacular *Divine Comedy*—was placed on the Vatican's Index of Forbidden books in 1554 and was not removed from the list until 1881. Well before then, on September 8, 1335, the Dominicans at Santa Maria Novella in Florence prohibited novices from reading and studying any books composed by the man "called Dante in the common tongue."[17] But at least for now, the poet's physical remains were spared censure and desecration. Although no official document corroborating Boccaccio's account is known to exist, several pieces of evidence line up to make the threat to Dante's bones credible. Giannozzo Manetti affirmed, based on the testimony of "a certain great professor of law," that the poet "was condemned to be punished for heresy" because his "unusual work seems to be directed against the shepherds of the Roman church." Pope John XXII was himself not averse to making such threats. In a letter of April 30, 1325, he called for the exhumation and burning of the cadaver of Matteo Visconti, the powerful ruler of Milan, dead for nearly three years, whom John had accused of heresy and excommunicated in 1320.[18]

Most important, the men recognized for keeping Bertrando del Poggetto from burning Dante's body along with copies of his book were known for working closely with the cardinal. Ostasio I da Polenta, who had murdered Rinaldo da Polenta, Guido's brother, and taken control of Ravenna in 1322, reached an agreement with Bertrando granting papal authority over the city in 1329, the year in which Dante's bones were at risk. Pino della Tosa was no less influential as "a valiant and noble knight of Florence" with a long history of civic leadership distinguished by an admirable ability to negotiate and reach compromises with allies and adversaries alike. He was in Bologna at the time of the cardinal's fulminations and threats against Dante. His collaboration with Ostasio in this case made Dante an object of accord rather than contention between Florence and Ravenna. Perhaps della Tosa's intercession on behalf of his deceased compatriot signaled that the poet's native city would one day have a legitimate right to reclaim the body it had cast out.[19]

This collaborative spirit did not last for long. In the second half of the fourteenth century, Dante's city of origin again suffered by comparison with his final refuge and place of rest. Throughout the first, most extensive version of *Life of Dante*, written in the 1350s, Boccaccio harshly denounced Florence for its unjust treatment of the poet. Early in the biography, he rued the painful consequences of Dante's political activities. The poet was not free of blame—his civic engagement distracted from more important philosophical and literary pursuits—but wicked Florence bore the brunt of Boccaccio's attack. Eager to effect change by pursuing "the fleeting honors and vain pomp of public offices," Dante yielded to the urgings of leading citizens and made a name for himself through contributions to city governance. With no chance of steering a neutral course between the White and Black Guelph factions dividing Florence, Dante felt compelled to align himself with the Whites, the more reasonable and just of the two parties. This choice, however, meant that he was now more vulnerable than ever to the political machinations of his enemies. Sure enough, when Fortune turned against the White Guelphs and they fell victim to a coup, Dante was one of many who was "not only cast down upon the ground but cast out from it." Exile, Boccaccio sarcastically exclaimed, "was the reward that Dante reaped for the tender love he had cherished for his country! This was the reward that Dante reaped for his toilsome efforts to remove the evil discords! This was the reward that Dante reaped for giving all his care to the good, the peace and tranquility of his fellow citizens!" Anticipating the later lack of a suitable monument for Dante's bones, Boccaccio recast Florence's punitive exile as "the marble statue erected to him in eternal memory of his virtue." Like a perverse epitaph, this exile became "the letters in which his name was inscribed amongst the fathers of the fatherland on tablets of gold."[20]

Like Giovanni del Virgilio, Boccaccio set Florence—Dante's "wretched mother"—against venerable Ravenna. Immediately after reprinting del Virgilio's epitaphic Latin verses, he launched into a long rebuke dripping with acerbic disdain. "What frenzy, what recklessness possessed you," he asked "ungrateful" Florence, "that you chased into exile, with such strange cruelty, your dearest citizen, your chief benefactor, your unique poet?" Nor did he accept "the common madness" of the time as an excuse for such cruelty, for then "why, when passions had abated, did you not return to tranquility of mind and, repenting of the deed, recall him?" As another son of Florence, Boccaccio was eminently qualified to take Dante's side in calling on their malevolent mother to look with remorse on her actions, to feel shame for her sinful choice. Other cities proudly claimed native poets as their own—Homer by Athens (and other Greek cities), Virgil by Mantua, Ovid by Sulmona, Horace by Venusia, Juvenal by Aquinum—because they knew that "the lasting influence of these men would be, even after their own ruin, eternal splendors of their name." Florence alone, "clouded by some strange blindness," followed an opposite path. Rather than honoring the gifted son whose poetry would bring honor to her, she debased herself by banishing him. Boccaccio bitterly observed that the penalty Florence had placed on Dante's head—death—nature's eternal law had accomplished: "Dead is your Dante Alighieri, in that exile which you, envious of his worth, unjustly inflicted upon him."[21]

Dante's bones, after all, had been buried elsewhere. Boccaccio channeled the poet by holding Florence accountable on Judgment Day for how it had mistreated him in life and continued to do so in death. "He lies under another heaven than yours," he reminded Dante's native city, "and you do not need to see him ever again, except on that day when you shall be able to see all your citizens, and see their faults examined and punished by a just judge." Those who unjustly sentenced Dante to exile and still held a grudge, Boccaccio imagined, would not fare well before the throne of God at the Final Judgment. Along with this bitter condemnation, however, he foresaw a potential turning point, a way for Florence to redeem itself before it was too late. The poet's birth city, simply put, must "begin to seem like a mother, and no longer an enemy." To do so, Boccaccio urged his Florentine compatriots, "yield the tears that are due to your son, yield to him a mother's pity, and he whom when alive you rejected—no, chased into exile as one to be feared—desire to have back again, at least when he is dead."[22]

Thus began the centuries-long tradition of calling on Florence to repatriate Dante's bones to atone for the sin of having forced him to live and die in exile. Boccaccio explained why he offered this pastoral advice to Florence: "however ungrateful and tyrannical you were to him, he always held you in reverence as a son." Moreover, he explained to Florence, "[Dante] never desired to rob you—as you robbed him of your citizenship—of that honor which must of necessity attach to you because of his works." Boccaccio cherry-picked to spin Dante—the self-proclaimed "Florentine by birth, not by disposition"—into a son who, "however long his exile endured . . . still always placed [Florence] before any other city, and always loved [it]." His casting of Dante as the unconditional lover of his native city, true or not, seemed part of a calculated strategy to move Florence, through guilt, to seek repatriation of the poet's bones. If the "barbarians" not only "demanded the bodies of their dead again" but were "willing to die like men so that they might have them back," Boccaccio asked, then how could Florence— daughter of Rome and granddaughter of Troy—do less and not repatriate its exiled son? Priam, king of Troy, regained his son Hector's body by paying with its weight in gold; the ancient Romans retrieved the remains of Scipio Africanus the Elder. Neither a princely warrior like Hector nor a great liberator like Scipio, Dante nonetheless should not be "held their inferior, for there was never a time when arms did not yield precedence to knowledge." "Seek to be the guardian of your Dante," he demanded of Florence, "ask for him back."[23]

Even if Florence did not want to repatriate Dante, the city should still demand his bones, using "this fiction" as a way to diminish culpability and rehabilitate its image. In any case, Boccaccio taunted, "I am certain that he will not be surrendered to you," an outcome allowing Florence to have it both ways—look good by making the demand, rejoice at not having it met—in accord with its "innate cruelty." Reverting to the angry sarcasm with which he began his long denunciation, Boccaccio delivered the knockout punch: the dead poet, much better off where he was, would never leave Ravenna for Florence. "If dead bodies have any perception at all," he mused, there was no chance that "Dante's body could endure to depart from where it is for the sake of coming back to [Florence]. He lies in company far more desirable than any which [Florence] could give him." Ravenna, Boccaccio assured Florence—lest the latter felt inclined to assume an air of superiority—was "far more venerable than [Florence] for antiquity; and though her age has somewhat disfigured her, yet she was in her youth far more blooming than [Florence]."[24] Atonement through repatriation was out of the question because Florence was not worthy of that option after all.

By providing the home Florence denied, venerable Ravenna earned the right to preserve Dante's bones. But the Adriatic city was also a fitting final resting place because it was "like one great sepulcher of most holy bodies." It was far better for Dante to lie in Ravenna than among Florentine ashes that "preserve still the madness and injustice they had in life, and, at ill accord with one another, shrink from each other as the flames of the two Thebans did." Boccaccio's allusion to Eteocles and Polynices, the Theban brothers whose joint funeral pyre produced a flame that split in two to show their continuing enmity, captured the lingering effects of Florentine divisiveness. It was a fitting image in the context of Dante's life and poetry. A victim of the "madness and injustice" fomenting and resulting from violent political discord, the poet had used the same classical reference to highlight the eternal rancor of Ulysses and Diomedes, former comrades in arms suffering within a divided flame in Hell for the sinful crimes they committed together in the Trojan War. Dante's dead body, Boccaccio suggested, would suffer among the mortal remains of Florentines as hostile to one another in death as they had been in life.[25]

Still, Ravenna's great joy in preserving the bones of one "whose works hold all the world in admiration" could not erase its envy of Florence for being able to "boast the title of his origin." Whenever Ravenna would be remembered for Dante's death, Florence would be remembered for his birth. "Remain with your ingratitude," Boccaccio concluded his rebuke of Dante's native city, and let Ravenna rejoice in knowing it will win lasting glory as the poet's final resting place. His call for Florence to seek repatriation of Dante's bones ultimately served as a rhetorical ploy to disparage the city further. Boccaccio recognized Florence's indisputable and everlasting claim as his place of origin while denying it any chance of giving his dead body a home. That title rightfully belonged to Ravenna alone.[26]

No inscription—by Giovanni del Virgilio or anyone else—embellished Dante's tomb when Boccaccio visited Ravenna and wrote his *Life of Dante,* a period extending from the 1350s through the early 1360s. Murky, misleading, and contradictory sources make it difficult to pin down dates and other facts, but experts now believe that one or more epitaphs were inscribed on or near the stone sarcophagus in the second half of the century.[27] Del Virgilio's eulogistic verses of 1321, with their denunciation of "ungrateful Florence" and exaltation of "pious Ravenna," probably never appeared on the face of Dante's tomb, though perhaps a plaque or tablet inscribed with the epitaph was placed nearby between 1365 and 1370, only to be removed within a few years. Its removal doubtless coincided with the introduction of other epitaphs placed on or close to the sarcophagus.

Meneghino Mezzani, who knew Dante in Ravenna and honored the poet's legacy by producing a manuscript of the *Divine Comedy* in 1363, is conventionally assigned authorship of an epitaph possibly inscribed on the wall above the tomb sometime in the 1370s.[28] This epitaph, which, like del Virgilio's, was subsequently removed from the mortuary chapel, provides only the most basic information—name, city of birth, date of death—while praising its subject to the skies: Dante, "whose glorious fame penetrates the entire universe," is the "founder of eloquence, light and honor of the muses."[29]

The epitaph that ultimately triumphed, the one we read today on the front of the tomb, consists of six Latin lines in hexameter couplets:

> The rights of monarchy, the heavens, the Phlegethon, the cleansing waters
>> I sang while roaming, so far as destiny allowed,
> But because the wandering part of me withdrew to better citadels
>> And, happier, sought its creator among the stars,
> Here I, Dante, am confined, an exile from my native shores,
>> Born of Florence, a mother of little love.[30]

Today attributed to Rinaldo Cavalchini da Villafranca (1291–1362), a friend of the poet Petrarch in Verona, these words were long believed to have been written by Bernardo di Arpinello ("Canaccio") degli Scannabecchi, a member of an exiled Bolognese family that befriended Dante in Verona. Because of the epitaph's first-person voice—"I sang while roaming"; "Here I, Dante, am confined"—many people thought the poet himself had composed it. Leading with Dante's celebration of "the rights of monarchy," the epitaph was most likely inscribed on the tomb around 1377, a time in which Ravenna, having just freed itself from papal authority, was once again hospitable to such a strong pro-Ghibelline, proimperial sentiment. The epitaph's finale strikes another note that rang loud and clear at the poet's death in 1321: an exile in death as in life, Dante lies in Ravenna because he was born to "a mother of little love." A lasting condemnation of Florentine neglect was here etched in stone for all the world to see.

Florentine Remorse

Florence, long sad but joyful at last, warmly congratulates its poet
Dante, who has come back to life and to his homeland for a glorious
crowning after an absence of two centuries.

—MARSILIO FICINO

Giovanni Boccaccio's call for Florence to retrieve Dante's corpse appears
in retrospect to have been primarily an elaborate literary conceit. The city's
abusive treatment and subsequent unworthiness of Dante enabled Boccaccio
to fulfill the principal aim of his biography—notably titled a "treatise in praise
of Dante"—by casting the poet and his work as "divine." Later generations
of Florentines took calls for repatriation more seriously by amplifying and
periodically acting on them. Dante's bones, cherished no less than the remains of a saint, acquired the aura of holy relics for many of these worshipers.
Giannozzo Manetti, an early fifteenth-century biographer, thus implored
his native city, "do at least one thing you are certainly capable of doing: summon
back your poet's sacred bones from exile—from the place where you stub-
bornly refused to recall him . . . for many a year while he was still alive." The
recovery of Dante's "sacred ashes," he argued, would allow Florence not only
to cleanse itself of infamy but to attain a measure of "glory and honor." If
nothing else, the attempt would prevent others from blaming the city for of-
fending Dante in death as it had in life.[1]

Manetti overturned the accusations of heresy leveled at Dante by Cardinal
Bertrando del Poggetto and the Dominican preacher Guido Vernani a
century earlier. He viewed the poet's remains as not just respectable but, like
the holy body of a saint, worthy of outright veneration. Other Florentines had
already begun taking great pride in their exiled ancestor and seeking his posthumous return even before Manetti's call for repatriation in the 1440s. The
earliest sign of a Florentine attempt to retrieve Dante's bones appears in a

Latin epistle ignored or barely mentioned in existing accounts of the poet's graveyard history. Antonio da Legnago wrote this letter to his friend Pietro da Ravenna on December 5, 1378. Antonio was a notary who had risen to the upper echelons of power in Verona, serving as councilor at the court of Bartolomeo and Antonio della Scala from 1376 until his death in 1385. All we know of his correspondent is that this Peter was a native of Ravenna who probably taught in Ferrara.

The letter's date is significant because it means the "tomb of our Florentine poet," which Antonio saw "among other illustrious monuments in this famous city," already displayed the epitaph maligning Florence as the exile's "mother of little love." If Florence now sought to atone for this neglect, Antonio's letter suggests, then Dante's birthplace only managed further to debase itself—and to exalt Ravenna—by offering to buy the poet's remains. "O happy you," he congratulated his friend from Ravenna, for being "born of a land that valued the ashes of its virtuous guest over the gold of this most wealthy people." Prosperous Florence would employ other methods—some less crude than the offer of money, others more so—to obtain Dante's bones in years to come. But, as this initial failure presaged, it would be difficult if not impossible "to take this treasure" from Ravenna.[2]

Florence again took up the issue of repatriating Dante's remains less than twenty years later, this time officially and as part of a larger civic initiative. The Council of the People met on December 22, 1396, to vote on a proposal to build monumental tombs for five Tuscans with Florentine roots who had achieved fame while mostly living elsewhere. The renowned jurist Accursius (Francesco d'Accorso, ca. 1182–1260), who taught law for many years in Bologna, was the first of these illustrious citizens. In the *Divine Comedy*, Dante had damned him for sodomy among the "great and famous scholars" pelted by an eternal firestorm on the scorched inner ring of the seventh circle of Hell.[3] The next four were dead poets "still considered alive by the glory and fame of their virtue." Dante (1265–1321) headed this list, followed by Petrarch (1304–1374), the poet and papal secretary Zenobi da Strada (ca. 1312–1361), and Boccaccio (1313–1375). The proposal called for the tombs to be erected in the main church of Florence, Santa Maria del Fiore, better known today as the city's Duomo. Worthy of the men and the city, these "large, magnificent, honorable" monuments would be adorned with marble sculptures and other ornaments. Since they were each buried elsewhere—Accursius in Bologna, Dante in Ravenna, Petrarch in Arquà, Zenobi in Avignon, Boccaccio in Certaldo—their bones first had to be brought to Florence and then placed in the tombs for the "perpetual fame and celebrated memory" of the men and the Republic. The proposal, approved by a vote of 153 to 51, called for construction of the mausoleums even in the absence of physical remains, but they were not built. Whether the requests for repatriation were rejected by Ravenna and other cities or were never sent at all, the bones of Dante and his distinguished compatriots stayed where they were.[4]

Hopeful of a better outcome, Florence appealed directly to the ruler of Ravenna three decades later. Leonardo Bruni, the Florentine chancellor (and Dante biographer), wrote a formal Latin letter on behalf of the city's *signoria,* or governing council, to Ostasio da Polenta seeking the restitution of the poet's bones. Dated February 1, 1429, Bruni's letter affirmed that the young lord—the third and last ruling member of the da Polenta family named Ostasio—should not wonder at the "unique, even special affection and delight" binding Florence's leaders and all its citizens to the "celebrated, immaculate memory of Dante Alighieri, the great and famous poet." Dante's glory was such that "it brings praise and splendor to the city, the light of his genius illuminating his homeland." Recalling the earlier proposal to erect "magnificent tombs" for Dante and Petrarch in Florence, the council now sought to achieve that goal in the case of the former. Florence therefore entreated Ravenna's ruler to allow the return of Dante's "ashes and bones" so they could be venerated in a monumental tomb built in his native city.[5] Bruni's letter reveals how Dante was used, as an expert on the poet's reception in Renaissance Italy writes, "to promote a certain vision of Florence as a preeminent capital of culture and learning, one which encompasses both the contemporary revival of classicism and the earlier legacy of Trecento vernacular poetry."[6]

A request for Dante's bones less than fifty years later confirmed that the proposal of 1429, like those before it, had gone unfulfilled. The petitioner in this case was none other than Lorenzo de' Medici (1449–1492), the Florentine ruler whose political and cultural achievements earned him the title of Il Magnifico. Lorenzo's request for the transfer of Dante's "most worthy bones" from Ravenna to Florence was promising for two interrelated reasons: Ravenna was now controlled by Venice, and Lorenzo had a strong personal and professional relationship with Bernardo Bembo, a powerful Venetian humanist, statesman, and diplomat. Bernardo came to know Lorenzo and his court well during his time as Venice's ambassador to Florence. He arrived in January 1475 to celebrate the alliance of Venice, Florence, and Milan. An assembly of Medici followers named Lorenzo and his younger brother,

Giuliano, as Florence's leaders after their father Piero's death in 1469, though Lorenzo in effect ruled the city. Letters show that Bernardo exploited his political position for personal gain by securing loans for himself and family members from Lorenzo. Another letter reveals that the Medici ruler in turn hoped his friendship with Bernardo would enable Florence finally to bring Dante home.

The author of this letter, written to Lorenzo on April 13, 1476, was Antonio di Tuccio Manetti (1423–1497), a respected Florentine mathematician, astronomer, and architect. A great admirer of Dante, Manetti applied his scientific knowledge to the *Divine Comedy* in an attempt to map out the location, dimensions, and shape of the poet's underworld. The earliest Florentine printed editions of the poem included Manetti's calculations, and later thinkers—including Galileo Galilei—drew upon his study in their analyses of the site, size, and form of Dante's Hell.[7] Inspired by his devotion to Dante, Manetti reminded Lorenzo of a conversation that took place after the Medici ruler had visited the Venetian ambassador not long after the funeral of Matteo Palmieri, a Florentine humanist and city official who had died in 1475. Bernardo Bembo had promised to secure the "repatriation of those bones" after he arrived home, information that Lorenzo had subsequently shared with Antonio Manetti. "Those bones" could only mean Dante's remains, which Manetti fervently hoped Lorenzo would make sure Bernardo kept his promise to repatriate.[8]

But Lorenzo soon had far more pressing concerns than the retrieval of Dante's dead body. He worried most of all how not to become a corpse himself. Lorenzo nearly lost his life on April 26, 1478, when political enemies, led by prominent members of a rival banking family, viciously attacked him and his brother, Giuliano, during mass in the Florentine cathedral. Giuliano bled to death on the church floor while Lorenzo narrowly escaped with a knife wound. The people refused to rise up against the Medici, as the Pazzi and their accomplices had hoped, and Lorenzo's supporters executed or banished ringleaders of the conspiracy, allowing him to restore order in the city. Lorenzo's punishment of his enemies drew Florence into war with the papacy and the Kingdom of Naples, but he emerged even stronger after his bold mission to Naples in 1479–1480 reaped a peace treaty with King Ferdinand, forcing Pope Sixtus IV to cease hostile actions against Florence. Repatriating Dante's bones was understandably not Lorenzo's highest priority in this period.

Gifted members of Lorenzo de' Medici's inner circle meanwhile found a different way to bring Dante back to Florence, one perfectly in keeping with their humanist enterprise centered on the preservation, veneration, and transmission of works by eminent philosophers, theologians, and poets. Florence surpassed other cities in manuscript production of Dante's *Commedia* in the second half of the fourteenth century. The poet's popularity continued to grow in the 1400s, with more codices made in this century than in the previous one. Over half the surviving fifteenth-century manuscripts came from Florence, most of them produced to satisfy reading demands of the thriving merchant class. Dante's poem was at that time "the privileged means by which Florentine men and women learned to write and then to read."[9] With the advent of the printing press, however, Florence fell behind other Italian cities in the dissemination of Dante's work. The first printed edition of the *Commedia* was produced in Foligno, in central Italy, in 1472, followed by five printed editions published in Venice, Milan, and Naples in 1477–1478. These "foreign" achievements pushed the Florentine humanist Cristoforo Landino "to produce what was to become the most famous and influential Renaissance printed edition and commentary."[10]

Published by Niccolò di Lorenzo della Magna on August 30, 1481, with a large print run of twelve hundred copies, this celebratory edition was "a monument to Florentine nationalism and Neoplatonism."[11] It accordingly placed great emphasis on Dante's unbreakable bond with his native city. In addition to the text of the poem and Landino's commentary on it, the work included a long *proemio,* or prologue (with a letter by Marsilio Ficino), and copperplate engravings (*intagli*) by Baccio Baldini based on Sandro Botticelli's illustrations. Landino (1424–1498) taught grammar, rhetoric, and poetry at the Florentine *studium,* or university. An author of various vernacular works as well as Latin poetry, dialogues, and commentaries, he "played a central role in refounding Tuscan as a literary language able to develop humanist concerns and themes."[12] Ficino (1433–1499) was a leading Florentine translator and scholar of Plato's works and Neoplatonic writings whose philosophy was deeply imbued with Christian hermetic thought. Botticelli (1445–1510) is best known for paintings on both religious and secular themes—his *Primavera* (ca. 1477–1482), *Madonna of the Magnificat* (ca. 1483), and *The Birth of Venus* (ca. 1485) are masterpieces of Italian Renaissance art—but he also undertook the ambitious project of illustrating all one hundred cantos of Dante's poem (ninety-two drawings survive, a few with color added).

With contributions by Landino, Ficino, and Botticelli—three leading lights of Laurentian Florence—the illustrated book partially compensated for the city's failure to reclaim Dante's body. The work at least presented itself this way. In Landino's ceremonial presentation of the book to the Florentine governing council, he left no doubt about the civic spirit motivating this new edition of Dante's poem. Reiterating points from the prologue's opening chapter, he took credit for "liberating" the poet from the barbaric, corrupting idioms of foreign editors and commentators. Landino's "pure and simple Florentine" version of Dante allowed the poet "to return home after his long exile and be honored in his native tongue, a language superior to all other Italian idioms."[13]

This textual and linguistic repatriation cast an unforgiving light on Dante's continued physical absence from Florence. In the prologue, Landino digressed from the topic of chapter 8—Florentine commerce (*mercatura*)—to argue passionately for the repatriation of the poet's bones and their burial in a marble tomb built to honor him in the city's main cathedral. He imagined readers who, upon hearing his account of Florence's many virtues, would have good reason to accuse the city of ingratitude for unjustly banishing such a worthy citizen as Dante and for compounding its disgraceful blunder by not recalling him from exile during his lifetime. Landino attempted to blunt this legitimate criticism—and thereby save the Florentines—by attributing the injustice to "a vice of the times, not the nature of the people." On the contrary, his revisionist history argued, only a small group of powerful citizens then in charge committed this "vile act," and "not without the profound sorrow of the people." By blaming Dante's unjust exile on the wickedness of earlier leaders, Landino somewhat exonerated Florence by recalling how, once the poet's enemies lost power after his death, the people were free to pass a decree (in 1396) calling for the construction of an ornate marble tomb for Dante in the city's main church.[14]

Acknowledging Florence's failure to follow through on this conciliatory gesture to Dante—again due to the "envy of the powerful few"—Landino urged the city's current leaders to answer the people's prayers and show their devotion to "the father of [their] homeland" by reclaiming the poet's remains from exile and bringing them back to Florence for burial in the Duomo, his "proper and honorable" final resting place. Just as the most deserving citizens of Athens were honored in public buildings, so "Dante's merits and the Florentine people's devotion" demanded the placement of a "lasting monument to him in a holy and majestic public space." Landino believed Dante's burial in the city's principal cathedral was what "divine precepts wanted," what "human laws commanded." Anticipating Ugo Foscolo's famous verses on the bones of Michelangelo, Machiavelli, Galileo, and Alfieri in the Florentine Church of Santa Croce ("Dei sepolcri," composed in 1806), Landino celebrated Dante as an immortal whose outstanding achievements had the power to inspire the living to follow in his footsteps. "Who does not know," he asked rhetorically, "that the fame and glory of those who in death remain alive is a brilliant flame constantly driving human hearts to the highest virtues and learning?"[15]

Landino repeated his call for the poet's repatriation in his commentary on one of the *Inferno*'s most consequential episodes: Dante's encounter with Guido da Montefeltro, a warlord from Romagna condemned to the circle of fraud for counseling Pope Boniface VIII to defeat his enemies with a false promise. During their conversation, Dante informs Guido that tyrants with "war in their hearts" continue to dominate his region. Landino exploited the poem's mention of Ravenna, the Adriatic city ruled by the da Polenta family, to report on Dante's posthumous state. "The body of the poet lies with honor in Ravenna," he admitted. But this disposition of Dante's body, no matter how honorable, was unacceptable. "All wise and learned men are of the opinion," he announced, "that the Florentine people should bring it back to his homeland and honor it with a tomb worthy of such a poet."[16]

Practically speaking, Landino and his collaborators knew it could take a long time before Dante returned *in corpore* to Florence—if ever. Absent physical repatriation, what better way was there to honor their illustrious ancestor than by using their scholarly, literary, and artistic talents to celebrate his body of work, his great poem of the afterlife above all? Late in life, when he had probably abandoned all hope of ever again entering his native city, Dante movingly entertained the fantasy of returning to receive the laurel crown at the Florentine baptistry, his portal to the faith that sustained him and shaped his work in exile. Having ascended to his birth constellation—Gemini—in the Celestial Paradise, Dante envisioned himself being crowned for his faith by Saint Peter. The idea of this religious coronation prompted Dante to imagine his great labor—the "sacred poem / to which both Heaven and earth have set their hand / so that it has made me lean for many years"—overcoming Florentine cruelty and winning him the highest honors as a poet in his birthplace.[17]

Marsilio Ficino welcomed the Florentine edition of the *Commedia*—annotated by Landino and adorned with engravings of Botticelli's illustrations—as the belated fulfillment of Dante's fantasy. Ficino's Latin letter and its Italian translation fill the penultimate chapter of the volume's prologue. The opening words leave no doubt that Florence's first printed publication of the poem amounts to Dante's glorious return: "Florence, long sad but joyful at last, warmly congratulates its poet Dante, who has come back to life and to his homeland for a glorious crowning after an absence of two centuries." Ficino has Florence address the poet directly, telling "my Dante" that his wish, should "piety overcome impiety," to return to his homeland and receive the laurel crown has not been in vain. Apollo, moved by Dante's long exile and Florence's tears, sends Mercury down to earth, where—in the guise of Cristoforo Landino—the god is instructed to "awaken you [Dante] from sleep with his sacred wand, take you upon his wings, bring you inside the walls of Florence, and finally crown your temples with Apollo's laurel."[18] Part homage to Dante, part blurb for the Florentine book and its editor, Ficino's contribution neatly folded the poet's fifteenth-century resurgence into their native city's own political and cultural renaissance.

As Florence celebrated Dante's return with its first printed edition of his *Commedia*—annotated, illustrated, and produced by the city's scholarly, artistic, and editorial luminaries—Bernardo Bembo found another way to honor the poet. Sent by Venice to govern Ravenna in 1481–1483, Bernardo did not have Dante's bones transferred to Florence, as he had promised Lorenzo de' Medici in 1475 or 1476. Keeping his word on repatriation would have proved difficult even if he had wanted to do it. Relations between Florence and Ravenna had already begun to fray by the time Bernardo assumed power in Ravenna. After Lorenzo's alliance with King Ferdinand of Naples in 1479, Venice and Florence moved in different political directions. When Venice and the papacy waged war on Ferrara in May 1482, Florence joined Naples, Milan, and Bologna in support of Ferrara.

Instead of compelling Ravenna to give Dante's bones to Florence, Bernardo ordered a major renovation of the poet's tomb, the first since his burial in 1321. At that time Guido Novello da Polenta had Dante's corpse placed in one of the many plain marble tombs scattered around Ravenna. Guido's plan to construct a monument befitting Dante's stature was thwarted, as we saw in Chapter 1, by the coup in 1322 that condemned the poet's benefactor to exile for the rest of his life. Dante's original sepulcher was housed in a small chapel connected by a portico to the larger Braccioforte chapel. The two buildings—their entrances facing each other—were only about ten meters apart along an east-west axis running along the northern side of the Church of Saint Francis. The small chapel was named for the Madonna because an image of the Virgin Mary had been painted on one of its walls. Dante's tomb was set along the back of the chapel, which abutted the wall of the Franciscan convent's cloisters.[19]

By the time Bernardo assumed power in Ravenna, not only did Dante lack the dignified monument Guido had intended, but his mortuary chapel and the surrounding structures—the portico and Braccioforte—had fallen into a deplorable state. Bernardo, at his own expense, commissioned Pietro Lombardo (ca. 1435–1515) to remodel the tomb and chapel. Pietro was an architect and sculptor mostly active in Venice but then living in Ravenna with his sons, Tullio and Antonio, both of whom followed in their father's professional footsteps and probably assisted him in his renovations. Pietro's most striking contribution was his architectural and artistic embellishment of the wall area behind and above Dante's tomb. Its centerpiece is a bas-relief of the poet, standing in profile, as he faces a book on a lectern. Dante wears a laurel headdress and ceremonial robe, his left hand raised to his chin while his right hand rests on another volume lying open on a small table-shelf holding, underneath, other books and an ink pot. Carved in Istrian marble, Dante is intensely engaged in his work. Debra Pincus, an art historian who has closely studied the renovated tomb, conjectures that the two open books are the Bible (on the lectern) and Virgil's *Aeneid*. Pietro's portrait captures Dante not reading or writing but, rather, deep in thought as he draws knowledge and inspiration from the two foundational texts.[20]

The sculptor framed the scene with rectangular strips of African marble—red with white veins—probably taken from an ancient monument, and he set all this within Grecian marble (white) topped by a lunette repeating the same colors and framing. The lunette contains a roundel displaying the words "virtuti et honori" within a garland of palm and laurel. The palm leaves, traditional symbol of victory through martyrdom, recognize Dante's virtue in enduring years of exile, while the laurel leaves honor his poetic excellence. The words in nominative form (*virtus et honor*) and the branches, which Bernardo used as his personal motto, also appear on a plaque that now decorates a convent wall next to the chapel but is thought to have once adorned the arch over the building's entrance. The motto on this plaque contains an additional Latin phrase, "his non cedo malis." By "my virtue and

3.1. Dante's tomb remodeled by Pietro Lombardo (Photo: Elisa Valentini, July 2016)

3.2. Pietro Lombardo's bas-relief of Dante (Photo: Elisa Valentini, July 2016)

honor," Bernardo has Dante say, "I do not yield to misfortune," a powerful testament to the poet's triumph in the face of hardship. The two phrases, along with wreaths of laurel and palm, were later repeated in the ornamental pattern of the wrought-iron fence erected between Dante's chapel and Braccioforte in 1921.[21]

The art historian Mary Garrard has posited a theory for the origin of Bernardo Bembo's motto that highlights the role of Dante's tomb in Florentine-Venetian relations. Garrard argues that a young Florentine woman laid claim to "virtue and honor" several years before Bernardo appropriated the words to express his devotion to Dante and Florence as well as to the woman—Bernardo's Platonic lover—by having Pietro Lombardo chisel them above Dante's tomb and on the front of the chapel. Leonardo da Vinci painted a small portrait of Ginevra de' Benci in the 1470s, perhaps to commemorate her marriage to Luigi Niccolini at age sixteen in 1474. The words he painted on the back of the panel today read, "virtutem forma decorat" (beauty adorns virtue), but infrared reflectography has revealed that the motto was originally "virtus et honor." The words are "written" on a scroll connecting two branches—one of palm leaves, one of laurel leaves—and

3.3. Roundel with Bernardo Bembo's motto above Dante's tomb (Photo: Elisa Valentini, July 2016)

wrapping around a sprig of juniper (*ginepro,* in honor of Ginevra) at the center of the emblem.[22]

Scholars took this figure on the back of the panel to mean that Bernardo commissioned the painting—or, at the very least, he owned the panel before Leonardo executed his portrait of Ginevra de' Benci. They interpreted the change from "virtue and honor" to "beauty adorns virtue" to mean that Bernardo modified his own motto to praise the painting's beautiful subject. Garrard has challenged this interpretation. She thinks it more likely that, since Bernardo's first verified use of the motto is at Dante's tomb, he took his beloved's emblem as his own (same words, same trees) and applied them to Florence's great poet. Unhappy with Bernardo's appropriation of her original words, Ginevra meanwhile sought to reclaim her identity by adopting a new motto—"beauty adorns virtue"—that recognized her inner and outer worth, her intelligence and poetic ability as well as her moral virtue and physical beauty. Whatever the motto's origin, Lorenzo de' Medici and other leading Florentines, participants themselves in the conventions of Platonic romance, would have understood Bernardo's homage to Dante also as a sign of his affection for Ginevra de' Benci and Florence.[23]

Bernardo Bembo may have thought to smooth the waters with Florence, especially with Lorenzo de' Medici, by renovating Dante's tomb and chapel. If so, the inclusion of an emblem in praise of his adored Ginevra de' Benci—one perhaps first devised by the woman herself—could have strengthened, even inadvertently, his conciliatory gesture toward Florence and its ruler.[24] The tomb and its surroundings, in any case, were in poor condition and benefited immensely from Bernardo's intervention, as he boasted in the Latin epitaph he wrote for the occasion. Bernardo's verses speak directly to the poet. "You were lying here, Dante, in a paltry grave," the epitaph laments, "the squalid site barely making you known to others, but now you rest beneath this marble vault, shining for all with brighter adornment." The refurbished funereal abode was Bernardo's gift to Dante, the poet "whom the Etruscan muses cherished most." He had a plaque inscribed with his epitaph placed on a wall of the chapel on May 27, 1483.[25]

Dante's sarcophagus was itself a focus of Pietro Lombardo's work commissioned by Bernardo Bembo in 1481–1483. Pietro kept the original marble tomb but reduced its overall size and sculpted a fish-scale design on the cover, a common feature of ancient tombs. He added a marble strip around the perimeter between the base and cover and set the tomb atop a pedestal mirroring the design of the upper strip. The nature and extent of this operation leaves little doubt that Pietro had to open the tomb and remove Dante's bones before rearranging them in the shortened, narrowed base.[26] Bernardo also had Pietro preserve the epitaph beginning "Iura monarchiae" (the rights of monarchy), the words today attributed to Rinaldo Cavalchini da Villafranca, for the newly designed sepulcher. Pietro engraved the epitaph, originally inscribed on the tomb in the late 1370s, on a marble relief imitating a rectangular piece of cloth tacked to the front of the tomb. The capital letters "S.V.F." centered above the epitaph confirm Bernardo's attribution of the words to Dante himself. Like many others, he took the first-person account—"Here I, Dante, am confined"—to mean that the poet composed the verses for his own grave, *sibi vivens fecit* (he wrote this while he was alive).

By having Pietro Lombardo keep this epitaph, so prominently displayed, on the remodeled tomb, Bernardo Bembo also kept alive the memory of Florentine mistreatment of Dante. The poet remains an exile even in death because, in the epitaph's final words, he was "born of Florence, a mother of little love." Bernardo did not just renege on his promise to have Dante's bones returned to Florence. Seen in the harshest light, he rubbed salt in the wound by improving the conditions of the poet's gravesite but not the reputation of his "native shores." The refined tomb and chapel further enshrined "the rights of Ravenna's people" to keep Dante in their city, his final refuge after being cast out of Florence.[27]

If Bernardo's renovations exacerbated tensions between Ravenna and Florence—and harmed rather than repaired his own relationship with Florentines—Cristoforo Landino's reaction gave strong evidence to the contrary. He had bonded with Bernardo over their shared humanist interests during the Venetian senator's earlier stays in Florence. Bernardo was among those in Florence who heard Landino's famous lectures on Dante. Landino also composed poems celebrating Bernardo's fervent—if Platonic—love for Ginevra de' Benci, the young married woman he worshiped. Landino lavished praise on both Bernardo, "a salutary star / sent from the city of Venice to the Tuscan lion," and "lovely Bencia," whose beauty "surpasses the goddesses in heaven." In singing of Bernardo's love for Ginevra, he declared his own love for Bernardo to be greater than the love forging such legendary male friendships as Pylades and Orestes; Pollux and his brother, Castor; and Pirithous and Theseus. It is small wonder, then, that when Landino heard of his friend's major overhaul of Dante's gravesite, he expressed admiration and gratitude rather than dismay and resentment. "All the people of Florence," Landino wrote to Bernardo, were indebted to him for bringing "its citizen—its poet— from squalor to splendor."[28]

Landino sent this letter not long after he presented his edition of Dante's *Commedia* to Florence on August 30, 1481. He regretted not having learned sooner of the renovations then under way in Ravenna. On behalf of Florence, he would have gladly acknowledged Bernardo's great gift to Dante in his commentary, twelve hundred copies of which had already been printed. Landino promised to correct this oversight in future publications. Until then, he hoped his Venetian friend would derive pleasure from an epigram, enclosed with the letter, that he composed in honor of Dante's renovated sepulcher:

> Ancient Ravenna made a new tomb,
> Built with refined artistry, for Tyrrhenian Dante.
> But hostile fate harms sacred tombs,
> Covering everything beautiful with ugly neglect.
> But you, Bernardo, favorite of the Venetian Senate,

You, Bembo, great protector of the holy song,
You took what envious time had worn down with its gnawing tooth,
And made it new with snow-white marble.[29]

Landino simultaneously praised Bembo and promoted his own work by sending a special copy of the 1481 edition to his friend. Held today in the Bibliothèque Nationale in Paris, Bembo's personal copy displays the senator's coat of arms and motto (*virtuti et honori*) and includes a page with Landino's letter and epigram.[30]

Even while gushing over Bernardo Bembo's efforts to improve the state of Dante's tomb and mortuary chapel, Landino could not help but betray a hint of Florentine pride and determination. Ravenna, it was true, held Dante's remains. But Landino spoke for his compatriots when he reminded his Venetian friend that the poet was and will always be Florentine. He is still "their citizen"; he is "their poet." This plain truth motivated the next generation of influential Florentines to resume calls for the repatriation of Dante's bones. A Florentine edition of Dante's *Commedia* and a major renovation of his tomb in Ravenna were simply no substitute for the return of his body.

4

Holy Grave Robbers

And it being believed that he had in his lifetime, in body as well as in spirit, made the journey through the Inferno, Purgatorio, and Paradiso, so in death it must now be assumed that in body as well as in spirit he has been received and welcomed into one of those realms.

—CARLO MARIA NARDI

Exploiting a propitious confluence of events at the start of the sixteenth century, Florence dispensed with polite petitions and turned to power politics to achieve its goal of repatriating Dante's bones. Spearheading the project this time was not an informal if dynamic cohort of like-minded cultural and political leaders but a small yet formidable organization with a charter, funding, and official functions. Ravenna was now controlled not by the Venetian Republic but, following the victory of the League of Cambrai over Venice in 1509, by papal Rome. Finally and most promising, the Medici ruler sanctioning and acting on Florentine claims to the poet's remains was not Lorenzo the Magnificent but his son Giovanni, better known as Pope Leo X. All the stars were aligned for what Florence had been trying to do for well over a century: retrieve Dante's bones from the city in which he had died and bury them in his place of birth.

Members of the Sacred Academy of the Medici (Sacra Accademia Medicea) were literary, artistic, and political leaders of Florence who saw themselves as "spiritual heirs" of the Platonic humanists gathered around Marsilio Ficino in the late fifteenth century. If the earlier group coalesced around shared interests in Florentine civic and cultural life, the new incarnation enjoyed the privileges and rights of an officially recognized academy. Like their predecessors, these prominent citizens sought to advance Florentine supremacy by celebrating and drawing on the glories of earlier times. Active from 1515 to 1519, the organization included at least two members of the extended Medici family (Pierfrancesco and Gerozio) and had such close ties to its

Florentine patron in Rome that it was sometimes called "his sacred academy." The pope allocated an annual budget to the academy bearing his family's name and approved a charter granting the power to crown poets and orators. The group met regularly for poetry readings, musical performances, and lectures on Dante and other poets.[1]

Giovanni de' Medici (1475–1521), the second son of Lorenzo, was installed as Pope Leo X on March 11, 1513. At least five letters sent by or on behalf of the Sacred Academy of the Medici urged the pope and his representatives in Rome to support Florentine efforts to take Dante's bones from Ravenna and entomb them in his native city. The first letter, which is remarkable for its origin, content, and history, has not received the attention it deserves. The letter was drafted by Girolamo Benivieni (1453–1542), an influential poet and humanist who was the "driving force" behind this determined Florentine campaign to repatriate Dante's remains. A member of the Sacred Academy, Benivieni wrote the letter for Lucrezia de' Medici Salviati (1470–1553), the pope's older sister, on March 15, 1515. Paul Oskar Kristeller, the renowned scholar of Italian Renaissance philosophy, published the portion of the letter provided in the catalog from the auction at which it was sold in 1936. After the owner loaned the document for display at the National Dante Exhibition in Rome in 1965, the complete text was published that year in the journal *Il veltro*.[2]

In this extraordinary letter, Lucrezia plays the family card to convince her brother to authorize the repatriation of Dante's bones. She reminds Leo of their father's close relationship with Bernardo Bembo during the time of the Venetian nobleman's ambassadorship in Florence. Bernardo, she recalls, had promised to Lorenzo the Magnificent that he would deliver to Florence "the bones of our truly divine poet Dante from Ravenna, where they are buried." But stronger even than Lorenzo's desire to repatriate Dante's body was the "love of foreigners for this poet," a love motivating Bernardo's "praiseworthy renovation of his gravesite, which had fallen into disrepair over time." Now, she informs her brother, members of the academy—"intellectuals, friends of theirs"—"thought the time had come in which these bones, after their long and undeserved exile, can and must, without delay, be returned to their homeland." Holding nothing back, Lucrezia exhorts Leo to fulfill their father's desire by taking this action on behalf of herself, the academy, and the entire city.[3]

Succeeding where others (including his illustrious father) had failed, the Medici pope would burnish his legacy by ending Dante's posthumous exile. He would win the praise of his fellow Florentines, certainly, but also of people throughout Italian lands. Lucrezia need say no more because she knows that, "for such a holy task, it suffices just to mention it and then let the just man respond to the stimulus of love." The pope's sister is confident he will seek to repatriate Dante's bones out of respect for "the celebrated and immortal name of such a great poet and compatriot," for "the poet's many lovers and admirers," and above all, for "the memory of his father and of his homeland." Florence is keen to worship "at least those few relics of such a great son." By providing this sacred treasure, Lucrezia assures her brother, "you will receive more lasting glory and honor than any city has ever bestowed on a citizen." The letter was sent in Lucrezia's name to the Supreme Pontiff "for the return of Dante's bones."[4]

The Sacred Academy of the Medici also presented its case for Dante's post-humous repatriation directly to Pope Leo X and prominent members of his court in Rome. In a letter dated June 1, 1515, less than two months after Lucrezia's personal appeal, the academy wrote to Pietro Bembo (1470–1547), whose father, Bernardo, had renovated Dante's tomb in 1483. Pietro, whose fame owes largely to his choice of the Tuscan vernacular (exemplified by Petrarch) as the model for Italian literature, served as Leo's secretary in Rome. The letter follows up on a visit in which Florentine ambassadors had asked Pietro to speak on their behalf with the pope. Rejoicing over positive reports from the ambassadors, the academy now thanks Pietro for having secured Leo's authorization for Florence "to repatriate the blessed bones of our sacred poet Dante." Ever attentive to its audience, the academy adds that these bones had been "reinterred and preserved with great devotion by the venerable memory of Your Lordship's father."[5]

Echoing Giannozzo Manetti's veneration of Dante's "sacred ashes" from a century earlier, the Sacred Academy of the Medici wrapped the poet's body in the language of sainthood. It sought not just to bring the remains of its "sacred poet" from Ravenna to Florence but to "translate" them (*translatare*), the technical term for the ritual movement of a saint's dead body to its most suitable location, typically a church closely associated with the holy person's life and legacy.[6] In what amounts to a deal with Pietro Bembo, the Florentines insisted on repaying their debt by giving something in "exchange"— *cambio*—for his role in convincing Leo to allow the repatriation. Once the "translation of these bones" took place, they promised, Florence would honor his father, Bernardo, with a plaque or other ornamentation on the new marble tomb built for Dante in the poet's native city. Unmentioned in the letter, this sign of gratitude to Bernardo Bembo would double as a tribute to his son Pietro for honoring Bembo *pére*'s word to Lorenzo de' Medici years earlier to repatriate Dante's bones.[7]

The Sacred Academy sought confirmation of papal backing two week later. In a letter of June 13, 1515, to Giulio de' Medici, it rejoiced with the cardinal over his cousin Leo's "concession" to Florence—his "most glorious city"—to "repatriate the blessed bones of our divine poet Dante." By enabling this repatriation, the pope would make Florence "fully bloom with virtue and immortal fame, as his ancestors have always done." Not wanting to pester His Holiness, the academy asked Giulio to help it bring the "sacred work" to fruition by reminding him that "the more he nurtures and favors it, the more his virtue will rise to heaven and shine on the whole world like the rays of the sun."[8]

If Pope Leo X was quick to promise, he was slow to act. On October 23, 1516, over a year after the initial letters, the academy bypassed the pope's most influential confidants and went straight to the man himself. It increased pressure on Leo to transfer Dante's remains from Ravenna to Florence by adding a theatrical flourish to its impassioned letter. The academy told the pope that its president, "enflamed with love and zeal for this sacred school" and wishing for "the repatriation of the bones of our divine poet Dante," reported hearing a voice at different hours at different times of year but always close to dawn, when true dreams occur. In these early morning hours at the home of the Sacred Academy, where President Antonio d'Orsino Benintendi resided, a loud voice proclaimed, "Now, now, now is the time for me to leave my loathsome tomb in Ravenna because, as I foretold, piety vanquishes wickedness."[9]

"O Most Holy Father," the writers explain to their papal patron, "the divine poet invokes the name of Your Blessedness." In a clever rhetorical ploy, the academy has Dante's ghost call on Leo for immediate repatriation by saying the time has come for him to leave his grave in Ravenna. In answering "the fervent prayers of his Academicians" to bring Dante's bones to Florence, Leo therefore answers "the most devout prayer of the divine poet." For this merciful act on behalf of Dante and the academy, the pope would win glory on earth and in Heaven. The academy assures Leo, moreover, that it has a plan and the resources to carry out the repatriation in a dignified manner, an operation it is sure the pope will approve. By conjuring the poet's ghost to give its request "a more urgent, impassioned, and authoritative air," the Sacred Academy of the Medici showed that it was also the Sacred Academy of Dante.[10]

Pope Leo X waited another three years before taking action, and then only after the Sacred Academy sent him a formal Latin letter written in a grand, solemn style. This time many prominent members of the organization personally signed the petition. They listed among the pope's favors to the academy his approval "for the transfer of Dante Alighieri's bones and ashes from Ravenna to his native soil." Included among the twenty named signatories to the letter, dated October 20, 1519, were two members of the Medici clan as well as the vicar of Cardinal Giulio de' Medici, Archbishop of Florence (Andrea Gammaro), distinguished Florentine poets and historians (Girolamo Benivieni, Bartolomeo Cerretani, Jacopo Nardi, Lorenzo Strozzi), and a descendant of the family of Dante's beloved Beatrice (Pietro Portinari).[11]

One name stood apart from the rest of these esteemed Florentines: "I, Michelangelo, sculptor, likewise supplicate Your Holiness." The only member of the academy to sign in Italian, not Latin, Michelangelo was also the only one to use his signature to bolster the case for repatriating Dante's bones. He offered, in his flinty vernacular prose, "to make a worthy tomb for the divine poet in an honorable place in this city." The great and versatile artist—sculptor, painter, and architect—was gathering marble for the façade of San Lorenzo during this period (the endeavor lapsed in early 1520) and beginning work on the Medici Chapel and Laurentian Library, projects that would occupy him for most of his remaining time in Florence before he left the city for good in 1534. In Leo's good graces for undertaking these monumental tributes to Medici power and influence, Michelangelo encouraged papal support for Dante's repatriation by promising to build a suitably grand tomb for the city's supreme poet. For a pope obsessed with cementing the legacy of his family's Florentine dynasty, this offer may have been the incentive needed to drive him to action.[12]

Michelangelo's well-known admiration for Dante, born of deep knowledge of the poet's *Commedia,* is evident in his artistic production over many years.[13] Michelangelo also expressed his reverence for Dante in his own poetry. His poems, like his painting and drawing, "often have a quality that can best be described as sculptural," and the two sonnets he wrote on Dante support this observation.[14] Composed over twenty-five years after the 1519 petition, Michelangelo's verses praise Dante as a "shining star" bringing unmerited glory to Florence. The gates of Heaven may have been opened for Dante, but those of his "ungrateful native land" were "closed to his just desire" with his banishment from Florence. "Just as no exile was ever less deserved than his," Michelangelo says of Dante, "so no one of like worth or greater was ever born."[15]

Urging the transfer of the poet's bones from Ravenna to Florence, Michelangelo and other members of the Sacred Academy of the Medici sought to end Dante's exile with their formal letter to Pope Leo X. The Florentine artist was destined for a similar posthumous experience forty-five years later. After Michelangelo's death in Rome on February 18, 1564, a few weeks before his eighty-ninth birthday, the painter and art historian Giorgio Vasari acted on the authority of Duke Cosimo I de' Medici to have his fellow Tuscan's body transferred to Florence for burial in the Church of Santa Croce. A year before Michelangelo's death, Vasari and Vincenzio Borghini, a Florentine historian and Benedictine prior, had anointed him "head, father, and master" of their newly founded Academy of Design (Accademia del Disegno), the "first academic institution devoted to art in the West." Michelangelo was indifferent at best to the professional honor, but the elaborate funeral ceremonies that Vasari and Borghini staged for him in Florence lent legitimacy and prestige to their fledgling academy while at the same time reconciling the great artist's legacy with the Medici house.[16] By petitioning the pope to reconcile Dante with his native city in 1519, Michelangelo and his colleagues in the Sacred Academy likewise aimed to honor their Medici patron while advancing their own interests.

Unlike previous entreaties, this request for repatriation—sweetened by Michelangelo's offer to sculpt Dante's tomb in Florence—bore tangible if unanticipated results. Pier Desiderio Pasolini (1844–1920), an Italian senator and distinguished historian of Ravenna, his native city, provides a vivid account of how papal intervention enabled Florence finally to act on its desire to seize Dante's bones. When the president of Romagna, Bernardo de' Rossi, imposed a new tax on Ravenna (150 gold *scudi* per month) in Leo's name, ostensibly to pay for the president's Swiss guard, local residents promptly rioted. In response to the city magistrate's refusal to comply, Bernardo had the official and other rebellious citizens taken from Ravenna and held in the nearby town of Cesena. Two deputies from Florence's Sacred Academy, accompanied by the regional president and a team of master masons, were thus assured of meeting no resistance when they entered Dante's mortuary chapel at night. Once inside, they approached the marble tomb "ever so quietly, almost like thieves (though by permission of the pope)." With considerable effort, the masons removed the heavy marble cover that Pietro Lombardo had remodeled over thirty-five years earlier. But when the Florentines peered inside, they saw by the light of candles that "the tomb was empty!"[17]

Jacopo Nardi (1476–1563), a celebrated Florentine historian and poet, was one of the twenty prominent members of the Sacred Academy of the Medici who had signed the decisive petition to Pope Leo X in 1519. If Jacopo was not one of the academy's two envoys sent to retrieve Dante's bones from Ravenna, he would have heard the shocking news soon enough from his crestfallen colleagues: other grave robbers had beaten them to the punch and already removed the poet's remains from his tomb. Passed down from generation to generation, the story of Dante's empty tomb was known to Carlo Maria Nardi when he wrote a biography of his illustrious ancestor in 1735. Carlo recounted and commented on the moment of revelation in exquisitely Dantean terms. "The eagerly desired translation came to naught," he wrote, "because when the two deputies from the Academy arrived at the tomb, they found Dante neither in soul nor in body; and it being believed that he had in his lifetime, in body as well as in spirit, made the journey through the Inferno, Purgatorio, and Paradiso, so in death it must now be assumed that in body as well as in spirit he has been received and welcomed into one of those realms." Since Dante's living body visited the afterlife, Nardi's sardonic logic goes, his dead body must have once again joined his soul there. With Dante's bones gone missing, the Florentines were unable to transfer them like the remains of a saint—a "translation" (*traslazione*)—to the poet's native city for burial in the tomb that Michelangelo promised to make.[18]

Dante's bones, it turns out, did not travel far at all from their original tomb in Ravenna, much less to an infernal circle below the earth's crust or to a purgatorial terrace in the southern hemisphere or to a heavenly planet. After the box of bones with Dante's name on it was accidentally discovered during excavations close to his mortuary chapel in 1865, subsequent investigations produced a reasonably clear picture of how, when, and by whom his remains were taken from the tomb before the Florentines had a chance to do the same.

It was not difficult to determine who had preemptively stolen Dante's bones: Franciscan friars had both motive and means to conduct what they considered a legitimate violation of the poet's gravesite, a "holy theft" as noble as those that brought the remains of saints from one location to another. They aimed, however, not to move Dante's bones to a more sacred site but to protect them against an illegitimate "translation" from his final refuge in life to the city that had punished him with unjust exile. In foiling Florentine plans to repatriate Dante, the local Franciscans acted not only from loyalty to Ravenna. They also raided the poet's tomb because they thought his Franciscan inclinations made them the rightful custodians of his remains.

Dante's admiration and affection for Saint Francis of Assisi is deeply embedded in his thought and poetry. The poet's views on evangelical poverty and papal authority, major themes of the *Divine Comedy*, owe a great deal to Francis and his followers. Dante repays this debt with a powerful eulogy to Francis, spoken by Thomas Aquinas, in the sphere of the sun and with the saint's exalted position in the celestial rose of Paradise. Saint Francis, "all seraphic in his ardor," was ordained by divine providence as a prince of the church, along with Saint Dominic, whose wisdom made him "resplendent with cherubic light" on earth. When Dante says he went "to the schools of the religious orders and to the disputations held by the philosophers," he probably refers to his education—even if informal—at the *studia,* or schools, of Santa Croce and Santa Maria Novella, the principal Franciscan and Dominican churches, respectively, in Florence. At Santa Croce, just a few blocks from his house, Dante encountered the ideas of renowned Franciscan authorities like Pietro di Giovanni Olivi and Ubertino da Casale on the fraught role of poverty and material possessions in the mendicant orders and the church in general. Dante's strong Franciscan inclinations have led some commentators to take the wayfarer's wearing of a cord—a distinctive feature of Franciscan identity—in the afterlife as a sign that the poet was himself a lay (tertiary) Franciscan or even, less plausibly, a Franciscan novice. True or not, this belief greatly appealed to the friars in Ravenna, for whom guarding Dante's bones—and keeping them in the city—was a way to reciprocate the poet's love of Saint Francis.[19]

The location of the Franciscan convent in relation to Dante's tomb allowed the friars to take physical possession of his remains before the two Florentine envoys, backed by Pope Leo X, could repatriate them. The chapel in which Dante was buried in 1321 stood just outside the cloisters of the convent. The chapel's entrance faced Braccioforte to the west, with Dante's marble tomb sitting along the back or eastern wall beneath Pietro Lombardo's bas-relief of the poet in profile. The tomb and Lombardo's decorations rested on a remnant of the original cloister wall, with the back of Dante's tomb actually lodged in this wall. When Lombardo had remodeled the sarcophagus in 1483, he inserted a marble strip—just over four inches high—between the base and cover along the three visible sides of the tomb. He understandably opted not to waste precious marble at the back of the tomb, fixed in the primitive cloister wall, but instead filled the four-inch gap between the base and cover of this hidden side with a double row of bricks. Physical evidence reveals how the Franciscans exploited this architectural feature to extract Dante's bones with impunity and to cover their tracks.[20]

To access Dante's tomb surreptitiously, the Franciscans had only to break through their cloister wall from the inside and create an opening in the old cloister wall, in which the back of the sarcophagus was lodged. Just over a foot of empty space—thirty-four centimeters—separated the new and old cloister walls. The friars probably decided to rob the grave after catching wind of Florentine requests to the Medici pope for permission to take the poet's bones from Ravenna, perhaps acting on their plan soon before the foreign envoys arrived in 1519. Corrado Ricci imagined a group of Franciscans waiting until late at night, when the city was asleep, before sneaking out of their cells and gathering in the cloisters. By the light of torches, they found the part of the wall corresponding to the location of Dante's tomb on the other side and began using a hammer and chisel to create an opening.

Ricci tested this hypothesis on April 14, 1890, when he had workers scrape away the surface of the cloister wall. The underlying stonework showed unmistakable signs of having been repaired. The straight line of bricks was interrupted by an uneven mixture of rocks and broken bricks used to fill the hole. Once the friars broke through their cloister wall, they reached the back of Dante's tomb just over a foot away, lodged in a remnant of the old cloister wall. Since Pietro Lombardo had set bricks between the cover and base at the back of the tomb, the Franciscans could now see the bones simply by removing a few of these bricks. Perhaps, as Ricci fancied, they recited the prayer of the dead as they illuminated the inside of the ancient sarcophagus and extracted, one by one, Dante's bones, probably needing tongs or another tool to reach more distant parts of the skeleton.

Overall this procedure worked well. A Franciscan friar could extend his arm through the gap between the base and cover of the tomb to grab, with his hand or the tongs, the poet's vertebrae, ribs, tibias, and other bones—even the large femurs—and pull them into the cloisters of the convent. The opening was too narrow for one part of the skeleton, however. Even without the lower mandible (already gone missing), Dante's skull could not pass through the four-inch space. To rectify this, the friars took a chisel to the top of the base, taking off enough marble to enlarge the opening to nearly six inches (fifteen centimeters) in diameter, wide enough for them to extract the poet's skull with ease. It was far better to damage the marble tomb, obviously, than to break the bones venerated for once housing "the brain that envisioned the realms of the afterlife in the immortal poem!"[21]

Today visitors can find a plaque marking the spot on the wall through which the Franciscans gained access to Dante's bones, an exhumation from their perspective at once holy and patriotic. Placed on the cloister wall after Ricci's excavation in 1890, the inscription reads,

4.1. Traces of the hole through which the Franciscans raided Dante's tomb in 1519 (Corrado Ricci, *L'ultimo rifugio di Dante Alighieri* [Milan: Hoepli, 1891], 342)

4.2. The back of Dante's tomb showing the gap between the cover and base (Corrado Ricci, "L'arca lapidea," in *Ricognizione delle ossa di Dante fatta nei giorni 28–31 ottobre 1921*, ed. Santi Muratori, Corrado Ricci, Giuseppe Sergi, and Fabio Frassetto [Rome: Reale Accademia Nazionale dei Lincei, 1923], 15)

Traces of the hole
Through which the Franciscans
In the early sixteenth century
Extracted Dante's bones
From the sepulcher
Then attached to the wall on the other side
Thus saving his bones for Ravenna

The Florentine envoys must have noticed damage to the back of Dante's tomb, where marble had been chipped off the top of the base, several broken pieces having fallen to the bottom. Given the tomb's proximity to the cloisters, they must have also quickly realized who had taken the bones and how they did it. This near certainty leads us to wonder why the Florentines chose not to exploit their powerful position to convince the Franciscans, through force if necessary, to return the stolen bones. This is one of the great unanswered questions of Dante's graveyard history: Why the papal-backed deputies and their companions did not raid the convent, as the friars had raided Dante's sepulcher, and subject the perpetrators—or their brothers in the know—to extreme methods used by secular and religious authorities alike to extract confessions, particularly as there was an actual crime here to confess. If they pursued this course of action, no record of it has come down to us.

A response composed within a few years of the theft confirmed that the Florentines and their papal patron and compatriot took no such drastic measure to retrieve Dante's bones, inaction that left the sixteenth-century commentator as perplexed as later ones. Leo X died on December 1, 1521, and after the short pontificate of Adrian VI, another Medici—Leo's cousin Giulio—was elected pope on November 19, 1523. If repatriating Dante's bones, no matter how important to Florence, could not compete with other items on Leo's agenda following the botched mission to Ravenna, it paled in comparison to the epochal events bedeviling Pope Clement VII. Under increasing pressure to stem the tide of the Protestant Reformation, Clement was at the same time caught in hostilities between the Holy Roman Emperor Charles V and King Francis I of France, a conflict that led to the emperor's sack of Rome in 1527.

A Florentine writer of the time nonetheless felt that the continuing absence of Dante's body from Florence—because of the Franciscans' preemptive theft—was a subject well worth Clement's consideration. In a sonnet, the anonymous author reminded Clement that when his "brother Leo, the supreme shepherd," had courteously asked the Ravennese "only for the bones of our orator," they responded by removing Dante's remains from the tomb and taking them elsewhere. If only Leo had apprehended and tortured the thieves or those who knew them, "the bones would have returned from wherever they were," for which the pope would have won "praise and honor." Florence beseeched Clement to turn his attention to Dante, the "light and splendor of your homeland." "If not to Dante," the Florentine writer wittily asked Pope Clement VII, then "to whom would you show clemency?" He urged Clement to use his power, since Leo had not, to have Dante's bones brought to Florence and buried there "for the eternal fame and glory of his name."[22] We do not know if Clement ever received this lyrical appeal to force the Franciscans to produce Dante's body for burial in Florence. If he did, the chance of him acting on it during such tumultuous times was slight at best.

5

An Empty Tomb

No,—she denied me what was mine—my roof,
And shall not have what is not hers—my tomb.

—LORD BYRON

So began a stretch of nearly 350 years during which Dante's bones lay somewhere outside their tomb. If the original gravesite was home to the poet's body, then the Franciscans' stealthy exhumation, no matter how pure their motives, initiated a new stage of displacement. To prevent Florence from repatriating Dante, and so ending the political exile that had shaped the poet's life and work, the friars had removed his physical remains from their sepulchral abode. A victim of his own law of poetic justice, Dante was an exile in death as in life. The theft made him a posthumous exile twice over: in one case from his native city, in the other from his original tomb. The absence of the poet's bones, however, did not prevent further changes to the small chapel housing the empty sarcophagus. Taking place as if the corpse were still there, renovations in the 1600s and 1700s marked a major shift in the debate over claims to Dante's bones and their final resting place. In these instances, the regional rivalry between Florence and Ravenna took a back seat to the intramural conflict between Ravenna's Franciscan friars and the city's political leadership.

The friars claimed possession of Dante's chapel on the basis of Archbishop Filippo Fontana's granting of the church (then called San Pietro Maggiore) and surrounding properties—"the piazza, the cemetery, houses, and other structures"—to the Franciscan order in 1261. They reaffirmed control of the chapel in the middle of the seventeenth century by making significant changes to the building and the grounds around it. In 1658–1660, they had the colonnade connecting the chapel to Braccioforte taken down and replaced with a wall. As part of these renovations, the chapel itself was detached from the cloisters of the Franciscan convent and rotated ninety degrees: the eastern wall with Dante's tomb and Lombardo's sculpted relief of the poet, previously attached to the cloister wall, now became the southern wall of the chapel. In this new orientation, Dante's tomb faced north, where the chapel entrance (previously facing Braccioforte) opened onto the street. They also installed a small gate—locked with a key—in front of the arched entranceway. Finally, as if declaring ownership of the chapel by signing their work, the friars paid for the painting of an effigy of Saint Francis and the coats of arms of four Franciscan pontiffs—Sixtus IV (1471–1484), Sixtus V (1585–1590), Nicholas IV (1288–1292), and antipope Alexander V (1409–1410)—on the new façade.[1]

Investigations following the discovery of Dante's remains in the nineteenth century confirmed that the Franciscans were in possession of the bones even while caring for the chapel as if they were still inside the original tomb. Over time, ordinary friars may not have known about Dante's stolen bones, but the conventual leadership clearly did. After the confiscation in the early 1500s, high-ranking Franciscans passed the bones down to their successors, one generation to another. Writings on the makeshift coffin found in 1865 show that Antonio Santi had viewed the bones on June 3, 1677, and moved them four and a half months later, probably to another hiding place in the convent. Documents in the convent's archives enabled researchers to verify, from handwriting analysis, that the Brother Santi who recorded these interactions with Dante's bones was in fact chancellor of the convent at that time. Born in Ravenna on August 3, 1644, Antonio Santi was already the convent's chancellor by 1672, a position that involved managing the friars' business affairs. Just a few weeks after viewing Dante's bones, he recorded a proposal, approved by the brothers, to sell five or six casks of white wine at the best price possible. Highly respected, Santi became the convent's *guardiano,* or father superior, in 1700, three years before his death.[2]

Perhaps because the friars knew Dante's bones were safe inside their convent, they paid less attention to the inside of the chapel when they detached the building from the cloisters, rotated it ninety degrees, and turned the façade into a tribute to Franciscan glory. Disregard of the interior space took a heavy toll over time, with conditions reaching an appalling state by the last decade of the seventeenth century. Not only was the chapel run-down and littered with debris, but intruders climbed over the gate during the night and behaved in ways that made other offenses to Dante's tomb seem mild by comparison. At one point, city authorities were summoned to keep "vagrant women from defiling Dante's monument with their sordid acts," the precise form of these acts apparently best left unmentioned. The chapel's deterioration impelled Ravenna's magistrate, joined by the pope's cardinal legate, "to have the place cleaned and barred with an iron gate to prevent easy access bringing all kinds of filth," the word for "filth" (*lordure*) echoing Dante's deprecating description of sins punished in the lower depths of Hell.[3]

City officials asserted their right to clean and refurbish Dante's chapel because they believed it fell within Ravenna's jurisdiction, not that of the Franciscan order. They cited several factors in their favor to justify the city's work on the chapel in 1692. Removed from the church and convent, the chapel was an isolated building facing a public street. Dante's tomb, originally belonging to Guido Novello da Polenta and later remodeled by order of Bernardo Bembo, governor of Ravenna for the Republic of Venice, came under Ravenna's dominion in 1511 when Pope Julius II invested the city's *signoria*, or ruling council, with full legal rights to what had once been subject to Polentani and then Venetian rule. For a long time the commune, not the Franciscans, had kept the key to the chapel gate. The friars themselves had implicitly recognized Ravenna's legal authority over Dante's chapel in 1687, the city magistrate argued, when they sought his permission for a project—later abandoned—that would have required the relocation of the poet's tomb.[4]

The magistrate, supported by the papal legate Domenico Maria Corsi, a Florentine cardinal, ordered workers to begin cleaning, repairing, and redecorating Dante's chapel on May 22, 1692. When the friars, while reciting morning prayers in the church, realized what was happening, they sent two brothers to confront the workers inside the chapel. Informed that a city official had issued a public order for the project, the Franciscans replied that the chapel was not under city jurisdiction and told the workers to leave the premises, which they did. Just two days later, however, the friars were awakened at eight o'clock by the sound of hammers, shovels, and pickaxes pounding walls supporting the chapel's iron gate. After a protesting brother was presented with Cardinal Corsi's ordinance forbidding the Franciscans from harassing or otherwise preventing the men from doing their job, a flock of friars rushed out of the convent and, "armed with poles, brooms, rolling pins, and similar objects," fought the workers. "Overwhelmed by the ardor and number of the disciples of the pious friar of Assisi," the men "were forced to flee, taking with them the holy marks of so many blows!"[5]

The workers—masons and artists—were not alone when they returned six days later. In petitions opposing the renovations, Franciscans called it an "attack" (*attentato*) each time the men came to work on the chapel, but on this day the loaded charge was not entirely unfounded: the six workers who arrived at noon on Wednesday, May 30, were accompanied by a captain leading thirty to forty armed guards. Protected by this show of force and in the presence of a large crowd of onlookers, stone masons immediately set to tearing down part of the front wall so they could remove the iron gate. The convent's father superior threatened the men with excommunication, but to no avail. Over the next six days, a phalanx of ten to twelve armed guards, refreshed with periodic changes, stood watch near the main entrance to the convent, only a few steps from the chapel. Thus shielded from Franciscan interference, the renovators worked day and night on the exterior and interior of Dante's chapel. In the event that the friars put up resistance, a bell would summon all soldiers in the city to come and defend the guards and workers. "A sorry episode of such petty animosity" was how a later commentator assessed this confrontation between the city and the convent.[6]

Actors in the restoration project enumerated changes made to the building in 1692. On the outside, master mason Cicognini reported that he and his men rebuilt the front wall and installed a new iron gate with a lock. Above the arched entranceway, they replaced the tributes to Saint Francis and the Franciscan pontiffs with marble tablets displaying the coat of arms of the papal legate Cardinal Domenico Maria Corsi, flanked by those of vice legate Giovanni Salviati and the Commune of Ravenna. Inside the chapel, they repaired the walls and ceiling vault, painting the surfaces white, and redid the pavement with terra-cotta tiles.[7]

Cicognini also oversaw the placement of an epitaph on the right-hand side (entering the building) recognizing the contribution of these renovations to Dante's physical afterlife. Finding the mausoleum erected by Guido Novello da Polenta and decorated by Bernardo Bembo "nearly laid to waste from the injuries of time," the council and people of Ravenna, led by Cardinal Corsi and Monsignor Salviati, took it upon themselves to "repair, renew, and adorn the precious chamber as if it were their own." While Ravenna asserted its dominance over the Franciscan convent by renovating Dante's chapel, the epitaph struck a note of triumphalism over the city's other rival for the poet's posthumous affection. "Exiled from Florence," Dante was "generously received by Ravenna, which honored him in death as it had rejoiced in him in life," the epitaph began. This familiar opposition between guilty Florence and pious Ravenna set up the later recasting of the renovations as Ravenna's way of "reconciling the ashes of the great citizen to his homeland."[8] Ravenna's benevolence extended not just to Dante but to the city that had exiled him.

Another worker, Girolamo Domenico Bertos, recalled sculpting the three coats of arms placed on the façade and having his assistants clean and polish all the marble fixtures inside the chapel, including "the marble tomb holding (so they say) the bones of the poet Dante." The sculptor's offhand remark—"so they say"—betrayed a lack of confidence in the actual presence of the bones. Franciscans in Ravenna were apparently not the only ones who knew Dante's tomb was empty. After the friars stole the bones in the early 1500s, rumors of the empty tomb "always swirled among the common people," but a trail of evidence to this effect only emerged in the late eighteenth and early nineteenth centuries.[9] Even then, interested sides refrained from broadcasting such an inconvenient truth, preferring instead to express it through innuendo, ambiguity, and obfuscation. It was as if there were a tacit agreement among those in the know, a conspiracy to keep the secret for one's own benefit: for the Franciscans, to avoid having outsiders discover or confirm that the friars had stolen the bones and demand their "repatriation" to the tomb or, worse, to Florence; for Ravenna—perhaps for Florence, as well—to avoid the embarrassment of admitting that it had lost the body of Italy's supreme poet and ancestral father. Informed parties understandably thought it best to maintain the comforting illusion that Dante's bones still lay in the marble sarcophagus chosen by Guido Novello da Polenta in 1321, remodeled by Pietro Lombardo (for Bernardo Bembo) in 1483, and repositioned by the Franciscans when they detached and rotated the chapel in 1658–1660.

Ravenna's renovations to Dante's chapel in 1692 hardly ended acrimonious debate between the city and the Franciscan convent over rights to the site. On the contrary, the two sides continued to fight over jurisdiction until the next major overhaul, nearly a hundred years later, produced the *tempietto*—"little temple"—that we see today. Competing claims to the chapel resurfaced when it received unusual visitors just two years after Ravenna completed its renovations. On August 26, 1694, Giuseppe Morena, a convicted criminal from Faenza, a town not far from Ravenna, escaped from prison and, accompanied by two guards he had corrupted, sought sanctuary. Pursued by law enforcement, the three men first tried to enter the Church of Saint Francis; when that failed, they grabbed the iron gate in front of Dante's tomb and refused to let go. The ruckus drew a large crowd that shouted for the police to respect ecclesiastic immunity. This in turn alerted the father superior, who poked his head out the convent window. Protesting to the police chief, he called on witnesses to keep the officers from violating the chapel's immunity. The police backed off, but a short while later, when the papal vice legate ordered the immediate capture of the fugitives, they pulled the men from the gate and brought them back to prison.[10]

The debate over sanctuary did not end there. Unhappy with the city's forcible removal of the fugitives from the chapel gate, Ravenna's episcopal vicar filed a protest. The argument against immunity, in his report, rested on the claim that Dante had been declared a heretic after his death. The chapel therefore "remained polluted even if it were a sacred place and so could not enjoy ecclesiastic immunity." He concluded, however, that this argument did not apply because the poet's bones "were no longer in the chapel or mausoleum." The vicar willingly betrayed knowledge of Dante's empty tomb to have the chapel, unpolluted by a heretic's remains, retain its immunity. Ignoring the question of heresy, the Congregation on Immunity in Rome concurred, affirming on September 28, 1694, that Dante's chapel was truly a sanctuary as part of the Franciscan convent. Whether under the jurisdiction of Ravenna or the Franciscans, the chapel was connected with the convent, just as family chapels were still part of a church, and so earned the right of immunity. The Congregation called for the transfer of the captured fugitives from the city jail to a church prison.[11]

Recognition of immunity left unresolved the question of jurisdiction. City and convent battled over rights to Dante's chapel even as its condition deteriorated. This time the Franciscans took the lead, as they had in the mid-1600s, in sprucing up the place. Acting on their claim of ownership, the friars hired workers to pave the street in front of the chapel in 1735 and, eight years later, in 1743, to clean the façade and brighten the interior with a fresh coat of paint. Nor did Ravenna intervene when the friars had the artist Andrea Barbiani redecorate the wall above the entrance with images the city had removed in 1692: Saint Francis and the order's four pontiffs once again welcomed worshipers to the chapel housing the tomb in which Dante's body was buried in 1321 and was said still to lie.[12]

That visitors were in fact venerating an empty grave was confirmed—though not publicly acknowledged—when another papal legate tied his legacy to Dante's by remodeling the poet's mausoleum. Cardinal Luigi Valenti Gonzaga (1725–1808) decided to fund the construction of a mortuary chapel worthy of Dante in 1780, two years after he began his first term as the papal legate in Romagna. A champion of the arts and sciences, Cardinal

Gonzaga commissioned several major projects in the region, including the redesign of the Ravegnana road, the main thoroughfare connecting Ravenna with Forlì and eventually, feeding into Via Emilia, with Tuscany. He became the librarian of the Holy Roman Church in 1802, a prestigious position he held until his death in Rome in 1808. On May 7, 1780, Ravenna's governing council signed a resolution expressing the city's gratitude to "our most worthy legate" for "generously giving, at his own expense, a more elegant and decorous appearance to the mausoleum of the eminent poet and scholar Dante Alighieri." In honoring Dante, the renovation will also "add to the beauty and dignity of this city."[13]

For the major redesign of Dante's chapel, Gonzaga chose Camillo Morigia (1743–1795), a highly regarded architect from Ravenna's nobility. Noteworthy among Morigia's other projects were his completion of the façade of the Church of Santa Maria in Porto (1775–1783) and his redesign of several rooms and the atrium of the library for the monks of Classe (now the Classense Library). Morigia's neoclassical style, characterized by pure geometric lines and modest decorative flourishes, is evident in his conception of Dante's renovated chapel. Made of ashlar blocks—dressed rectangular stonework—the exterior walls rose up to a small cupola topped by an ornamental pine cone. A cornice of Istrian marble ran beneath a large lunette framing the door below and wrapped around the building, with the lunette repeated on the two sides. Morigia inserted a triangular pediment between the lunette and cupola, the triangle's interior—the tympanum—adorned with an ouroboros, the tail-biting serpent, traditional symbol of eternity. Three Latin words inscribed above the doorway—"DANTIS POETAE SEPULCRUM"—announced what lay inside the chapel, "the tomb of the poet Dante." On a ledge just above the inscription, Morigia placed the Gonzaga family's coat of arms. The cardinal, like previous sponsors of the major changes to Dante's chapel, made sure that he received full credit for his contribution.[14]

Inside the chapel, Morigia placed white stucco medallions with portraits of Virgil, Brunetto Latini, Cangrande della Scala, and Guido Novello da Polenta in the pendentives, the four triangular corners connecting the walls to the cupola. A festooned band circled the base of the spherical ceiling. The rectangular marble tablet with Bernardo Bembo's epitaph from 1483—the one beginning "in a paltry grave" (*exigua tumuli*)—dominated the wall to the right (entering the chapel), while an epitaph commemorating the latest renovations stared back from the left-hand wall. These new Latin verses, composed for the occasion by Abbot Stefano Morcelli, celebrated Dante as

5.1. Dante's chapel remodeled by Camillo Morigia in 1780–1782 (Corrado Ricci, *L'ultimo rifugio di Dante Alighieri* [Milan: Hoepli, 1891], 315)

the "first poet of his age, the restorer of the most refined culture." Acknowledging previous patrons of Dante's physical afterlife—Guido and Ostasio da Polenta for raising the original monument, Bernardo Bembo for embellishing it as the poet deserved—Morcelli's epitaph honored above all Cardinal Gonzaga for enlarging and restoring the mausoleum, which "the neglect of earlier generations had ruined." Although the epitaph dated the renovations commissioned by Gonzaga to 1780, the work was not completed until two years later, with the inauguration held on June 22, 1782.[15]

Morigia's substantial remodeling of Dante's chapel afforded another opportunity to verify or disprove rumors that the tomb was empty. Cardinal Gonzaga was not the sort of man to pass up this chance. Individuals present in Ravenna at the time confirm that he had the tomb opened to see what if anything it contained. Brother Tommaso Marradi, sacristan of the Franciscan convent, wrote a four-line record of the inspection on the cover of a mass book. Discovered in 1865 among the convent's papers, Marradi's note said that after "nothing at all was found" in the tomb, "it was then sealed up again with the Cardinal's seal and the whole thing was kept secret."[16] Everyone's interests were better served by retaining the belief that Dante's bones still lay in their tomb.

Camillo Spreti (1743–1830), a respected historian from Ravenna, corroborated the friar's account. In his history of the city, published in 1822, Spreti recalled that Cardinal Gonzaga "insisted on opening the sarcophagus—in a public forum with authorities present—to confirm the authenticity of such precious contents." At this point, however, Spreti diverged from Brother Marradi's straightforward report to forge a masterful piece of rhetorical obfuscation, a head-spinning sentence worthy of the most skillful spokespersons for scandal-prone politicians. Instead of admitting, as the Franciscan sacristan had, that "nothing at all was found," Spreti wrote that "they found there what was necessary in order not to doubt"—they "found" confirmation, in other words. But of what? Was the tomb empty or not? The rest of the sentence hardly clarified the matter: "And to the memories that the tomb enclosed," he spun, "others were now added to make known to posterity the indubitable truth without objection that Ravenna alone could boast of possessing the remains of such a great poet." Without actually lying, Spreti succeeded in avoiding the awkward truth: Dante's bones lay somewhere in Ravenna, just not in his tomb.[17]

To judge from the experience of famous visitors at Dante's tomb after these latest renovations, Cardinal Gonzaga succeeded in keeping knowledge of the poet's missing bones from going public. Vittorio Alfieri (1749–1803), a celebrated eighteenth-century Italian poet best known for his tragedies, wrote in his autobiography of a journey he took in 1783 from Siena to Venice and back again, visiting other Italian cities along the way. He had recently published his first ten tragedies and completed four of five odes inspired by the American Revolution (*America libera*)—he composed the final ode in Venice (June 8–10, 1783) after learning of the signing of the Treaty of Paris (September 3, 1783) that ended the war between England and the United States of America. Tyranny, freedom, and the exercise of power are recurring themes in Alfieri's works. His life, "both as he lived it and as he narrated it," writes a scholar of modern Italian literature, "was that of an exiled intellectual defying political oppression in all its forms."[18]

"From Bologna," Alfieri recalled of his travels in 1783, "I went out of my way to visit the tomb of the Poet in Ravenna." Less than a year after the inauguration of the remodeled chapel, he approached the tomb to worship, his behavior betraying no doubt about Dante's physical presence. "I spent an entire day there," he wrote, "dreaming, praying, and weeping." His journey tapped a "new and copious stream of tender rhymes." Sonnets flowed from his pen nearly every day. Inspired by his visit to Dante's tomb, he composed one of those poems on May 31, 1783. In the sonnet, Alfieri imagines himself in conversation with "great father Alighieri." Dante looks down from Heaven on his "not unworthy disciple," who, prostrate before the sarcophagus, "draws deep sighs from his heart." Imploring the master to illuminate him, Alfieri asks if a poet seeking eternal glory "must take up arms against envy and cowardice." Speaking from experience, Dante bemoans the high cost of engaging one's detractors. "Son," he says, "I took up arms, and it pains me greatly, because in this way I gave fame to people so vile they were not worth trampling with my feet." Do not lower your gaze, Father Dante commands Alfieri, but rather "go, thunder, conquer." Should you find envious adversaries at your feet, better just to "pass over them" without even looking, a rejection even harsher than Dante's dismissal of cowardly souls on the outskirts of Hell.[19]

When Cristoforo Landino, writing in the fifteenth century, honored Dante as "the father of your homeland," the *patria* in question was naturally Florence, the city to which Landino sought to repatriate Dante textually—with the first Florentine printed edition of the *Divine Comedy*—if not physically. Vittorio Alfieri's paean to "great father Alighieri" in the late eighteenth century pivoted on the poet's admiration for Dante as a personal father figure.

Identifying with his late medieval precursor, Alfieri came to view himself as, in the literary scholar Joseph Luzzi's words, "a kind of second Dante." Alfieri's sonnet also revealed an emerging national consciousness glorifying Dante as the father of a potential Italian nation-state. The poem's bellicosity—"take up arms," "go, thunder, conquer"—reflected an appreciation of the intimate connection between literature and politics in Dante's work. The poet Giuseppe Parini, Alfieri's contemporary (1729–1799), noted this connection when he praised Dante as "the first Italian who, transferring his enthusiasm for political freedom even into literary affairs, dared to shake off the revered yoke of the barbarous Latin-centeredness of his times." Cherishing the civic value of Dante's poetry at a time when Italian freedom was thwarted by foreign rulers and their proxies, Parini and Alfieri were instrumental in fashioning Dante into the founding father of Italy's liberation movement.[20]

Dante's emergence as Italy's literary, spiritual, and political father in the late eighteenth and early nineteenth centuries was hardly surprising. Many talented Italians readily identified with the medieval poet's experience of exile as they, too, fell victim to foreign domination and manipulation of Italy's weak and fractious civil society. That Dante's estrangement from Florence lasted beyond his death, with his bones thereafter lying in Ravenna, made his lesson even more poignant to Italian patriots compelled by their political activism to live—and often die—abroad. The poet-soldier Ugo Foscolo exemplified this identification with Dante. Born in 1778 on Zacynthus, a Greek island then under Venetian control, Foscolo completed his studies and fought valiantly as a military officer in Italy before political enemies drove him into exile, eventually in 1816 to England, where he died and was buried in 1827. Following Dante in death as in life, Foscolo also endured a complicated graveyard history, but with a happier ending: one year after Rome became the final major piece of the new Italian nation, his corpse was exhumed from its grave in Chiswick, England, and transported to Florence. On June 24, 1871, the repatriated poet received a state funeral before his remains joined those of Machiavelli, Michelangelo, Galileo, and Alfieri in the Church of Santa Croce.

A fervent proponent of Italian independence, Foscolo welcomed Napoleon as Italy's liberator when the young French general invaded Italy in 1796 and defeated Austrian forces and their allies. Applying Enlightenment-inspired ideas and reforms of the French Republic, Napoleon created a republican regime in Lombardy and merged other conquered and occupied lands into the Cisalpine Republic. Although the victorious general's sacrifice of Venice to Austria in the Treaty of Campo Formio (October 17, 1797) infuriated Foscolo, he again joined Italian patriots in fighting alongside the French when Austria and Russia invaded Italy in 1799. Set in this period, Foscolo's first major work, the epistolary novel *Last Letters of Jacopo Ortis* (published in 1802), features a love-sick patriot seeking creative and political inspiration from monuments honoring great Italians from earlier times. At the same time, these physical tributes to Italy's glorious past call attention to its squalid present state and its failure to honor cultural heroes during their lifetimes.

Less than a year after witnessing the deplorable condition of Petrarch's villa in Arquà (November 1797), Jacopo visits Florence, where he trembles with emotion while approaching the tombs of Galileo, Machiavelli, and Michelangelo. Wondering if Santa Croce's impressive mausoleums were built to expiate the sins of earlier generations, he grasps the bitter truth that many who are persecuted in their own day are venerated by posterity. If these distinguished Italians suffered during their lifetimes, they eventually found the respect they deserved in the disposition of their mortal remains. The same could not be said of Dante, the first and greatest Italian for Jacopo and his creator. So it is a visit to Dante's tomb, fittingly, that gives the tormented patriotic soul the strength to follow through on his resolution to die. "On your funeral urn, Father Dante!" he exclaims, "As I embraced it I became all the more determined. Did you see me? Father, did you not inspire me with such strength of mind and heart while I genuflected, with my forehead pressed against the marble of your tomb, and meditated on your high-mindedness, and your love, and your ungrateful native city, and your exile, and your poverty, and your divine intellect? I parted from your shade more resolved and more joyful." An exile even in death, Dante is the figure with whom Jacopo—and Foscolo—most intensely identifies. The young Italian reveres "Father Dante" as the quintessential example of greatness ("high-mindedness," "love," "divine intellect") accompanied by misfortune ("ungrateful native city," "exile," "poverty").[21] This misfortune, of course, was even worse than Foscolo imagined, for Dante's exile in death was twofold: denied to Florence, the poet's bones were also denied repose in his tomb in Ravenna. If Dante "saw" his petitioner in 1799, he did not do it from the marble "funeral urn" before which Jacopo Ortis knelt, a reverential act probably drawn from the author's own experience in imitation of Vittorio Alfieri's emotional visit sixteen years earlier.

Also oblivious to the missing contents of Dante's tomb were Italian representatives of the Cisalpine Republic who celebrated the poet as a fellow traveler on the road toward democratic, anticlerical governance. Leading this republican refashioning of Dante was Vincenzo Monti (1754–1829), a renowned poet, translator, and professor whose political allegiances changed with the times, from papal apologist to Napoleonic republican to Austrian sympathizer. During the republican period, Monti and his associates organized a procession to Dante's tomb, where a solemn ceremony was held, followed by a festive gathering with speeches and poetry readings in honor of the poet at Ravenna's city hall.

Paolo Costa, a respected Dante commentator and the moderator of Ravenna's Constitutional Association, and Jacopo Landoni, a poet serving as the association's secretary, wrote a notice that, posted throughout the city, invited the public to attend the commemoration. Under the heading of "Liberty—Equality," two of the three Enlightenment ideals championed by the French Revolution and popular with republicans, their announcement incorporated the third term of the motto—*fraternité*—in its salutation to the "Ravennese People, Brother and Sister Citizens." "It is not unknown to you," Costa and Landoni reminded their compatriots, that "the divine Dante," "Lord of the Supreme Song," "is our fellow citizen." Well versed in republican political rhetoric, they lionized Dante as the "ancient Destroyer of the Sacerdotal Fraud," complementing this antipapal sentiment with an invitation to witness the poet's "glorious memory democratically honored" at the afternoon ceremony in his chapel. "Let us all hasten to strew myrtle and laurel leaves," they concluded the public notice, "and to bathe his Tomb with tears that fall from the Patriot's eyes on the Holy Ashes of the meritorious Geniuses of Humankind."[22]

On January 3, 1798, Vincenzo Monti and other republican leaders, accompanied by militia members and a marching band, walked from city hall to Dante's chapel, embellished for the occasion with sumptuous wall hangings and laurel festoons. Holding aloft "the sacred volume of the *Divine Comedy* crowned with laurel," a prominent citizen headed the procession. After Commissioner Luigi Oliva opened the ceremonies with solemn words in honor of Dante at the entrance to the chapel, Maria Laderichi and Giuditta Milzetti—wives of Count Cristino Rasponi and Paolo Costa—removed Dante's poem from its laurel covering and laid it on the marble tomb; the women also placed two wreaths, one of laurel leaves and one of roses, under Dante's sculpted image. The leaders and their entourage then returned to city hall, where

Monti praised Dante as the "father of the Italian language" and extolled the virtuous qualities of his "republican soul" despite the poet's ardent defense of empire in his *Monarchia:* if republican Italy could forgive and honor Virgil, whose *Aeneid* exalted the Roman Empire, how could it not do the same for Dante? asked Monti.[23]

Vincenzo Monti's passionate speech drew its power from the assumed presence of Dante's bones in the tomb. The poet today receives the "precious title of your citizen," Monti told his audience in Ravenna, an honor befitting "his great virtues, his painful misfortunes, and his holy ashes, which have been sleeping here for five centuries." At this revolutionary moment in Italian history, "his bones stir, riled up by the cry of jubilation that awakens them." If Monti wanted to spoil the festive day with sorrow, he could easily bring tears to the eyes of his listeners by leading them back to "that cold marble holding the silent ashes." With the tomb's cover removed, he would "point to that dust, the pitiful remains of such a great man," a sight at which no eye could stay dry. Raising a fistful of Dante's dust, he would cry, "Citizens, here is Dante Alighieri, here is the proud and virtuous republican who used his pen to strike down the tyrants of his homeland and the greedy murderers of all Italy." Monti's exaltation of Dante for the republican cause naturally fingered religious authority as the enemy. Dante was the thinker who used history and philosophy to "penetrate the labyrinth of falsehood and reveal the crimes of the destructive and hypocritical Minotaurs of the Vatican." Observing that "the few relics of Dante's venerable remains are still warmed" by Ravenna's long-standing devotion, Monti exhorted citizens to "come and touch them, feel the new coloring of life that moves them as you honor his memory today with new kindness." "Your guest," Monti concluded in full republican spirit, "has become your brother."[24]

Vincenzo Monti would have wreaked havoc had he turned rhetoric into reality by opening Dante's tomb in 1798. When, instead of the poet's "venerable remains," he revealed an empty sepulcher, Monti and his republican compatriots would have realized sooner or later that the Franciscan friars were the likely culprits. At a time of open hostility to religious institutions in Italy, it is entirely conceivable that the friars would have then felt the wrath they had so far escaped following their confiscation of Dante's bones nearly three hundred years earlier. But the tomb remained sealed, as did the lips of those who knew the unpleasant truth that it was empty. Ignorance and secrecy therefore kept Ravenna's secular authorities from acting on their anticlerical fervor. Local clergy members, for their part, were incensed by the city's celebration of Dante as a republican hero. Father Benedetto Fiandrini was one such person angered by politicians coloring Dante with the religious rhetoric of sainthood ("holy ashes," "venerable remains") while simultaneously idolizing him as the "Destroyer of the Sacerdotal Fraud." Mocking the "ridiculous procession" and denigrating its leaders as "fanatical" (Cristino Rasponi) and "impious" (Paolo Costa), Father Fiandrini took a dim view of the ceremonies in his firsthand account.[25]

Napoleonic reforms raised concerns even outside the church in Italy. Laws banning the burial of corpses in city churches and graveyards motivated Foscolo to write his major poem, "Of Tombs." Celebrating the power of tombs of worthy ancestors to inspire the living, he believed Florence was blessed for gathering in one sacred place—the Church of Santa Croce—the mortal remains of such Italian "glories" as Machiavelli, Michelangelo, Galileo, and Alfieri. Their presence in Florence only exacerbated Dante's absence. Memorably calling the missing poet "the exiled Ghibelline," Foscolo set the stage for a bitter battle over Dante's political symbolism in the nineteenth century. While proponents of the emerging nation-state claimed the medieval poet as Italy's father and prophet, propapal forces embraced him as a neo-Guelph advocate of the Catholic Church's territorial and civic authority.[26] Whether visitors to Dante's mausoleum honored an illustrious exponent of the pope's civil authority or—like Foscolo and Lord Byron—the prophet of a nation free of foreign and papal rule, they all had one thing in common: they worshiped an empty tomb.

Composing "Of Tombs" in 1806, Ugo Foscolo had no knowledge that Dante's body was missing not only from Florence but also, since 1519, from his tomb in Ravenna. The poet's bones probably resided in Ravenna's Franciscan convent throughout this long period, with occasional viewings and rearrangements like those documented by Brother Antonio Santi, the convent's chancellor, in 1677. When the Napoleonic suppression of religious institutions reached Ravenna in 1810, the friars had to decide what to do with Dante's bones as they abandoned their collective home in the city. Turning the poet's remains over to civil authorities was out of the question, as was entrusting them to the Archbishop of Ravenna, Antonio Codronchi, an ambitious prelate working closely with French and Italian republican leaders. Nor could the friars run the risk of taking Dante's bones with them as they ventured out in the world. Hiding them in a safe place close to the convent seemed the best option. With luck, Dante's bones would still be there once the revolutionary fever had subsided and the friars came home to their convent.[27]

The friars found their hiding spot in a wall that had once allowed passage between the Braccioforte chapel and the church cemetery. Corrado Ricci has shown that this doorway, located just outside the convent's cloister, a stone's throw from the empty tomb in Dante's chapel, did not even exist before 1701, thus debunking the assumption among witnesses to the discovery of bones in 1865 that Brother Antonio Santi hid the pine box there in 1677. Sometime before 1810, however, the door had been removed and the opening in the wall filled with cement. When or soon before the Franciscans left the convent in 1810, they hollowed out the former passageway to create a cavity large enough to accommodate the box measuring thirty inches in length and less than a foot each in width and height. The hole in the wall, starting just over a foot and a half above ground level, was about three feet across, thirteen inches high, and a foot deep. A friar hid the chest of bones by sealing the opening with bricks, no doubt "hoping to remove them again if God were to allow him to return to his cell!"[28] Where the broken wall once stood, visitors today find a rectangular marble block. "A remnant of the walled-up doorway," the inscription reads, "where Dante Alighieri's stolen bones—hidden by the Conventual Friars Minor in 1810—were discovered on May 27, 1865." Since the Franciscans never returned to their cells in Ravenna, Dante's bones lay untouched in their hiding place until the stone mason Pio Feletti's pickax fortuitously dislodged them fifty-five years later.

5.2. Pine chest that held Dante's bones (Museo Dantesco / Istituzione Biblioteca Classense)

5.3. Tablet indicating the wall in which Dante's bones were hidden (Photo: Elisa Valentini, July 2016)

So the bones no longer resided within the convent, but neither were they in their tomb when the English poet George Gordon (Lord) Byron came to worship there in 1819. Like Foscolo, Byron drew literary, political, and personal inspiration from Dante's tomb in Ravenna. Although Foscolo and Byron never met, they held (for the most part) a favorable opinion of each other's work, and their lives followed a similar geographical trajectory but in opposite directions: whereas Foscolo was born on a Greek island (1778) and died in exile on the outskirts of London (1827), Byron was born in London (1788) and, following the breakup of his marriage, embarked on an adventurous life in exile that ended with his death in Missolonghi (1824) during Greece's war of independence. But Italy, past and present, occupied the center of their lives and imaginations. Mining Italian history and literature for raw materials with which to shape and enrich their own art, the poets at the same time actively participated in Italy's struggle to overcome foreign oppression and become a free and united nation.

Byron endowed Dante with unique status in Italian history in *Childe Harold's Pilgrimage* (1812–1818), the poem that launched him to stardom. Claiming that "Dante's brow alone" had worn the laurel "wreath" before the glory days of Renaissance Ferrara, Byron lauded the medieval poet as the foundation of Italy's literary tradition, the "Tuscan father" and "Bard of Hell" whose "comedy divine" was the unsurpassed model for such later epic poets as Ludovico Ariosto (1474–1533) and Torquato Tasso (1544–1595). Byron symbolically crowned Dante not just for his poetic achievement but for his political and civic meaning. Embodying the harmonious union of artistic, intellectual, and political excellence, Dante prompted Byron to resurrect the names of other great Italians as a rallying cry for Italian independence and national unity. Following Foscolo's lead, he recognized Santa Croce's special place in Italy's destiny, the church's "holy precincts" holding "ashes which make it holier, dust which is/even in itself an immortality." In the Florentine church lay "Angelo's, Alfieri's bones, and his, / the starry Galileo, with his woes," Bryon wrote; "here Machiavelli's earth return'd to whence it rose." Like the primordial elements, the mortal dust of these Italian heroes "might furnish forth creation" with the establishment of Italy as a modern nation-state.[29]

Byron saw Santa Croce for himself during a one-day visit to Florence, in which he also admired the sculptures and paintings in the Uffizi museum and the Pitti Palace, while showing far less appreciation of the Florentine rulers—"fifty rotten & forgotten carcases [*sic*]"—buried in the Medici Chapel. In a letter to his publisher John Murray (April 26, 1817), he recounted this visit, writing that the tombs of Machiavelli, Michelangelo, Galileo, and Alfieri made Santa Croce "the Westminster abbey of Italy." As much as Byron venerated the Italians interred there, he found nothing to approve in the tombs themselves, calling them, with his acerbic wit, "overloaded" with figures and inscriptions ("all your Allegory & eulogy is infernal"). Memorials to these men, whose eminence spoke for itself, ought to have been simple and direct, containing no more than a bust, a name, and "perhaps a date" for the "unchronological—of whom I am one." The church was made "holier" by the immortal "dust" of the Italians buried there, not by ostentatious monuments to their glory. Byron's paean to the Italian luminaries buried in Santa Croce was also an act of homage to Anne-Louise-Germain Necker, Baroness of Staël-Holstein, another star in the constellation of European Romanticism, whose death in the summer of 1817 saddened the poet. His passage on the tombs breathed new life into Madame de Staël's belief that the church boasted "perhaps the most brilliant assembly of the dead in Europe."[30]

And yet, for all this brilliance, the creative elements necessary for Italian regeneration were incomplete. Michelangelo, Alfieri, Galileo, and Machiavelli may have found their final resting place in Florence, but their presence could not but direct attention to the absence of the three great Tuscan writers whose bones, in tombs far less grandiose than the monuments in Santa Croce, lay elsewhere. "But where repose the all Etruscan three," Byron wondered, "Dante, and Petrarch, and, scarce less than they, / the Bard of prose, creative spirit! he / of the Hundred Tales of love." Alas, the bones of Italy's resplendent *tre corone*—her "three crowns"—did not augment the holiness of the Florentine church, for they were buried in Ravenna, Arquà, and Certaldo (Boccaccio's native town). "Santa Croce wants their mighty dust," Byron declaimed, but "ungrateful Florence" had only itself to blame for Dante's absence. The city's most famous son "sleeps afar," a victim of the cruel sword of divisiveness wielded by rival political factions that "in their worse than civil war / proscribed the bard whose name for evermore / their children's children would in vain adore / with the remorse of ages." Florence's loss is another city's gain: "Happier Ravenna," on whose shore "honoured sleeps / the immortal exile."[31]

Byron had not yet visited Ravenna and set eyes on Dante's tomb when he wrote those verses. That changed after he met the last great love of his life. The talented and handsome English lord was introduced to Teresa Guiccioli in Venice shortly after her marriage at age eighteen to Count Alessandro Guiccioli, a wealthy nobleman from Ravenna nearly forty years her senior. This was the count's third marriage. Byron and Teresa became lovers when they met again in Venice a year later, in April 1819. Before she departed, Teresa invited Byron to visit her in Ravenna, using Dante's tomb and other local attractions as a pretext to sweeten the invitation. Two months later, following a flurried exchange of love letters, Byron left Venice to join her there. Unhappily, she was very ill when he arrived on June 10, and they could see each other only in the presence of others. The next day a frustrated Byron wrote to Teresa that he was trying to distract himself by visiting the local sites, but even the little that really interested him—Dante's tomb and a few items in Ravenna's renowned library—he viewed with "an indifference made pardonable by the state of [his] heart."[32]

Perhaps Byron downplayed his excitement at seeing Dante's tomb to impress upon Teresa his distress at not enjoying time alone with her. Or maybe his mood changed because events with his *amica* took a sudden turn for the better. Either way, a note in the poet's hand on the flyleaf of his personal edition of the *Inferno* indicates that he was hardly indifferent to Dante's tomb when he returned there the following afternoon: "This edition, in three volumes, of 'La Divina Commedia,' I placed with my own hands upon the tomb of Dante, in this city, at the hour of four in the afternoon, June 12th, 1819. Having thus brought the thoughts of Alighieri once more in contact with his ashes, I shall regard this work, not with higher veneration, but with greater affection, as something like '*a copy from the author.*'" Byron's lifelong friend John Cam Hobhouse, who transcribed this note, recalled that the poet "habitually" had this copy of the *Inferno* on his person while living in Ravenna.[33] Byron did not know that, with Dante's bones no longer in the tomb, his reverent gesture of reuniting "the thoughts of Alighieri" with "his ashes" was even more theatrical than intended. But this hardly emptied the gesture of meaning. On the contrary, Dante's symbolic blessing of Byron's personal copy of the *Divine Comedy* inspired the English supplicant in his own literary pursuits.

Having taken lodgings "within fifty yards" of Dante's tomb, Bryon soon forged a deep connection with the sacred spot. He dismissed the exterior of the building—the renovations of Camillo Morigia in 1780–1782—as "a mere modern Cupola" but held a more charitable view of the interior, commenting on the "well preserved" state of the "effigy & tombstone" designed by Pietro Lombardo in 1481–1483. Byron paid another solemn visit to the mortuary chapel less than a week after sanctifying his personal copy of Dante's *Divine Comedy*. On June 18, witnesses report, Byron was accompanied by his friend Francesco Aglietti, a celebrated Italian physician whose treatment of Teresa Guiccioli, at Byron's insistence, would soon have "so good an effect" on the countess's health that she could accompany her husband on a tour of his estates two months later. Byron again entered the sanctuary bearing a book of poetry, this time not Dante's volume but one of his own works. Observing a respectful silence, absorbed in his thoughts, Byron placed his book above the tomb, as if making an offering to Dante.[34]

Giovanni Sabbatini, the venerable secretary of the Guiccioli family, described the scene years later to Frances Elliot, an Englishwoman who spent most of her adult life abroad—primarily in Italy, where she died and was buried in 1898—writing travel literature and novels with Italian themes. "Even though he was only a stone's throw away from the Piazza, milord arrived there in a solemn manner to visit Dante's tomb," Sabbatini recalled: "All his servants were decked out in formal attire. He himself wore a splendid uniform, as would be fitting if Dante were a living monarch. Accompanied by Dr. Aglietti, he carried in his hand a volume of his works—beautifully bound in calfskin—to place above the altar where Dante's death mask was displayed. Milord stood still in front of the tomb with his arms crossed over his chest and his eyes fixed on the mask." "That night," Sabbatini told the novelist, Byron "shut himself in his room and on this very table began to write the *Prophecy*." The poet indeed conceived and wrote *The Prophecy of Dante* during his stay in Ravenna, its first words penned in the evening after a meditative visit to the tomb: Byron recorded the date, June 18, 1819, at the beginning of his autograph manuscript of the poem.[35]

The Prophecy, Byron explained in the preface, was born after "it was suggested to the author that having composed something on the subject of Tasso's confinement, he should do the same on Dante's exile—the tomb of the poet forming one of the principal objects of interest in that city, both to the native and to the stranger." In *The Lament of Tasso,* Byron had dramatized the imprisonment of the epic poet Torquato Tasso in Ferrara. A dedicatory sonnet to *The Prophecy* confirms that it was Teresa Guiccioli who suggested Byron likewise memorialize in verse Dante's artistic triumph in the face of adversity. "Thou art the cause," he says to his beloved, since "for thee to speak and be obey'd / are one." Teresa herself remembered how she "begged" Byron, who was then always by her side, to "gratify" her by "writing something on the subject of Dante, and, with his usual facility and rapidity, he composed his *Prophecy*." Several years later, Byron again credited the countess with urging him to write the poem, adding that "the sight of his tomb, which I passed in my almost daily rides, inspired me." If Teresa Guiccioli was Byron's partner in the poem's conception, Dante's tomb—like the book that led Francesca and Paolo to act on their illicit desire in the *Inferno*'s famous episode—moved the lovers to plant and nurture the fruitful seed.[36]

The Prophecy of Dante, Byron announced to his publisher in 1820, was "the best thing I ever wrote," before quickly hedging, "if it be not *unintelligible*." Finally published, after a series of delays, in April 1821, the poem is a dramatic monologue written in terza rima, thus imitating Italy's "great 'Padre Alighier,'" as Byron in the preface calls Dante, who invented this rhyme scheme for his *Commedia*. The reader hears Dante speak shortly before his death in 1321, "foretelling the fortunes of Italy in general in the ensuing centuries."[37] Recalling how his love of Florence was rewarded with unjust banishment from the city, Byron's Dante sees his own fate in Italy's future. He imagines a time when Florence will regret her cruelty. "The day may come when she will cease to err," the poet allows,

> The day may come when she would be proud to have
> The dust she dooms to scatter, and transfer
> Of him, whom she denied a home, the grave.

Florence may one day seek to repatriate his remains, "but this shall not be granted." Instead, Dante insists, "let my dust / Lie where it falls," his native soil having relinquished its right to his "indignant bones." Because Florence "denied me what was mine—my roof," the prophesying poet declares, she "shall not have what is not hers—my tomb."[38]

Byron, true to his subject, creatively applied Dante's law of *contrapasso,* the ironclad logic by which the punishment in Hell fits the sin in life: just as Florence denied a home to Dante ("what was mine—my roof"), so she will be denied "what is not hers," the poet's grave. And this retribution, like Dante's infernal punishments, lasts forever. When her "angry gust" subsides, Florence will change course and, lifting her sentence of exile ("repeal'd her doom"), attempt to gather in death what she banished in life. But she will fail, for not even the interventions of princes, popes, and poets can overcome a fundamental fact: Florence forfeited her claim to Dante's "indignant bones."

Like Foscolo, Byron rued the harsh reality that brave and creative spirits like Dante—those fated "in life, to wear their hearts out, and consume / their days in endless strife"—are often appreciated only after they "die alone." Posthumous praise, while welcome, arrives too late, for the dead poet is "but a name" to future admirers who "spread his—by him unheard, unheeded—fame." The "future thousands" coming from far and wide to visit Dante's tomb would therefore be "wasting homage o'er the sullen stone."[39] Unaware that Dante endured a second exile after death, Byron did not know how truly prophetic these words were. Stolen in 1519, the poet's remains had been missing from their tomb for three hundred years, held nearly all of this time by the Franciscans in their convent. Since the evacuation of the friars in 1810, the plain box of bones languished behind a bricked-up wall close to the poet's mortuary chapel. All this time pilgrims to Dante's chapel in Ravenna, from tourists and students to kings and popes, unknowingly paid their respects to an empty grave.

Several months after writing *The Prophecy of Dante,* Byron was still in Ravenna, picking up where he left off the preceding year on *Don Juan,* his mock-heroic epic recounting the amorous adventures of the title character while satirizing contemporary society, most of all Byron's critics and fellow literati. Digressing from Juan's story, Byron reflected on the irony of fame, how the renown of warriors and poets grows in time even as their lives and civilizations fade into oblivion. Not even Dante's tomb will long withstand the ravages of time. "I pass each day where Dante's bones are laid," Byron wrote, knowing that the "little cupola, more neat than solemn" will "protect his dust" for only so long, before it too succumbs to neglect and decay. The Romantic poet could hardly have imagined that his brooding fatalism assumed too rosy a picture. Franciscan graverobbing, not the passing of time, already deprived Dante's dust of the protection of its original sepulcher in Camillo Morigia's "little temple" and would continue to do so until the poet celebrated his six hundredth birthday in 1865.[40]

Prophet of Italy

*Dante did more for Italy, for the glory and the future of our People,
than ten generations of other writers and statesmen.*

—GIUSEPPE MAZZINI

The *New Monthly Magazine,* a London publication, included a section,
"Foreign Varieties," that briefly informed readers of news and events from
around the world. Attesting to Byron's celebrity status in English society, the
November 1818 issue reported, under Italian news, that the aristocratic ex-
patriot "still continued at Venice late in September last, pursuing his poetical labours with indefatigable ardour." Readers learned that Byron "devotes
his mornings entirely to study, and spends his evenings chiefly at the Theatre, receiving the visits of his friends in his private box." On the same page,
wedged between news of the discovery in Rome of documents pertaining to
the House of Stuart and an item on a Florentine exhibition of casts of the
Elgin marbles, appeared this notice: "A subscription has been opened at Florence, for a monument to be erected in honour of Dante. It is well known
that the prince of Italian poets, when in banishment, like Gibelin, was reduced
to beg for shelter and a morsel of bread in foreign countries. The monument
will be erected in the church of Santa Croce, the Pantheon of Tuscany."[1]
Recognizing the improbability of repatriating Dante's bones, leading Florentines formed a committee to raise funds for a monumental cenotaph—an
intentionally empty tomb—to join the actual graves of Machiavelli, Michelangelo, Galileo, and other great Tuscans in Santa Croce. They launched
their campaign with publication of the project manifesto on July 18, 1818. An
expression of Florentine pride as well as resignation, the marble cenotaph—
completed by Stefano Ricci in 1829 and installed the following year—also
marked the elevation of Dante to a symbol of the emerging Italian nation.

The regional rivalry embroiling Florence and Ravenna during the Renaissance, culminating with the theft of Dante's bones to prevent their repatriation (with papal backing) to Florence, was no longer raging in the early nineteenth century. Nor were the Ravennese municipality and the Franciscan order waging an intramural battle for control over Dante's tomb, though proprietary fires still flared up on occasion. As the Italian liberation movement—energized by the French Revolution—gained momentum despite inevitable setbacks, Dante came to represent, more than anyone else, the prophetic father of a free and united Italy.

Although Byron never addressed Florentine plans for Dante's cenotaph, he undoubtedly heard of the subscription in 1818 to fund the project. His *Prophecy of Dante,* composed the following year in Ravenna, suggests that he held a strong opinion on the matter, and it was not favorable to Florence. At the end of the poem, Byron's Dante foresees Florence erecting a tomb to honor the poet, as in fact came to pass, but—too late in recognizing his worth—it must remain empty. "Florence!" Dante declares, "when this lone spirit shall return / to kindred spirits, thou wilt feel my worth, / and seek to honour with an empty urn / the ashes thou shalt ne'er obtain—Alas!" Showing no mercy toward the Florentines for his death and burial in exile, Dante envisions a time "when Truth shall strike their eyes through many a tear, / and make them own the Prophet in his tomb."[2] That time had come.

Following in the footsteps of Alfieri, Parini, Monti, and Foscolo, Byron fashioned Dante as a patriot, the ancestral father of Italy's national liberation. "They made an Exile—not a slave of me," Byron has the poet say of his enemies in 1321, with an eye toward Italy's future. This Dante knows from experience that to overcome foreign oppression and achieve freedom, Italians must heal their own factional divisions. "What is there wanting then to set thee free, / and show thy beauty in its fullest light?" he asks. The answer is "to make the Alps impassable," and "we / her sons, may do this with *one* deed—Unite!"[3]

Moved by Florence's proposal to honor Dante with a cenotaph in Santa Croce, Giacomo Leopardi likewise spoke through the medieval poet to call contemporary Italians to arms. "On the Monument to Dante Being Erected in Florence" was one of two patriotic poems Leopardi wrote ("To Italy" is the other, more famous canzone) soon after the announcement of the cenotaph in 1818. He recognized, as Foscolo had, the power of sepulchral monuments venerating famous Italians to inspire later generations in grand cultural and political pursuits. Leopardi was therefore appalled by the absence of even a "stone" honoring Dante in Florence, a city known throughout the world for its native son's literary masterpiece. Since the cenotaph promised to rectify this disgraceful omission, Leopardi showered the Florentine promoters of the project with praise, urging them on with the promise of glory and gratitude for their patriotic act. Honoring Dante, the "noble father of Tuscan poetry," amounts to loving Italy, "this unhappy country," a mother "grieving" for her sons who died fighting for a foreign tyrant—Napoleon during his Russian campaign (1812)—not their native land. If his compatriots should ignore the legacy of their illustrious ancestors, then Leopardi believes Italy is better off without them. "Arise and go," he bluntly implores the uninspired, for if Italy is "the home of cowards, / better she be a widow and alone," as Dante famously described Italy in his devastating diatribe against the toxic combination of venal foreign rulers, papal interference, and factional warfare keeping it in servitude.[4]

The committee for the monument to Dante did its part to promote the national cause by capitalizing on the poet's patriotic appeal. This energetic group of influential citizens sought the funds and other resources required to create a work of funereal art worthy of placement inside the Florentine church that English Italophiles amiably called the "Westminster Abbey of Italy." Santa Croce, immortalized by the likes of Foscolo, Madame de Staël, and Byron for housing the tombs of Machiavelli, Michelangelo, Galileo, and Alfieri, was an easy choice. But whereas those sculpted monuments held the mortal remains of the luminaries they honored, by 1818 the Florentines knew they had no realistic hope of repatriating Dante's bones and so planned from the start to commission a cenotaph.

Addressing the manifesto to residents of Tuscany, the committee members loosened Florence's grip on sole ownership of Dante, while, less altruistically, they expanded their donor base for financial assistance. The invitation for subscriptions called on "all Tuscans to enrich themselves with a new glory" by contributing a portion of their material wealth. Admitting that Dante "raised a monument to himself more lasting than marble and bronze" with his *Divine Comedy,* the committee was nonetheless moved to repay the poet for the fame his work brought to his native land "with a public and splendid demonstration of gratitude." The "homeland" that thus honored its deserving citizens, the manifesto writers reasoned, was both "just and wise" because such a tribute would also speak to later generations. Anticipating Leopardi's poetic commentary on the proposed cenotaph, they impressed upon their audience the urgency of honoring Dante with a fitting monument as the five hundredth anniversary of his death fast approached (1321–1821). The foreign visitor to Florence, they imagined, "filled with veneration for those rare individuals who in every age have illuminated Tuscany, anxiously seeks the monument to this man who soars like an eagle higher than all others." This visitor, "amazed not to find it," understandably "reproaches" Florentines.[5]

Contrary to popular opinion, plans for Dante's cenotaph in Santa Croce did not originate with Ugo Foscolo's famous poem "Of Tombs" in 1806. When Marco Lastri and Marquis Gaetano Capponi founded La Società degli Amatori della Patria—the Society of Lovers of the Country—in 1802, they commissioned the architect Luigi Cambray-Digny, the future *gonfaloniere,* or mayor, of Florence, to sculpt the monument. Political turmoil, however, prevented Cambray-Digny from proceeding beyond the design stage. Only in 1818, with an eye toward the 1821 milestone anniversary of Dante's death, was another group of influential Florentines able to set the cenotaph on course to completion. But not everyone shared their enthusiasm. The idea of honoring Dante in Florence by constructing "a tomb without mortal remains" because Ravenna refused to relinquish them "seemed absurd to some."[6]

Absurd or not, the Florentine committee decided the time had come finally to demonstrate the city's devotion to Dante's memory by "raising a monument to the supreme poet and greatest Italian writer."[7] With the approval of the Grand Duke of Tuscany, Ferdinand III, they awarded the prestigious commission to Stefano Ricci (1765–1837), a master sculptor at the Florentine Academy of Fine Arts. A talented practitioner of the neoclassical style then in vogue, Ricci was strongly influenced by the works of Antonio Canova (1757–1822), the Venetian sculptor who created Vittorio Alfieri's monumental tomb for Santa Croce in 1806–1810. Having already achieved distinction for several sculptures in and around Florence, including the tombs of Michal Skotniki (an aristocratic Polish painter) and Pompeo Signorini da Mulazzo (a prominent Tuscan judge and minister) in Santa Croce, Ricci was a natural choice for the design and execution of Dante's cenotaph. After he completed his sketch of the monument in 1819, however, Ricci took over ten years to model and sculpt figures large enough to blend harmoniously with the church's other grandiose marbles.

Stefano Ricci's cenotaph honoring Dante, competed in 1829, was presented to the public in Santa Croce on March 24, 1830. Covering the solemn yet celebratory event, the *Gazzetta di Firenze* could now affirm that "to the pilgrim in search of a monument of the *Divine Poet* in his native land, we will no longer have to answer with the painful account of the reasons for which it was missing." The long article also served as a quasi-apology for Florence, a large portion of it cataloging the reparatory actions of Dante's birthplace—editions, commentaries, biographies, and other manifestations of Tuscan (particularly Florentine) admiration and love for Dante over the centuries. Not coincidentally, the official source for information on the cenotaph, Melchior Missirini's book published on the occasion of the unveiling in Santa Croce, is titled "On the Memories of Dante in Florence, and of the Gratitude of the Florentines for the Divine Poet."[8]

The cenotaph's promoters therefore presented the work as a way to bury the hatchet and heal old wounds, and not only those inflicted by Dante's banishment from his homeland. They also used the monumental if empty tomb to defuse lingering tension between Florence and Ravenna over the fate of Dante's bones. Taking the moral high ground, the Florentine newspaper spun Ravenna's refusal to relinquish the bones into a sign of devotion to the poet, an echo of Cristoforo Landino's praise for Bernardo Bembo's renovation of Dante's sepulcher in the fifteenth century. Later Florentines could at least find comfort in the fact that the "denied ashes" still lay, after all, in Italy. Missirini likewise shaped his discussion of the cenotaph with language intimating Italian aspirations toward nationhood. He urged praise of "the strong and illustrious Tuscan Nation" for its largesse in bringing the undertaking "magnificently to completion," thus giving the rest of Italy a "great example of how to love one's homeland and honor its most distinguished citizens."[9]

The prominent inscription on the base, composed by the scholarly abbot Giovanni Batista Zannoni, congratulates Tuscans for giving this "honorary tomb" to Dante. The monument, its promoters crowed, brought to fruition the "decree made by our ancestors three times in vain."[10] The inscription probably refers to the Florentine proposals of 1396, 1429, and 1519, though there is one glaring difference between those efforts and the sculpture installed in Santa Croce in 1830. Earlier generations proposed a monumental tomb for Dante in Florence with the expectation that it would hold his repatriated remains. No bones meant no tomb. The Tuscans who commissioned Stefano Ricci to sculpt Dante's funerary monument, on the contrary, envisioned a cenotaph when they launched their campaign to fund it. The monument's meaning derived in part from the absence, not the presence, of the poet's remains.

Even and especially absent Dante's bones, the monument expresses the poet's powerful symbolism for all Italy. The pyramidal structure features

6.1. Stefano Ricci's cenotaph for Dante in Santa Croce (Scala / Art Resource, NY)

three interrelated figures framing the raised tomb in the center. At the apex of the pyramid sits Dante in thoughtful repose, his right hand supporting his laurel-crowned head (his eyes are shut, his mouth turned downward), with his right elbow and left forearm resting on a book in his lap. This volume, Missirini reasonably infers, is the *Divine Comedy,* the poem in which Dante revealed and condemned the personal, political, social, and spiritual ills of his world in order "to restore Italian civilization to a measure of liberty." Below Dante, to his left, is a bent female figure, her crossed arms draped over a book covering a corner of the tomb. Personifying poetry, she lays her head of disheveled hair on her arms. Her left hand rests on the book—another copy of the *Divine Comedy*—opened to a page displaying Dante's poetic credo. "I am one who, when Love inspires me," he tells another poet in *Purgatorio,* "take note and, as he dictates deep within me, so I set it forth." This "sweet new style," Bonagiunta da Lucca realizes, distinguishes Dante from him and other vernacular poets. Distraught Poetry, with a laurel garland seeming about to fall from her right hand to the ground, conveys the consequences of losing Dante's unique talent. Now that he is gone, she fears never finding another poet worthy of her crown.[11]

While Poetry, recalling the *mater dolorosa*—the grieving mother of Jesus—often depicted in art at the foot of the cross, pays tribute to Dante's revered place in the Italian Catholic imagination, the female figure standing on the other side of the tomb embodies the poet's national symbolism. Originally meant to represent only the Tuscan region (La Toscana), and so conceived in Stefano Ricci's sketch in 1819, the figure grew to encompass all Italy by the time his monument was unveiled in 1830.[12] Antonio Canova's tomb for Vittorio Alfieri in Santa Croce also depicts Lady Italy. But whereas Canova's figure is "more anti-French than pro-unification" in her grief over Alfieri's death, Ricci's statue honors Dante's memory by promoting a triumphalist vision of Italy. Proudly facing forward, she holds a scepter in her right hand—symbol of Italy's "continuing supremacy in the arts of genius and of the soul"—while her left arm extends upward toward Dante, her favorite son. Ricci projected Italy's glorious cultural legacy onto a brighter political future by transforming the wretched servant and abandoned widow lamented by Dante and Leopardi into a victorious queen. The star rising from her crown symbolizes nothing less than the "wisdom by which Italy was such a great light among Nations" even before joining their ranks as an independent and unified state.[13] A regional achievement with national implications, the cenotaph soon joined memorials to other heroes within the Italian collective consciousness.

Giuseppe Mazzini welcomed works by Foscolo, Byron, Ricci, and other patriotic poets and artists recognizing Dante's foundational role in Italian culture and politics. A leading figure—along with Giuseppe Garibaldi, Camillo Cavour, and King Victor Emmanuel II—in Italy's independence movement, culminating in the Risorgimento (Resurgence) of 1859–1861, Mazzini freely used Dante's life and poetry to inspire his compatriots to unite and fight to free themselves from foreign and papal rule. When, in 1841, Mazzini addressed an article on Dante to Italians working in England, where he (like Foscolo) lived in political exile, he began by mentioning the cenotaph installed just over a decade earlier. "In the Church of Santa Croce in Florence, among the names of many great Italians," he wrote, "a monument erected not many years ago bears the name of DANTE ALLIGHIERI." Mazzini failed to mention, of course, that this monument—unlike those dedicated to other illustrious Italians in the church—was by design an empty tomb. For his purposes, memorializing the medieval poet, entrusting his name "to the memory of an entire people," sufficed. What must Dante have done for "the Nation," he wondered, that "after five and a half centuries it continues to admire him and to pass his memory down to future generations?"[14]

Mazzini answered this question by focusing on Dante's political convictions and experiences. What set the poet above even the other great Italians, the source and animating principle of his power, was his unequaled love of Italy. No one really appreciates, Mazzini insisted, that over the course of Dante's life—during his darkest days in exile through to the moment he died—he remained true to the belief that "Italy would one day be a Nation and would for the third time direct European civilization," with Rome as central to the new Italy as it had been to the Roman Empire and the medieval church. Mazzini asserted that "Dante did more for Italy, for the glory and the future of our People, than ten generations of other writers and statesmen." The perfect citizen, Dante was the prime inspiration for other great Italians who "contributed to the progress of the National idea" over the centuries. Mazzini followed tradition in anointing Dante as the father of the Italian language ("Padre della nostra Lingua"), but the title now carried heightened political meaning: the "common Language" created by the poet "will one day represent National Unity among us all."[15]

Dante represented for Mazzini the perfect fusion of thought and action, the pen and the sword, the potent combination of theory and praxis needed to achieve the unity and liberty of Italy. If this goal remained elusive during the poet's lifetime despite his talent and patriotism, it was only because, as shown in Mazzini's sketch of medieval Italian politics, "the time was not ripe for the Nation." Dante appealed to proponents of Italian independence in more favorable times because he "was always with the People, that is, with the basis of the future Nation." Mazzini closed his tribute to Dante by recounting how, when Dante was asked one day by a friar what he was searching for, the poet replied, "pace," the "peace" that no one was able to give him on earth. Mazzini consequently called on Italians to bring Dante this long-sought peace by fulfilling his dream of a free and united Italy. Only "when you will have become worthy of Dante in love and in hate," he told his compatriots, "when your land will be *yours* and not another's—when Dante's soul will be able to look on you not with sadness but with joy at all this holy Italian pride—then we will raise a statue of the Poet on the greatest height in Rome, and we will inscribe on its base: TO THE PROPHET OF THE ITALIAN NATION, FROM ITALIANS WORTHY OF HIM."[16]

Mazzini again bestowed this title on Dante a year later, this time ascribing it to Ugo Foscolo, his fellow Italian patriot in exile. Foscolo had written an extensive commentary on the *Divine Comedy*. Left unfinished at Foscolo's death in 1827, his final work was edited for publication by his friend Mazzini in 1842. In the volume's preface, which Mazzini signed as "An Italian," he avowed that Foscolo "sought in Dante not only the poet, not only the father of our language, but the citizen, the reformer, the religious apostle, the prophet of the nation." The poet and Dante scholar Gabriele Rossetti (1783–1854), father of the poet-artist Dante Gabriel Rossetti and the poet Christina Rossetti, similarly recognized Dante's prescient patriotism. Finding refuge in England, as Foscolo and Mazzini did, after being exiled from Italy for his revolutionary politics, Rossetti strongly identified with Dante. Those who "love their country and are not prepared to suffer for its ills," he has Dante say in a poem, "are either cowards or fools." Rossetti took Dante's advocacy of a supreme earthly ruler as a prophetic sign of Italy forming "a single national body." The same year these words appeared in print, in Rossetti's 1826 commentary, Mazzini wrote his first piece of literary criticism. "The subject was Dante," he recalled, "whom during the years 1821 to 1827 I had learned to revere not only as a poet, but as the Father of the Nation." In that article, titled "On Dante's Patriotic Love," Mazzini urged all Italians to study Dante, the "divine Alighieri," who was first among those whose writings, like their lives, sought the good of their homeland. Repeating the lesson of Foscolo and Leopardi, Mazzini told Italians "to never forget that the first step in making great individuals is honoring those who came before."[17]

Mazzini and other leading cultural and political voices joined in calling on Dante's example to support Italian aspirations for nationhood in the nineteenth century. The poet's moral authority, political philosophy, and paternity of the language confirmed his place as Italy's ancestral father and prophet. Models for modern Italy, as the historian Adrian Lyttelton has shown by examining the legacy of the Lombard League (an alliance formed in 1167) and the Sicilian Vespers (an uprising in 1282), were often grounded in a "new, positive evaluation of the Middle Ages." Dante, more than any other individual or event from the past, enabled Italian patriots of all stripes to imagine an independent and unified country—the sort of "imagined community" identified by the political scientist Benedict Anderson with the modern nation.[18]

A literary icon who championed Italy's Roman and Christian heritage while calling for an end to the foreign oppression, civic factionalism, and papal interference that kept Italy "enslaved," Dante inspired artistic and political proponents of various Italian narratives, even those advancing more moderate and conservative versions of nationhood. Count Cesare Balbo (1789–1853), for one, took a more conciliatory position toward Austria and included the papacy in his proposal for an Italian confederation headed by the Kingdom of Piedmont-Sardinia, which he served as prime minister in 1848. Dante, Balbo wrote in his influential biography of 1839, is "a large part of the history of Italy, . . . the Italian who more than any other gathered in himself the genius, virtues, vices, and fortunes of our country." The poet, in sum, is "the most Italian Italian who has ever existed." Vincenzo Gioberti (1801–1852) was a priest, philosopher, and statesman who supported Italy's independence and unification. He, too, preferred a confederation of stakeholders but envisioned the pope—not a secular ruler—as the nation's president. Gioberti believed the "resurrection of Dante" in the nineteenth century "was the necessary condition for the resurgence [risorgimento] of Italian thought and talent."[19]

The visitor's log once kept in Dante's chapel contains palpable evidence of the poet's national significance during the Italian independence movement. The year that generated the most enthusiasm was 1848, a year of high hopes (soon dashed) for Italy's liberation. An entry signed by a lieutenant and five other officers in the Sardinian navy explained how, on leave from fighting on the seas near Trieste for "the holy cause of Italian freedom and independence," they came to Ravenna to see the tomb holding "Father Alighieri's sacred ashes." Citing Dante's scathing depiction of Italy as a "pilotless ship in a fierce tempest," the navy officers declared that, having understood the poet's words, they followed "a single flag, united in one idea from the Alps to Sicily, and a single cry: *War on the foreigner*." With this rallying cry, the sailors wrote, "we move against Austrian tyranny." Signing off with "Viva l'Italia!" they asked "great father" Dante to "pray for the holy cause of [their] redemption."[20]

The volume beginning in 1846 ends with the entry of Pope Pius IX, who visited the tomb on June 24, 1857. The pope, like the seamen, included verses from the *Divine Comedy* with his signature. He cited, appropriately, the words of a penitent in Purgatory proclaiming the transient nature of fame and power, how it is "nothing but a gust of wind . . . changing name with every new direction." The winds of change had certainly begun to turn against the papacy and were gathering strength. The years 1859 and 1860, with much of Italy finally achieving independence and unification, saw another uptick in recorded visits to Dante's tomb. On October 2, 1860, not long after the victory of the Piedmontese army over badly outnumbered papal troops at Castelfidardo, King Victor Emmanuel II paid his respects to Dante and signed the guest book. During Italy's struggle for freedom from foreign rule, wrote one patriotic poet in 1865, "the *Comedy* for us, like the Bible for the Israelites in exile, was the symbol of the homeland and nationality."[21]

The Italy that finally arose—*risorgimento* literally means "rise again"—was a parliamentary monarchy far more pleasing to Dante's neo-Ghibelline admirers than to the neo-Guelph camp that favored some form of papal governance, though the arrangement was not nearly democratic enough for the likes of Mazzini and Garibaldi. After a series of military victories and political annexations, the Kingdom of Italy was proclaimed on March 12, 1861, in Turin, the nation's first capital. Italy's map covered most of the peninsula (including former papal states) as well as the islands of Sardinia and Sicily, with Venice (and surrounding territory) and Rome slated for future possession. The poet Giannina Milli (1825–1888), who had won acclaim as a young woman for her performances of improvised verses, devoted several pieces to Dante. In a sonnet recited in Siena in 1862, Milli observed how Italy had nearly achieved Dante's vision of Italian unity by "crushing her tyrants." Now more than ever, she declared, "we hail you as our poet and prophet!"[22]

Saint Dante

The Commission congratulates Ravenna, to whom the heavens reserved the good fortune of revealing Dante's sacred bones to resurrected Italy, and hopes they will be preserved like a treasure of the
nation that reaffirmed its unity in Dante's name.

—REPORT OF THE NATIONAL
COMMISSION ON THE DISCOVERY
OF DANTE'S BONES

With Dante's six hundredth birthday falling in 1865, the same year Italy
moved its capital from Turin to Florence, plans took shape for festivities
doubling as a lovefest celebrating the new nation and the poet in his native city.
Italy signed a pact with France on September 15, 1864, calling for the French
to remove troops from Rome within two years. The Italians for their part
agreed to respect papal sovereignty over Rome and to transfer the seat of government to Florence, thus seeming to relinquish their claim on Rome as
the nation's capital. In truth, writes the historian David Kertzer, Italy's
leaders "clearly made the agreement in bad faith," knowing that "if they
could get the French troops out of Rome, . . . they would eventually find
some pretext to annex it." Meanwhile the massive movement of government resources—human and material—took place in the fall, allowing King
Victor Emmanuel II to open the ninth legislature in the Palazzo Vecchio
on November 9, 1864. The king himself officially moved to Florence on
February 3, 1865.[1]

The proposal to celebrate Dante's six hundredth birthday in Florence originated in the late 1850s and was unanimously approved by the city council
on November 14, 1863. There was no denying the overtly political nature of
the festivities planned for May 14–16, 1865. "It was less to Dante the Poet,

than to Dante the Patriot, that these honours were to be rendered," wrote Henry Clark Barlow, a distinguished scholar from England who attended the ceremonies. "It was less for Dante the founder of Italian literature, and the father of the Italian language," he continued, "than for Dante the founder of the true policy of the Italian nation, and the father of his country, that Italy flocked to the city of his birth to glorify the greatest of her sons." Dante's national symbolism, however, hardly diminished his local importance to Florence. On the contrary, as Mahnaz Yousefzadeh shows in her in-depth study of the centenary celebrations, lionizing Dante as a national hero enhanced the city's status as the new Italy's political and cultural center. A Sicilian official vividly captured Dante's unique role in Italian unification. Towns and organizations all through the land should send representatives to honor Dante in Florence because "in one body he reunited Italy's scattered limbs." In anticipation of this momentous event, Florence sought one more time to repatriate the remains of the "one body" that belonged to Italy's father and prophet, its secular saint.[2]

Contributors to the *Giornale del Centenario di Dante Allighieri,* a periodical created to inform the public of plans and activities related to the festivities, voiced strong support for Dante's posthumous repatriation and suggested why and how it should now happen. One writer celebrated Italy's newfound unity as an opportunity for Ravenna and Florence to strengthen their fraternal bond through the transfer of Dante's bones. He called for the return of "the Divine Poet's ashes to his native land" so they could be buried "in the Pantheon of great Italians in Santa Croce." Other writers cited the poet's poignant homecoming wish in *Paradiso*—to receive the laurel crown in the Florentine Baptistery, his "beautiful Saint John"—as a reason to break with tradition and erect a tomb for his "sacred bones" in that church. Baron Giacomo Baratta clothed his appeal in religious rhetoric. Praising the "Fathers of the Florentine Commune" for their "noble and holy petition to Ravenna for the ashes of the Great One," Baratta cast repatriation as the chance for Florence, thanks to favorable political conditions, finally to atone for the sin of exiling Dante. Imagining the transfer of Dante's "venerated relics" as if it were a national celebration of the poet's sainthood, he unabashedly proposed an event "at once religious and civil." Using the technical term for the transportation of a saint's remains, Baratta called on Florence's best architects and artists to raise a triumphal arch marking for posterity "the glorious memory of the translation [*traslazione*] of Alighieri's ashes to his homeland." He, too, chose the Baptistery as the poet's final resting place but dispensed with the magnificent tomb. Surpassing "any mausoleum in grandeur, any epitaph in eloquence" would be a tablet inscribed with one word: *Dante*.[3]

Giving an official face to these public appeals for the transfer of Dante's bones was a man who would play a major role in subsequent chapters of the poet's graveyard history. Born near Pistoia in 1810, Atto Vannucci was a liberal Catholic intellectual and priest who taught classical literature and ancient history while advancing the cause of Italian independence and unification. After supporting the uprisings of 1848 with journalistic work, he served in the provisional Tuscan government in 1849. Vannucci went into exile following the restoration of the Grand Duchy of Tuscany, living in France, England, and Switzerland before returning to Italy in 1854. He was appointed director of Florence's Biblioteca Magliabechiana and professor of Latin literature at the Istituto di Studi Superiori in 1859 and was elected as a deputy to the Italian parliament the following year.

Vannucci made the case for repatriation to the Florentine Commission for the Dante Centenary on April 14, 1864, sending his report the next day to Giulio Carobbi, the city's mayor (*gonfaloniere*) serving as president of the commission. Without the presence of Dante's remains in Florence, Vannucci argued, the celebrations planned for 1865 would not be "beautiful and complete." He therefore urged the commission to do what was required to open the festivities "with the entrance into Florence of Dante's bones, recalled at last from an exile lasting five and a half centuries." Vannucci believed that Italy's independence and unification, a new political order that Dante's vision helped bring about, augured well for the poet's repatriation. Calling on the support of other Italian cities and distinguished citizens, Vannucci framed Florence's petition for the remains as a national issue, while insisting that "Dante's ashes," when all was said and done, "belong to us"—Florence—"in particular." Confident in Ravenna's acquiescence to "this honest request made in the name of mother Florence and the entire great Italian nation," he foresaw vast numbers of Italians coming "to affirm again, swearing on the sacred bones, the unity of Italy."[4]

After the commission unanimously endorsed Vannucci's proposal, the Florentine city council formed a committee to draft a resolution to petition Ravenna for the return of Dante's bones. By the overwhelming margin of twenty-two to one, the council approved the resolution seeking to obtain from Ravenna, "as a fraternal gift, one as noble as it must be sorrowful, the restitution of Dante's bones." Three days later, on May 7, 1864, Giulio Carobbi wrote to the mayor of Ravenna, Gioacchino Rasponi, to convey Florence's desire for "the Remains of the Great One." While the resolution placed blame for Dante's exile squarely on the shoulders of the poet's compatriots, Carobbi closed his letter by shifting culpability from those earlier Florentines to "the wretched times in which they lived," a distinction that ultimately mattered little in the face of Ravenna's masterful management of the petition.[5]

Responding to the petition on May 18, 1864, Mayor Rasponi wrote that Ravenna needed time to study carefully such a delicate matter. He made sure, in the meantime, to approve the "noble Italian sentiment" motivating Florence to seek Dante's bones and expressed "deep confidence" that, no matter Ravenna's decision, "bonds of friendship and political brotherhood" between the cities would only grow stronger. This friendship, after all, was nurtured by the "profound, quasi-religious devotion" of Ravenna and Florence toward "the great Italian Prophet Dante Alighieri." Over two months later, on July 27, Ravenna's city council held an open meeting to discuss the Florentine petition. Mayor Rasponi, as president of the council, presented a resolution that skillfully denied the petition by turning each Florentine argument on its head. Whereas Florence saw the centenary as a chance to honor the promise of earlier generations to repatriate Dante, Ravenna countered that it could not honor the poet properly by "abandoning to another those sacred remains that were and are the object of such veneration and love by the Ravennese citizens." In its boldest stroke, Ravenna used Italian nationhood to nullify Florence's complaint that Dante's burial outside his native city perpetuated his unjust exile. In a free and united Italy, the resolution maintained, Dante was as much at home in Ravenna as anywhere else on Italian soil.[6] Demonstrating the power of Dante's national symbolism, Ravenna's rejection of the Florentine petition for the poet's bones also revealed the persistence of regional rivalries in the new Italy.

Florence failed in its attempt to crown the 1865 centenary with the return of Dante's bones, but the poet and Italy received many other gifts. The festivities, in turn, were a gift to the nation's new capital, which hosted between fifty thousand and one hundred thousand visitors over three days. Dante became a prime business opportunity for Florentines across socioeconomic strata, their efforts aided by little or no regulation of the markets. Henry Clark Barlow spoke from personal experience when he complained of a "golden age" for hotel owners, carriage drivers, and porters, dryly remarking that "the felicitous occasion afforded for fleecing *forestieri* will never be forgotten." Merchants of every kind exploited Dante's "patronage" by putting his "sacred head" on cards, medals, portraits, jewelry, and buttons: "Whatever was said, or sold, or done, had a reference to Dante."[7]

A call for poems elicited a flood of lyrical salutes to Dante and his works from professional writers and amateur enthusiasts alike. "Sonnets fell in showers, and biographical memoirs sprang up out of the ground," observed Barlow in his firsthand account. Poems written for the centenary fill nearly four volumes of Carlo del Balzo's anthology of literary tributes to Dante over the centuries. The downpour even included a poem on Ravenna's rejection of Florence's request for the poet's bones. Gabriele Fantoni, an author of patriotic histories from the Veneto region, composed a sonnet contrasting the city that, by abandoning Dante, had made him great (Florence) with the one that, loving the poet, stayed by his side (Ravenna). The poem's title, "Ravenna's Great Refusal of Florence and the Sixth Centenary," pulled no punches. It also commented on the petition with delicious irony by repurposing a famous line from the *Divine Comedy*. When Dante encounters neutral souls in the periphery of Hell, he singles out "the shade of him / who, through cowardice, made the great refusal" without giving a name. Celestine V, the pope whose abdication allowed the ascension of Dante's enemy, Pope Boniface VIII, is the most likely candidate for this wretched shade, tormented like his peers by stinging insects while chasing a flag. Ravenna's "great refusal" to relinquish Dante's bones cast harsh light on Florence's abandonment of the poet, one of the fateful consequences of Celestine's cowardly refusal to don the papal mantle.[8]

The most spectacular gift by far was Enrico Pazzi's massive marble monument to Dante. Piazza Santa Croce, covering nearly fifty thousand square feet, had been transformed into an elaborate amphitheater for May 14, 1865, the opening day of the ceremonies. In the middle of the piazza stood the Dante monument, "the image of Him whom all Italy had assembled to honour" concealed beneath "a mountain of white drapery." Delegations from Italy's provinces and representatives of various civic associations stood at attention, their "gorgeous canopy of brilliant banners" creating a colorful scene. A stage had been erected for bands and choirs in front of the church. "Ladies and privileged guests" were ushered to reserved seats on a raised platform along the right-hand side of the piazza, while common folk—so long as they were "decently dressed"—were permitted to watch from a larger public space on the left. The entire viewing area in and around the piazza accommodated eighteen thousand people. Covered in green cloth, the prime space between the monument and the church held a dais with a throne for the king and chairs for his ministers. "The effect was splendid," recalled Barlow, "the sensation great."[9]

King Victor Emmanuel II, accompanied by military and government leaders, arrived at eleven o'clock in the morning to shouts of "Viva!" Count Luigi Cambray-Digny, the Florentine mayor, then gave a speech drenched in patriotic rhetoric, his words tightly binding Dante to the new nation. "Today we not only pay due homage to the Supreme Poet, illustrious Philosopher, and great Citizen," he declared. More important, citizens throughout Italy, "from the August Monarch to the representative of the most humble town," hastened to Florence "to affirm again, before the whole world, the glorious resurrection of the Italian Nation, our indissoluble unity, our independence." Giambattista Giuliani, a priest and Dante scholar from Florence, next took the stage to dedicate the statue. "With flushed cheek and beaming eye, like one inspired," he exhorted all Italians to "honor the most lofty poet," words spoken in praise of Virgil in Dante's *Inferno*. "Providence decreed," Father Giuliani declared, "that Dante would triumph in the hour of Italy's preordained Renewal." Reminding his listeners that the poet sought a free and united Italy, Giuliani concluded his impassioned oration with a heartfelt appeal: "Let us join in a new bond of love around our great Father Alighieri, let this be his resplendent and inviolable Crown, this his glorious triumph."[10]

As soon as Father Giuliani finished speaking and the king shook his hand, the orchestra burst into song as the white veil opened to reveal "the majestic figure of Dante." Men removed their hats, the crowd shouted Giuliani's call to "honor the most lofty poet," the bells of Palazzo Vecchio rang out, and a rocket went up from a nearby tower to announce the joyous event. "Well might the heavens smile propitious," Barlow wrote, "and the sun of Italy shine out in all his glory."[11]

Enrico Pazzi's monument to Dante—its inscription reading "To Dante Alighieri, Italy," followed by the year 1865—was a belated birthday present from Italy to its prophetic father. In 1856, Ravenna had commissioned Pazzi, a native son, to design a statue of Dante for installation there, but the city found his model aesthetically and politically disagreeable. Dante looked grim, and the sculptor's alignment of the poet with Italy's independence movement jarred with Ravenna's status as a papal state. Two years later, influential citizens proposed raising a large monument to Dante in Florence. Pazzi's conception, while still criticized for its severity, gained admirers, and Florence accepted his model after Tuscany joined the Kingdom of Italy in 1859. As planning proceeded for the 1865 centenary, a special committee hired Pazzi

7.1. Inauguration of the monument to Dante in Piazza Santa Croce in Florence
(Photo taken May 14, 1865; Alinari/Art Resource, NY)

to make the monument, and on March 17, 1864, the Florentine city council
approved its placement in Piazza Santa Croce. The sculptor, who had by then
lived so long in Florence that he was considered a resident, produced the colossal marble statue in time for the opening of the festivities on May 14,
1865.[12]

About nineteen feet tall from toe to head, Dante stands atop an even taller
pedestal so that the entire monument rises nearly forty feet above the piazza.
Designed by the architect Luigi del Sarto, the quadrangular base holds four
lions, each displaying a tortoise-shell tablet with the title of one of Dante's
minor works centered in a wreath: *Vita nuova* in laurel, *Convivio* in olive, *De
vulgari eloquentia* in various flowers, *Monarchia* in oak. Dante naturally dom-
inates the monument. Crowned with laurel, he grasps his robe with his left

7.2. Enrico Pazzi's monument to Dante (Photo: Fratelli Alinari, ca. 1890; Alinari / Art Resource, NY)

hand, pulling it close to his body, while his right hand holds the *Divine Comedy*. An imposing eagle, symbol of the Roman Empire, stands at Dante's feet, looking up at him, while the poet glares ahead with an expression of "anger and sadness because no strong hand rises to break the chains of Italy, an inn of sorrow, and allow the eagle to soar." The monument celebrates the freedom Dante sought by displaying around its base the emblems of principal Italian cities as if to confirm his prophecy of their union.[13]

Dante's admirers from other countries joined citizens from all over Italy to celebrate the young nation's independence and the poet's six hundredth birthday. His national symbolism, a unifying theme of the three-day festival, received a grand send-off at an unofficial banquet held for foreign dignitaries on Wednesday, May 17, a day after the conclusion of events. England's Henry Clark Barlow, one of our eyewitnesses to the centenary, and representatives of France, Germany, Belgium, Russia, Hungary, Poland, and the United States were the guests of many eminent Italians—there were nearly 130 participants in all—including Gonfaloniere Luigi Cambray-Digny (the Florentine mayor), Father Giuliani, Enrico Pazzi, and several generals and government ministers. Champagne and words flowed freely over the course of the evening, with speakers occasionally supplying fresh takes on the centenary amid the general bonhomie of the gathering.[14]

After Mayor Cambray-Digny toasted the foreign guests, Barlow and Monsieur Mezières spoke in turn on behalf of England and France. The US representative then rose to speak in his native language, but as few in the room understood English, James Montgomery Stuart—a reporter for London's *Morning Post*—translated the speech into Italian. At the mention of "gli Stati Riuniti"—"the re-United States"—the room erupted with applause, a poignant reminder that Italy celebrated its first years as an independent and (mostly) united nation just as the United States of America emerged from a gruesome war fought to preserve the union and make it "more perfect"—more free—by eradicating slavery. The American speaker, Charles Volney Dyer (1808–1878), was in Florence to represent his country because President Lincoln had appointed him as a judge on the tribunal created by the 1862 treaty with Great Britain for the suppression of the slave trade. A fervent abolitionist and active station manager for the Underground Railroad in Illinois, Dyer knew Lincoln well from Chicago politics and was an obvious choice for the international commission aimed at stopping slavery. Fond of European travel when not on duty in Sierra Leone, Judge Dyer was in Rome when he learned of the president's death on April 15, 1865, from the bullet fired by John Wilkes Booth at Ford's Theatre the night before—exactly one month before the festivities in honor of Dante and Italy in Florence. Now there to speak for his country, Dyer "paid a beautiful and touching tribute of affection to the apostle and martyr of freedom." At the mere mention of the name— Abraham Lincoln—"every Italian in that vast assembly of distinguished men rose reverently to his feet, and stood in profound silence."[15]

Another American abolitionist, the poet Henry Wadsworth Longfellow, participated in the Dante centenary in a different way, while also highlighting parallel struggles for freedom in Italy and the United States. Longfellow received a copy of the *Divine Comedy* in Rome on April 11, 1828, and by the end of 1837 wrote that Dante "excites [him] more than any other poet."[16] Inspiring sonnets like "Mezzo Cammin" in 1842 and "Dante" in 1845, providing material for Harvard lectures (1838–1854), and culminating in publication of the first American translation of the entire poem in 1865–1867, Dante accompanied Longfellow for nearly his entire adult life. Longfellow became the first president of the Dante Society of America, one of the nation's oldest scholarly societies, a year before he died at age seventy-five in 1882. Although he could not be there in person, Longfellow sent a copy of his *Inferno* translation— privately printed—for display during the Florentine festivities in honor of Dante and Italy.[17]

Dante's pervasive message of freedom—spiritual liberation from sin but also political emancipation—rang true and timely to Longfellow's ears as the divided nation fought over the fate of Southern slavery. Throughout the war years, he drafted and revised his translation of the *Divine Comedy,* completing a first version of the *Inferno* on April 16, 1863, by writing a canto a day during the month after Charley, his eighteen-year-old son, left home to fight for the Union.[18] Longfellow was deeply pained by the war's horrific toll in death, mutilation, and destruction on both sides in the conflict, its devastation hitting close to home when Charley was badly wounded in battle. But the monstrosity of chattel slavery was an injustice he could not bear. Dante stood as a harbinger and symbol of freedom on both sides of the Atlantic, as Longfellow showed in a sonnet written on March 7, 1866, to accompany his translation of the *Paradiso.*

Longfellow's Dante is "the star of morning and of liberty," the prophet of Italian independence. But this great liberator is not for Italians only. His message reaches "all the nations" as his "fame is blown abroad from all the heights, / . . . and a sound is heard, / as of a mighty wind." Dante's liberating "sound" was indeed heard clear across the ocean in the nineteenth century, inspiring New England Brahmins like Longfellow and Senator Charles Sumner, and African American "freedom readers"—the title of an Italian literature scholar's book on the subject—such as the orator Frederick Douglass and the poet Henrietta Cordelia Ray. In American abolitionist circles, Dante held a place "on a par with none less than Lincoln," Dennis Looney argues.[19] For Italians, he played the composite role of Lincoln and Washington as the nation's "star of morning and of liberty" and its ancestral father.

The evening's final speaker, Count Terenzio Mamiani della Rovere (1799–1885), was a highly respected Italian intellectual and patriot, having led a long and storied political life before the centenary in 1865. Arrested, imprisoned, and exiled after the failed uprising of 1831, he lived in France until 1847. More practical reformer than zealous revolutionary, he served as prime minister (later foreign minister) in the government of the Papal States, trying unsuccessfully to persuade Pope Pius IX to relinquish political authority and support Italian independence in 1848. Mamiani also played a leading role in the formation of the government of the Kingdom of Sardinia-Piedmont. He was elected to parliament in 1856 as a supporter of Cavour, whom he helped assume power after the war and annexations of 1859–1860. He served as minister of education in 1860–1861 and was a special envoy to Greece in 1861–1863, before being nominated senator the following year. He would continue to fill important positions in Italy's government after Rome became the nation's capital in 1871. The count greatly impressed Barlow, who described him as a small, slender man with fine features exuding intelligence, kindness, energy, and authority. Mamiani's physical presence, combined with his gift for eloquence, made him seem "cast by Nature in that generous mould of Poet, Philosopher, and Politician, of which Dante was the culminating example."[20]

Count Mamiani had always been driven by his liberal Catholic beliefs to advocate on behalf of marginalized and underprivileged groups in Italy and abroad. So his speech before other Italian elites and eminent foreign guests unsurprisingly placed Dante's milestone birthday and Italian unification ("of which he is the symbol") within a larger geopolitical context. Mamiani was proud that Italy, unlike many other countries, had achieved its independence because (for the most part) different parts transcended local interests to unite into one nation without class persecution, reprisals, and despotism. He hoped Italy's "new and salutary example" would not be lost on his foreign guests, whom he saluted as "brothers." Mamiani used this name "not by chance, not by any rhetorical habit, but with profound and appropriate meaning" at a time when "across the ocean, the last chains of a suffering portion of the human race fall broken."[21]

The count's words assumed deeper meaning when his speech was printed in the Florentine newspaper two days later. On the same page appeared an article describing how Italians in the United States had paid their final respects to Abraham Lincoln. Three hundred Italian workers, the reporter wrote, attended the slain president's memorial service in Washington, DC, with others joining processions that met the funeral train carrying Lincoln's body (and that of his son Willie, who had died in 1862) from Washington to Springfield, Illinois. At the stop in New York City, which drew over one hundred thousand mourners, Italians were summoned by their nation's consul (the first one), five hundred of them marching in public for the first time behind Italy's flag.

Mamiani used a striking image to convey the lesson of Italian nationhood for the world. "Scarcely risen from our tomb," he told the foreign dignitaries, "we already offer some practical policies any people can use to their advantage." He pictured the arrival of Italian liberation and unification not as a birth but as a rebirth or resurrection—as a return from the dead. This was also how the French writer Victor Hugo described Italy's nascent nationhood in his congratulatory letter for the centenary. Accepting the invitation of Mayor Cambray-Digny to add his voice to the celebrations, Hugo sang the praises of Dante and Italy. His elegant paean to Italian glory, dated May 1, 1865, was printed in French on the third day of festivities (May 16) in the Florentine newspaper *La Nazione,* the city's major newspaper and de facto media outlet for the new nation. The author of *Notre-Dame de Paris* (1831) and *Les misérables* (1862) insisted that Dante and the nation were one, the poet's life and masterpiece foretelling Italy's triumph over adversity. Italy was "embodied" in Dante, the nation's "soul." Even during the bleakest times, when Italy was politically dead, it managed to shine as a beacon for literature, science, exploration, art, and architecture. "Ah, yes, she lives!" exclaimed Hugo: "From the depths of her sepulcher, she protested with her brilliance. Italy is a tomb from which arose the dawn." Newly resurrected, Italy now promised new wonders.[22]

Italy, as we saw in the Prologue, was not the only one risen from the grave. On May 28, 1865, two weeks after tens of thousands of people came to Florence to celebrate Italian nationhood on Dante's six hundredth birthday, *La*

Nazione printed a piece of "latest news" suggesting that the poet had already been absent from his tomb for many, many years. "We have been informed of the following extremely important dispatch sent yesterday from Ravenna to the Minister of Education and to the Gonfaloniere of Florence," the notice began: "This morning at 10 A.M., while knocking down part of an old chapel close to Dante's tomb, workers found a wood chest containing bones, with the following inscription on the inside—*Dante's bones viewed again on June 3, 1677*—and another inscription on the outside: *Dante's bones placed here by me, Brother Antonio Santi, on October 18, 1677.*" The message arrived while the city council was in session, allowing the Florentine leadership immediately to convey its "joy" to Ravenna by telegraph. But while Ravenna's communication just stated the facts—what workers found at a site close to the poet's tomb on Saturday, May 27, at ten in the morning—the Florentine response readily assigned the bones to Dante. As remains of the "divine poet," therefore, they were not just bones. They were "precious relics."[23]

In examining the bones on the day of the discovery, Drs. Claudio Bertozzi and Giovanni Puglioli likewise assumed they belonged to the poet. "The bones that belong to Dante's cadaver are well preserved," began their preliminary report. This statement seems more like an assumption based on first impressions and Antonio Santi's inscriptions than a conclusion drawn from careful analysis of the physical remains. Vincenzo Rambelli, a notary from Ravenna, included the doctors' assessment in his official report of the day's dramatic events, from the discovery and collection of the bones to their examination and repackaging. In Ravenna, no less than in Florence, Dante's bones acquired a saintly aura as "mortal relics" and "holy remains," their discovery bringing "indescribable joy" to the citizens. Rambelli gave a public reading of the report inside Dante's mausoleum at the end of the day. Intended "to solemnly certify the discovery of the bones of the divine poet," the formal document was signed at five o'clock by twenty participants and witnesses—from the politicians, doctors, and engineers "down to the lowest workers"—before Rambelli and two other notaries, Saturnino Malagola and Pietro Bendazzi, notarized it.[24]

If these bones really were Dante's, then the tomb in which he had been buried in 1321—the tomb Pietro Lombardo had remodeled in 1481–1483—no longer held his remains. The only way to make sure was to see what, if anything, lay inside the tomb announcing, "Here I, Dante, am confined." Meeting at the end of May, Ravenna's city council resolved to open the poet's original sarcophagus a week later, on June 7, 1865. This date would allow for all members of a national commission to observe the operation and issue an authoritative report on the bones found in a wall not far from the poet's mausoleum. The Italian government formed the commission soon after news of the discovery reached Florence. Baron Giuseppe Natoli, Italy's minister of education, selected six highly respected men to perform this national service: Giovanni Gozzadini, an archeologist and historian from Bologna, was joined by three Tuscans—Atto Vannucci, Giambattista Giuliani, and Luigi Paganucci—and, from Ravenna, by Mayor Gioacchino Rasponi and Alessandro Cappi, esteemed director of the city's Classense Library. Natoli appointed Gozzadini, whose wife, Teresa Serego-Alighieri, was a descendant of Dante, president of the commission.

The prospect of this national commission—appointed by the Italian government in Florence—coming to oversee the opening of Dante's tomb did not sit well with Ravenna's leadership and ordinary citizens. Even before the group's first meeting on June 6, the day before the opening, there was "in the air a certain diffidence if not open animosity" toward Florentines already on hand to represent Dante's native city in the centenary ceremonies planned for Ravenna at the end of June. Ravennese diffidence toward the Florentines intensified following the unexpected if timely discovery on May 27, 1865. If these bones belonged to Dante, who was to say that Florence might not enlist the aid of national leaders to take them? This would not be the first time Florence exploited favorable political circumstances to attempt "repatriation" over Ravenna's objections. One Florentine in particular caused concern: Atto Vannucci, a leading voice in the failed campaign to bring Dante's remains to Florence for the recently concluded festivities there, was present for all actions taken the day of the discovery—he and two Florentine deputies (Vincenzo Malenchini and Cirillo Monzani) signed the May 27 report as witnesses—and now served on the national commission.[25]

Writing for the Milanese newspaper *La Perseveranza* on June 3, a citizen of Ravenna described the city's immediate response to this concern. Addressing the topic of Dante's bones—"these days our ancient city is concerned exclusively with this matter"—the author told readers that "the mayor, the executive council, and the Ravennese people were somewhat alarmed by the appointment of this Commission, and the mayor left immediately for Florence." Only after Mayor Rasponi received assurance that the commission's sole purpose was to investigate and authenticate the discovery "did alarm die down and tranquility return" to the Ravennese people, who—the writer from Ravenna quickly added—"are rightly possessive of the relics of the great Italian!" Public animosity toward Florence was contained for the time being, but it found an outlet and led to threats of violence soon after the original tomb was opened and examined on June 7, 1865.[26]

The day before opening Dante's tomb, authorities added safeguards to protect the bones that—according to Brother Santi's inscriptions—had once occupied it. After examination of the bones on May 27, they had been returned to the crude wood box that mason Feletti's pickax had dislodged from the wall. The box had then been set inside a newer pine chest tied crosswise with a white cord and locked, its key deposited by Mayor Rasponi at city hall. The Italian National Guard kept the reinforced box of bones under constant watch in Dante's little temple. Now, on Tuesday, June 6, the double box of bones was enclosed within a third container made of metal and closed with four locks, each key given to a different individual. Hoping the next day's operations would confirm that these bones were Dante's, the mayor and other city leaders wanted to make sure they stayed put until then.[27]

To ensure credibility, the tomb opening was planned as a public affair. On June 5, Ravenna's executive council announced that the event would take place two days later as "the natural consequence of the miraculous discovery of Dante's bones," a marvel "over which you rightly rejoiced, O citizens, and by which the entire nation was moved."[28] Workers maximized space directly behind the mausoleum by erecting a platform—with two levels—to allow the national commission, local officials, and as many citizens as possible to witness the event. Filippo Lanciani, local head of the Corps of Civil Engineers, offered details not mentioned in the official report of June 7, 1865. Unacknowledged in previous studies, Lanciani's recollection of the discovery of bones and the tomb opening is contained in long letters that his father, Pietro, sent to the editor of the newspaper *L'Osservatore Romano* soon after the events. Lanciani recalled that officials and the public began gathering in the tomb area on Wednesday morning at seven o'clock, but when he and Romolo Conti, Ravenna's chief civil engineer, initiated the operations an hour later, members of the national commission had yet to appear. Lanciani and Conti first had a large strip of sandstone shaped to fit around the tomb's cover so it could be safely lifted off the base, a wise precaution given existing cracks in the marble. However, the commissioners objected when they arrived to find the protective device already in place. The engineers directed masons to remove the sandstone mold, thus enabling observers to verify the cover's integrity, and then to reattach it. This was all unnecessary, a frustrated

Lanciani remarked, because the presence of three notaries public from the start "should have removed every suspicion."[29]

Work proceeded at a brisk pace over the next few hours. Masons immediately began dismantling the rear wall of the mausoleum, cutting through the stonework from the outside to reveal the back of the tomb, partially lodged within the wall. Spectators filling the mausoleum's backyard had an excellent view of the event's main attraction. When the sarcophagus appeared, they noticed that a double row of bricks sealed the gap between the back of the base and the cover—less than four and a half inches wide—corresponding to the marble strip that Pietro Lombardo had wrapped around the three internal (i.e., visible) sides of the tomb. Inside the mausoleum, meanwhile, masons removed the plaster binding the cover to the base and to the decorative wall behind the tomb. A high-ranking representative from Florence, Prior Giovanni Balzani Romanelli, arrived as a witness at ten thirty, just in time for the moment of truth. At a quarter to eleven on June 7, 1865, Dante's tomb was opened in the presence of official witnesses—representing Ravenna, Florence, and Italy—and a large crowd of local residents.[30]

The official report states only the basic facts: Mayor Rasponi and the other six commissioners inspected the tomb and "found it entirely empty." Fortunately more personal testimony exists. Primo Uccellini (1804–1882) may not have ranked high enough in the social hierarchy to sign the official report, but this Italian patriot (he had been imprisoned for five years during Austrian occupation), employed since 1861 as a librarian in the Classense Library, gave a brighter picture of the response when Dante's tomb was opened. As workers prepared to remove the cover, "all the spectators, hearts thumping, turned their eyes to the tomb." This, according to Uccellini, is what he and other anxious observers then saw, felt, and heard: "Little by little the cover slid off the marble base, and when the tomb was seen emptied of the recently gathered remains, our spirits were filled with an indescribable joy and the bells of the public tower immediately announced, ringing in celebration, the good news to citizens anxiously awaiting it." Uccellini wrote his account on June 12, while the events of five days earlier were still fresh in his mind. Henry Clark Barlow corroborated this response to the empty tomb, writing that "a universal shout of joy burst from all present at this conclusive fact." He also voiced an unsettling consequence of the happy revelation. If the tomb had lain empty "for nearly two centuries" (actually closer to three and a half centuries), then "the gifted of all countries, poets, philosophers, and historians, who as pilgrims had come to bow down before Dante's sacred remains, had knelt before an empty urn, and returned to their homes perfectly satisfied."[31]

Still, an "empty urn" meant the bones discovered on May 27 almost certainly belonged to Dante, a conclusion that aligned well with what many people in Ravenna previously feared (and now hoped) but were afraid publicly to admit: the poet's bones had been missing from their gravesite for a very long time. One young man from Ravenna, busy preparing for university exams in Bologna at the time of the discovery, was stunned by his compatriots' enthusiasm for someone dead for over five hundred years. Pier Desiderio Pasolini (1844–1920) could not fathom "how in Ravenna all citizens of every class were so excited by Dante's bones, which everyone knew were not where they were said to be." Yet, this future Italian senator observed, "one was careful not to repeat it too much," treating this knowledge "as if it were a family secret." He confessed to doing this himself. Engineer Conti, in his report written soon after the discovery, claimed that older citizens had recalled hearing from Franciscan friars at the beginning of the century "the mysterious words" that a "great treasure" was hidden in Braccioforte. Reporting on the events of 1865, Barlow acknowledged this tradition, adding that the treasure "had indeed come to light, though few, if any, had ever suspected what that treasure might be."[32]

In truth, at least some observers had good reason to view the opening of Dante's tomb as a mere formality, a "simple confirmation" that it was empty. They knew that Melchior Missirini (1773–1849) claimed in his popular biography of Dante (first published in 1840) to have heard from current Franciscans of their predecessors' graverobbing; "if true," this meant the poet's bones "would no longer lie in their tomb." Filippo Mordani, a native of Ravenna who figured prominently in his city's Dante commemorations in 1865, reported more specific knowledge of the empty tomb and efforts to conceal it. Dionigi Strocchi (1762–1850), a writer and professor living in Ravenna, could not contain himself from revealing to Mordani what he had been told by the Archbishop of Ravenna. "Oh enough," Strocchi said on July 1, 1841, "I want to tell you something, since we're all alone here. You should know that Dante's tomb is empty, the bones aren't there anymore. Your Archbishop Codronchi told me this. But please don't breathe a word of this, because it has to be kept secret."[33]

Despite ample evidence of this poorly kept secret, a few very important people could not help harboring a lingering doubt about what they would find in the poet's tomb. They feared above all the appearance of another set of human bones, "resulting in two skeletons of Dante." No one worried more about this nightmare scenario than Ravenna's mayor, Gioacchino Rasponi. He understandably craved an even higher degree of certainty before the tomb was opened in the presence of a national commission, not to mention local citizens and foreign visitors. Details vary, but separate reports based on a common credible source show the mayor conducting a preemptive, clandestine examination of Dante's sarcophagus not long before the public opening on June 7, 1865. Count Luigi Guaccimanni, a member of Ravenna's executive council who signed the official reports of May 27 and June 7, shared his firsthand knowledge of the secret operation many years after the fact. Mayor Rasponi, accompanied by just a few close colleagues and trustworthy workers (possibly including mason Pio Feletti and engineer Romolo Conti), sneaked into Dante's mausoleum late at night to verify that the tomb was empty. They could have done this, as Santi Muratori explained in 1918, by boring a small hole in the tomb—most likely somewhere between the base and the cover—and then inserting a wire or other flexible instrument to detect the presence of any solid objects. The mayor and his accomplices were undoubtedly ecstatic at having their hopeful assumption confirmed. They also knew they would have to feign that same joyful relief when the tomb was revealed to be empty during the public event.[34]

To everyone's relief, the opening of Dante's sepulcher in Ravenna did not unearth a second skeleton to cast doubt on the identity of the one found in the wall less than thirty feet away. Nor was the original tomb completely empty, however. Mayor Rasponi and Giovanni Gozzadini, president of the national commission, found piles of dust and pieces of dried laurel leaves—lasting evidence of the glory with which Dante was buried in 1321—as well as marble chips that had fallen to the bottom of the tomb when the Franciscans chiseled away part of the base to create an opening large enough to extract Dante's skull in the early sixteenth century. Rasponi carefully collected these materials and handed them to the notary Vincenzo Rambelli, who presented them to witnesses before they were placed in crystal vases for preservation. Most important, Rasponi and Gozzadini found among the stone and floral remains two small hand bones, and Drs. Puglioli and Bertozzi later discovered a small foot bone while sifting through the dust. The three bones were wrapped in paper sealed with red wax displaying Ravenna's coat of arms. Labeled "Dantis Ossa," the packet earned that designation when, four days later (June 11), the doctors conducted a more thorough examination of the skeleton dislodged from the wall of Braccioforte. They concluded that the three phalanges did in fact "match those found earlier," thus giving "further proof that the bones so fortunately discovered belong to the Divine Poet— something which in any case is shown by documents, tradition, and history to be beyond doubt."[35]

Official statements and reports note that something else was found inside Dante's original tomb on June 7, 1865, though they conveniently fail to mention the nearly fatal consequences of this discovery. Staining the interior of the tomb, along the sides and bottom, was a substance—almost black in color—that traced the contours of a human body. Doctor Puglioli scraped samples of the dark matter from an area corresponding to the location of the supine corpse's head and buttocks. Mayor Rasponi then enclosed the scrapings within four carefully labeled sheets of paper and immediately handed the samples to Giovanni Gozzadini, president of the national commission. Gozzadini was entrusted with the task of having the material submitted for chemical analysis. This analysis, the reports tell us, confirmed the supposition of the commissioners and other observers of the opened tomb that the dark material conforming to the outline of Dante's cadaver was "animal matter," meaning hardened residue of the poet's decomposed body.[36]

Official documents provide all this information. But they do not tell the whole story. By jumping from the gathering of the tomb scrapings to the reporting of test results, authorized sources ignore the drama surrounding possession of the material that took place in the short interval between these two moments. Fortunately for posterity, eyewitnesses recounted details elsewhere that untangle links in the chain of custody of the corporeal matter scraped from Dante's tomb.

Engineer Filippo Lanciani, whose memories of the tomb opening were published by his father, Pietro, in Rome's *L'Osservatore Romano* newspaper just a week later, claimed that he helped the two doctors collect the dark residue. Most of the substance covered the spot in the tomb corresponding to the midsection of Dante's cadaver. Lanciani confirmed that Gozzadini, as head of the commission, was entrusted with the task of submitting the samples for chemical analysis. He went far beyond the official record, however, in revealing details of what happened as soon as the public became aware that Mayor Rasponi had placed material removed from Dante's tomb—presumed traces of the decomposed body—in the hands of a man not from Ravenna. Giovanni Gozzadini was an eminent Italian, for sure, but a "foreigner" nonetheless.

Ravenna's leaders had sung the praises of Italian brotherhood by using the fact of unification to deny Dante's perpetual exile and so to deny Florence's claim to his bones in the 1864 petition. The public, on the other hand, had no inclination to respect even the pretense of national harmony when the scrapings were given to Gozzadini. "This arrangement," on the contrary, "so upset the people nearby that many of them began voicing their objections as soon as the consignment took place. The ill humor subsequently grew to the point that a bunch of common folk headed over to the inn where that gentleman was staying, with the aim of preventing his departure."[37] To ordinary citizens in Ravenna, the president of the national commission was not just any "foreigner." Distrustful of Florentines' intentions following their petition the year before—a move that no doubt brought to mind the city's attempt to steal the bones three and a half centuries earlier—local residents were already on high alert. A dangerous rumor soon accompanied news of Gozzadini's possession of the tomb scrapings. The near victim spoke afterward to others of the peril in which he found himself on that solemn June day in 1865. Writing over twenty-five years after the fact, Corrado Ricci still had Gozzadini's revelation of his close call fresh in mind: "The late count told me," Ricci recalled, "how, after the false rumor had spread that he was a Florentine sent to ask for Dante's bones or to transport them to Florence, a crowd of Ravennese citizens gathered under the windows of the Hotel Spada d'Oro, where the senator was staying."[38]

To this agitated group, Gozzadini was a Florentine—worse, a Florentine intent on accomplishing by stealth what the diplomatic petition had failed to do. It is little wonder, then, that his possession of any trace whatsoever of Dante's remains—no matter how provisional and legitimate—incited public outrage. The mob that had formed outside the hotel of the suspected Florentine agent "erupted in a demonstration so noisy and hostile," Ricci wrote, "that Count Gozzadini was forced to take refuge in a secluded area [within the hotel] away from where the protestors were shouting him down." No fool, Gozzadini took the threat seriously. "Seeing how things had taken a turn for the worse," Lanciani reported, "he hurried to hand the material over to the mayor, a measure which calmed the spirits of the citizens and allowed him to leave Ravenna without harm." Gozzadini, in truth, was not even Tuscan (much less Florentine) but rather a citizen of Bologna. "Once the misunderstanding was resolved," the apprehensive citizens, to their credit, promptly reversed course: allowing Gozzadini to exit the hotel, they greeted him with "enthusiastic applause." We do not know at what point in the standoff the count returned the scrapings to Mayor Rasponi, but he must have been relieved to get them off his hands.[39]

President Giovanni Gozzadini was not Florentine, but other members of the national commission were. Though not born in Florence, Atto Vannucci and Giambattista Giuliani were distinguished, longtime residents of the city. Luigi Paganucci, citizen of a neighboring Tuscan town, also had strong ties to Florence, where for many years he taught courses on anatomy; as president of the committee that brought to fruition Enrico Pazzi's statue of Dante (unveiled in Piazza Santa Croce a few weeks earlier), he also served on the Florentine commission for the Dante centenary.[40] Chewed up by the rumor mill, these men, like Gozzadini, faced the threat of being lynched by an angry Ravennese mob.

Federico Fabbri, a veteran of the Risorgimento who later became a prominent political journalist, worked in Ravenna's administration when Dante's bones were discovered on May 27, 1865.[41] A witness to events in the days to follow, Fabbri recalled the reaction of his compatriots to news of the consignment of the tomb scrapings to Gozzadini and (it was believed) his Florentine colleagues. Fabbri's recollection, published in the newspaper *Corriere della Sera* in 1900, was still vivid thirty-five years after the fact:

> I remember! When in 1865 they discovered the box that Brother Santi
> had immured in the vicinity of [the Church of] S. Francesco and that
> contained Dante's bones, I was in Ravenna. There ran a rumor then
> that a few scrapings from the sarcophagus that was supposed to hold
> the remains of the divine poet had been given to Atto Vannucci, G. B.
> Giuliani, and other Florentines. The whole town was in turmoil and
> objected, and there were even public protests under the windows of the
> Hotel S. Marco, where the Florentines were staying. To calm the anger
> of the Ravennese, it was not only promised but solemnly declared to
> them that not a particle of the remains of Dante's body would leave the
> city walls.[42]

To corroborate Fabbri's testimony, the newspaper informed readers of Giovanni Gozzadini's similar experience. Appointed by Minister of Education Giuseppe Natoli to the national commission "charged with verifying the fact of the discovery of Dante's bones," Gozzadini and his colleagues were bound by duty to observe and report on the examination of Dante's tomb. When they returned to their respective hotels later that day, they hardly could have imagined, as the editor wryly put it, that their souls would "very nearly be sent to Heaven!" Their bodies, less poetically, nearly required tombs of their own.[43]

The indignation of the Ravennese citizens, however misplaced, showed that their claim on Dante's bones extended even to material scraped from his tomb. They objected to the loss of an iota of those bodily traces no less than they would have to the loss of an entire rib or femur. Dante may have been born in Florence, and he may have stood for all of Italy; but each and every speck of him belonged to Ravenna, the legitimate custodian of his mortal remains. The angry citizens who nearly attacked Gozzadini and other members of the national commission during the brief time in which they held the scrapings showed "how the Ravennese are jealous of Dante's bones" and—as a warning—"how unwise any plan to take them elsewhere would be."[44] Calm was restored with the return of the tomb scrapings to Mayor Rasponi, who submitted them for analysis the following day, June 8, 1865.

Drs. Puglioli and Bertozzi conducted a more thorough examination of Dante's bones three days later (June 11, 1865) before the national commission and other important persons. In addition to verifying that the three small bones from the tomb belonged to the skeleton found on May 27—confirmation of their identification of the remains as Dante's—the physicians now drew conclusions from their detailed measurements of the poet's cranium. Capable of holding an exceptionally voluminous brain, the cranium's large size and harmonious shape indicated a man of "vast" and "superior" intelligence.[45] The national commissioners also focused an inordinate amount of attention on Dante's skull in their official report to the government issued the next day (June 12, 1865). But whereas the two doctors dismissed phrenology—the theory of the German physiologist Franz Joseph Gall (1758–1828) that the skull's outer surface indicated mental character and abilities—as a pseudoscience "already discredited in the same country in which it was born," the commissioners created a psychological profile of the poet even as they claimed "not to concern themselves very much with phrenological doctrines." Dante's cranium, following Gall's system, showed "a philosophical mind" with highly developed affective and intellectual faculties as well as talents and qualities touching on music, art, satire, religion, benevolence, independence, and pride.[46]

The national commission's main task, however, was to verify the identity of the skeleton, and on this matter its members showed no ambivalence. Historical and anatomical evidence confirmed, "now more readily than before, [the commissioners'] conviction that those bones belonged to the supreme poet." Consistent with how Dante was celebrated during the Florentine festivities a month earlier, they concluded the official report by interpreting the discovery of his bones as a divine sign of Italy's political fortune. Congratulating Ravenna, "to whom the heavens reserved the good fortune of revealing Dante's sacred bones to resurrected Italy," the commission hoped these remains would be "preserved like a treasure of the nation that reaffirmed its unity in Dante's name." The religious rhetoric of this national report took physical form when, two weeks later, the poet's skeleton received the sort of public veneration usually reserved for the corpse of a political or spiritual leader that lies in state.[47]

The presence of Dante's bones that made the centenary celebrations "beautiful and complete" happened not in Florence, as Atto Vannucci had hoped when he lobbied for their repatriation, but in Ravenna on June 24–26, 1865. The city "spared neither money nor means" on its own Dante festival. The new and "peculiar feature" of the event—the display and reburial of the poet's bones—raised expectations for an attractive program of accompanying activities, from processions, banquets, speeches, and conferences to illuminations, musical recitals, horse races, and raffles. The Braccioforte chapel, with its four open sides framed by graceful arches, was an ideal venue for displaying Dante's skeleton to the public. An altar-like dais nine feet long, four feet wide, and five feet high was raised inside the chapel. Red cloth with gold fringes—colors of the Commune of Ravenna—embellished this platform and the area around it. The dais held a transparent reliquary casket, its sides and hipped cover formed by crystal plates trimmed in gold. Eight feet long, the receptacle measured about two and a half feet across and stood nearly five feet high. Angels adorned the corners, and a gilded vase stood atop the glass coffin, which rested on lion's-paw legs.[48]

The day before the start of the festivities, Drs. Puglioli and Bertozzi placed the bones in their correct anatomical position and fastened them to an unobtrusive mechanical frame. Ravenna's citizens and visitors awoke on the morning of June 24, a Saturday, to the salvos of an artillery salute. The city was already coming to life, its streets filling with local residents and people arriving from the countryside and other parts of Italy, as Dante's reassembled skeleton was brought to the Braccioforte chapel. The doctors carefully laid it out on a white satin bed inside the crystal casket, which was veiled by a large white cloth. Tricolored flags already brightened buildings and streets, and the area around Braccioforte and the poet's mausoleum was decked out for the special occasion. Piazza Dante Alighieri (today Piazza Garibaldi), a short distance from the tomb, was lined with banners and pennants, their poles wrapped in ivy and laurel. A concert stage was set up in the center of the piazza, and taller poles displaying the gonfalons of Rome, Venice, Florence, and Ravenna rose from its four corners. Echoing the Florentine festivities a month earlier, the privileging of these four cities—two of them not yet part of the nation—highlighted significant progress toward fulfilling Dante's dream of Italian unity while urging its completion. At the entrance to Via Dante Alighieri, the street leading to the mausoleum, stood a majestic triumphal arch bearing the coat of arms of the House of Alighieri and an epigraph announcing that on June 24–25, 1865, "the people of Ravenna celebrate Dante's six hundredth birthday and the discovery of his bones."[49]

Led by members of the National Guard, a festive procession departed from city hall at noon. Representatives of Ravenna, Florence, and other cities were joined in the march by military, cultural, and national leaders, including Minister of Education Natoli. Last in line—but first in honor—were the Florentine prior Nicolò Nobili (representing his city), Mayor Rasponi of Ravenna, and Count Serego Alighieri, the poet's descendant. Music, bells, and applause greeted the procession along the route, with the Venetian flag—darkened as if in mourning—drawing the loudest ovation. Arrived at their destination, Mayor Rasponi, Prior Nobili, and Count Alighieri entered the Braccioforte chapel. After Rasponi lifted the white veil from the crystal coffin and laid two laurel wreaths at its base, he praised Dante's cultural achievement and its preeminence in Italian nationhood. The "initiator of a new civilization," Dante, for Rasponi, was not just a poet and philosopher but a political visionary for whom the unity of the Roman Empire prefigured the unity of Italy. Bones of the "divine poet" were "precious relics," an "incomparable treasure . . . returned to Italians in these fortunate days when Italy unites as an independent country and retakes its ancient seat among the nations of Europe!"[50]

That day and the next—June 24–25, 1865—residents and visitors gathered at Braccioforte to view Dante's skeleton and pay their respects. Spanning the chapel's four archways, an iron railing protected the poet's treasured relics while allowing worshipers to view them from a short distance away, as seen in the photograph in figure 7.3. During the hot summer evenings, residents illuminated their homes with candles, while lamps and torches lit up the

7.3. Display of Dante's skeleton in the Braccioforte chapel on June 25, 1865 (Corrado Ricci, *L'ultimo rifugio di Dante Alighieri* [Milan: Hoepli, 1891], after page 368)

streets. Illuminations transformed Via Dante Alighieri into a "truly wondrous dream," and tricolored lamps—white, green, and red—flooded the Braccioforte chapel with light, thus allowing crowds to view Dante's bones bathed in Italy's colors all through the night. When not looking in wonder at the divine poet's relics, festival-goers enjoyed concerts, harness races, lectures, theatrical performances, fireworks displays, and other events in Dante's honor.[51]

Giovanni Andrea Scartazzini, one of the nineteenth century's greatest Dante scholars, was in his late twenties when the poet's bones were discovered in 1865. He later recalled how Italians and foreigners came "with all speed to Ravenna" to view them at the end of June, the influx of visitors creating "golden days for the local innkeepers!" Commercial opportunism, no matter how unwelcome, seems not to have spoiled the pleasurable solemnity of the occasion. Henry Barlow, the English representative to the festivities, found it "a strange and touching spectacle here to behold the bones of him laid out whom all Italy and the civilized world delight to honour." Dante's bones, in clear view, showed "a dark warm brownish tint." The poet's cranium appeared "most beautiful in shape and proportion," making it all the sadder that "the lower jaw was missing to complete the head." The skeleton naturally had a powerful effect on young minds. Writing some twenty-five years after the event, Corrado Ricci slips out of his objective narrative to inform readers that "naïve children were also shown the poet's skeleton so that, when they one day understood the greatness of the man to whom it belonged, they could say with the sweet satisfaction felt by the writer of these pages that they had seen it." Another writer recalled the "profound impression left on everyone— particularly on us kids—by the imposing spectacle of the square portico of Braccioforte, with that crystal urn raised in the center, holding the skeleton of the Poet, as if he had risen up in our easily excited imaginations!" Even the elderly and infirm, Ricci remembered, were brought there and assisted by others so they could participate in the ritual viewing.[52]

Dora D'Istria, an honored guest at the festivities in Ravenna, was deeply moved by the power of Dante's displayed bones to unite Italians in their devotion to the poet and the nation. A Romanian princess of Albanian origin, Dora was a celebrated cultural figure in postunification Italy, Florence in particular, where she lived from 1860 until her death in 1888. Accompanied by Mayor Rasponi's royal mother—Luisa Murat Rasponi was the daughter of Joaquim Murat (king of Naples) and Carolina Bonaparte Murat, sister of Emperor Napoleon I of France—Dora observed the spectacle from a window overlooking the Braccioforte chapel. Strong proponents of Italian independence and unification, the two princesses took pleasure in the "enthusiasm of a people happy to become a nation."[53]

Dora believed that Italy's success—and that of other free nations—demanded the emancipation of its female population, largely through improved educational opportunities for girls and young women. She raised this issue at the banquet at the end of the first day of the festivities. Dante's Beatrice, Dora told the gathering of dignitaries and other esteemed guests, provided an authoritative model for such female empowerment. Beatrice was "the final word in that great moral revolution that Plato foresaw and the apostles preached—the fulfillment of which Dante made possible." She was not "the eternal child of Roman law"; she was not "the woman of early Christianity condemned to silence on religious matters." Beatrice, instead, had "a pure and refined ability—as penetrating as the wisdom of the philosophers—to reveal the mysteries of heaven and earth."[54]

Not everyone appreciated how Dante's bones received saint-like veneration outside specifically religious confines and practices. Pier Desiderio Pasolini, the university student back home in Ravenna for the occasion, found the display highly distasteful. "It was a scandalously pagan scene" that the poet never would have sanctioned. "Poor Dante's bones were exhibited like those of a reptile," Pasolini complained on the day of the unveiling, "like a petrified crocodile displayed in a geological collection." Even the venue was wrong. Instead of being viewed in the Church of Saint Francis with the appropriate religious accoutrements, Dante's remains were "encased within four plates of glass and surrounded by gas-lit lamps inside a flower-strewn portico that seemed set up for a picnic." Pasolini was offended by the civic ceremony passing itself off as a church ritual. If authorities wished to sanctify Dante's bones, they at least owed him the dignity of a proper ceremony in the right setting.[55]

A priest conducted the reburial ceremony on June 26, 1865, though the father in question was the patriotic Dante professor Giambattista Giuliani. The ceremony began when the leading citizens present at the unveiling of Dante's bones two days earlier (minus Minister Natoli) gathered again at the Braccioforte chapel. Father Giuliani had attributed the confluence of Dante's milestone birthday and Italian nationhood to divine providence when he dedicated Enrico Pazzi's monument to the poet in Florence the previous month. He now praised the discovery of Dante's bones as "perhaps a miracle to fulfill the prophecy of the long-sought unity and prosperity of Italy." "These bones tell me," Giuliani relayed to his audience, "that Dante's triumph prepares and inaugurates the complete triumph of Italy and the best civilization in the world." Giuliani also used this eulogy to call for the erection of a "grandiose temple" with a "glorious tomb" worthy of holding the poet's "precious relics."[56]

Right after Father Giuliani's speech, Drs. Puglioli and Bertozzi opened the crystal display casket, disassembled the skeleton, and checked the number and state of the bones against the lists from the examinations on May 27 and June 11, 1865. Mayor Rasponi then placed the bones in a walnut casket sheathed by a protective lead container measuring three feet long and just under a foot each in width and height. The mayor also set inside the casket the sample material—traces of Dante's decomposed body—scraped from the marble tomb when it was opened on June 7, 1865. A sealed crystal tube holding a written record of this episode in the afterlife of Dante's "sacred relics," from their discovery on May 27 to their reburial on June 26, 1865, was placed in the casket with the bones and tomb scrapings. After the cover of the walnut coffin was fastened with ten screws and the lead cover was soldered to the base, four pallbearers—Mayor Rasponi, Florentine prior Nicolò Nobili, regional prefect Giuseppe Alasia, and Senate vice president Giuseppe Pasolini (father of young Pier Desiderio)—carried the casket to Dante's mausoleum and placed it in his marble tomb. Under the direction of engineers Conti and Lanciani, workers finally reset the cover on the sarcophagus and repaired the back wall of the mausoleum—inside and outside—so that it looked the same as before.[57]

On June 29, 1865, just three days after the reburial of Dante's bones, an article in the local newspaper (*Ravennate*) spelled out the political implications of Father Giuliani's speech and other key moments of the festivities in Ravenna: "Rest in peace, dear bones, consecrated by the devotion of all Italians and the world, and bathed by the tears of Venice and Rome." "Once you are placed in a fine monument raised for you by Italy and the world," the article continued, "those cities, too, will remove the dark veil that today covers their flags." Because that grand new monument never materialized (a funding campaign launched in 1890 fizzled out), Dante's physical remains, blessed and bathed as they were, continued to reside in their original sarcophagus (remodeled in 1481–1483) within the "little temple" built in 1780–1782. Both the bones and the scrapings—hardened residue of Dante's body—were still there when the tomb was next opened in 1921, the six hundredth anniversary of his death. By that time, the poet reigned supreme not only as Italy's saintly father, prophet, and liberator but as the nation's redeemer of its outstanding territorial claims.[58]

Two

Fragments of Redemption and Warfare

8

The Redeemer

And now he stands still, and seems to wait, at Trent.
—GIOSUÈ CARDUCCI

In 1865, the year of Dante's six hundredth birthday, Italy's most important "unredeemed" lands—its major missing pieces—were Venice and Rome, Italian centers of cultural, political, and (in the case of Rome) religious power. Political leaders and average citizens alike looked to Rome, the city that Dante believed was divinely ordained as the seat of imperial and papal rule, as the nation's future capital. On the eve of the festivities in 1865, the Provincial Council of Florence presented King Victor Emmanuel II with a sword, a finely worked, richly adorned commemorative gift. One side of the blade bore the inscription, "Dante al primo re d'Italia"—"From Dante to the first king of Italy"—while the other side flashed one of the *Commedia*'s most politically charged passages: "Come and see your Rome and how she weeps, / widowed and bereft, and cries out day and night: / 'My Caesar, why are you not with me?'"[1] The message was clear and provocative: Victor Emmanuel II, King of Italy, was called upon here, as Dante had once called upon the Germanic emperors Albert I of Austria and Henry VII of Luxemburg, to fulfill his duty to make Rome, free of papal interference in temporal affairs, once again the center of Italian political life.

The following day, May 14, 1865, the king presided over the opening ceremonies in Piazza Santa Croce, its four corners adorned with banners of the cities most important to this joint celebration of Dante and the young Italian nation: Florence and Ravenna—the cities of Dante's birth and death—represented on the east side of the piazza, Rome and Venice with pride of place on the west side. Giambattista Giuliani addressed the king and the crowd just before the unveiling of Enrico Pazzi's monumental statue of Dante in the middle of the piazza. He cleverly used the stern demeanor of Dante's marble face to extend the poet's lament for Rome to include Venice as well. "Nor could the austere semblance of Alighieri put off its severity and clothe itself in a smile of entire satisfaction," he declared, "while Rome still weeps, and Venice, beneath the indignant yoke of a foreign oppressor, in pain and suffering, beats her troubled breast."[2] After receiving the king's congratulations, Giuliani thanked him for all he had done for Italy. "I have done what I could, and am ready to do what remains to be done," replied the king. These were "memorable words that made a deep impression on all who heard them," recalled one witness, noting that they "were subsequently confirmed."[3]

Italy added Venice to the national map with its victory over Austria the following year—and its army wrested control of Rome from Pope Pius IX in 1870—but the end of overt hostilities with Austria failed to secure other cities and provinces with large Italian populations living on the wrong side of the nation's northeastern borders. Thus began the irredentist movement (*irredentismo*), the long-term effort to gain those territories still "unredeemed" after 1866—Matteo Renato Imbriani (1843–1901), a hero of the Risorgimento, coined the phrase *terre irredente* in 1877. Already during the festivities of 1865, however, Italy claimed these "oppressed" or "occupied" lands as its own. They, in turn, displayed their allegiance to Italy through their devotion to Dante. Delegations from Istria and Trieste marched alongside representatives of Rome, Venice, and all fifty-nine provinces in the Kingdom of Italy. With financial contributions for the erection of Pazzi's colossal Dante, Trent and Istria wrote their attachment to the national body in stone, their coats of arms chiseled alongside those of other Italian cities on the frieze of the statue's pedestal.[4]

Italian inhabitants of "unredeemed" cities under Austrian control who were unable to attend the festivities in person found other ways—at times very creative ones—to honor Dante on his six hundredth birthday. Participation took various forms in these regions, from solemn ceremonies and artistic tributes—poems and musical compositions, bronze busts of Dante, commemorative medals—to academic conferences and the acquisition of the poet's works for libraries. Dante's worshipers in these Italian regions outside the nation's borders sometimes paid a high price for their activities. Citizens of Gorizia, now an Italian commune bordering Slovenia, suffered arrest and persecution for turning a celebration of Dante into a display of Italian pride. Italian students there found a less dangerous but curiously effective way to show their love of Dante and Italy. Since Austrian authorities refused to excuse them from school on the poet's birthday, young patriots honored Dante by leaving their books at home and showing up for class dressed all in black. The students' morbid fashion statement—not to mention their arrival at school with no books—may seem like a shabby way to celebrate the birth of Italy's greatest writer. Given the political context, however, their provocative gesture made sense: not being allowed to honor properly the father and prophet of the Italian nation, whole and free, was to them legitimate cause for grief and protest.[5]

Not all Italians, not even all those within the nation's borders, identified Dante with Italy. The country's Catholic hierarchy understandably opposed the celebrations in Florence glorifying the medieval poet as the prophet and proponent of the modern nation-state. Under no illusions that government leaders had their eyes set on Rome as Italy's future capital, the papacy and its supporters mocked and challenged the appropriation of Dante by liberal and secular Italians. An article in *L'Osservatore Romano,* the Vatican newspaper, led with "Alighieri and the Present Italian Revolution" to argue that it was anachronistic to give Dante "foolish ideas today in vogue with respect to the independence and unity of Italy, and to transform him, like a government minister, into a kneejerk adversary of the popes' temporal sovereignty."[6]

Civiltà Cattolica, the major Jesuit periodical, likewise rebuked Italian leaders and festival organizers for spreading the message that Dante, "a Catholic poet and intellectual," was really "a republican, Florentine soul who foretold the unity of Italy and the fall of the temporal dominion of the Pope." This writer considered the Dante festival a distasteful pagan event ostensibly in sync with the wishes of most Italians but actually an elite affair inaccessible to the masses. Traffic control and highly restricted seating, he observed, ensured that most of the festivities excluded the greater public. From this fiercely propapal, antigovernment perspective, the joint celebration of Dante and the new Italy amounted to having the king thrust his sword—its blade inscribed with the poet's lament for a weeping, widowed Rome—right through the heart of the church.[7]

The political nature of Italian tributes to Dante only intensified after the discovery of his bones on May 27, 1865. These tributes continued to rally Italians to the cause of completing unification by "redeeming" lands under foreign rule. After Ravenna announced a public display of Dante's bones, to be followed by a solemn reburial ceremony, an invitation to the historic event was sent out to leaders (*podestà*) of Italian cities, including several then located outside Italy's northeastern borders: Venice, Verona, Mantua, Padua, and Trieste. The invitation, dated June 15, 1865, portrays Dante as a figure like John the Baptist and other biblical prophets, a unifying force announcing future redemption: "The presence of representatives of the principal Italian cities at the viewing of *The Bones of Dante Alighieri,* and at their entombment, which will solemnly take place, following the festivities, on the 26th of this month, will be the most eloquent honor that Italy could give to the Sublime Poet, the forerunner [*preparatore*] of national unity."[8] Like the faithful called to honor a saint's remains when they are moved or "translated" to their final resting place, typically near the altar or in another prominent location within the church most devoted to the sacred body, witnesses from all over Italy—and from Italian lands yet to be "redeemed"—flocked to Ravenna for the viewing and reburial of the man who laid the groundwork for national unity.

Dante's capacity to bring people and places outside the nation's borders within this united Italy was born of his writings. Cherry-picking passages from the *Commedia,* irredentists and their supporters turned Dante into Italy's cartographer of choice, the unimpeachable arbiter of the shape of the nation's body. His divine poem established truth with the force of Holy Scripture, in this case what naturally—therefore rightfully—belonged to Italy. It was Dante, asserts Theodore J. Cachey Jr., an expert on geographic mapping in medieval and early-modern Italian literature, who "first recognized the key role that the map of Italy needed to play if any kind of cultural unification were to be achieved."[9] When describing the circle of heresy in Hell, Dante compares the raised tombs holding the suffering spirits—those who "hold the soul dies with the body"—to the sepulchers dotting the burial grounds "at Arles where the Rhone goes shallow" and "at Pola, near Quarnero's gulf, / which hems in Italy and bathes her borders." For irredentists, Dante's geography located Pola (Pula) with the rest of Istria (today split between Slovenia and Croatia, with a sliver in Italy) and the Dalmatian shoreline bathed by the Gulf of Quarnero (Croatia's Kvarner Gulf) all within Italy's boundaries, not in Austria.[10]

Dante's placement of South Tyrol, including the city of Trent, on Italy's map proved more binding, as this land later became part of the nation. He assigns this region to "fair Italy" when referring to Lake Garda (Benaco in Dante's day) as the source of waters emptying into a swampland where the

prophetess Manto settled and died, her dead bones serving as the foundation of Mantua, the city of Virgil's birth.[11] Reinforcing irredentist claims
was the poet's inclusion of the language spoken in Trent among the Italian
dialects discussed in his *De vulgari eloquentia*. There he writes that the
cities of Trent, Turin, and Alessandria "are situated so close to the boundaries of Italy that they could not possibly speak a pure language." Although
Dante dismisses the dialects of these border towns, necessarily contami-
nated by other languages, as "appalling" (*turpissimum*), all that mattered
from a later political perspective was that the people speaking them were
Italian.[12]

At the end of the nineteenth century, the Italian community of Trent, a
city then under Austrian rule, honored Dante with a large monument. The
poet's sixteen-foot figure stands atop a tiered pedestal, the entire structure
rising nearly sixty feet high.[13] Unveiled in Piazza della Stazione (today Piazza
Dante) on October 11, 1896, Cesare Zocchi's imposing bronze statue, like
Pazzi's Florentine colossus, was a public display of Italian ethnic and cultural
pride. "To Dante, to our Father," reads the inscription around the base of the
monument, "from the Trentino with the praise and assistance of the Nation."[14] The political import of this statue was not lost on anyone. The poet
Giosuè Carducci, a powerful irredentist voice, composed an ode for the occasion, its final verse neatly encapsulating Dante's position at the vanguard
of the movement to "redeem" this land for Italy: "And now he stands still, and
seems to wait, at Trent."[15]

What other writers lacked in verbal artistry, they made up for in passion
for the cause. One of the official anthems of the irredentist movement began,

> Long live Dante! This pure
> most sweet word
> consoles five peoples
> and unites them in one thought.[16]

Written by Riccardo Pitteri and set to music by Ruggero Leoncavallo,
composer of the popular opera *Pagliacci* (premiered in 1892), these words
expressed the yearning for Italy—through love of Dante—by Italians still
living under Austrian rule after the war of 1866. Pitteri, a poet from Trieste, was also president of the Lega Nazionale, for which he composed this
hymn. One of the two major irredentist organizations, the Lega, founded
in 1891, represented the interests of Italian communities in the Trentino,

eastern Friuli, Trieste, Istria, and Dalmatia—the "five peoples" consoled and united by Dante.

Not to be outdone in devotion to Italy's ancestral father, the other major irredentist association was named the Società Dante Alighieri. First proposed by refugees from Trent living in Rome, "La Dante Alighieri," or simply "La Dante," was founded in 1889 by prominent Italian cultural and political figures, including Carducci and Menotti Garibaldi, one of Giuseppe's sons. Ostensibly created to promote the diffusion and preservation of Italian language and culture abroad, the organization "was clearly political in intent," aiming above all to prevent Austria from destroying "the *italianità* of the *terra irredenta*."[17] The group's founding manifesto signaled this political intent in its opening words, though only in generic terms—no doubt to avoid running afoul of Austrian authorities in the "unredeemed" lands. "Intent on achieving the political unity of the nation," the founding members announced, "we Italians seem at times to forget that the homeland is not all within the material borders of the State."[18] To close this gap between ethno-cultural entity ("patria") and politico-juridical concept (state), they emulated efforts by other nation-states to keep the language and traditions alive among Italians living in other nations: "Wherever an accent of our language is heard, wherever our civilization has left its traditions, wherever our brothers must and wish to remain with us," they asserted, "there is a piece of the homeland that we cannot forget."[19]

Providing access to Italian books, language education, and cultural activities, La Dante saw knowledge and practice of the language as the best way to prevent Italians living outside Italy from losing "consciousness of the homeland." It used this approach not only with the growing number of Italian emigrants to distant lands but first and foremost with compatriots at risk of losing their Italian consciousness because of "the particular conditions of the places in which they reside"—those living under Austrian rule. Counting on the Italian language to reinforce Italian identity, the society's founders knew that one name above all others would "most worthily consecrate" their mission: Dante Alighieri.[20]

Isidoro del Lungo, arguably the most eloquent and influential voice enlisting Dante in the irredentist campaign, belonged to neither the Lega Nazionale nor the Società Dante Alighieri. But he was one of the founding members of the Società Dantesca Italiana in 1888, the main Italian organization devoted to Dante scholarship. A leading light in Dante studies and medieval

Italian history, del Lungo was president of the society from 1920 until his death in 1927. He also belonged to the Accademia dei Lincei and the Accademia della Crusca, Italy's most venerable scholarly associations. Before and after his appointment to the Italian Senate in 1906, he made a strong case for "redeeming" occupied Italian lands in the name of Dante.

Del Lungo's rhetoric soared when he made his case for Dante's Italy. Dante had served his one and only term as a Florentine prior from June 15 to August 15 in 1300. Decisions made that summer set the stage for Dante's exile the following year—and thus for the poem beginning "midway in the journey of our life," or Easter week of 1300, by Dante's reckoning. For the six hundredth anniversary of Dante's fateful priorate and (poetic) descent into Hell, the Commune of Florence invited del Lungo to deliver the commemorative lecture in the Salone dei Cinquecento, the largest and most important chamber in the Palazzo Vecchio, Florence's city hall. Dante was the "shining genius of the Italian homeland," declared del Lungo. Transcending partisan divisions, the medieval poet inspired Italians of 1900 to "raise a flag of national and moral justice," a "symbol of redemption for all those regions where [the language of] *sì* prevails and unites."[21]

In this moment of heightened national consciousness, del Lungo deftly exploited the anniversary of Dante's exile to raise the poet's iconic status. More than the father of the Italian language and culture, more than the prophet of Italian independence and unity, Dante then reigned supreme as the nation's tutelary deity. The two national societies bearing Dante's name complemented each other in lifting the poet to these Olympian heights. While the Società Dantesca Italiana (with del Lungo serving as its vice president in 1900) worked to illuminate and communicate knowledge of the poet's words, the Società Dante Alighieri aimed to transform these words into "the standard bearer of the nation's rights 'through virtually all the regions,' as Dante proclaimed, 'to which this tongue of ours extends,' from the eastern shores to the Istrian peninsula, from the Alps of Trent to the sea of Sicily."[22]

If Dante was Italy's god, his tomb was the nation's altar. Councils of the Società Dante Alighieri from all over Italy planned to worship at the poet's tomb-altar in Ravenna three months later, in September 1900, on the anniversary of his death: "We shall kneel, O Divine One, before your tomb, and we shall tell you of the united purpose and virile hopes for the future of this fatherland that you were the first to proclaim in your immortal song."[23]

Marking Italy's hopes for the "patria" as strongly masculine ("speranze virili"), del Lungo's vow to Dante hinted at the transformation of the poet from a national to a nationalist figure. Charles Davis, a Dante scholar and historian of medieval Italy, usefully defines nationalism "not merely [as] patriotic pride in a region or language or ethnic group but also as devotion to a national state, to a political entity which embodies and intensifies these loyalties."[24] Loyalties to the Italian nation-state intensified in the final decade of the nineteenth century as irredentist claims on lands under Austrian control dovetailed with colonialist ambitions in the Horn of Africa. Through negotiations with King Menilek II of Ethiopia, Italy won recognition of occupied territory along the Red Sea, officially establishing a Colony of Eritrea on January 1, 1890. Italy and Ethiopia understood the terms of their agreement very differently, however, and relations between the two countries soon turned hostile. Italian forces from Eritrea were routed by the larger, better-prepared Ethiopian army at the Battle of Adwa (Adua in Italian) on March 1, 1896, "the worst defeat ever inflicted on a colonial power in Africa."[25] Dante's evolution from a national to a nationalist symbol in del Lungo's address in 1900—only four years after the humiliating defeat at Adwa—thus occurred against the backdrop of a country struggling to regain its footing and renew hope in its future. What better place to do so than at Dante's tomb in Ravenna, the altar of the nation's father, prophet, and earthly god?

At this tomb eight years later, Isidoro del Lungo was again at the center of events promoting the poet's deification by a nation seeking to "redeem" lands thought to be occupied by a foreign power. The occasion in 1908 added a distinctive feature to Dante's mortuary chapel that we still see today: a votive lamp, its flame fueled by oil, suspended from the ceiling in front of the poet's marble tomb.[26] An offering of the Società Dantesca Italiana to Dante, the lamp produced a flame with oil provided by the Commune of Florence (its supply guaranteed each year in perpetuity), the Florentine oil to be held in a decorative amphora given by Italians living under Austrian rule in Trieste and other "unredeemed" lands. Dedicated in solemn yet politically tinged ceremonies held in Ravenna on September 13, 1908, the anniversary of Dante's death, the gifts were accompanied by a formal document. Printed on parchment patterned on an illuminated page of a Medici codex in Florence's Biblioteca Laurenziana, the words by the Dante scholar Guido Biagi (treasurer of the Dante Society) give full voice to Dante's god-like power in Italian national consciousness:

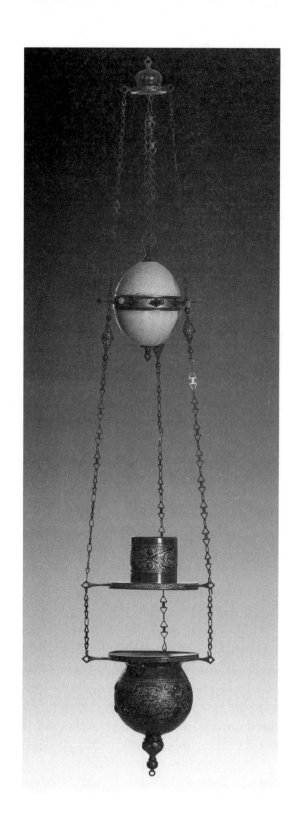

8.1. Original votive lamp
for Dante's tomb (Museo
Dantesco / Istituzione
Biblioteca Classense)

So That, Nourished By Olives
From The Land From Which He Was Banished,
An Expiatory And Wishful Flame
May Burn At The Tomb of Dante
The Società Dantesca Italiana Offered This Votive Lamp
The Commune of Florence Offered The Oil By Which It Shines
In Perpetuity
The Italians Of Trieste, Istria, Gorizia, Trent, Dalmatia, and Fiume
Offered
The Amphora To Hold It And The Wreath That Circles the Marble Stand
Both Made With Silver Collected From Their Homes
In Concert They Made These Offerings
In Concert With Him
Who In His Immortal Verse
Marked The Future Borders
Of The Italian Fatherland[27]

The ornate parchment was placed in an elegant leather case. Decorated in silver, the case displays the Alighieri family coat of arms with the year of Dante's death, 1321, and the emblem of the Società Dantesca with the year 1908. Florence gave a second sheet of parchment, also beautifully designed, to Ravenna that fixed in writing Florence's promise always to provide oil from its hills to keep the votive lamp burning.

The afternoon of September 12, 1908, a Saturday, a delegation departed from Florence to bring the lamp to Dante's tomb in Ravenna. Representing the Società Dantesca were Senator del Lungo (vice president), Guido Biagi (treasurer), and Pietro Stromboli (vice president of the organization's Florentine chapter). The aristocrat Cesira Siciliani Pozzolini represented the "Comitato delle Signore Patronesse," a committee of noblewomen who funded the illuminated parchment with Biagi's inscription. The calligrapher who created the decorative document (Amedeo Nesi) joined the delegation, as did the artist who designed the lamp (Enrico Lusini) and the artisans who fashioned it (Vittorio and David Manetti). Also embarking on this "devout pilgrimage" to Ravenna were the mayor of Florence and other city officials accompanied by pages and trumpeters in traditional costume and an honor guard bearing the city's gonfalon.

The Florentines were welcomed at the train station in Ravenna that evening by municipal authorities and other leading citizens. Illuminated and brightly decorated, Ravenna's streets were abuzz with crowds of locals and visitors from all over the country. The excitement grew the next day as people awaited the arrival of over a thousand "dear brothers and sisters" from Trieste, Istria, and cities and towns "where 'sì' is heard" along the eastern Adriatic coast. After a difficult, wind-tossed crossing, four boats flying the Italian flag arrived at the Darsena, Ravenna's marina. The entire city seemed to have gathered at the dock to greet the new arrivals, who brought the amphora, silver wreath, marble stand, and other offerings to Dante from their "unredeemed" lands. As the weary travelers disembarked, civic and cultural associations displayed banners and waved pennants, and bands belted out well-known patriotic songs. After the exchange of greetings and embraces, the Ravennese and their guests walked in procession to the "palazzo municipale," or City Hall, which had been set up for a festive and restorative banquet. As officials brought the gifts to the "little temple sacred to Dante," the rest of the entourage proceeded to the Classense Library for the inauguration of the Sala Dantesca and the Museo Dantesco, a special hall and museum space furnished with over four thousand codices, editions, translations, and studies of Dante's works as well as Dante-inspired artwork and memorabilia. Ferdinando Gallina, Ravenna's mayor, recounted the history of the Dante hall and museum, explaining how a campaign initially aimed at erecting a monument to Dante was used instead to fund the collection, a selection of which was on display for the guests. The group then walked a few blocks to the Teatro Dante Alighieri for the solemn presentation of the lamp and other offerings.

By the time the presentation began, at three o'clock, the theater was packed—both the stalls and the four-tiered gallery—with the visiting delegations and local residents from all walks of life. Trumpeters announced the entrance of the Florentine mayor, Francesco Sangiorgi, and the executive council accompanied by pages in full costume carrying the city's gonfalon. Mayor Sangiorgi and Attilio Hortis, a leading intellectual and activist from Trieste, were among the speakers who moved the audience to rousing cheers. But it fell to Isidoro del Lungo, on behalf of the Società Dantesca, to highlight the significance of the main event, the offering of the lamp to Dante. He made clear from the start that Dante's sepulcher was where the spiritual and the political met, where "the religion of tombs" joined with "the religion of the fatherland." His tomb was an altar, and there was no altar "more noble, more bounded with universal veneration" on which Italians could consecrate their faith in the nation.[28] It was therefore appropriate for Italians to gather at Dante's tomb in spirit and in person, as they did on September 13, 1908, to

8.2. Amphora for the lamp
oil provided by Florence
each year (*Società dantesca
italiana: Atti e notizie* 2
[1907–1908]: after page 84)

make the votive offering of a perpetually burning lamp. The flame, he explained, was both "espiatrice" and "augurale": expiatory insofar as Florence,
whose hills provide oil for the lamp, atoned for having sent Dante into exile
but also a wish—an "augurio"—for the possession of Italian lands still cut off
from the nation, lands that honored Dante by offering the amphora for the
Florentine oil. Giovanni Mayer, the artist who modeled the container for the
oil on an ancient amphora, set the bowl in a ring supported by five female figures standing for the "unredeemed" provinces of Trieste, Istria, Gorizia,
Dalmatia, and Trent, their Latin names inscribed around the vessel. Italian
women living in these lands donated silver utensils and other household items
to be melted down and used in the gift. Collectively, these offerings to Dante

signified the nation's determination to complete itself by redeeming its exiled populations.

The "most solemn moment of this unforgettable sacred ceremony" finally arrived: the lighting of the votive lamp, which workers had installed in Dante's mausoleum, suspending it from the ceiling in front of the tomb, during the afternoon speeches.[29] The Dante Society delegation, the mayors of Florence and Ravenna, and representatives from Trent, Trieste, and other contested cities walked from the theater to Dante's temple, moving slowly through the crowded streets. They had an even more difficult time making their way into the small mausoleum, already overflowing with locals and foreigners who came to admire the lamp, the decorative amphora of Florentine oil, and its marble stand. Signora Pozzolini removed the parchment from its leather case, gifts from Italian noblewomen to Dante and Ravenna, and presented it to Mayor Gallina. After the author of the written dedication, Guido Biagi, read his words aloud to the assembled witnesses, Attilio Hortis poured oil from the silver amphora—a gift from "unredeemed" Italians—into the lamp's font. Isidoro del Lungo took a silver matchbox, a personal gift from Riccardo Zampieri, director of the *Indipendente,* an Italian newspaper in Trieste. He read the inscription on the box, "To raise the flame," adding, "words and light! Precious light that comes to us across the Adriatic." On behalf of the Società Dantesca, del Lungo then struck a match and handed it to Mayor Sangiorgi of Florence, giving him the honor of lighting the "the expiatory, wishful flame at Dante's tomb." The lamp lit, Mayor Sangiorgi proclaimed, "Glory to Dante, now and forever!"[30]

The Florentine mayor's words of praise echoed those used in Catholic liturgy to praise God. "A Dante gloria, ora e nei secoli" tellingly substituted Dante for God in what is known as the minor (or lesser) doxology, *doxa* being the Greek word for "glory" or "praise," a prayer used in the Western Church since the seventh century: "Gloria Patri, et Filio, et Spiritui Sancto. Sicut erat in principio, et nunc, et in saecula saeculorum" (Glory be to the Father, and to the Son, and to the Holy Spirit. As it was in the beginning, is now, and will be forever).[31] The mayor's listeners would not have missed the allusion—the Italian version begins "Gloria al Padre" and ends "ora e sempre nei secoli dei secoli"—nor would they have questioned the wisdom of treating Dante as a deity at his tomb, on the anniversary of his death, in 1908. Dante was a god in the Italian imagination at this time in the nation's history, a god who inspired and sanctified efforts to redeem Italian populations still exiled from the "patria," or homeland.

Official documents signed and ceremonies concluded, Dante's "little temple" remained open to the public late into the night. Ordinary citizens made a "devout pilgrimage" there to see the little flame—"symbol of the stead-fast veneration of Italians for Dante"—and the votive gifts.[32] Ravenna's mayor meanwhile hosted a convivial banquet at Hotel Byron for the visiting delegations and other illustrious guests. Electrified by the spirit of patriotism and civic harmony, they toasted Italy's "sister cities who tirelessly defend and pay honor to the Italian language, which is constantly battered and threat-ened with all forms of cunning and violence."[33] When representatives of those "sister cities" departed the following day, filled with the spirit of Dante, many of them returned to Austrian territory aboard ships flying the Italian colors. Ceremonies and symbolic gestures, however, would hardly suffice to bring these lands and their people home to Italy. Italians on both sides of the Adri-atic knew this. It would take actions and ships of another order to accom-plish this goal, the kind of ship named after Italy's father, prophet, saint, and—ever more—its god of war.

With the addition of Rome to the Italian Republic in 1870, Dante's national significance had declined somewhat as unification gave rise to new heroes such as Giuseppe Garibaldi.[34] The poet awoke with a vengeance in the early twentieth century, his symbolism bleeding into increasingly militant forms as the movement to "redeem" occupied lands gained steam before, during, and soon after the Great War. Embodying Dante's more bellicose image on a grand scale was the *Dante Alighieri,* the first dreadnought—the class of large battleships introduced by the British Royal Navy in 1906—built by Italy in its naval race with Austria. Launched in the presence of the king and queen in 1910, the ship was not fully outfitted until 1913 and saw only limited action in the war but was a tangible sign of how Italy called on the poet to rally sup-port for military action in defending and expanding its borders.[35]

After war broke out in 1914, Italian interventionists deployed Dante as a major weapon in their campaign to convince the nation to fight. Although part of the Triple Alliance with Austria-Hungary and Germany, Italy had no obligation to take the side of its allies—who were the first to declare war—because of the defensive nature of the agreement. While neutrality was fa-vored by the majority of Italians and their elected leaders, most of those clam-oring for intervention were motivated by animosity toward Austria for its occupation of Trent, Trieste, and other "unredeemed" lands. The combative poet-daredevil Gabriele D'Annunzio led the charge in exploiting Dante's popular authority to persuade Italy to take up arms. A charismatic nationalist who backed up his oratory with bold actions, D'Annunzio exploited Dante's god-like stature to promote intervention. In a speech for the unveiling of a monument to Garibaldi in Genoa, D'Annunzio recast the Beatitudes, the first part of Jesus's Sermon on the Mount, as a war cry in Dante's name.

His radical adaptation of the biblical text exalted not those who were typically situated at the margins of power—groups held in high regard by Jesus but despicable to D'Annunzio—but those who were cheered by the prospect of war. Whereas Jesus blessed the meek, the patient, and those who mourned, D'Annunzio blessed twenty-year-olds (for their innocent minds and hardened bodies), the enraged (eager to rip out their hatred and make an offering of it), and those who "have not wasted their power but conserved it in the discipline of a warrior." Those who "hunger and thirst" shall have their fill of "glory" rather than biblical "justice." Whereas Jesus's "peacemakers" shall be counted as children of God, D'Annunzio's pacifists—yesterday's opponents of the war—shall see the light and be among the first to fight. Both Jesus and D'Annunzio blessed the merciful, who themselves shall receive mercy (Jesus) or shall be called as medics and nurses to "dry a splendid flow of blood and dress a shining wound" (D'Annunzio). The "pure of heart," finally, shall not—or not only—"see God," as Jesus would have it, but shall "return in victory, for they shall see the face of a new Rome, its brow crowned again by Dante with the triumphant beauty of Italy." Rome–Dante–Italy: this was the Holy Trinity preached by D'Annunzio to infect his congregation with war fever.[36]

D'Annunzio's highly anticipated speech was printed in its entirety in Italy's most influential newspaper the same day he delivered it. His words also drew international attention. The *New York Times* reported that the finale "brought all to their feet waving handkerchiefs and tossing hats in the air." Whipped into a frenzy by D'Annunzio's oratory, his listeners "sang the Marseillaise, cried out for war, and thronged forward to carry him away in triumph—while suddenly on the top of the monument, a large poster was unrolled, bearing the one word, TRIESTE."[37] Intervention promised the liberation of Italian lands from foreign occupation, a view that allowed public figures like D'Annunzio to use Dante's authority to rally the country to fight.

The strategy worked: after signing the secret Treaty of London with the Entente powers on April 26 and renouncing the Treaty of the Triple Alliance on May 4, 1915, Italy declared war on Austria less than twenty days later. Paolo

Boselli, senior member of the House of Deputies and president of the Società Dante Alighieri, was chosen to chair the special commission charged with approving legislation granting special powers to the government—military, economic, financial—in the event of war. Announcing the commission's unanimous support of the law later that day—effectively a declaration of war—Boselli claimed that entering the conflict was a "promise of freedom" for populations "supremely Italian by the decrees of nature, by the perpetuation of language, by the spirit of thought, by the ties of history."[38] The law was immediately—and decisively—approved by the House on May 20 and unanimously approved by the Senate the following day. Italy delivered an official declaration of war to Austria on May 23, 1915. Boselli wrote to his colleagues at the Società Dante Alighieri two days later, framing the war in irredentist terms. The society kept faith "in the fate of Italy and in our most Italian brothers and sisters of the Trentino, the Giulia region, and Dalmatia, believing in our mission as a forerunner and exponent of their hoped-for freedom," always remembering that Dante "established with his immortal decree the destiny of the Nation."[39]

With Italy at war with Austria and (fifteen months later) Germany, Dante soon became enmeshed in the machinery of wartime propaganda. Dante-themed postcards were a popular form of political art during the war years, often put to the service of laying claim to "unredeemed" territories that Italy hoped to win from the conflict. These shorthand avowals of love for Italy—and hatred of the enemy—attested to Dante's power in the collective Italian imagination. One striking example portrayed Dante—wearing a laurel crown—and a German soldier, tiny in comparison with the poet. The soldier stands on a ladder so he can hammer a Prussian nail into the back of Dante's huge head. The caption reads, "Dante ha la testa dura," meaning that Germanic civilization, or *Kultur,* was unable to penetrate Dante's "hard head," emblematic of Italian culture's resiliency.[40]

As Germany launched a series of major attacks on the Western Front in advance of the arrival of American troops in the trenches, the deteriorating Austrian-Hungarian army was left on its own to fight Italy—now supported by French and British divisions—in the spring and summer of 1918. King Victor Emmanuel III rallied the troops with a visit to the front. On his return, he stopped to review a division from Ravenna in the pine forest of San Vitale. Accompanied by the mayor and other officials, the king then entered the city to visit a hospital and to greet veterans and military families gathered in Piazza Vittorio Emanuele.[41] On May 18, 1918, amid the fanfare of a

Dante ha la testa dura
(da una cartoliua di guerra)

8.3. Wartime postcard:
"Dante has a hard head"
(Maria del Vasto Celano,
ed., *Dante e la guerra*
[Rome: Nuovo Convito,
1917], 113)

royal visit, the sovereign paid his respects at Dante's tomb. The "little temple" was covered at that time by sandbags to protect it against bombings like the one by Austrian naval aircraft that had damaged the nearby Basilica of Sant'Apollinare Nuovo on February 12, 1916.[42] "With that pale, gaunt, mournful face in which we all saw the face of the Nation," the king knelt before Dante's marble sepulcher, as if to pray at the high altar of Italy's god.[43] Alluding to the poet's lament to "serva Italia," he expressed his hope for imminent triumph: "Italy no longer a servant to the enemy in any of her lands!"[44]

Italy was virtually guaranteed victory with the rout of enemy troops at the Battle of Vittorio Veneto (October 24 to November 4, 1918). Austrian-Hungarian soldiers in flight from the battle were mowed down by gunners on Allied warplanes. But like other nations, Italy suffered horrific losses from the war: Over 650,000 Italian service members died in the conflict or soon thereafter, as many as a million were wounded in action, and half a million civilians died, the vast majority from illness (Spanish influenza) and starvation. This sacrifice was even harder to accept because territories promised to Italy by Britain and France in the Treaty of London (April 26, 1915) in exchange for intervention did not become part of the nation after the war. Areas with large (usually majority) Italian-identified populations included Venezia Giulia (with the cities of Trieste and Gorizia), Alto Adige (with the city of Trent), Northern Dalmatia, and Istria as far as the Gulf of Quarnero (with the port city of Fiume, today Rijeka in Croatia).

Italy succeeded in annexing Trieste and Trent (and surrounding areas) after the war, but Britain, France, and the United States rejected its claims to Northern Dalmatia, Fiume, and most of Istria at the Paris Peace Conference in 1919. The three dominant powers instead redrew the map of Europe to include these territories within the new nation of Yugoslavia. President Woodrow Wilson took an especially firm stand against Italy by refusing to recognize the 1915 agreement, to which the United States (having entered the war in 1917) was not a party, and by strongly opposing Italian claims to contested areas along the Adriatic coast. This betrayal by erstwhile allies confirmed the worst suspicions of irredentists and ultranationalists like Gabriele D'Annunzio. In an article on the first anniversary of the disastrous Battle of Caporetto, a year before the end of the war, he feared Italy's victory would be "mutilata," the first recorded instance of the phrase—"mutilated victory"—that came to define the nation's disappointment in the outcome of the war.[45]

Italian leaders and much of the public became angry and bitter as D'Annunzio's dire warning came to pass. They believed the addition of these territories was required to complete the work of Italian unification begun in the previous century. The native words for these "Italian" areas still outside Italy's geopolitical boundaries—*irredento*—and the movement to reclaim or annex them (*irredentismo*) said it all. These "unredeemed" lands were parts of Italy cut off from the nation's body. Irredentism acted on the determination to reattach or incorporate them. The religious resonance of the term was not insignificant. Recognizing the fervor with which Italians outside the nation's boundaries—Italians by language and heritage—sought inclusion in the homeland, it also underscored the mission, almost sacred in nature, of the nation to "redeem" lands and people believed to belong rightfully to Italy.

Refusing to accept the international rejection of Italian claims, D'Annunzio headed a militia that occupied Fiume on September 12, 1919, thus laying claim to the farthest Italian outpost marked by Dante. The poet's Gulf of Quarnero "kept itself Italian for Fiume over the centuries," D'Annunzio said to the "Fiumani" and other Italians, this "Italian spirit radiating from Fiume" along the eastern Adriatic coast and out to its islands.[46] As commander of the Italian Regency of the Quarnero, he stamped the introduction to Fiume's new charter, essentially its constitution, with Dante's seal of approval for the city's Italian identity.[47] Even after the Italian navy ended D'Annunzio's dream by shelling his palace on Christmas Day in 1920, the rebel leader continued to invoke Dante's authority in rallying his troops. Writing from Lake Garda on April 3, 1921, he congratulated the founders of a new order of legionnaires by citing, in this "year of Dante," the words of the poet's ancestor Cacciaguida in response to the senseless, disloyal actions of his companions in exile: "It will be best for you / to become a party unto yourself," he advised his steadfast comrades from the failed occupation.[48] Later that month D'Annunzio intimated Dante's sacred role in Italian national life by addressing his men as "Brothers in Christ and in Dante."[49] Just three days later, on April 30, 1921, Pope Benedict XV published an encyclical in anticipation of the milestone anniversary of Dante's death. In it, the pontiff claimed for the Catholic Church a "special right to call Alighieri hers."[50] Benedict's Dante was an ardent supporter of the church (the papacy in particular) who led others to Christ, while D'Annunzio put the poet on a par with Christ as Italy's savior.

D'Annunzio, worshiping Dante but feeling betrayed by his government and the military in which he had served, refused an invitation to come to Ravenna and deliver a major speech to an adoring crowd for the commemorative event. Ever the political showman, he nonetheless managed to turn his absence into a dramatic highlight of the ceremonies, as big a nonevent as the absence of Giuseppe Garibaldi had been during the national celebrations in 1865—the Risorgimento hero stayed away from the festivities to avoid stealing the spotlight from Dante and King Victor Emmanuel II or to prepare an operation aimed at seizing control of Rome.[51] D'Annunzio still felt the sting of his brutal expulsion from Fiume, and he admitted that while he would have gladly humbled himself before Dante—the "disdainful Hero"—he had no such inclination to do so before representatives of the "triumphant Beast," the politicians and military leaders who had crushed his patriotic dream to win the city for Italy.[52] He thought it plain wrong to address free Italian citizens when other Italians were deprived of liberty in unredeemed lands.

Unable to honor Dante in person, D'Annunzio found another way—at once poetic and combative—to make his presence felt at the ceremonies in Ravenna. At the request of Mayor Buzzi, he and his entourage plucked laurel leaves from various locations along the western shore of Lake Garda. They gathered enough leaves, each of them "whole and perfect," to fill three sacks. D'Annunzio then recruited three fellow aviators—"three princes of the wing" who had flown in the "glorious squadron of the Quarnero"—to fly their planes to Ravenna with the "votive offerings."[53] D'Annunzio sent the gift of laurel leaves not only to honor Dante but also to pay tribute to Italians who died or were wounded fighting for the nation. And the nation, for D'Annunzio, included "unredeemed" territories with large Italian populations—like Fiume—outside Italy's internationally recognized borders. He made this point in his accompanying message, which the mayor read at the civil ceremonies in Ravenna on September 13, 1921. The sacks of laurel leaves, D'Annunzio wrote, "enclose a Delphic flame visible only to the initiated," and he had the words "Inclusa Est Flamma" (the flame is inside) printed in large letters on each sack.[54] The erudite poet refers here to the eternal flame in the temple to Apollo at Delphi, the hearth of ancient Greece that supplied sacred fire to Greek cities following their victory over Persia at the battle of Plataea in 479 BCE. As the sanctuary at Delphi was "the common hearth of Greece, the origin of its fire, the center of its world," so Dante's tomb—D'Annunzio's cryptic message says to the "initiated"—supplies the sacred, regenerating force of the Italian people.[55]

Just as the festivities in Florence for Dante's six hundredth birthday had doubled as a celebration of Italian liberty and unification, so the ceremonies in Ravenna marking the six hundredth anniversary of his death honored the sacrifice of Italian soldiers and sailors in the Great War. The commemorative activities took place over four days—Sunday, September 11, to Wednesday, September 14, 1921—and involved Italians from all walks of life. But Italy's armed forces were the stars of the spectacle, and they worshiped Dante as their god.

9

Tomb of the Poet-Soldier

The most solemn affirmation of the idea of Italy must take place, as the
people of Romagna and citizens of Ravenna have fully understood, at
the tomb of the divine Poet!

—GENERAL UGO SANI

• Dante was more than the inspirational father, prophet, and secular saint
of Italy to soldiers and sailors who fought for their country in World War I.
If veterans worshiped him as a national deity soon after the war, it was also
because, like so many of them, he had experienced firsthand the horrors of
battle. Dante, the universally acclaimed poet, had put his life on the line for
a cause greater than himself when he fought at age twenty-four for Florence
and its Guelph allies against Arezzo and the Ghibellines at the Battle of Campaldino on June 11, 1289.

Florence and other Tuscan cities and towns honored Dante's military patriotism on the six hundredth anniversary of his death. On the morning of
Friday, September 16, 1921, members of the military joined local dignitaries
and a large crowd of spectators at Campaldino for the unveiling of a tall monument, known as the "Column of Dante," in recognition of the poet-soldier's
participation in the battle. The ceremony began at eleven o'clock sharp with
troops from all the armed forces lining up around the column. Guglielmo
Pecori-Giraldi, a decorated general from World War I and former governor
of the Trentino and Alto Adige, represented the Ministry of War. Other generals and national leaders, including the minister of education and various
senators and deputies, were also on hand, along with representatives from
nearly every Tuscan province and commune. Two marching bands and hun-
dreds of flags created an atmosphere of local and national pride. On behalf
of the Italian army and navy, General Pecori-Giraldi paid homage to the "first
champion of Italy" and presented the commemorative column, erected by

initiative of the Ministry of War, to the mayor of Poppi, one of the places that hosted Dante during his years of exile.[1] The cover was removed and the column revealed to great acclaim as the soldiers presented arms and the bands struck up the Italian national anthem. An inscription at the base of this column erected at the site of fraternal warfare declared that it stood for "the strength of the nation's armed forces in defending Italy's rights."[2]

The six hundredth anniversary of Dante's death fell only three years after the end of the war, a period in which Italy and other nations sought a modicum of meaning (if not closure) to the unimaginable bloodletting by "rendering sacred the bodies of the fallen."[3] So it was inevitable that commemorative events centered on the tomb of Italy's deified father, himself a soldier, would double not only as a celebration of the nation's victory but as a tribute to the lives lost and bodies maimed in achieving it. Nowhere was this more evident than in the opening ceremonies in Ravenna. Santi Muratori, the respected librarian and Dante scholar from Ravenna who wrote the official account of the centenary, thought it right for the military "to be first to pay homage to the Prophet of the Homeland." To Dante, who had called Italy "a slave and an inn of sorrow," the army could now present "mother Italy" finally "free within almost the entirety of her shoreline and mountains." Having borne the brunt of the sacrifice required to realize this expansive liberation, "the army of 600,000 dead" came to Ravenna "to lower its flags on the tomb-altar of the Hero who turned his suffering into the living essence of the Nation."[4] Dante, in his triumph over adversity, was viewed as a model for Italy and—as the soldier of Campaldino—its victorious but mourning armed forces.

On September 11, 1921, Ravenna took center stage as the heart and soul of Italy. The train station became the focus of attention in the morning as crowds of local residents and people from all over the country moved through the streets, passing brightly festooned houses and public buildings, to descend on the station piazza. There they found troops already in formation, with others lined up from the Church of San Giovanni Evangelista all the way to Corso Garibaldi. The train carrying Italy's minister of education, Mario Orso Corbino, arrived from Rimini at eight o'clock, soon followed by a train from Bologna bringing other national figures surrounded by flags and gold pennants. All eyes turned to the glittering group of decorated officers who escorted the standard-bearers, leading them outside the station into the square formation of soldiers standing at attention. "Bayonettes and swords flash in the sunshine," reported an observer, as "warplanes roar overhead, swooping like falcons in circles; a battery of canons fires the 101-gun salute."[5]

The procession was a feast for eyes and ears. Every division of the Italian army was represented, from the infantry, cavalry, alpine troops, and *bersaglieri* (elite infantry) to artillerymen, grenadiers, engineers, medical units, royal guards, and *carabinieri* (military police). Active and retired officers, along with veterans' groups and the association of mothers and widows of fallen servicemen, also marched in honor of Dante, as did a delegation of Italian senators and other political and civic leaders. Adding splendor to the event were the banners, or gonfalons, of Ravenna, Florence, Rome, Trieste, and Ferrara, followed by a "forest of flags" of many civic groups and cultural organizations, including student associations and the Dante Society of Florence. Honor guards and trumpeters dressed in historical costumes provided additional color, and military bands kept spirits high with patriotic song.

The focal point of the spectacle was a wagon carrying the silver and bronze wreath to be laid at the foot of Dante's tomb as a permanent offering from Italy's army and navy to the prophetic poet-soldier of the nation. When the procession passed in front of Dante's mausoleum, the music stopped, and all flags, pennants, and gonfalons were lowered. The marchers then entered Piazza Alighieri, where standard-bearers and representatives from all over Italy mounted a large stage draped in purple cloth.

Crowds of ordinary citizens joined military and civilian representatives in the piazza for the presentation of the funeral wreath in honor of Dante. The privilege of delivering the main address and presenting the wreath fell to General Ugo Sani, a wounded war hero in command of the army division from Bologna.[6] In an impassioned speech, his strong voice piercing the air like a trumpet's blast, the general praised Dante as the model soldier inspiring Italians to defend their nation and claim its rightful lands. Italy's armed forces venerated Dante as the embodiment of national consciousness. Playing the role of educator, Sani reminded his listeners that what most said "Italy" in the late Middle Ages was the language, "the Italic idiom of which Dante was, if not the first, the most confident and brilliant shaper, almost its creator." Dante understood this language—the basis for the various dialects spoken throughout the land—as the thread uniting the Italian people into a nation. So it was in Dante's name that aspirations toward an independent, unified homeland took shape over the centuries, with the poet, "following the hand of God, marking with his hand the borders of this destined land of ours!" As the nation's divine cartographer, Dante motivated and sustained Italians in unredeemed lands outside the nation's borders, his sculpted image in the recently "redeemed" city of Trent a living monument to Italian suffering and perseverance. For all these reasons, the distinguished general declared, "the most solemn affirmation of the idea of Italy must take place, as the people of Romagna and citizens of Ravenna have fully understood, at the tomb of the divine Poet!" And the military, in its special relationship to Dante as guardian of the nation he had envisioned, earned the right to add "the glory of its victorious arms" to this "beautiful" idea of Italy by laying a permanent wreath at this tomb.[7]

Dante likewise inspired Italians—military personnel above all—as the "lord and master" of duty. As the "tutelary spirit of the nation who at Campaldino fought as a soldier in the service of his faith," Dante personified and exalted the harmony, discipline, valor, and spirit of sacrifice exhibited by Italian soldiers in the war. General Sani quoted Eugenio Barbarich, a commander in World War I known for his writings on military campaigns, who claimed that Dante's work made warfare "the most tragic and redemptive event of human experience." The *Divine Comedy,* Sani elaborated, was cherished by Italian soldiers as "a Bible and an Iliad," a potent fusion of divine truth and epic heroism motivating them to fight for the nation: "Dante the soldier could not create purer, more worthy soldiers in his own image."[8]

The general concluded his address by calling on Italians of all ages, classes, and faiths to show solidarity at the "sacred Tomb" of "the greatest Italic spirit." Asking officers and soldiers to present arms, and civilians to remove their hats, he prayed that Dante's worshipers might become "apostles of a religion of peace," leading to a "straight path that has as luminous beacon and goal the Nation."[9] In this way, the votive flame lit in 1908 and kept alive in Dante's mausoleum, in illuminating his tomb and the wreath given that day by the army and navy, "will burn in the thought and the will of the entire Italian people."[10] As the war hero finished his prayer-speech, quoting stirring words from a patriotic ode by Giosuè Carducci, "a thrill, like a heroic gust of wind, ran through the large crowd."[11] At no time more than on this historic anniversary of Dante's death did his tomb serve so well as the altar of Italy's secular god.

Fortunato Buzzi, mayor of Ravenna, then took the podium to accept the wreath, his words speaking volumes about the national nature of the event:

> I have the honor of receiving the wreath that the Army and Navy offer
> to the first and greatest of Italians. Indeed: Ravenna has good reason
> for insisting that only this tribute be laid at the poet's tomb. Those of us
> combating for the nation in other ways say to the Army and Navy that

fight on our borderlands and seas: *Evviva!* We gathered in this piazza at another time before proceeding to the poet's tomb: then he inspired us to fulfill our national destiny. Today, having achieved that long-sought goal, today Italy seeks another victory: that of harmony. Along the streets of the procession our women threw flowers over our glorious flags. You—wounded warriors, widows, war orphans, and fighters—you lowered your flags before the Poet. Ravenna shouts out to you: *Evviva:* long live the Army, the Navy, long live Italy![12]

Commemorating Dante's death enabled Italians to honor recent wartime sacrifices, while encouraging them to recall the six hundredth anniversary of the poet's birth fifty-six years earlier, when the serendipitous discovery of his bones occurred in the midst of progress toward unification. Factionalism among Italians from and within different cities and regions—speakers of a common language across a range of dialects, heirs to ancient Rome—was one of the evils that most vexed Dante during his lifetime. Mayor Buzzi idealistically drew on this theme in 1921 to exhort Italians to complete the promise of the Risorgimento. The military, in its victory and subsequent expansion—however incomplete—of Italy's borders, had earned the right to lay the one and only wreath at Dante's tomb. But another, even more elusive Dantean "victory," that of peaceful "harmony," still seemed a long way off. Peace, as we shall see, was far from the minds of another group of World War I veterans who came to Ravenna for the milestone anniversary of Dante's death.

After the speeches in Piazza Alighieri, the dignitaries and military escort proceeded to Dante's tomb. Flowers thrown by orphaned girls—"those who have been touched by misfortune, who know every kindness"—rained down on the marchers as they moved along Via Dante.[13] It took six strong *carabinieri* to carry the heavy wreath made of bronze (with silver inlay) to the mausoleum. There it was welded to a decorative plate already attached to the porphyry pavement at the foot of the marble sepulcher. The ceremony inside the small building was brief (by Italian standards), the narrow space not designed to hold a large number of people comfortably for an extended period of time. Besides, this was a place for prayer and meditation, not speeches or sermons.[14]

Architect Ambrogio Annoni, superintendent of monuments in Ravenna, speaking on behalf of the minister of education, presented the freshly decorated chapel to the municipal authorities. Mayor Giannetto Valli of Rome then unveiled a striking new addition to the building. On behalf of the

9.1. Dante's tomb, with bronze wreath (Photo: Elisa Valentini, July 2016)

"eternal city" that embodied Dante's religious and political ideal, Mayor Valli presented a set of doors made with bronze from an Austrian canon "brought down from the highest peak that the foreign enemy fought in vain to hold, there where the statue of the Poet protects and watches over the new borders of Italy."[15] Dante, the mayor continued, must be rejoicing on this occasion—six hundred years after the day in which "his sacred ashes were still warm"—to find Italy "no longer a grieving servant but a land free and unified, strengthened in thought, revitalized in action, queen for the third time in finally reaching its holy goals."[16] Addressing soldiers in the audience, Valli declared that the laurel wreath they laid "like an offering" on Dante's tomb symbolized not only the poet's greatness but also Italy's victories in war. The wreath was a fitting tribute to the poet-soldier who famously decried the lack of worthy contenders for Apollo's leaves, the honor given both for military triumphs of emperors and artistic achievements of poets.[17] No one applauded Mayor Valli's words—a suitable nonresponse in the somber presence of Dante's remains—but "a murmur of heartfelt agreement" arose from those gathered inside the chapel.[18]

The mayor of Rome also addressed representatives of the various Italian communes that donated another votive offering to Dante: a silver *campana*, a bell whose tolling would call Italians to gather "around the most sacred altar of our people."[19] Guido Biagi, a founding member and president of the Società Dantesca Italiana, came up with the idea of the communal bell in honor of Dante. Designed by Duilio Cambellotti and made by Eugenio Lucenti, the bell weighed six tons, stood almost five feet tall, and was over three and a half feet wide at its mouth.[20] Following a solemn ceremony, the bell was installed in the small tower erected at the top of a stairway behind Dante's tomb. One of the most moving passages in the *Divine Comedy* not coincidentally describes the tolling of a bell. As the sun sets on Dante's first day on the Mountain of Purgatory, he, a wayfarer in the afterlife (and exile on earth), reflects on the heartache felt at that hour by sailors who miss the friends they left behind, on the pang of homesick love felt by pilgrims upon hearing the distant ringing of a bell:

> It was now the hour that melts a sailor's heart
> and saddens him with longing on the day
> he's said farewell to his beloved friends,
> and when a traveler, starting out,
> is pierced with love if far away he hears
> a bell that seems to mourn the dying light.[21]

Presented on the anniversary of Dante's death, the bell was inscribed with these famous verses in two bands—one for each tercet—circling its top portion. The bottom was decorated with laurel and palm branches—symbols of glory and victory—embracing the coats of arms of Florence, Ravenna, and Rome, cities of the poet's birth, death, and highest politico-religious ideals.[22]

Corrado Ricci and Santi Muratori, natives of Ravenna with unsurpassed knowledge of Dante's tomb and appreciation of its importance, had strong impressions of "la campana di Dante" when it was presented in 1921. Ricci lyrically captured the scene that took place when the bell tolled at the end of each day: "Toward sunset various groups of people gather in the area around Braccioforte in Ravenna: they come from different classes, rich and poor, educated and uneducated, students and workers, priests and soldiers, professors and farmhands, even simple housewives and children. As evening falls 'Dante's bell' begins to ring out. Everyone listens in silence. Then, after the final sound, they move off in silence as if absorbed in prayer or in the memory of people or places far away."[23] Muratori repeated his friend's description of the bell's power to pull on the heartstrings of its listeners at sunset, as Dante had imagined happening at that time of day to sailors and other travelers away from home. But Muratori saw another potential purpose in the bell, one consistent with the strongly patriotic—often militarist—mood pervading the commemoration in 1921: the tolling of Dante's bell as the nation's call for the "gathering of its male citizens"—that is, a call to arms.[24] The bell, along with other votive offerings to Dante, notably the lamp and amphora given in 1908, were all instruments of a ritual with existential meaning for Italy. In honoring Dante, they embodied the nation's spirit. "If ever there comes a generation that fails to honor the ritual," wrote Muratori, a generation "that lets die the echo of Dante's daily greeting, that extinguishes the lamp's flame, that lets the oil in the amphora dry out—that day there would no longer be a country."[25]

Given the extraordinary power invested in Dante's bell, it was a matter of no small importance to find a person worthy to toll it. As the sun set on September 11, 1921, the day on which the bell was inaugurated, that honor was given to "good Fusconi," a war hero who had served with Italy's elite infantry (*bersaglieri*) in some of the fiercest fighting against Austrian troops before losing the use of his right leg to a wound.[26] This would not be the last time Antonio Fusconi played a significant part in the drama of Dante's physical afterlife.

The civil ceremonies honoring the six hundredth anniversary of Dante's death took place in Ravenna two days later on Tuesday, September 13, the traditional date of the poet's passing from this life. These celebrations were even more grandiose than the military-led events, with Italy now more broadly represented. In addition to Ravenna, pride of place in the day's procession and ceremonies went to Florence and Rome, closely followed by lands recently liberated and joined to the nation (Trieste and Trent) and—poignantly—the city of Fiume and other "unredeemed" parts of the Dalmatian peninsula. The commemoration also took on an international flavor. Official dignitaries and other representatives from a wide range of nations—France, England, the Netherlands, Sweden, Czechoslovakia, Argentina, Egypt, Japan, and the United States—came to Ravenna to pay respects to Dante. Not everyone believed the poet would have liked all the attention he received during the centenary. The writer Janet Ross, an English expatriate who had been living in Italy for decades, even felt sorry for "poor old Dante," imagining "how bored he would be if he could hear and read all the rubbish people are howling and scribbling about him and his Beatrice."[27]

Americans on hand for the commemorations included students from Stanford University and the Catholic University of America (Washington, DC) as well as journalists from Italian American newspapers (*Il Progresso, Il Carroccio*).[28] A group of 150 US college students, accompanied by several professors and Monsignor John T. Slattery, president of the Dante Memorial Association, had visited Ravenna the previous month to show "admiration for the life and genius of Dante and to bear witness to [their] love and [their] homage to his revered memory." After attending a mass celebrated by Father Slattery in the Church of Saint Francis, the students visited Dante's tomb, where they unveiled a handsome bronze plaque paid for with funds they had raised in American universities. On the evening of August 4, 1921, the Harvard Glee Club gave a "magnificent" concert of early music to an appreciative packed house in Ravenna's Teatro Dante Alighieri under the direction of Archibald T. Davison.[29] Back home, Americans celebrated the Dante centenary by unveiling statues of the poet by Ettore Ximenes (still standing today) in New York City (across from the Metropolitan Opera House) on November 5, 1921, and in Washington, DC (in Meridian Hill Park) on December 1, 1921.[30]

The groups included in the great procession in Ravenna on September 13, 1921—and the order in which they lined up at eight o'clock in the morning along Viale Farini—demonstrated the dominant role of Italy's armed forces and unresolved geopolitical issues even in the civil celebration. At the head of the procession marched legionnaires—soldiers from Ravenna, Bologna, and Forlì who had participated in the occupation of Fiume—bringing the three sacks of laurel leaves sent by D'Annunzio from Lake Garda. Three "courageous aviators"—Bottella, Granzarolo, and Tessone—had flown to Ravenna the previous day from an airfield in Brescia (Olivari di Ghedi), each bearing one sack of leaves.[31] A portion of each sack was used to fill wicker baskets carried by one hundred little girls in white dresses so they could scatter them as the procession approached the area around Dante's tomb. Behind the legionnaires walked Ravenna's municipal guards and firefighters, followed by the band of the Twenty-Eighth Infantry Division and the banners of Rome, Florence, and Ravenna accompanied by pages and heralds in traditional costumes. Political leaders and other civil authorities, framed by a phalanx of *carabinieri* in dress uniform, were next in line, prominent among them Mayor Fortunato Buzzi of Ravenna, Mayor Giannetto Valli of Rome, Assessor Alfredo Cipriani representing Florence, Minister of Education Corbino, Vice President of the Senate Filippo Torrigiani, Senator Luigi Rava (former mayor of Rome), other members of parliament, and representatives of various Italian communes. Other civilians in the procession included the Dante scholars Pio

Rajna and Guido Biagi (with the banner of the Società Dantesca Italiana), members of other Italian cultural organizations, and foreign dignitaries. Also participating were widows and mothers of fallen soldiers, workers' unions, athletic societies, political parties, marching bands, veterans' associations, and various military units.

The parade route ran from Viale Farini to Piazza Vittorio Emanuele (today Piazza del Popolo), passing through Corso Garibaldi, Via Girotto Guaccimanni, Via Mazzini, Via Guido da Polenta, and Via Dante Alighieri. Marchers were regaled along the way by enthusiastic crowds and showered with flowers thrown from windows. When the procession reached the corner of Via Guido da Polenta, the music stopped, and the crowd grew quiet. Dante's tomb was in sight. As the marchers walked in silence, Dante's bell rang out, "a sound of death, a sound of glory."[32] The legionnaires of Fiume were the first to pass in front of the tomb. There they halted and pointed their flags downward in a sign of respect. Young girls, meanwhile, reached into their baskets and, gliding gracefully around Dante's mortuary chapel, scattered D'Annunzio's laurel leaves, their sweet bouquet filling the air. "Was this Ravenna? Was this Romagna?" mused Santi Muratori. "Where were we? In the presence of the ancient Eleusinian Mysteries? On the Via Sacra? We seemed to be waiting for a sign, a marvel, an omen. It felt as if we were in the presence of a divine power." In honor of Italy's divine poet—the nation's god of war—soldiers and other worshipers bared their heads, while Florentine trumpeters raised their silver horns and sounded clarion notes. So Dante's native city "saluted its great exile and, restraining its grief, acknowledged reality and fate." Muratori, showing himself a true son of Ravenna, added that Florence no longer sought to repatriate Dante's bones because Ravenna was their "worthy guardian." Besides, as his compatriots had reminded their Florentine counterparts during the debate over the poet's remains fifty-six years earlier on the anniversary of his birthday, ever since Italian unification, Ravenna was no longer "a land of exile."[33]

The sculpted figures of Saints Apollinare and Vitale, looking down from their perches atop twin columns in Piazza Vittorio Emanuele, beheld a sea of humanity after the procession had made its way into Ravenna's main square, filling it to capacity. Banners displaying the city's coat of arms—lions against a vivid red-and-gold background—hung from windows around the piazza, and laurel festoons adorned the Palazzo del Commune, or city hall. The crowd was no less vibrant. Military units, veterans' groups (including red-shirted Garibaldini), civic associations, and pages and heralds from Florence and other cities combined to paint the scene, at once solemn and celebratory, with "a hundred colors, thousands of faces."[34] After an officer called the troops to attention, the crowd fell silent, and the mayor of Ravenna stood to speak on the balcony overlooking the piazza.

Fortunato Buzzi did not disappoint his listeners. His remarks exploited the occasion of the "glorious centenary of Dante Alighieri" to bind the history and fate of Italy to its supreme poet. "Every Nation," he declaimed, "when it wishes to express and affirm its proper place and worth in the history of civilization, points to one of its glorious children." This Italian, spoken with one voice by all the nation's citizens—"the most learned and the most humble"—could be but one: Dante.[35] Repeating Mazzini's nineteenth-century contention that Dante "did more for Italy, for its future and for the glory of our people, than had ten generations of other writers or political leaders," Mayor Buzzi zeroed in on Dante's tomb—"where the pure flame of Italian identity burns forever"—as the site of a rebirth of "sentiments of affection and tenderness" across political divisions, nothing less than the beginning of "the new history of Italy."[36] Consistent with the postwar religious atmosphere of the centenary, he concluded his high-minded speech by calling on Dante's spirit—his *ombra*—to rise up from this tomb and, surrounded by other great Italian heroes and martyrs, to keep watch over the nation's glorious future.[37]

But Mayor Buzzi's work was not done. It was his task then to read Gabriele D'Annunzio's telegram to the vast audience that the poet-warrior, had he accepted the mayor's invitation, would have directly addressed on the anniversary of Dante's death. D'Annunzio's words to the soldiers and civilians gathered in Ravenna—and, by extension, to all of Italy—justified his absence (and relative silence) as a sign of humble respect before the incomparable Dante but, even more, as a sign of protest before the powers of the official Italy (its political and military leaders) that had betrayed the promise of freedom for all Italians by refusing to fight for Fiume and other as yet "unredeemed" lands. To make this last point, he identified with one of Italy's most acclaimed war heroes, rhetorically asking if it would be possible for the "hard and reserved race of Francesco Baracca"—Italy's top fighter ace, who died when he was shot down on June 19, 1918—"not to understand this need for silence and solitude."[38] D'Annunzio sent three bags of laurel leaves, as we have seen, in honor of both Dante and Italy's fallen soldiers. He emphasized this dual function of his offering by requesting that a mother of one of the fallen or wounded soldiers from the Romagna region be permitted "to scatter a handful of these leaves into the sea breeze in glory of the sacrifice that the implacable Dante of the Quarnero received in his Paradise."[39] After the ceremony, the legionnaires of Fiume returned to Dante's tomb with the laurel leaves, and Countess Paolina de Biancoli, the mother of Francesco Baracca (the "lion of Romagna"), fulfilled this patriotic duty by scattering the leaves in honor of Dante and the soldiers who, like her son, had died in the war.[40] Dante's gravesite, now more than ever, served to commemorate the collective sacrifice of Italians on behalf of their country.

Mayor Buzzi's reading of D'Annunzio's words was the emotional high point of the ceremonies on September 13, 1921. Santi Muratori, a witness to the scene, was moved by the reaction of the soldiers to D'Annunzio's simultaneous praise of Dante and indictment of the government and military leaders for abandoning Fiume: "Young warriors, the flower of Italy, accustomed to staring death in the face, emerged from the hidden powers of our race. They offered to Dante awareness of the heroic actions made in his name along with the sorrow of betrayal. In the packed piazza a single shout resounded: 'For Italian Fiume, *eja, eja, alalà!*'"[41]

Every listener understood *"eja, eja, alalà!"* as the battle cry of Italy's best fighters—the *arditi* (daring ones), or shock troops, many of whom were among D'Annunzio's most loyal followers in the occupation of Fiume in 1919–1920. D'Annunzio himself coined the phrase—combining a Latinate exclamation (*eja*) with the battle cry of ancient Greek soldiers (*alalà*)—to replace the traditional *hip hip urrà* ("hoorah" in English) in World War I.[42] The rousing cry was then naturally adopted for the enterprise in Fiume, as heard in the resounding cheer of Italy's "young warriors" in response to D'Annunzio's stirring if self-serving words for the Dante centenary.

After Mayor Buzzi finished reading D'Annunzio's message, the Florentine representative—Assessor Alfredo Cipriani—addressed the lively crowd. Stressing Florence's solidarity with Ravenna, he declared that "the city that had the good fortune to be the cradle of Dante Alighieri feels itself on these days to be one in spirit with Ravenna, final refuge of the great exile and faithful guardian of his tomb." Cipriani even went so far as to accept Ravenna's long-held argument that Dante's exile had ended with unification, thereby eliminating any need for the transfer of his remains to Florence. "The spirit of the Poet who intuited and upheld the language and history and unity of our people," he acknowledged, "who foresaw its future borders matching its ancient ones, is no longer an exile in Italic lands because every town and every city in which our sweet tongue is heard now sees in him the same purest symbol of the nation."[43]

Dante's exile may have ended with unification, but it should not be forgotten that he had served as comfort and inspiration for other Italian exiles over the centuries—as Senator Luigi Rava of Ravenna (a former mayor of Rome) reminded his compatriots in his speech to the soldiers and civilians gathered in Ravenna on September 13, 1921. He recalled how Dante's tomb in Ravenna, the most tangible sign of the poet's exile from Florence, had been an especially influential source of that comfort and inspiration to Italians facing challenges in foreign lands, from Foscolo and Mazzini in the early nineteenth century to soldiers and prisoners during the recent war. Even for Italian emigrants "who want to remember the native country and its language, civilization, and culture, it is in the name of Dante that they pursue this noble goal."[44] The crowd in Piazza Vittorio Emanuele erupted in applause, as it frequently did during the speeches. Military bands struck up patriotic songs as the civil ceremonies came to an end.

The name of one group of participants did not appear in the official program of events in Ravenna, but they were still a conspicuous presence during the ceremonies honoring Dante in 1921. Like the legionnaires of Fiume and other followers of Gabriele D'Annunzio, this group was also composed largely of disaffected veterans and other angry young men, but they swore fealty to another charismatic leader, one as much on the rise as D'Annunzio was in decline. Their rebellion was fueled less by international affairs than by Italy's sclerotic domestic politics and the perceived threat of rival groups. They, too, enjoyed shouting the war cry of Italy's assault troops (*eja, eja, alalà*), even attaching it to the refrain of a version of their signature song, which also included verses in praise of Dante.[45] "The vision of Alighieri / shines today in every heart," they sang, along with the other verses of "Giovinezza," the fascist anthem, as they marched into Ravenna on Monday, September 12, 1921. A vanguard of these "black shirts" had in fact already entered the city center on September 10, the day before the first day of the commemorations. They chose Ravenna because it was known as a vibrant center of the Italian Socialist Party, the party to which Benito Mussolini had belonged (serving as editor of its official newspaper, *Avanti!*) before being expelled in 1914 for his advocacy of Italian intervention in the war.

September 12, 1921, the second day of the ceremonies in Ravenna, fell on a Monday. It was supposed to be a relatively low-key day, a break between the military procession and presentation of the wreath on the first day and the massive civil celebration on the third day. Arrangements were made for visits to the basilicas, churches, and monuments—Sant'Apollinare Nuovo, San Vitale, San Giovanni Evangelista, San Francesco, Santa Chiara, the Mausoleum of Galla Placidia—for which the city was rightfully famous. But September 12 turned out to be anything but a leisurely day of sightseeing. Instead, Ravenna was overrun by a force of some three thousand militant fascists set to attack the property and persons of their enemies—socialists and communists, above all. This was no ragtag gang of marginal hotheads but a disciplined paramilitary unit led by two rising stars in the fascist movement: Italo Balbo, a war hero whose fomenting of fascist violence paved the way for Mussolini's dictatorship, and Dino Grandi, Mussolini's future minister of foreign affairs and ambassador to Great Britain.[46]

Santi Muratori announces in his official report on the commemorative events for September 12 that he will only touch "indirectly" on the fascist gathering in Ravenna because it was not in the formal program. His brief remarks, while not downplaying the bellicose trappings of this "gathering of fascists," nonetheless set their assault on the city in the more flattering light of a holy pilgrimage: "They were 3000 young men who came from all over the Emilia region. Proceeding in military fashion, they were accompanied by their armored cars, their flags, and the song of their anthem, 'Giovinezza.' They came by foot, covering tens of miles like soldiers or pilgrims to Rome to renew their vows and strengthen their faith at the tomb of the Poet of Italy."[47] In reality, this fascist "March on Ravenna," as it came to be known, far more closely resembled a crusade than a pilgrimage. Intent on intimidating if not terrorizing their victims, these black-clad *squadristi*—fascist action squads—devastated the city's Camera del lavoro (the center for workers and unions), cooperatives, and other sites associated with socialists and communists. Forces of order, amply represented in Ravenna for the commemoration, largely turned a blind eye to the attacks, thus allowing for the destruction of property and, when victims fought back, numerous injuries and several deaths.[48] The fascist marauders, seeking to spin their criminal activities as righteous acts on behalf of Italy, perversely took a victory lap in front of Dante's mausoleum. Having learned from D'Annunzio "how politic it is to claim that Italy's great poet is on their side," many fascists remained in Ravenna the following day to march in the procession in honor of Dante.[49]

By omitting mention of this violence and praising the perpetrators' devotion to Dante in coverage of the event, Muratori appeared to endorse or at least tolerate fascist activities during the commemorations in Ravenna. Other commentators took a stronger stand—pro or con—on the matter. Catholic clergy and institutions—while no friends of the targeted socialists and communists—were themselves on the receiving end of insults and threats if not physical aggression by the *teppisti,* or "thugs," as a writer for *Civiltà Cattolica,* a Jesuit publication overseen by the Vatican, called fascists in a report on the events in Ravenna. "It was enough to witness the excesses and brutality of the fascists," the writer concluded, "to understand the substance of their involvement in the glorification of Dante."[50] As an overview of the ceremonial events tersely put it, the fascists arrived in Ravenna on September 12 "to create their usual disorder all over the place."[51] Another Catholic periodical, the *Bollettino del Comitato Cattolico per l'omaggio a Dante Alighieri,* was produced by Ravenna's Catholic committee for the centenary commemorations. It ran from January 1914 through December 1921. This bulletin mainly reported on the many ways that Catholic organizations paid homage to Dante before and during the anniversary celebrations. Noteworthy among these tributes was a meeting of the Catholic Federation of Italian Universities in honor of Dante, culminating with a visit to his tomb on September 1, and a gathering of three thousand members of the Union of Italian Catholic Women on September 6. After a mass celebrated by the archbishop in Sant'Apollinare, the women walked in silence, preceded by white banners, to Dante's tomb. There they heard "the most beautiful words that could be said in honor of Dante, who had elevated woman to be the messenger of divine wisdom and mercy."[52]

In the Catholic committee's coverage of the "fascist demonstration" on September 12, it could not help but decry "incidents that disturbed for a moment the serenity of the celebrations and spread more than a little panic among foreign visitors." Showing more solidarity than the Jesuit periodical with other victims of fascist violence, the bulletin acknowledged attacks on socialist and communist centers, including acts of arson. But the committee was outraged above all by "the curses, the licentious and irreligious songs, and the insults thrown at priests and other Catholics"—not to mention unspecified threats made against members of the Catholic centenary committee itself, including Bishop Celso Constantini. Unlike for the more viciously abused socialists and communists, this fascist aggression was viewed by the Catholic press as an "ugly parenthesis" that however took nothing away from the positive public reception of Catholic tributes to Dante and the overall success of the centenary.[53]

Fascists and their sympathizers, for their part, saw the March on Ravenna as cause for celebration, not indignation. Crashing commemorations of the six hundredth anniversary of Dante's death was a momentous event in the movement's history for them. A party official from Ravenna recalled the arrival of the fascist squads as an "unexpected homage" to Dante, one that—unlike the empty official ceremonies and meaningless literary tributes—the poet actually appreciated. He imagines that Dante welcomed the powerful cry shouted by thousands of black shirts as they marched by his tomb: "To Rome!"[54] As Dante did for Italians at other pivotal moments in the nation's history, he exerted a "moral force of undeniable power" from beyond the grave.[55] Those who were inspired and those who were appalled by the gathering of black shirts in Ravenna would have agreed on one point: the fascist fashioning of Dante began at his tomb in Ravenna on the six hundredth anniversary of his death, a year before the March on Rome that would bring Mussolini to power.

10

Ill-Gotten Remains

If all [the fragments] were retrieved, they all weren't returned.
—CORRADO RICCI

If the bones of Italy's prophetic father had been treated like those of a saint in 1865, it followed that the faithful would go to great lengths to procure pieces of his skeleton to venerate as precious relics. They dutifully obliged. No matter the precautions taken by civic leaders, doctors, and law enforcement to ensure the integrity of the body at the time of its discovery, examination, and reburial in 1865, the temptation was just too great for determined bone collectors—including several of those very officials—not to indulge their craving for a cherished piece of Dante by pocketing a small prize from the area where the remains had been found.

Size seems not to matter when it comes to relics. Victricius of Rouen made this point in his letter *Praising the Saints* from the late fourth century. Since "the whole can be in the part," he reasoned, "we can no longer complain of smallness." Truth sees even "small relics and a little blood" as "brighter than the sun," for "there is nothing in relics which is not complete."[1] Saint Gregory of Nazianus, Archbishop of Constantinople in the fourth century, likewise insisted that "even a drop of blood from a saint or martyr was quite as efficacious a relic as the whole corpse. A finger was as good as a foot."[2] In even the tiniest portion of holy remains, Peter Brown observes, "the chilling anonymity of human remains could be thought to be still heavy with the fullness of a beloved person."[3] This belief motivated the crowd that gathered around the fresh corpse of Thomas Becket, Archbishop of Canterbury, after he had been savagely murdered in his church on December 29, 1170. Those arriving on the scene wasted no time "in accumulating as many parts of Thomas as there were to be had."[4] Intoxicated with a holy bloodlust, "some daubed their eyes with blood, others who had brought little vessels made away with as much as they could, while others eagerly dipped in parts of their clothes they had cut off."[5] Purported samples of Becket's blood eventually found homes in finely crafted reliquaries, such as a small silver box or casket made soon after his canonization in 1173.[6]

The division of saintly and martyred bodies not only was permissible but became "central to the Christian cult of matter" in the Middle Ages, writes Caroline Walker Bynum—so much so that "the faithful sat by the beds of dying holy people, hoping to get a fragment of the body as soon as the bones were prepared for distribution."[7] This understanding of "wholeness in partition" entered the secular world when medieval aristocrats and monarchs began seeking greater power and more prayers in death by having their mortal remains present at multiple places of worship.[8] Dante hardly sought to increase his influence or enhance his spiritual state through dissemination of his body parts, but the prevalence of relics in churches throughout Italy naturally conditioned the thinking and behavior of nineteenth-century Italians. When Dante's remains were discovered in the wall of the Braccioforte chapel on May 27, 1865, many people were therefore driven by sincere devotion, sheer avarice, or their combination to possess a relic of the divine poet. Some exploited their proximity to the discovery site to steal a small bone or two amid the chaos and confusion, while others used their privileged social or professional connections to acquire the relic from its original owner. Either way, all believed the object in their possession to be legitimate. They thought they owned a physical piece of Dante. The history of relics, alas, is littered with false claims of authenticity. This chapter on bones lifted from the discovery site of Dante's skeleton is no exception. Then again, it takes only one true relic to justify informed consideration of the many pretenders.

By the six hundredth anniversary of Dante's death in 1921, all known bones and fragments said to belong to the skeleton discovered in 1865 had made their way back to Ravenna's municipal authorities in one way or another. But they had not been placed in the tomb with the rest of the bones for one simple reason: their authenticity had not been verified. No one in 1865 had wanted to find a second skeleton inhabiting Dante's marble sepulcher when the wood box claiming to hold his bones fell out of the wall of Braccioforte (at least no one admitted harboring that macabre wish); likewise, no one in 1921 wanted to face the awkward situation of adding, say, a piece of a shoulder blade to a tomb already containing two that were intact. City authorities thus proposed having the alleged relics scientifically examined and—if authentic—reunited with the bones in Dante's tomb on this grand occasion. Corrado Ricci's strong endorsement of this proposal virtually guaranteed its acceptance and implementation. Born in Ravenna in 1858, Ricci was an accomplished art historian who served as the city's superintendent of monuments from 1897 to 1906, when he was appointed director general of antiquities and fine arts in Rome. There he spearheaded major excavations of the imperial forums. Even while living in Rome, however, Ricci was frequently consulted as an expert in the recovery and preservation of Ravenna's artistic and architectural heritage. In particular, no one commanded more respect than Ricci on questions pertaining to Dante's tomb and remains, about which he had written so well in his monumental book on the city where Dante spent the final years of his life.[9] An invaluable historian of events surrounding the 1865 discovery of Dante's bones—as a child he had seen the skeleton on display in the Braccioforte chapel before its reburial—Corrado Ricci played a central role in the 1921 commemoration of Dante's death and in renovations of the area around the tomb in years to come, right down to his own death in 1934.

Determining the authenticity of presumed relics required the exhumation of Dante's skeleton in order to verify if the stolen bones belonged to it. Since disinterring Dante's bones was a matter of not just local but national interest, Ravenna formally requested the approval and involvement of the Italian government, specifically the Ministry of Education. On June 2, 1921, the Dante Committee of Ravenna put forth a proposal for an examination of the poet's bones.[10] This would be the first time they were removed from the tomb since they had been returned there in 1865. Fortunato Buzzi, mayor of Ravenna, soon reached an agreement with the Ministry of Education to arrange for the exhumation and examination. At the mayor's request, Ricci wrote to Antenore Cancellieri, director general at the ministry, stressing the absolute necessity of the new examination and laying out precise guidelines for doing it. In his letter, dated July 11, 1921, Ricci explained the reasons for opening Dante's tomb once again.[11] He more than anyone else was aware of the troubling consequences of human error, poor judgment, and scandalous behavior in 1865 that could only be rectified with another look at Dante's bones.

By 1921, for one thing, the sciences concerned with evaluating human remains had made significant progress since the examination of the bones fifty-six years earlier. The doctors who conducted the examination were "good men," Ricci acknowledged, but they had scant training, for instance, in anthropometry—the study of human measurements (especially on a comparative basis)—a field then at an early stage of development. Modern experts saw deficiencies and glaring mistakes in the report of Drs. Puglioli and Bertozzi that "on this occasion must absolutely be corrected."[12]

But there was another purpose for exhuming Dante's bones in 1921. When workmen accidentally found the box containing Dante's bones in 1865, Ricci reminded the government official, people present at the site abused their position to pocket bone fragments. Other citizens meanwhile picked up pieces of other bones in the area around Braccioforte, a former burial ground, and promptly sold them off as parts of Dante's skeleton. Stolen bones and fragments made their way back to city authorities over the years as owners succumbed to external pressures or the sting of remorse or as heirs acted to repair a dearly departed one's moral lapse. This was the time to rejoin any authentic pieces to the rest of the skeleton in Dante's tomb and to discard the false relics. Dante's wandering body parts simply "must find peace in their tomb!"[13]

Once the skeleton was unearthed, it would be easy to determine which pieces legitimately belonged to Dante, Ricci assured the official—first and foremost, of course, by making sure there was no duplication between the bones under consideration and those lying in the tomb. Another criteria of verification was particular to Dante: the poet's bones, as noted in the earlier reports, had a distinctive dark-reddish-orange appearance—similar in color to rust—that Ricci attributed to the decomposition in humid conditions of the red garment in which Dante had been buried.[14] Any purloined bones missing from the skeleton should show this same coloration.

Ricci called on the assistance of the Ministry of Education in selecting two experts fit for the job of examining Dante's bones and making these determinations. Professionally and personally, they had to be good and serious individuals, scientists capable of conducting the "necessary and delicate and devoted work" without leaking or sharing the results for the sake of fame or publicity.[15] Secrecy was of the utmost importance to Ricci in what he hoped would be the final, definitive examination of Dante's remains. He understandably wanted to limit the number of participants and observers to just a few trustworthy persons, but he also insisted that there be no photographs taken or casts made of the bones. Knowing how "indiscretions or thefts" might allow reproductions to appear in "the Sunday papers or on two-cent illustrated postcards," Ricci feared the worst: "Dante's skull shown this way," he warned, "would bring shame to the city of Ravenna and to the Nation!"[16]

10.1. Master mason Pio Feletti at the site where he discovered Dante's bones on May 27, 1865 (Corrado Ricci, *L'ultimo rifugio di Dante Alighieri* [Milan: Hoepli, 1891], 359)

Ricci's outrage at such an imagined indiscretion might have been a sign of his own guilty conscience at work. His coverage of Dante's bones in his 1891 tome was itself rich in photographic reproductions, including images of the site where Dante's bones had been found and of the wooden box that held them. A scrupulous historian of art and architecture, Ricci adorned his book with over fifty illustrations, including reproductions of many photos taken by his father, who worked as a photographer, painter, and stage designer.[17] On

May 28, 1865, Luigi Ricci (1823–1896) aimed his lens at Pio Feletti, the master mason who had found the bones the day before; Feletti, pickax in hand, faces the camera while sitting in profile in front of the brick wall that had concealed the treasure.[18]

The younger Ricci surely committed no violation of privacy or decency by reproducing this image in his book. But in light of his prohibitions for the 1921 examination, his use of a photo we saw before may have raised eyebrows: above the caption "Esposizione delle ossa di Dante nel 1865" (display of Dante's bones in 1865), Ricci inserted the photograph of the Braccioforte chapel (open on all four sides) showing Dante's skeleton, visible inside a clear crystal urn set in the center of the building, as it was being viewed by well-dressed visitors on June 25, 1865 (see figure 7.3). Ricci said the image was an enlarged, touched-up version of a "very small photo" of the scene taken that day by Count Annibale Facchinetti. More tellingly, Ricci admitted that the count, an amateur photographer, had taken the photo on the sly—*clandestinamente*—apparently through a small attic window overlooking Braccioforte, thus suggesting that prohibitions in place around the display of Dante's bones in 1865 were every bit as severe as those Corrado Ricci wished to impose on the examination in 1921.[19]

Ricci himself confirmed this suspicion in 1891, though he held nothing back in excoriating municipal authorities for forbidding photographs of Dante's skeleton in 1865. "With great harm to history and science," he railed, "the city government at that time, with the usual small-mindedness of uncultured people having little understanding of their duty to civilization, would not allow photographs or drawings of the chapel's interior or of Dante's bones (his cranium in particular), while putting forth concerns and scruples that were completely unjustified." Count Facchinetti may in fact have falsely claimed authorship of the prohibited photograph of Dante's skeleton to protect his dependent—professional photographer Antonio Guglielmi—from legal sanctions that could not be enforced against the count.[20]

A city elder himself in 1921, Ricci apparently came to appreciate the same cautionary measures he had criticized so harshly thirty years earlier. In his letter to Director General Cancellieri, he recognized the potential value of reproducing photographs of Dante's bones in journals published by reputable scientific organizations, such as the Reale Accademia Nazionale dei Lincei, an association of distinguished scientists and academics founded in Galileo's day and to which Ricci proudly belonged.[21] But what would then prevent "indiscreet persons" from using the images to turn a quick profit? "And so, I say, extreme measures for extreme dangers," he thundered, "no photographs and no casts!"[22] Fortunately for posterity—not least for later studies of Dante's bones—Ricci soon reverted to his earlier position and agreed to the necessity of having a professional photographer create a visual record of the examined remains.[23]

With the approval and financial support of the Ministry of Education, Ravenna's city council met on October 7, 1921, to discuss the proposal to exhume and examine Dante's bones. The council set three main goals for the operation: first, to replace authentic bones and fragments of Dante's skeleton that had been taken by individuals present at the discovery of the bones in 1865; second, to verify the current state of the bones and take action to prevent future deterioration; and third, to correct and complete anthropometric and anthropological analyses conducted by Drs. Puglioli and Bertozzi.[24] The final four days of October were selected for the exhumation, examination, and reburial of Dante's bones. Mayor Buzzi asked two illustrious Italian scientists to conduct the examination: Professor Giuseppe Sergi (1841–1936) from Rome (on Ricci's suggestion) and his former student Professor Fabio Frassetto (1876–1953) from Bologna. Both men were physical anthropologists. Sergi founded the Roman Society of Anthropology and the Laboratory of Experimental Psychology, while Frassetto—who also held a degree in medicine and surgery—founded the Institute of Anthropology at the University of Bologna. He specialized in comparative craniology.[25] Sergi and Frassetto enthusiastically accepted the invitation to examine Dante's bones and to determine if any of the alleged relics were genuine. They were told that "a sense of duty and principles of high morality demand that such fragments, once their authenticity has been established, be reunited with the other bones and placed for eternity in the ancient tomb."[26]

After the professors had removed and listed the bones, they arranged them in their natural order and proceeded to ascertain if any bones or fragments taken from the discovery site and later turned over to city authorities belonged to Dante. Owing to the excellent condition of the exhumed bones, it took less than an hour to assess the authenticity of the entire collection (at least thirteen specimens). The alleged relics spoke volumes about the desire of Italians in 1865, soon after the nation's birth, to honor and connect with their ancestral father. That Dante wrote the world's most famous account of communion with the dead only inflamed the desire for pieces of his revered body and the coffin that held it.

Relic fever therefore ran high among workers and onlookers on May 27, 1865, when a box of bones bearing Dante's name spilled out of the wall of Braccioforte chapel where a former passageway to the cemetery had been sealed with bricks. Townspeople hurried to the scene as soon as they heard the words "Dante" and "bones," many of the new arrivals joining those present in the rush to gather the bones and the planks of the broken box and carry them the short distance to Dante's sepulcher. Bones and pieces of the coffin inevitably fell along the way, but "if they all were retrieved, they all weren't returned."[27] Just as troubling, some people furtively picked up a bone or two from the area—a former church cemetery—that they believed or claimed was part of Dante but may have actually belonged to another body.

Three bones taken from site were turned over to authorities not long after the discovery. The collectors were residents of Ravenna with no official role in the excavations that unearthed Dante's bones or in the efforts to collect and secure them. Two of the men seemed to know each other quite well. Luigi Personali, a lawyer, collected two bones from among the "infinite number of bones of infinite dead bodies" in the excavated area with no reason to conclude they belonged to Dante beyond their location close to the discovery site.[28] Soon after, Personali gave one of the bones to Adolfo Borgognoni, a teacher of literature and history at Ravenna's Technical and Professional Institute who authored numerous essays on Dante. Three days later, as news of this "relic" spread through Ravenna, Mayor Rasponi demanded that Borgognoni hand it over, which he did through the services of an attorney, Gaspare Bartolini, on May 30. This forced restitution did not, however, prevent the mayor from firing the professor from his job, effectively "putting him out in the street."[29] Knowing that the city government meant business, Personali handed over his "relic" the following day. In his letter to the mayor on May 31, Personali told how Borgognoni begged to have one of the two bones; not satisfied, he insisted on having the other fragment as well. Personali refused Borgognoni's demand, but he could not refuse the mayor. Nor could Maurizio Pancerasi, who responded to an official note demanding the return of "the bones known to be in his possession" by handing over the one bone he had on June 8, 1865.[30] In his accompanying letter, Pancerasi said he found the bone "about three steps" from the spot where Dante's remains had been discovered, adding the bizarre twist that he already put two other bones back where he found them, as if this somehow lessened his guilt. Why the man would replace two bones while keeping one raises questions that only further impugn his character. Did he think only one of the three bones was authentically Dante's? Did he fear appearing too greedy a body snatcher?[31]

On June 11, 1865, just three days after Pancerasi relinquished his remaining bone, Drs. Puglioli and Bertozzi declared that the three small bones found in Dante's tomb when it had been opened on June 7 were part of the skeleton discovered on May 27. They used this comparison with the discovered remains as an opportunity to see if the same was true of the bones handed over to city authorities by Borgognoni, Personali, and Pancerasi. They first concluded that the objects retrieved from Borgognoni and Personali were really two parts of a single piece of bone, in this case a fragment of a femur or thighbone, the largest bone in the human body. Since Personali had found both bones close to the discovery site (and then gave one of them to Borgognoni), it was no surprise that they fit together—like two pieces of a jigsaw puzzle—to form one larger bone fragment. The doctors quickly determined this relic to be false: the fragment did not belong to Dante because his skeleton already had two perfectly whole thighbones. Also declared false was the bone specimen found by Pancerasi some "three steps" from the discovery site.[32]

Drs. Puglioli and Bertozzi confirmed their view that these bones "do not belong and have no relation to Dante's bones" when Ravenna's executive council asked them to look at alleged pieces of Dante's body on March 11, 1882.[33] Containing the three items retrieved and rejected in 1865, the collection had by this time grown to seven bone specimens: one radius, or outer forearm bone (thin and whitish in appearance and missing an end); one piece of a shoulder blade; one piece of a metacarpal, or hand bone; one round piece of an unidentified bone; and pieces of two ribs, in addition to the femur fragment. The radius and piece of shoulder blade were immediately rejected for the same reason the thighbone specimen had been declared false: Dante's skeleton already boasted two intact radii and shoulder blades. More damning still, the shoulder-blade fragment and one of the rib fragments were not even human. The other three items met this basic test but were deemed extraneous to Dante's skeleton because their coloration was wrong and they were filled with dirt. The poet's bones, by contrast, were "very clean, almost shiny."[34]

An eighth bone—another rib fragment—had somehow joined the collection by 1921. Upon examination of the exhumed skeleton on the afternoon of October 29, Professors Sergi and Frassetto easily determined that this specimen of unknown provenance, like the ones examined by Drs. Puglioli and Bertozzi in 1865 and 1882, did not belong to Dante. Two items contained in separate packages presented more complicated and intriguing cases. These packages, like the collection of eight bone fragments, had been held in Ravenna's renowned Classense Library. Santi Muratori, the library's director from 1914 to 1943, was second only to his friend Corrado Ricci in shedding light on the history of Dante's tomb and remains. And like Ricci, Muratori was himself an influential character in this chapter of that history covering the pivotal events of 1921.

Muratori, author of the "Verbale," or official minutes, of the exhumation and examination of Dante's bones in 1921, described the items in detail. One package contained a small glass box about three inches long (7.8 centimeters), an inch and a quarter wide (3.3 centimeters), and an inch and a half high (3.6 centimeters). The box was wrapped in paper with official seals and an announcement of what lay inside: "Precious object—Fragment of the bones of a little finger belonging to Dante's skeleton, given back to the Municipality of Ravenna by the heirs of F. Mordani, who died in 1886."[35] The note added that the municipality transferred this alleged relic to the Classense Library on April 13, 1893. Opening the glass case in 1921, Professors Sergi and Frassetto found a piece of bone, solid in texture and reddish-brown in color, measuring just under two inches at its longest (4.5 centimeters) and half an inch at its widest (1.3 centimeters). On a separate sheet of paper, Filippo Mordani had written instructions for its disposition after his death. He also told readers how to respond to the "precious object":

My Good Reader
Don't Be Scandalized
But Bow Down
And Kiss This Little Urn
16 October 1865
I, Filippo Mondani,
Placed Here
This Fragment of a Bone
of *Dante Alighieri*
Given To Me
By He Who Secretly Took It
From the Box
In Which P[adre] Antonio Santi

A Friar Minor of the Convent in Ravenna
Had Gathered The Relics
Of The Divine Poet
After My Death
I Wish For Such A Noble Relic
To Be Preserved Forever
In The Library of Ravenna.[36]

The name Filippo Mordani was well known to the scientists and other participants in the events of 1921, as it had been to citizens of Ravenna when Mordani accepted this "noble relic" of the "Divine Poet" from an unnamed person present at the discovery of Dante's bones on May 27, 1865. He placed the bone in the glass case or reliquary five months later. Born in Ravenna in 1797, Mordani was a patriotic professor of literature whose works include a celebratory biography of Lord Byron (1841). He was imprisoned in 1849 for his political activism and sent into exile in 1850. He later represented Ravenna in the National Assembly in Bologna (1859) before moving to Forlì. Following the discovery—"so unexpected, almost miraculous"—of Dante's skeleton, Mordani returned home to Ravenna "to venerate the bones of the divine poet" and to witness their reburial, which he did on June 26, 1865.[37] He published a book of inscriptions for the occasion, including one for a plaque placed at the site of the discovery:

The Glorious Bones
Of
Dante Allighieri
Hidden Inside This Wall
In 1677 On October 18
By Antonio Santi Of The Friars Minor In Ravenna
Were Found
On May 27 In 1865.[38]

Mordani erred in believing that Antonio Santi placed the crude pine box of bones in the wall in 1677—that probably occurred when the Franciscans were forced out of their convent by the Napoleonic reforms in 1810. He also erred in believing that his "noble relic" was the fragment of a finger bone belonging to Dante. The scientists determined the specimen to be part of the surface of a long bone, and they doubted this bone was Dante's.[39]

Professors Sergi and Frassetto likewise doubted the authenticity of the last of the alleged relics consigned to the Classense Library for safekeeping. This item had also been turned in by a surviving relative, though not in fulfillment of the deceased owner's written wishes, as in the case of Mordani. Signora Elettra Zanotti, widow of Saturnino Malagola, apparently took it upon herself to give the fragment—another outer piece of a long bone—to an authority after the death of her husband. Contained in a small wooden box with a glass cover, this piece was smaller than Mordani's fragment—just over an inch long (2.7 centimeters) and a quarter of an inch wide (1.1 centimeters)—but had similar solidity and showed the same reddish-brown color. The person to whom widow Zanotti entrusted the alleged piece of Dante's skeleton was none other than Corrado Ricci. She gave it to Ricci soon after Malagola's death on October 1, 1884. Ricci, in turn, gave it to city officials on September 24, 1900.

That it took Ricci a full sixteen years to deposit the fragment with proper authorities severely compromised the moral force of his denunciations of Malagola, Mordani, Borgognoni, and others for procuring a memento of Dante and holding onto it.[40] Borgognoni, after all, lost his job for keeping his ill-gotten remain for a mere three days. Perhaps Ricci, like the other bone collectors, just could not resist the pull of the relic and let go of an object alleged to be part of Dante's remains. But Ricci eventually did let go, and his righteous anger at Malagola, hypocritical or not, was well founded. The relic's power certainly worked its magic on the respected notary.

Malagola's actions were all the more reprehensible because of the role he played in the events of 1865. He was one of the three notaries public who wrote up and confirmed the validity of the official reports on Dante's bones, including those documenting their discovery on May 27, their examination following the opening of the tomb on June 7, and their reburial on June 26.[41] Trusted to ensure the legitimacy of an operation of national and historical interest, Malagola instead violated the high ethical standards of his profession and may have broken the law by pocketing a bone fragment from the area in which Dante's remains had been found. The poet, who believed in an intimate, almost causal relationship between characters' names and their fate in the afterlife, would have had a field day with notary Malagola. Meaning "evil throat," Malagola calls to mind Malacoda (evil tail) and other Malebranche (evil claws), the malicious demons who guard and torture grafters—corrupt public officials—in the fifth pit of Dante's eighth circle of Hell, also known as Malebolge (evil pouches). This site of eternal punishment in Dante's underworld seems made for a sticky-fingered notary public like Malagola—

unless he sincerely repented before his death, for then he would be saved and win Paradise after purifying his soul on the terraces of Mount Purgatory. In this happier scenario, the prayers and good works of Malagola's loved ones— such as his wife's restitution of the stolen bone fragment—would expedite his journey up the mountain toward eternal glory in Heaven.[42]

This concluded the examination of all bones and fragments contained in the urn of relics held in the Classense Library. If the work had ended here, Dante's skeleton would have had no new additions and remained just as it was. But Santi Muratori, the library's director, kept hope alive when he presented three more items to be examined, each claiming to be a genuine piece of Dante. Professors Sergi and Frassetto quickly rejected two of the objects. One had the shape of a little horn, about an inch and a half long (3.5 centimeters), that had been set in gold like an amulet or pendant. This horn consisted of compact, osseous material but had none of the specific features of human bones, much less those belonging to Dante. Moreover, documentation purporting to verify the authenticity of the specimen did just the opposite: the jeweler Achille Vignoli declared in writing on February 26, 1904, that "a few years after the 1865 centenary, Cesare Nanni gave him a yellowish, horn-shaped bone to set in gold, telling him in confidence 'of having found it among Dante's bones as he helped gather them from the ground,' and that 'when he picked up this little horn and saw that it wasn't one of the bones, he put it in his pocket without being seen because he wanted to keep a memento of the precious discovery of the bones.'"[43] However, the trinket's later owner believed the object was part of Dante's skeleton—or at least pretended to believe in its authenticity for financial gain: he offered to sell it to an Italian for one thousand lire (about US$607 in 2019), a bargain in light of the fact that a wealthy American wanted to purchase it for five times as much.[44]

The other rejected relic had a more promising appearance and history, but its claim to legitimacy also quickly collapsed. Accompanying a small crystal box was a note describing the contents as "Piece of the chest that held Dante's bones" and "Fragment of Dante's bone taken in Ravenna during the discovery." That the stated date was off by a month—June 27 instead of May 27, 1865—should have given pause in accepting the note at face value. It was signed "D.S.," the initials of Demetrio Schiaparelli, a judge in Ravenna. Present at the discovery of the bones, he claimed to have taken the bone fragment and the piece of wood at that time. His wife inherited the crystal box after his death in 1903; after her death, it passed to her sister, who, in 1913, gave it to her son-in-law, the engineer Enrico Guagno. It was engineer Guagno, residing in Turin, who had the "generous thought" to send the crystal box and Judge Schiaparelli's explanatory note to Ravenna. Sergi and Frassetto removed a small bone fragment from the box, just over an inch in length (2.77 centimeters) and just under an inch in width (2 centimeters). At one end were two broken processes or projections surrounding an oval-shaped hole. Professor Frassetto identified this fragment as part of the bone of a sheep, specifically, a piece of the basisphenoid (a bone at the base of the cranium) of a young lamb.[45]

The third item exhibited by Santi Muratori was the least pretentious of all the contenders examined on October 29, 1921. Neither displayed in an elegant crystal case nor adorned with shimmering gold leaf, it was a small bone, plain and simple. It was also the only specimen that was what it purported to be: a missing piece of Dante's skeleton, a genuine relic. The bone was just over an inch and half long (4 centimeters) and varied in thickness from about a third of an inch at the center (0.8 centimeters) to about half an inch at either end (1.0 and 1.5 centimeters). Professors Sergi and Frassetto took only a short while to concur on the bone's authenticity, primarily because its reddish-orange color perfectly matched that of the other bones. They identified it as a small hand bone or phalange, probably from the index finger of Dante's left hand.[46] Reflecting on the life of this recovered finger bone, Muratori sentimentally imagined that it gave Dante's "final farewell to his ungrateful and negligent Florence, accompanied the rhythm of his grave thoughts, and clutched in the spasm of his final suffering when Fiduccio dei Milotti knew the great soul had departed, and Guido da Polenta, Piero Giardino, and Meneghino Mezzani lowered their heads and wept over the glorious corpse."[47]

Muratori was himself involved in the complicated afterlife of this bone. Adamo Benelli, an employee of the Feletti company of masons, had been working in the vicinity of the Braccioforte chapel when Pio Feletti discovered the chest of Dante's bones on May 27, 1865. As he helped fellow workers and others gather Dante's bones and transport them to the nearby sepulcher, Benelli decided to take a memento for himself. A thief, no doubt, but also kind, Benelli gave the bone to his friend Sante Sansoni as a gift a few days after the discovery. Some years later, Sansoni bequeathed the relic to his son. Angelo Sansoni, a leather worker with a shop on Via Cavour, jealously safeguarded the bone "with the intention of returning it when the occasion presented itself."[48] His desire to do so grew stronger over the course of many years until, motivated by a "generous impulse," he gave the bone "of his own

free will" to Santi Muratori on March 22, 1920, an action all the more praiseworthy because no one would have been the wiser had he not done so. Muratori congratulated Angelo, despite his having kept the bone for so long, for
fulfilling not only his "noble intention" but also a "high civic duty."[49] Muratori, in turn, kept the bone in his possession until April 11, 1920, when he
handed it over to the municipal government. The final links in the bone's
chain of custody were secured when it was examined by Professors Sergi and
Frassetto and returned to the tomb with the rest of Dante's skeleton at the
end of October 1921.

Adding even a single bone to Dante's skeleton may have been cause for
celebration, but there was also a sense in which, like the results of Italy's participation on the winning side in World War I, this was only a partial or
"mutilated" victory. After all, Dante's skeleton was still missing 77 of its 206
bones (as well as all 32 teeth) after the examination of 1921.[50]

11

Manly Mediterranean Bones

Dante therefore is the most glorious and authentic representative of the Mediterranean race.

—GIUSEPPE SERGI AND
FABIO FRASSETTO

· The military's laying of a wreath at Dante's tomb on September 11, 1921, anticipated its starring role less than two months later at another tomb. An even larger number of active troops and veterans joined thousands of other Italians in Rome for the burial of the Unknown Soldier in the National Monument to King Victor Emmanuel II.[1] A monument to Italian unification, the "Vittoriano"—derisively called the "wedding cake" or "typewriter" for its rigidly tiered form—is Italy's official "Altare della Patria," its national altar. The train carrying the casket of the Unknown Soldier departed from Aquileia in northeastern Italy on October 29 and arrived in Rome on November 2, 1921. The state funeral in which the body was buried and the tomb unveiled took place two days later.

Dante and the Unknown Soldier may appear at first glance to have little in common. Worshiping Italy's celebrated poet and prophet from the Middle Ages would seem unrelated to honoring an anonymous soldier killed in the Great War. Only on reflection do we see how they truly complemented each other, joining like two ends of a thread to bring healing closure to a grieving nation. Dante, after all, had no equal in Italian cultural life precisely because he ingeniously transformed the hardships born of political exile into the story of every individual seeking meaning in "our life." Likewise, the tomb of the Unknown Soldier marked not, as gravesites conventionally do, an identifiable person's death but rather the large-scale slaughter that in just a few years senselessly erased the lives of an unspeakable number of young men. While the Unknown Soldier was "special" by virtue of having been chosen to represent all his fallen comrades, he was at the same time an "everyman" allowing for collective as well as individual mourning.[2] Both tombs were doubly symbolic as memorials to two individuals—the best known and the unknown—whose bones had the power to transform personal loss into a unifying experience.

Despite Gabriele D'Annunzio's absence on both occasions, his influential role in events surrounding the tomb of the Unknown Soldier recalled his impact on the commemorations of the six hundredth anniversary of Dante's death. Even though his writings on a fallen comrade, Giovanni Randaccio, helped inspire the tomb, D'Annunzio refused an invitation to attend the burial of the Unknown Soldier in Rome, just as he had refused to attend and speak at the ceremonies in Ravenna. Whereas D'Annunzio had dispatched three pilots to Dante's tomb with laurel leaves in honor of the poet and dead Italian soldiers, he sent legionnaires from Fiume to lay a wreath at the tomb of the Unknown Soldier. Whereas D'Annunzio had requested that the mother of a fallen soldier be permitted to scatter the leaves at Dante's tomb, a war widow who had also lost a son in the fighting was given the task of selecting the Unknown Soldier by choosing one of eleven identical caskets brought from the battlefields into the basilica in Aquileia.[3]

Dante's centenary, and D'Annunzio's place in it, provided a blueprint for some of the mourning rituals observed in honoring Italy's Unknown Soldier. Momentous words from the *Divine Comedy* found new life in the funereal event. In the poem, Dante has Homer, accompanied by other ancient poets (Ovid, Horace, and Lucan), welcome Virgil back to his eternal home in Limbo. "Honor the most lofty poet," Homer exclaims, "his shade, which had left, has returned."[4] This modified last verse—"l'ombra sua ch'era dipartita è tornata"—was inscribed on the casket carrying the remains of the Unknown Soldier from Aquileia to Rome, the funeral train stopping in each town along the way to give Italians a tangible if symbolic body to mourn and honor. The inscription carried a potent emotional charge for viewers of the casket if only because the words came from the *Divine Comedy,* the great poem of the afterlife written by Italy's father and prophet, and conveyed the simple but profound message of homecoming as a return from exile to a place of loving familiarity. The Unknown Soldier, and all those unidentified dead soldiers his body represented, could finally rest in peace.

The context of Dante's verse deepened the meaning of its association with Italy's Unknown Soldier. The shade that "has returned" belongs to Virgil, and the place to which he has returned is the first circle of Hell. Limbo, as this region is called, perfectly captures the aura of poignant longing that surrounds the revered Roman poet in the *Divine Comedy:* Virgil can rescue Dante from the dark wood and guide him on his journey toward salvation, but he must eventually return home to Hell, where, like all those in Limbo, he lives "in longing" but "without hope."[5] Viewed in this light, Dante's poetry may have diminished the capacity of the Unknown Soldier to provide straightforward consolation, but perhaps that was the point. Only by grappling with the more nuanced sadness exemplified by Dante's beloved yet doomed Virgil could grieving Italians navigate the dark wood of personal and collective loss.[6]

As the Unknown Soldier made his way home amid great fanfare to be entombed in the nation's capital, Dante was once again secretly removed from his tomb in Ravenna. The purpose of this exhumation was to conduct a more accurate and thorough examination of the poet's bones than had been possible in 1865, as well as to determine which if any of the objects taken from the site of the discovery and later returned to authorities were missing parts of his skeleton: only one of these ill-gotten remains, as we have seen, proved to be an authentic relic. As the nation mourned its staggering losses in achieving a "mutilated victory" in the war (over 650,000 dead, the overwhelming majority lying in foreign lands) by burying the repatriated body of an unknown soldier, a small but distinguished group of worshipers oversaw the disinterment, examination, and honorable reburial of Italy's divine poet-soldier. Eyewitness accounts of these activities, no different from coverage of other key moments in Dante's graveyard history, exceeded objective or purely neutral description to reveal ideological views shaped by the time and place in which the events took place. In this case, the "scientific" deification of Dante as the virile embodiment of the Mediterranean race in 1921 anticipated fascists' fashioning of the poet in their own image over the next twenty-four years. This makeover happened not all at once but in stages, from renovations of the area around Dante's tomb to interpretations of his work as prophetic of Benito Mussolini, from plans for a Dante temple in Rome to a proposal for the rump fascist state to go out in a blaze of glory accompanied by the poet's bones at the end of World War II.

The last four days of October 1921 were allotted for the exhumation, examination, and reburial of Dante's bones. The scientific work was assigned, as we saw in reports on stolen remains purporting to belong with the skeleton, to two esteemed physical anthropologists, Giuseppe Sergi and Fabio Frassetto. At four o'clock in the afternoon on Saturday, October 28, a small group of trustworthy workers entered Dante's mausoleum and began preparations for lifting the cover off the marble sepulcher and removing the casket.

Architect Ambrogio Annoni directed the operations performed by master mason Cesare Bandini with the assistance of Giulio Rondoni and Armando Baggioni. Official witnesses to Dante's exhumation included three prominent citizens of Ravenna: Corrado Ricci, Santi Muratori, and Vittorio Guaccimanni (president of the Commission for the Conservation of Monuments).[7] After stopping for the night, work resumed the next morning at eight o'clock sharp.

Fearing disruptions caused by curious onlookers, the organizers took measures to avoid drawing public attention. Closing the area around Dante's mortuary chapel and Braccioforte to visitors, they created a clever decoy by setting up a scaffold outside the mausoleum (against the wall in which the tomb was partially embedded) to give the impression that it was required to support the building. So many renovations had been made in and around the chapel in the preceding weeks that planners hoped their current activity would be passed off as no more than the completion of some project suspended for the commemorative events in September. Observers easily might have surmised that a team was exploring the rear of the sarcophagus to shed light on how the Franciscans had managed to extract Dante's skeleton from the tomb in the early sixteenth century—an investigation that actually took place while experts, unbeknown to the public, examined the bones.

Late in the morning of Sunday, October 29, the lead box was removed from the marble tomb and brought into the nearby Sala di Montevideo, a room in the cloisters of the Franciscan convent that contained a precious collection of Dante mementos, including objects and documents pertaining to the discovery and display of his bones in 1865.[8] This lead casket protected, in turn, the walnut coffin that was used in 1865 to hold the bones. Santi Muratori recorded the reaction of observers when the coffin was opened and the bones extracted:

> At 2:47, within a religious silence—in the presence of the individuals
> named earlier as well as the mayor of Ravenna (Fortunato Buzzi), the
> municipal assessor (Giuseppe Carli), and the secretary general (Paride
> Piccioni)—the wooden cover was raised and the bones appeared. They
> were carefully arranged so that, from head to foot, they indicated,
> despite the restricted space, the body's natural order. After the passing
> of the wave of emotion that forced the men to bow their heads and
> focus their gaze on the divine head in which the spark of the sacred fire
> had shone and the ineffable work had been accomplished, the bones
> were removed one by one, and a list of them was made.[9]

11.1. Lead case removed from Dante's tomb on October 29, 1921 (Santi Muratori, "Verbale," in *Ricognizione delle ossa di Dante fatta nei giorni 28–31 ottobre 1921,* ed. Santi Muratori, Corrado Ricci, Giuseppe Sergi, and Fabio Frassetto [Rome: Reale Accademia Nazionale dei Lincei, 1923], 4)

After the "wave of emotion" had subsided, the men turned to the sober, practical work of cataloging Dante's bones. Yet Muratori and his companions knew they were participants in a solemn ritual. A "vague sense of unease delayed for a few moments the start of the operation."[10] They treated the poet's physical remains as if they were relics of a saint, the room becoming a crypt, the anatomical table a funeral bier. The scientific examination of Dante's bones partially resembled the *"recognitio exuviarum* [inspection of the remains] that proceeds the process of beatification."[11] The light cotton cloth on which Dante's bones had been laid out became a *reliquia mediata,* or secondary relic—a relic by way of contact with the poet's holy body—and was placed in a glass urn for posterity. Dante's cloth received the same veneration that Franciscan nuns had shown for wrappings that held the bones of Saint Francis of Assisi after they were discovered by Brother Bonaventura Zabberoni in 1818.[12]

When the examiners reassembled Dante's skeleton, they noted that the bones were in excellent condition and matched those listed in the anatomical report of 1865.[13] As we saw earlier, Dante's body was missing many of its 206 bones. The most conspicuous absences in 1921, as in 1865, were the lower

11.2. Dante's bones inside
the lead-encased walnut
casket on October 29, 1921
(Santi Muratori, "Verbale,"
in *Ricognizione delle ossa di
Dante fatta nei giorni 28–31
ottobre 1921*, ed. Santi
Muratori, Corrado Ricci,
Giuseppe Sergi, and Fabio
Frassetto [Rome: Reale
Accademia Nazionale dei
Lincei, 1923], 5)

jawbone (mandible) and a right lower-leg bone (fibula). Also missing were several vertebrae, one rib, nearly all the finger bones (twenty-five of twenty-eight phalanges), and most bones of the wrists, hands, feet, and toes.[14] After determining that only one of the returned objects taken from the discovery site in 1865 belonged to the skeleton, Professors Sergi and Frassetto checked their instruments and began a systematic examination of Dante's bones. It was four thirty in the afternoon of October 29, 1921. Over the next forty-eight hours, with breaks for meals and sleep, they measured and analyzed the poet's physical remains. The professors worked until seven fifteen and then, following a forty-five-minute break, from eight to eleven thirty, at which time they suspended work for the night. The moment had arrived to decide who would spend the night in the room with Dante's remains, both as an act of respectful religious observance and as protection against possible malfeasance. No one, given the travails of the bones in preceding centuries, wanted to leave anything to chance.

The examining committee had initially proposed to take turns keeping vigil through the night and early-morning hours. But Antonio Fusconi, already serving as custodian of Dante's tomb, asked for and was granted this honor.[15] Fusconi, a disabled veteran, had been tolling Dante's bell—a gift from Italian communes the previous month—thirteen times each day at sunset, the thirteenth being the date of Dante's death in September 1321. The ringing of the bell, he later said, gave "tongue to the grief of the exiled Dante sorrowing for his beloved birthplace of Florence."[16] While Fusconi remained alone in the room with Dante's bones, a unit of royal guards patrolled the area around the mausoleum and Braccioforte. The custodian refused even the small army cot set up for him, spending the night instead in a simple chair with only a thin blanket to cover him. Honoring Dante soldier to soldier, "the maimed veteran who lost a leg on Mount Hermada sleeps beside the soldier of Campaldino, the cavalryman who had seen the defeated troops walk out of Caprona in fear."[17] Respecting the authorities' desire to keep news of the exhumation from the public, Fusconi spoke of his vigil to no one, not even to his elderly mother. She and other relatives found it odd that he spent the night in that small room, having his supper passed to him through the closed gate.

Born in 1889 to a peasant family, Antonio Fusconi became somewhat of a legend for his selfless service as "Dante's watchman"—*la sentinella di Dante*—from 1921 until his retirement on January 1, 1966.[18] He was given a tiny office—a plain, damp cubbyhole behind the chapel—where he passed the time reading Dante's poetry, eventually learning it so well that he could quote and identify verses with ease. Small in stature, Fusconi walked with a limp (with the aid of a crutch) and was neither well-off—as his frayed coat cuffs attested—nor well educated. Yet he could be an imposing guardian of Dante's tomb. Elderly residents of Ravenna still recall how he would use his crutch to threaten people whose appearance or behavior he deemed disrespectful of the revered poet. Recipients of his rebukes ranged from children playing soccer and adults conversing too loudly under the laurel trees outside the chapel to visitors with the audacity to dress inappropriately or smoke in Dante's presence. When an army captain, told to remove his cap, said he was in uniform and that was enough, the resolute Fusconi retorted, "I'm in uniform too, as the custodian, and yet I still take off my cap." The officer promptly complied.[19]

Remarkably, Fusconi was absent only fifteen days during forty-five years as custodian of Dante's tomb—and that was when he visited battlefields where he had fought and cemeteries where his fallen comrades were buried. Just as remarkably, it was said that he never accepted a tip from visitors to the tomb, neither from simple tourists nor from heads of state or other dignitaries. He rode his bicycle each morning to the little temple, where he would spend the entire day watching over Dante's final resting place. After tolling the bell in the evening, he locked the heavy bronze doors to the building, closed the outside gate, and returned to his home, which he shared with his sister.[20] Fusconi was awarded a gold medal for his faithful service from the local Chamber of Commerce in 1957, and upon his retirement in 1966, at age seventy-six, he was given a gold watch by the president of the Republic, Giuseppe Saragat. Later that year Fusconi was named a Knight of the Order of Merit of the Republic. The day before his retirement, as the winter sun set at the end of a gray and humid day in Ravenna, the bell given by the Italian Communes in 1921 tolled, its thirteen peels marking the end of an era. Leaning on his famous crutch, Fusconi entered the chapel to place a bunch of red carnations on Dante's tomb. Pausing for a moment of silence before the tomb, he was so overcome with emotion that observers had to support him. Like Monsignor Giovanni Mesini, the priest from Ravenna who served on both the civil and Catholic committees for the Dante centenary, Antonio Fusconi was more than just one of the privileged few who had seen Dante's bones in 1921. Both men gloried in the honor of having kissed Dante's skull, Mesini recalling the powerful emotion felt by all present and Fusconi moved to say that "you don't get such a feeling even from kissing your own mother."[21]

After the first night of Fusconi's vigil, Professors Sergi and Frassetto, assisted by other committee members, recommenced their examination the next day, October 30, at eight in the morning, working until noon, then from two to six and again from eight to midnight. The professors created a visual record of the examination that day. Under their direction, Giuseppe Carli, a municipal assessor, took sixteen photographs of various bones, including Dante's skull, and Vittorio Guaccimanni, an accomplished artist, made two sketches of the skull.[22] At one point during the night, the light of candles became inadequate for the meticulous work. Thankfully, a resourceful worker managed to illuminate the room with electric lighting, though that made it

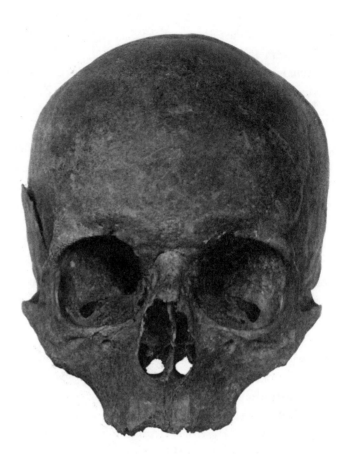

11.3. Dante's skull on
October 30, 1921
(*Ricognizione delle ossa di
Dante fatta nei giorni 28–31
ottobre 1921,* ed. Santi
Muratori, Corrado Ricci,
Giuseppe Sergi, and Fabio
Frassetto [Rome: Reale
Accademia Nazionale dei
Lincei, 1923], table 4)

absolutely necessary to cover all the windows to avoid a repeat of the night
before, when even dim candlelight drew the unwanted attention of several
passersby. After midnight, Antonio Fusconi once again remained alone with
the bones until morning. The examination resumed the following day,
October 31, at seven thirty, while preparations began for returning the bones
to the tomb. After Sergi and Frassetto's request for an additional day of
work was denied, the examination proceeded at a rapid pace. At four o'clock,
all the bones were checked against the master list and placed back in the
walnut coffin, which was still in excellent condition.

The same could not be said of the lead case for the coffin, even though both
had been made for the preservation of Dante's bones before they were re-
buried in 1865. Luigi Mazzavillani, a metalworker, was instructed to make
a new lead container because the inside of the current one showed signs of

corrosion from moisture that had entered through nail holes. (The nails had been used to fasten the lead case to the walnut coffin.) To further protect the walnut coffin and Dante's bones, this new case was over twice as thick (4.5 millimeters) as the original one. Professor Zanotti, a scientific expert, entered the room to take a small sample of the material scraped from the marble tomb on June 7, 1865, and test it for microfauna. The packaged scrapings were then placed back in the coffin next to the glass tube containing a document marking the events of 1865. Another glass tube was added—sealed with red wax and bearing the insignia of Ravenna—to hold parchment recording the 1921 examination for posterity.[23]

The Latin inscription on the new document cleverly combined the two notes that Brother Antonio Santi had written on the plain pine box in 1677:

> Dantis Ossa
> nuper revisa
> et hic reposita
> pridie Kal. Nov. MCMXXI

The date in the last line—"The day before the Calends of November, 1921"— was just a formal way of saying that Dante's bones, having been "seen again," were "placed back here" (in the original tomb) on October 31, 1921. The authenticating parchment was signed by participants and witnesses (except for Corrado Ricci, who had departed earlier that day), beginning with the mayor of Ravenna (Fortunato Buzzi) and two examining scientists (Frassetto and Sergi) and ending with the custodian of Dante's tomb (Antonio Fusconi) and the manual laborers.

After this document and other items had been placed in the coffin containing Dante's bones, Monsignor Giovanni Mesini, locally known as "Dante's priest," donned the robe and stole of his office and blessed the poet's remains according to Catholic practice. The cover of the walnut coffin was then shut tight with the original screws, one of which broke and had to be replaced with a wax seal. The lead cover of the container in which the coffin had been placed was finally welded to the base with a blowtorch. One task remained before transporting the lead-encased coffin from the "Room of Dante Mementos" back to the marble tomb in Dante's chapel. Using a screwdriver, Professor Frassetto etched the word *levante* (east) on the lead cover above the location of Dante's skull. This indicated to workers how to orient the coffin when they lowered it into the sarcophagus so that Dante would face the door of the chapel rather than the back wall.[24] As soon as Mayor Buzzi placed a laurel branch on top of the lead case, a mason entered the room to announce that, under the direction of architect Annoni, the small chapel—the *tempietto*—was now ready to receive Dante's remains.

In the fading light of autumn, the committee divided in two, one group standing inside the chapel, the other at the top of the stairway outside the examination room. With pitch-perfect timing, the bell in the campanile of the Church of Saint Francis rang out just then, as if to mark the end of the solemn ceremony. As arranged, other bells throughout Ravenna chimed the first note of Giuseppe Verdi's "Ave Maria"—an Italian version of the Latin hymn, attributed (falsely) to Dante, that the composer set to music—while the casket was lowered into the marble urn in the chapel. At 5:25 p.m. on October 31, 1921, Dante's "weary and holy bones" returned home once again.[25] However, as befits the poet of exile in death as in life, this exhumation in 1921 was not the last time in the twentieth century they would be forced to leave the tomb in which they had been laid to rest six hundred years earlier.

Dante's remains may have been treated like holy relics, but from the way Professors Sergi and Frassetto described them, this secular saint more closely resembled soldierly, dragon-slaying Saint George than humble, nature-loving Saint Francis. The scientists judged the poet's bones to be "perfectly preserved" in their official report written soon after the examination. Handling them had posed no risk because they were "robust and strong."[26] In Frassetto's more detailed study published ten years later, he doubled down on the strength of Dante's bones, coloring them with stereotypically masculine language that could not help but recall the pervasive machismo characteristic of fascist rhetoric and practice. Not only did Dante's pelvic bones show "strikingly masculine characteristics" in both shape and size, but his bones generally exhibited "toughness and virility"—the entire skeleton was marked by "strength and virility."[27]

Emphasis on the "manliness" of Dante's bones far exceeded the obvious point that they belonged to an adult human male. Virile strength so defined Frassetto's view of Dante that he used it to judge how well various portraits of the poet corresponded to his facial skeleton. The eminent scientist concluded that a miniature by an unknown artist in a fourteenth-century manuscript (Codex Palatino 313) best captures Dante in its "masculine and imperious profile," the various features of his face combining to express "strength and virility," physical characteristics "reflected in Dante's many activities, and in all aspects of his thought, whether moral or religious or poetic." Dante's masculine strength is a "noble force that we feel even today powerfully vibrating in the depths of our soul."[28] Frassetto's hypermasculine Dante surely owed less to the bones themselves than to the entrenched power of Italian fascism when he wrote those words in 1933, a time when virility—identified first and foremost with Mussolini's body—was the "master term" for a host of entwined fascist ideals, including "the cults of youth, of duty, of sacrifice and heroic virtues, of strength and stamina, of obedience and authority, and of physical strength and sexual potency."[29]

Frassetto compared his anthropological analysis of Dante's skull with existing representations of the poet's face and collaborated with a sculptor from Bologna, Alfonso Borghesani, to model Dante's full head "with the greatest exactness and the greatest possible attention to the form and the anatomical details."[30] This bust was the basis for an article Frassetto wrote for a glossy Italian magazine—published on February 6, 1938—and for a lecture he gave in English, titled "How Dante Really Looked," at the University of Berlin five days later. In the article, Frassetto muses that if only he had managed to overcome Corrado Ricci's "inflexible opposition" to physical reproductions of the "holy relics" during the 1921 exhumation, he would have had an exact copy of Dante's skull to use for his reconstruction. He knew then that he needed a plaster cast of the skull to create this scientifically accurate copy of the poet's face, a project he conceived when he and Sergi performed their examination. In defiance of Ricci's order, he therefore made two partial casts—on the sly, of course—one of Dante's palate (the roof of the oral cavity), the other of the midsection of the poet's face. Frassetto strategically chose these facial bones to copy because he would need their casts to create Dante's missing jawbone from scratch. He wisely decided not to reveal his violation of the prohibition against making casts until the article and lecture in 1938, four years after Corrado Ricci's death.[31]

If phrenology—the identification of character, personality, and behavior from shapes and measurements of the human skull—had already fallen into disrepute by the time Drs. Puglioli and Bertozzi examined Dante's bones in 1865, this so-called science of mind was certainly out of favor in scientific circles when Frassetto studied the bones in the early twentieth century.[32] But this hardly prevented him from trying to entertain his readers by deriving character from anatomy, personality from external appearances. Toiling in the even more tangled field of physiognomy, Frassetto created a psychobehavioral profile of Dante from the "anatomically correct" representation of his head. Acknowledging that his psychological interpretations might

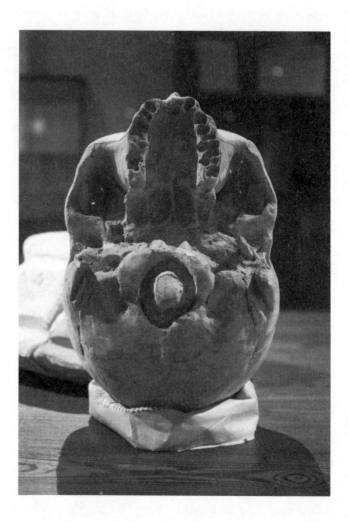

11.4. Cast of Dante's palatine bones by Fabio Frassetto (Alma Mater Studiorum University of Bologna–University Museum System–Museo di Palazzo Poggi; photo: Alessandra Altomare)

"seem somewhat extraneous to the nature of our anthropological studies and to science," he nonetheless justified them by calling on contemporary studies in endocrinology, psychology, and mental illness that argued for potential correlations of "forms, sizes, and particular bodily expressions (facial above all) with specific psychic states."[33] Frassetto here shows the influence of a former teacher: Cesare Lombroso (1835–1909), the famous Italian criminologist who postulated correlations—now discredited—between physical anomalies, such as unusual skull sizes and asymmetrical facial bones, and criminal pathologies.[34]

Speaking in English, Frassetto told his German audience in 1938,

In the reserved strength of this gaunt and severe face one feels the pallor of tense flesh, which must have been characteristic of Dante as a result of the never-ending unrest of his spirit. His personality is very clearly embodied in the great thoughtful eyes, made heavier by weight of the lids, in the unparted sensual lips expressing that knowledge of superiority that dominated him, in his haggard cheeks and also the haggard texture of the skin, the rugged nose and the prominent Adam's apple (signs of his strongly marked masculinity), and in each other decided and grave feature of his countenance.[35]

Frassetto combined Dante's virility—his "strongly marked masculinity"— with the "thoughtful eyes," knowing "superiority," and other "grave" features traditionally associated with the poet-genius of the *Divine Comedy*. The body confirmed what we knew about the man, and vice versa.

Dante's bones showed not only his pronounced virility but also his superior intelligence. Professors Sergi and Frassetto highlighted the large size of Dante's cranium, its volume—computed from measurements of length, width, and height—not merely *grande* or above average but surpassing cranial capacities of other Europeans known for their brainpower (Saint Ambrose, the poets Petrarch and Foscolo, the artist Raphael) and only slightly below that of the physicist Alessandro Volta, inventor of the electric battery. Employing the best experimental methods of the time, the professors achieved similar comparative results for the estimated weight of Dante's brain. At between 1,479 and 1,500 grams, it weighed well above what the scientists considered average (1,420 grams) for men between thirty-five and forty years of age.[36]

In Frassetto's 1933 study based on the data from 1921, he placed even greater emphasis on the exceptional size of Dante's cranium and brain. After noting the color of Dante's skull—"old walnut" (*noce vecchia*) with patches of dark orange—and the excellent condition of his cranial bones ("strong and resistant"), the scientist reported what mattered most: Dante's cranium, measuring 1,700 cubic centimeters in volume, was *molto grande*—"very large"—far superior to the average size of Italian male craniums (and European male craniums in general), which, in Frassetto's classification, varied between 1,450 and 1,550 cubic centimeters. He again gave Dante's skull high marks in comparison with those of other famous minds, this time concluding that the craniums of Dante and Petrarch—"the two great Italians"—closely resembled each other in both size and shape. Dante's brain fared even better. Applying three different methods for calculating Dante's brain weight, Frassetto concluded that it was "far above the average" for Italian adults and exceeded the "average weight of the brains of men of the highest intellect." Even in cases where Dante's brain weight (now pegged at 1.541 kilograms) was less than that of other illustrious thinkers, his overall body weight (estimated at 60 kilograms, about 132 pounds) meant his relative brain weight—a more accurate sign of "intellectual power"—was exceptionally high.[37]

Taken together, Dante's skull and other bones confirmed his manly genius for the scientists. Frassetto and Sergi may have given shorter shrift to the virility of Dante's skeleton in their 1921 report (published two years later), but even then they created a fascist-friendly Dante, "the most glorious and authentic representative of the Mediterranean race." This race had an illustrious five-thousand-year history, from the Minoan and Mycenaean civilizations to the glory days of Hellenism in Greece and Latin culture in Italy, and it entered a new age heralded by Dante himself.[38] Within this Eurocentric panorama, he shines both as heir to the great Mediterranean civilizations of the past and as harbinger of the next episode in the historical highlight reel, the European Renaissance at the dawn of the modern era. Unstated but glaringly obvious in this ethno-scientific celebration of Dante in racial terms is how well it aligned with a powerful force driving fascism just as the movement began to assert itself: Italy's yearning to reclaim its prominent place among nations in the succession of dominant civilizations.

The two scientists who examined Dante's bones in 1921 contributed to the fascist fashioning of Dante in complementary ways. Fabio Frassetto took the lead in accentuating Dante's virility, while Giuseppe Sergi was most responsible for seeing in the poet's bones a model of racial superiority. Sergi's work, spanning three decades and including over four hundred publications, "would form the bedrock of the Mediterranean school of racial theory." Propagated by devoted disciples, Frassetto among them, this school dominated Italian anthropology in the early twentieth century, its search for racial identity in the shape and structure of bones culminating in the use of x-rays for this purpose in the 1940s.[39] The injection of race in the 1921 report followed naturally from Sergi's earlier studies of European racial identity.

In Sergi's influential book on the Mediterranean race in 1895, updated and published in English in 1901, he argued that modern Europeans descended from a Eurafrican "species" in the Horn of Africa that branched into three distinct racial groups: African, Mediterranean, and Nordic peoples. These last two groups populated, respectively, the Mediterranean basin and northern regions of Europe. The "so-called Aryan races," for Sergi, were an

Asiatic variety of the Eurasiatic species and did not even include Germans and Scandinavians, who were instead Eurafricans "of the Nordic variety"—which was probably just as well because "the Aryans were savages when they invaded Europe: they destroyed in part the superior civilisation of the Neolithic populations, and could not have created the Greco-Latin civilisation."[40] Whereas German scholars and scientists celebrated the Nordic race as the true heirs of Aryans—whom they considered the foundation of Western civilization—Sergi instead hailed Mediterranean stock as "the greatest race in the world, one of the most grandiose phenomena in the history of the world and in human history."[41] Sergi and Frassetto's racially charged Dante emerged from this triumphalist vision of Mediterranean peoples, whom Sergi believed "were distinguished by their individuality, their desire to rise above the masses and become leaders in the arts, literature, or politics." As creators of the "Minoan, the Hellenic, and the Latin civilizations," the Mediterranean race possessed special artistic instincts that gave rise to a disproportionately large number of "inventors," "initiators," and overall "geniuses."[42] Dante therefore was la crème de la crème.

The physical anthropologist Giorgio Gruppioni and the literary scholar Alfredo Cottignoli, colleagues at the University of Bologna, have discovered unpublished writings by Fabio Frassetto that shed new light on this celebration of Dante as the supreme symbol of the Mediterranean race in fascist Italy. Having praised a racially marked Dante in his coauthored report with Giuseppe Sergi in 1923 and in his major study a decade later, Frassetto sought to capture the Italian poet's "true face" in the bust he created in 1938. He took his Dante bust on tour in Italy (beginning in Florence) and abroad, with displays at academic conferences in Germany and Poland.[43] Inspired by the enthusiastic reception of his work, Frassetto conceived of a documentary film narrating the afterlife of Dante's physical remains with emphasis on the scientific study of the bones, culminating with his 1938 bust as the best representation of how the poet really looked. Multiple versions of the film script and related documents from 1938–1940 (notes, correspondence, article drafts) reveal Frassetto's willingness to play the race card to reach a wider audience for his likeness of Dante.[44]

Given available technologies, Frassetto's procedure for representing Dante's face more faithfully was "absolutely original and ambitious."[45] He first took a skull similar to Dante's and made a plaster cast of it. Using the measurements (over one hundred), photographs, and unauthorized (partial) casts taken of Dante's skull in 1921, he spent two years shaping this prototype to

11.5. Plaster model of Dante's skull by Fabio Frassetto (Alma Mater Studiorum University of Bologna–University Museum System–Museo di Palazzo Poggi; photo: Alessandra Altomare)

correspond more accurately to the poet's cranium. In the end, he produced a bronze version in addition to numerous plaster copies. But to render Dante's face as accurately as possible, he needed to model the complete skull, including the missing mandible.

The jawbone had worried Frassetto from the time he ascertained its absence during his examination in 1921. Eight years later, he registered this concern as a guest at a séance in which Dante's spirit was summoned. The spiritual encounter took place on October 4, 1929, at a prestigious salon in Trieste hosted by the poet and occultist Nella Doria Cambon. As an authority on the afterlife, Dante was a popular "presence" at Cambon's gatherings. She dutifully documented the actions and words of the mediums through whom Dante's spirit manifested itself. During Frassetto's visit, he informed the medium—Romana Fornis—that he had been entrusted by the Ministry of Education and the mayor of Ravenna with examining

Dante's skeleton. He was impressed with the medium's physical description of Dante, how well it matched his study of the poet's skeleton "in its form and dimensions." When Frassetto asked about the missing jawbone, Dante tersely replied, "Don't search for my mandible. You won't find it." The poet's spirit added that, while this bone had been separated from his body, he was nonetheless "whole and free." "Do what you like with my bones," he told the anthropologist. "I really don't care!" When Frassetto asked about the prospects of his work, Dante foresaw it bringing him "glory and merit." The poet's confirmation that he left no death mask ("I didn't have time to think of this")—and that no existing portrait or sculpture accurately depicted him—undoubtedly encouraged Frassetto to show "how Dante really looked."[46]

To do so, he first had to face the daunting challenge of re-creating the missing jawbone. Frassetto began by selecting a mandible from Bologna's Museum of Anthropology that generally conformed with the rest of Dante's skull. He then made a plaster cast of this jawbone that he could shape to match more closely the other facial bones. Frassetto next worked like a plastic surgeon to put flesh on Dante's skull and re-create his face, the most conjectural stage of the project. The anthropologist employed the same procedure he had followed in 1933 to assess the accuracy of artistic portraits. He first gathered calculations of the average thickness of soft tissue taken by other scientists from predetermined points on the faces of cadavers, a technique previously used to identify remains of the Italian artist Raphael and the German poet and musician Schiller. He then supplemented this data with measurements derived from radiographic images (x-rays) of living individuals believed to resemble Dante in body type. Superimposing his rendering of Dante's face on the portraits, Frassetto ranked them in their faithfulness to the poet's actual appearance. To construct his three-dimensional model of Dante's face in 1938, he now returned to the most realistic artistic illustration—the miniature in the Codex Palatino—to flesh out parts of the face (lips, chin, nasal cartilage) not directly connected to bones. Finally, aware of the limits of his science, Frassetto collaborated with Alfonso Borghesani, drawing on the Bolognese sculptor's artistic expertise to create a bust—one version in marble, another in bronze—displaying Dante's "true face."[47]

Written between 1938 and 1940, Frassetto's documentary film project sought to exploit the popularity of cinema to publicize this more faithful model of Dante. Prefaced by a brief overview of the poet's graveyard history in Ravenna, the script relied heavily on Frassetto's 1933 study (*Dantis ossa*) and

11.6. Bronze bust of Dante
by Fabio Frassetto and
Alfonso Borghesani
(Museo Dantesco /
Istituzione Biblioteca
Classense)

his creation of the bust in 1938 to chart the anthropologist's work on Dante over nearly two decades, beginning with his examination of the bones in 1921. Dated December 21, 1938, the text celebrated Dante's virility and intellectual prowess—his "strong bones," "masculine temperament," and "high intelligence"—as deduced from his skeleton and brain size.[48] In the script, as in the earlier book, Frassetto attributed Dante's robust libido to his heightened masculinity. Despite unimpressive collar bones—even "smaller than average for a female"—Dante's skeleton displayed force and virility, qualities for which, wrote Boccaccio in the fourteenth century, "lust found an ample place not only in the years of his youth but also of his maturity."[49] Dante poetically confessed his lustful nature when, upon walking through fire on the Terrace of Lust in Purgatory, he claimed, "I would have thrown myself / straight into molten glass to cool myself, / so beyond measure was the burning there." Frassetto cited these "burning verses" as "the most authoritative confirmation of the anthropological data" suggesting the poet's high sex drive.[50]

Frassetto pitched his film to various fascist organizations and individuals, drawing a profile of the poet consistent with the regime's most primal ethno-racial impulses. The final line of the script he sent in November 1938 to the secretary of the University of Bologna's student fascist association (Gruppo Universitario Fascista) praises this virile Dante as the "symbol and supreme representative of the great and glorious Mediterranean race." Eager to make Dante's "true face" known to domestic and foreign audiences, Frassetto next tried to entice the cinematographic organization—Istituto Nazionale Luce—responsible for producing and distributing Italian films and documentaries favorable to Mussolini's government. He closed his letter of June 21, 1939, to the head of production with "fascist salutations." With no success on this front, he turned six months later to Alessandro Pavolini, head of the Ministry of Popular Culture, whose portfolio included the regime's propagandistic film-production company. In Rome on other business, Frassetto sought a meeting with Pavolini in late January 1940. The script he sent to the minister in anticipation of the meeting was titled *The Authentic Synthesis of the Race: Dante's Face Reconstructed after Six Centuries.* This version, like others, concluded with acclaim for Dante's "most noble features" as evidence of his embodiment of the superior "Mediterranean race." A central figure in a later episode of Dante's skeletal history, Pavolini was evidently no more receptive than others to Frassetto's film project despite the anthropologist's blatant appeal to belief in Mediterranean—and, by extension, Italian—ethno-racial superiority.[51]

In the end, Frassetto's celebration of Dante's Mediterranean racial identity may have scuttled his attempts to secure funding and technical support for production of the film. His rejection of the "improbable thesis" put forth by German scholars of Dante's "Nordic origins" was bound to backfire as Italy drew closer to Germany following Hitler's enthusiastic reception in Naples, Rome, and Florence in May 1938 and the formal alliance of the two nations a year later with the signing of the Pact of Steel.[52] Pavolini, who would fight alongside the Nazis against Italian partisans at the end of World War II, probably saw little upside in endorsing Frassetto's pro-Italian, anti-German identification of Dante's origins.

Glorifying Dante as the highest expression of the Italian people and Mediterranean race did not help Frassetto win backing for his film in 1938–1940, but nationalist claims for the poet otherwise found great favor under fascism. Overall, the virile, racialized Dante promoted by Giuseppe Sergi and Fabio Frassetto in their examination of his bones in 1921 flourished in Italy over the next twenty-four years. In their fascist fashioning of Dante, the anthropologists were joined by political, military, and cultural leaders (including scholars and journalists) up to and including the head of the regime himself.

12

Dante's Duce, Mussolini's Dante

Ravenna, the imperial city, rich in glorious memories and resplendent
with eminent monuments, today consecrates a dignified area of art,
science, and silence surrounding the venerable tomb of the Divine Poet.
—ARRIGO SOLMI

On March 26, 1904, a brazen young Italian man with socialist, antireligious inclinations debated Alfredo Taglialatela, a prominent Protestant evangelist, in Lausanne, Switzerland, on the existence of God. At one point in the precocious youth's argument, published in July 1904, he refuted the idea of a soul—divine, immortal, inalterable—existing separate from the body. Drawing on experimental work on psychic phenomena and human consciousness, he claimed the soul was nothing more than the product, through chemical reactions, of the human brain. He explained, moreover, that the "most recent deductions" revealed a new understanding of the brain and its function, namely, that "intelligence has its full force in brains weighing between a minimum of 1200 and maximum of 1800 grams; that the labyrinth of convolutions is more complicated in cultured races than in ignorant ones; that the two most important factors in intellectual development are culture and the amount of gray matter; and that, without falling for Gall's exaggerations, the idea of cerebral 'localization'—involving not definite regions but distinct centers whose destruction means the loss of activities—is in fact true." Hardly a scientist, the debater nevertheless showed himself conversant with accepted psychological and neurological understandings of the human brain at the start of the twentieth century. He also knew enough to reject the unscientific tenets of phrenology ("Gall's exaggerations") without discarding the notion that certain activities and behaviors are in fact localized in the brain. This twenty-one-year-old radical was Benito Mussolini.[1]

Over time, of course, Mussolini drastically changed his political views and even reached an accommodation with religion and the Catholic Church. He stayed true, instead, to a racist conflation of biology and culture in the years to come. Young Benito's distinction between "cultured" and "ignorant" races, based on cerebral complexity, opens a window onto thinking that would underpin hostile, exclusionary policies of the fascist regime, culminating in its violence against black Africans with the invasion of Ethiopia in 1935 and its discrimination against Italian Jews with the Racial Laws in 1938.[2] Mussolini's racist thinking on race and ethnicity was on full display in a preface he wrote to a book published in 1928.[3] Richard Korherr's *Regresso delle nascite: Morte dei popoli*—"Decline of births: death of peoples"—warned of the demise of Western civilization due to declining birthrates of white Europeans. In chapters with foreboding titles like "The Setting of the White Race," "The Foreign Races," and "War on Declining Birthrates," Korherr reduced demographic changes to a zero-sum game with civilizational consequences: lower birthrates of white Europeans compared with the birthrates of "foreign races" spelled the end of European power.

Mussolini, whose policies and laws to increase the Italian population had not yet borne fruit, held Korherr and his views on race and power in high esteem. Lamenting that in Italy, largely because of urbanization, "cradles are empty and cemeteries are expanding," Mussolini looked to reverse this trend. Foreseeing ten million additional inhabitants, he dreamed of "sixty million Italians making the history of the world feel the weight of their mass and power."[4] To encourage Italians to have larger families, Mussolini called on Hegel, "the philosopher of the State," to equate manhood with fatherhood ("he is not a man who is not a father") and stoked fears of an impending demographic catastrophe. "The entire white race, the Western race," he warned, "could be submerged by the other races of color that multiply with a rhythm unknown to our own." "Are black and yellow peoples," he asked ominously, "already at the gates?"[5]

Dante's virility and intellectual capacity, as deduced from his physical remains, made him the apotheosis of this great if declining Mediterranean race. A masterful demagogue, Mussolini easily grasped the advantage of claiming the poet for his cause, just as D'Annunzio had for irredentism and, before that, Mazzini had for the Risorgimento. In a famous speech at the Augusteo Theater in Rome on November 8, 1921, just one week after the exhumation of Dante's bones, Mussolini identified the poet as the inspiration not just for Italian nationhood but specifically for fascism. Rivaling D'Annunzio's outrageous rewriting of Jesus's Sermon on the Mount to enlist Dante as a proponent of intervention in World War I, Mussolini summoned him to make the case for fascism's transformation from a movement into a political party. Telling his listeners to remain true to fascism's "animating principle," the gifted orator ended his speech by reminding them that Dante had exalted Francis of Assisi for his marriage to poverty, after which "each passing day, he loved her more." Mussolini exhorted his fellow fascists to follow this example on behalf of the nation: each day to love more "this cherished mother who is called *Italy*."[6]

To judge from Mussolini's autobiography, published in English in 1928, Dante loomed large in his imagination from a young age. He recalled a visit to Ravenna with his mother during a summer vacation in his childhood. It was a short distance from the family home in the hamlet of Varano di Costa (in the Commune of Predappio) to Ravenna, but to young Benito "it was a great journey—almost like a journey of Marco Polo—to go over hill and dale to the edge of the sea—the Adriatic!" Ravenna, with its artistic legacy and illustrious history, left a deep impression on Mussolini, who credited the visit with enlarging his "concepts of life, beauty and the rise of civilizations." He was moved by Byzantine mosaics in the Basilica of Sant'Apollinare and fishing boats on the lovely Adriatic Sea, but his first recollection of Ravenna was of Dante's tomb, "inspiring in its quiet hour of noon."[7] When Mussolini later named poetry and philosophy—along with flying, fencing, motorcars, horseback riding, and music (he played the violin)—among his passions outside of politics, he boasted that Dante (among "the great poets") and Plato (among "the supreme philosophers") often occupied hours of his time.[8]

Mussolini no doubt exaggerated his devotion to Dante for purposes of self-aggrandizement. But he also understood the value of using the poet to legitimate and advance fascist ideals. Like D'Annunzio and other irredentists, Mussolini and his fascist followers called on the poet's unimpeachable authority in drawing what they believed to be the true map of a completely unified Italy. Contested cities and territories such as Fiume, Trieste, Dalmatia, the Trentino, and Alto Adige all fell within the "borders prophesied by Dante," borders "dear to every Italian heart." When this map expanded to embrace Trieste and Trent after World War I, it therefore conformed more closely to "the natural borders which Dante had prophesied and defined in the fourteenth century."[9]

Toward the end of 1921, Mussolini laid out a political program for his party when he spoke at a "great fascist meeting" in Trieste. He finished with a rousing affirmation of Italy's role as a leader among nations: "It is destiny," he roared, "that Rome again takes her place as the city that will be the director of the civilization of all Western Europe. Let us commit the flame of this passion to the coming generations; let us make of Italy one of the nations without which it is impossible to conceive the future history of humanity." In his autobiography, Mussolini recalls that he gave this speech during the year of Dante's centenary, an event that moved him to imagine the poet as the prophet of this fascist fantasy of Italian power. "I was dreaming," Mussolini wrote, "in the name of Alighieri: 'The Italy of tomorrow, both free and rich, all-resounding, with seas and skies peopled with her fleets, with the earth everywhere made fruitful by her plows.'"[10] Soon after assuming power in 1922, Mussolini made Dante Italy's ambassador to the wider world when he had a bust of the poet "placed in each Italian embassy and legation as a symbol of the mother country."[11]

Despite Mussolini's own reverence for Dante, he distrusted foreigners who held the poet in the same high regard. Dante effectively functioned as a litmus test for the paranoid leader. If representatives of other nations displayed knowledge of Dante, Mussolini took this as a sign that "they want to screw us with poetry." This sentiment was shared by his son-in-law (and foreign minister), Galeazzo Ciano. True to Ciano's belief that "in the end we work only to make Him happy," he was known to repeat many of Mussolini's colorful remarks, including this Dante-based warning against "foreigners."[12] No matter how much pride Mussolini, Ciano, and others took in Dante as a universal poet, they claimed him first and foremost for Italy. Francesco Giunta, one of the most militant fascist leaders before and during the regime's twenty-year reign, made this abundantly clear in a speech he gave to two hundred fascists who climbed to the peak of Mount Nevoso (in the Italian Alps) on September 14, 1921, to commemorate the poet's centenary. Giunta glorified Dante as the "symbol of the race" who foresaw a time when Italians would overcome fratricidal divisions to fight as one in defense of their rightful borders.[13]

Many fascist apologists restricted ownership of Dante even further by recasting him as the prophet not just of Italy or fascism but of Mussolini himself. To draw such a tight connection between Dante and the Duce, members and supporters of the regime relied more on the poet's allusions to some unnamed future savior of Italy and the world than on his yearnings for Italian unity within its rightful borders. To be fair, the *Divine Comedy* provided ample fodder for wildly anachronistic readings. Dante was rightly admired for his intellectual coherence and attention to detail in portraying even the most unreal environs of the afterworlds, but he also spun prophecies no less enigmatic—and therefore susceptible to far-fetched interpretations—than the prognostications of Nostradamus. His two most famous prophecies occur, appropriately, at dramatic moments in the poem, the first in the opening canto of *Inferno* and the second toward the end of the final canto of *Purgatory.*

In the first canto of the poem, just before Dante meets Virgil, who will lead him through Hell and to the summit of Mount Purgatory, where Beatrice will take over as guide, he is impeded by three beasts—a leopard, a lion, and a she-wolf—each more terrifying than the last. Only after the insatiable wolf has forced Dante back down to where "the sun is silent" does Virgil come forth from the shadows to rescue the Italian poet. Because the malevolent creature "lets no [one] pass her way," Virgil tells his frightened companion that they must make another journey: to escape the dark wood and climb to safety and salvation, Dante must first descend through the eternal circles of Hell, where he "shall hear despairing cries" of the damned. As for the wolf, Virgil foresees a time when a *veltro,* or "greyhound," will come and hunt her down in every city and village, finally destroying her and driving her back to Hell, from where envy had set her loose. This heroic hound, Virgil explains, will feed not on land or material possessions but on "wisdom, love, and power."[14]

While most medieval and Renaissance commentators interpreted Dante's prophesied *veltro* as an unidentified future leader—a messianic emperor or pope—if not Christ at the Second Coming, later critics proposed more specific answers to the riddle. The most widely held choice for this greyhound was Cangrande della Scala, Dante's host in Verona (1312–1318) and great hope for political renewal (*cangrande* means "big dog"), but other popular candidates ranged from Pope Benedict XI (died in 1304) and Emperor Henry VII of Luxemburg (died in 1313) to the Great Khan of the Tartars and even to Dante himself.[15] Some readers, invested more in using than in explaining or analyzing the poem, eagerly expanded the field to include names beyond those known to Dante and his medieval world. Searching for leaders from later times who in some way fulfilled Dante's prophecy, they entertained historic figures like Martin Luther (1483–1546), King Victor Emmanuel II (1820–1878), Giuseppe Garibaldi (1807–1882), and German Emperor William I (1797–1888).[16]

Soon after Mussolini seized the reins of power, fascist partisans exalted him as Dante's prophesied savior, the *veltro* who will slay the she-wolf and deliver "humble Italy" from evil.[17] One true believer who drew this line from Dante's hero to Mussolini was Giovanni Giuriati, a decorated veteran of World War I and participant in D'Annunzio's takeover of Fiume who marched on Rome in 1922 and served as a *gerarca*, or "hierarch"—a top official— in the fascist party. Writing on March 10, 1923, Giuriati professed "absolute faith" in his leader, declaring to Mussolini, "you are the 'Greyhound' prophesied by Dante."[18] In his memoirs written after the fall of the regime twenty years later, Giuriati reflected on how his faith in Mussolini as the embodiment of Dante's political philosophy was rewarded when the Duce succeeded where others had failed in resolving "the Roman question." For Giuriati, the Lateran Accords—the agreement signed in 1929 between the Vatican and Italy's fascist government—gave hope that Mussolini was "the man predestined to reunite in Rome, according to Dante's thinking, the two sacred symbols, the Cross and the Eagle," figures in *Paradiso* of religious warriors and just rulers. Mussolini's achievement would "therefore put to flight, not only from Italy, but from the face of the earth, moral and civil disorder, heresy and war."[19]

Giovanni Giuriati's emphasis on the cross and the eagle was not surprising. Luigi Valli had constructed an influential interpretation of the entire *Divine Comedy* around these two symbols in the early twentieth century. Inspired by a series of mystical studies of Dante's work by the poet Giovanni Pascoli, Valli came to see the "symmetry of the Cross and the Eagle" as "the fundamental theme that is secretly repeated in almost every passage of the Sacred Poem."[20] Dante's verses, in Valli's reading, convey the "secret" message that humankind's redemption requires both the Christian cross and the imperial eagle. In Dante's day, as in Valli's, this eagle was weak if not entirely absent. Domenico Venturini, who wrote the book on Dante and Mussolini from a profascist perspective, naturally saw the Duce as the incarnation of this missing emperor. He was not only the standard-bearer of the new political order but also the defender of the church, a role Dante assigned to the supreme earthly ruler. By raising again the banners of the "White Cross on a red background" and the "Roman Eagles," Mussolini was the strong ruler— lacking in the Middle Ages and even during the Risorgimento—destined to fulfill Dante's ideal of two suns: worldly and spiritual leaders as independent but complementary powers, each deriving its authority directly from God.[21] The Lateran Accords, Mussolini's achievement in reconciling church and state, would therefore have been "fully approved by Dante."[22]

Venturini, like Giuriati and other fascists, worshiped Mussolini as the "undisputed figure of the Greyhound, the liberator and restorer of Italy" foretold by Dante.[23] While also accepting the conventional identification of this messianic *veltro* with Cangrande della Scala, Venturini believed obstacles prevented the poet's champion from accomplishing his mission. Dante's prophecy could only be realized when the time was right and with the right leader. Instituting reforms not for personal gain but on behalf of the nation, freeing citizens from corrupt leaders, bringing peace by ending factional fighting, celebrating the glories of ancient Rome—such were the signs by which Mussolini's followers saw him as Dante's prophesied savior of Italy.

The second major prophecy in the *Divine Comedy*—truly a "difficult riddle," as Dante put it—gave fascist apologists even more reason to identify Mussolini as the answer to the poet's prayers.[24] In the Earthly Paradise atop the Mountain of Purgatory, Dante stages an allegorical representation of the historical relationship between the church and the empire. After an eagle, emblem of the empire, attacks the chariot of the church and leaves feathers inside it (symbolizing the papacy's harmful encroachment in secular matters), the chariot morphs into a terrifying monster, and Dante sees a lascivious, "disheveled harlot" (Pope Boniface VIII and malevolent successors) seated astride the beast. The harlot and a giant (King Philip the Fair of France) begin kissing until the giant, angered by his lover's wandering eye, beats her and drags her into the forest, violent acts signifying Philip's abuse of Boniface (leading to the pope's death in 1303) and the relocation of the papacy from Rome to Avignon, in southern France, by Pope Clement V in 1309.[25] Beatrice then offers a brainteaser no less bewildering than the strange events whose consequences it is meant to explain:

> The eagle that left its feathers on the car
> so that it first was monster and then prey
> shall not remain without an heir forever.
> For I see clearly and do thus declare:
> stars already near at hand promise us a time
> safe from all delay, from all impediment,
> when a Five Hundred Ten and Five,
> sent by God, shall slay the thieving wench
> and the giant sinning there beside her.[26]

Interpretations of this "Five Hundred Ten and Five," God's instrument of justice to free the world of the wicked harlot and giant, varied in specificity and believability. One popular—and reasonable—approach began by converting the Hindu-Arabic numerals (500, 10, 5) to their Roman equivalents, the letters *D, X,* and *V.* With some rearranging, combined with knowledge that *V* and *U* are interchangeable in Latin, advocates of this method arrived at a meaningful sequence, the word *DUX,* or "leader." Many critics, beginning with Dante's earliest commentators, drew from the usual pool of suspects to identify this heir to the eagle of imperial Rome. Cangrande and Henry VII often topped the list, with the Ghibelline leader Uguccione dalla Faggiuola also receiving votes.[27]

Domenico Venturini, by contrast, found Dante's *DUX*—a savior "sent by God"—in "any remarkable political luminary who, according to the circumstances of the time, achieves a magnificent transformation that brings the two powers [secular and spiritual] back within the sphere of their proper jurisdiction and defends the rights of the Church."[28] For Italy in the early twentieth century, Dante's heaven-sent leader, or *DUX,* could only be Mussolini, "our magnificent Duce."[29] Two days after Mussolini and Cardinal Pietro Gasparri (Vatican secretary of state) signed the Lateran Accords, Pope Pius XI told professors and students at the Università Cattolica del Sacro Cuore in Milan that to reconcile the Italian state and the Catholic Church, "perhaps, too, a man was needed like the one Providence had us encounter."[30] The pope's suggestion that God lent a hand to the agreement by supplying a political leader freed from the constraints of liberal democracy was reported and amplified by Italian newspapers, cementing the conviction that "only Mussolini, and Fascism, had made it possible."[31] This sentiment, not to mention the accords themselves, greatly concerned not just Italian Jews and other non-Catholics but anyone who believed the church had compromised its moral authority by giving its imprimatur to Mussolini's regime. Conversely, papal recognition of Mussolini's privileged role was music to the ears of diehard fascists like Venturini, who praised the Duce as "truly the man destined by Providence to bring to fruition the long awaited reconciliation in relations between the Church and the State."[32] In this worldview, Mussolini incarnated Dante's prophesied savior—symbolized by the greyhound and the *DUX*—not only as the great reconciler of the Italian nation and the Roman Catholic Church but also as the restorer of Italy's imperial aspirations.

Dante firmly believed the world was best served by a powerful and just emperor, with the Roman people rightfully filling the office of this ruler, whose authority came directly from God—this is the threefold argument of his Latin treatise, *Monarchia*. Mussolini, like Dante, "cherished the splendors of the Roman Empire."[33] The fascist dictator looked to classical Rome as the foundation of Italian glory and the model of a new civilization with Italy at its center. He appealed to national pride by presenting fascism as the modern realization of the "myth of Rome" across a broad swath of the Italian cultural landscape, from architectural, archeological, and engineering projects to monuments, exhibitions, and athletic events.[34] A spectacular example of this fascist *romanità*, the Via dell'Impero, or "Avenue of the Empire" (now Via dei Fori Imperiali, or "Avenue of the Imperial Forums") opened on October 28, 1932, the ten-year anniversary of the March on Rome. Connecting the Colosseum with Mussolini's headquarters in Piazza Venezia, this renovation symbolically joined the city of the emperors with the capital of fascist Italy, whose emblem—the *fasces,* or bundled rods with an ax head—represented ancient Roman authority.

Mussolini's imperialist politics played a major role in his foreign policy. Nowhere was this more evident than in Italy's invasion and colonization of Ethiopia. In his declaration of war on October 2, 1935, Mussolini exploited his compatriots' desire to avenge the devastating defeat at Adwa in 1896 and to overcome the alleged injustices that deprived Italy of enjoying "a little place in the sun" by expanding its colonies in Africa. "With Ethiopia we have been patient for forty years," Mussolini shouted; "enough now!"[35] Italian forces needed decisive victories, and soon, to back up their leader's warmongering, and they employed brutal methods to defeat the overmatched army of Emperor Haile Selassie. These included imprisonment of noncombatants, summary executions, indiscriminate bombing, even shelling and spraying Ethiopian soldiers and civilians with mustard gas and arsine, a poison gas made from arsenic.[36] By tolerating (when not ordering) such barbaric measures, even while projecting a sanitized version of the war to the Italian public and the rest of the world, Mussolini more closely resembled Machiavelli's pitiless prince than Dante's righteous monarch.

On May 9, 1936, four days after the fall of the Ethiopian capital of Addis Ababa, Mussolini announced Italy's victory from the balcony of Palazzo Venezia to a crowd of over four hundred thousand cheering supporters filling the piazza and streets below. The only note of suffering Mussolini mentioned in his short speech was the blood shed by Italians in their conquest. "Italy finally has its empire," he proclaimed:

> A fascist empire, because it bears the indestructible signs of the will and power of the Roman fasces, because this is the goal toward which the irrepressible but disciplined energies of the young, vigorous Italian generations have been directed for fourteen years. . . . The Italian people created the empire with its blood. It will enrich the empire with its works and defend it against any and all with its arms. In this supreme certitude, O legionnaires, raise high your banners, your blades, and your hearts to salute, after fifteen centuries, the reappearance of the empire upon the fateful hills of Rome.[37]

Mussolini spoke of an "Empire of peace"—*Impero di pace*—that waged war only when dictated by "peremptory, uncompromising necessities of life."[38] But this was only a pretext for subjecting native populations to unspeakable violence so that Italy could have its "little place in the sun" like other colonial powers. Dante, in stark contrast, championed empire as a source of peace not through conquest and occupation of foreign lands but through concord born of unity, with the emperor guiding humankind "to temporal happiness in conformity with the teachings of philosophy" and the pope leading humankind "to eternal life in conformity with revealed truth."[39]

The vast gulf separating these two imperial agendas hardly prevented fascists from claiming the poet's blessing for Italy's colonial ventures in East Africa. On the contrary, they enthusiastically transformed the Zona Dantesca—a major renovation of the area around Dante's tomb—into a monument to Italy's fascist empire. This tribute to Dante—also called the "Zone of Silence" (Zona di Silenzio)—was inaugurated on September 13, 1936, the 615th anniversary of his death. Following on the heels of Italy's conquest of Ethiopia, it inspired Italians to turn once again to Dante for legitimation, this time as the voice of the nation's imperialist ambitions. Giuseppe Frignani, a fascist deputy from Ravenna, fully appreciated the timing of the presentation of Dante's renovated gravesite to the public. In this year of empire, "Italy will come once again to bow before Dante," he wrote, "bearing the gift of accomplishments made in his name and in his honor according to the will of the Duce."[40]

Grotesque distortions of Dante's ideas and values aside, Mussolini's regime made good on its exaltation of the poet by funding and facilitating this major overhaul of his tomb's surroundings.[41] Corrado Ricci, the esteemed archeologist and art historian from Ravenna who had spearheaded the examination of Dante's bones in 1921, also played a major role in this chapter of the poet's graveyard history. As Ricci's reputation rose in the 1920s and 1930s—he established Italy's Institute of Archeology and Art History (L'Istituto Nazionale di Archeologia e Storia dell'Arte) in 1922, serving as its president over the next twelve years—his devotion to Dante's burial site in Ravenna never wavered. A supporter of Mussolini's regime, Ricci was named to the Italian Senate in 1923 and signed the "Manifesto of Fascist Intellectuals" ("Manifesto degli intellettuali fascisti") written by Giovanni Gentile, former minister of education under Mussolini, in 1925.[42] Even after moving to Rome, Ricci continued to exert unmatched influence on any proposal aimed at altering the buildings, grounds, and monuments surrounding Dante's mausoleum in Ravenna. He had strong opinions in these matters, and they carried substantial weight with local and national decision-makers—from the mayor all the way up to Mussolini himself—particularly after fascists assumed control of Ravenna's municipal government in 1923.

Architectural modifications to the Church of Saint Francis in 1921, the six hundredth anniversary of Dante's death, sought to re-create its presumed appearance when the poet's funeral took place there in the early fourteenth century. Since the church had been thoroughly remodeled in the late 1700s, these renovations largely entailed the removal or modification of eighteenth-century elements to produce a neomedieval style. Similar aesthetic criteria were applied to the Palazzo della Provincia, the large public building constructed along the southern side of Piazza Byron before it was renamed Piazza San Francesco. Palazzo Rasponi, an eighteenth-century palace remodeled into the luxurious Hotel Byron in 1888, had originally stood in this spot. Purchased by a socialist cooperative in 1918, the palace was burned to the ground by fascist *squadristi* led by Italo Balbo and Dino Grandi in the summer of 1922. Giulio Ulisse Arata designed the new building with late-Byzantine features, including alternating rows of arched and rectangular windows and a monumental portico topped with inverted pyramid-shaped blocks, harmonious with the Romanic façade of the church.

The Palazzo della Provincia, erected in 1925–1928, did not completely satisfy Corrado Ricci. But neither was it the disaster he feared would destroy the feeling of "mystery and respect" proper for Dante's tomb, "the most holy place not only in Ravenna but in all Italy."[43] Structures on the other side of the piazza were far more offensive. Santi Muratori, director of Ravenna's

Classense Library, shared his friend's fervent hope that the tomb area would recapture the sacred aura it had possessed "before the little shops of Piazza Byron became the Beehive, the Beehive expanded into a wine bar and beer garden, and small tables filled all the space in front of San Francesco, where they put on concerts and all the rest."[44] Photographs from the time depict a gritty hodgepodge of run-down structures, from the conspicuous watering hole—its main purpose, *Birreria,* announced in big block letters—and a modest fur shop (*pellicceria moderna*) to a plain brick wall displaying a large advertisement for Fernet-Branca *digestivo,* a popular *amaro,* or "bitter" after-dinner drink.[45] Marring the elegiac mood were not only houses, shops, and entertainment venues but vehicular traffic—wagons and automobiles—that flowed into the city and passed right in front of the tomb. This unsuitably rowdy and noisy environment made the strongest case of all for expanding what Ricci as early as 1924 called *la zona di rispetto*—"the zone of respect"—around Dante's gravesite.[46]

Renovations to the area around Dante's tomb aimed primarily at isolating it from traffic and noise. Ricci outlined the problem—and how to fix it—in a detailed reflection written on November 6, 1932. He complained most of all about the crowds and vehicles traversing the street in front of the mausoleum and disrupting the silence. The small road was so busy because of a basic feature of Ravenna's urban design: people from outlying villages and towns,

12.1. *Birreria* in Piazza Byron (Istituzione Biblioteca Classense)

12.2. Fur shop in Piazza Byron (Istituzione Biblioteca Classense)

12.3. Aperitif advertisement (Istituzione Biblioteca Classense)

including Forlì to the southwest, were funneled into the city along roadways that converged on the street passing in front of the little chapel. To make matters worse, an outdoor market was held twice a week in the neighboring Piazza Dante Alighieri (now Piazza Giuseppe Garibaldi), filling this street with a mess of vehicles (cars, vans, trucks, carts), chattering shoppers, and shouting merchants along with dust and mud—"all in all, a disgrace that the Head of Government and the leading citizens would like to see removed."[47] The solution, according to Ricci, was to reroute traffic by widening Via Angelo Mariani between Piazza Dante Alighieri and Via Giuseppe Mazzini (now Via Corrado Ricci) and by enlarging Piazza Byron to handle vehicles moving to and from Via Alfredo Baccarini, Via Girotto Guaccimanni, and Via Massimo D'Azeglio.

These renovations, in turn, required other changes—the demolition of the incongruous Beehive bar and unsightly modern houses on the northern side of Piazza Byron facing Dante's mausoleum—while maintaining the area's artistic and historical integrity. To this end, Ricci insisted that the small wall of the convent bordering the chapel preserve its "Franciscan humility," with no new building allowed to dominate the temple housing Dante's sepulcher, "a small structure, yes, but famous because individuals like Vittorio Alfieri, Ugo Foscolo, and others entered it and knelt before the tomb."[48] The architect Gustavo Giovannoni's proposal to create a more peaceful, reverent atmosphere by removing incompatible buildings and increasing green space accordingly met with general approval, though his plan to tear down Camillo Morigia's "little temple" and replace it with a more monumental home for Dante's tomb horrified Ricci. The senator was greatly relieved when, during a congressional meeting on December 6, 1927, Mussolini pulled him aside to say that "he would never, on any account, permit the demolition of Dante's chapel, which had become glorious from such a long history."[49] The Duce himself visited Ravenna and reviewed the planned renovations in the summer of 1932. At that time, he approved the work plan and authorized a significant financial contribution from the government toward its completion. Records from 1933 show a payment of four million lire (over US$268,000) toward the project. From this point forward, the fascist regime embraced the proposed improvements to the area around Dante's tomb, stressing the importance of honoring the poet as the "prophet of the Empire and precursor of Fascism."[50]

Authorities anticipated and promoted the creation of this "Dante Zone" or "Zone of Silence" by declaring a special holiday in the poet's name—a Sagra

Dantesca—in 1932, one year before work began on the project. For this popular pilgrimage, which became an annual event, special trains at reduced fares were dispatched from towns and cities up and down the Italian peninsula to bring Dante's worshipers to Ravenna. Mussolini's supporters naturally put themselves front and center at these commemorative events. Covering the Dantean holiday in 1933, one local newspaper (*Corriere Padano*) observed that "the most elite representatives of fascist Italy marched in an interminable procession before the humble tomb in which the ever alert genius of the poet-founder of Italianità—the first to give explicit, eloquent expression to the feeling of the common national destiny of the people—watches over the future of the Nation."[51] The groundbreaking ceremony took place that year on the anniversary of Dante's death. To dispel any doubt about the fascist regime's propagandistic appropriation of Dante for imperialist purposes, Mussolini donated a statue of Julius Caesar to Ravenna for the occasion.

Corrado Ricci, the most influential force behind the renovations, was given the honor of delivering the keynote speech before a large, pennant-waving crowd in Piazza San Francesco. "Today, finally, by the will of the Duce," he announced, "we inaugurate work aimed at removing the sounds of traffic (unconscionably disrespectful) from the tomb where Dante rests—work not of frivolous pomp but of reverent devotion."[52] Ricci reassured his enthusiastic audience that the words "zone of respect" (*zona di rispetto*) were never more appropriate because they really mean "zone of silence" (*zona di silenzio*), "and silence is the most profound expression of reverence."[53] To foster this atmosphere of respectful silence, Via Dante Alighieri and Via Guido da Polenta, the small streets running in front of the chapel, were closed to traffic, which was diverted to other roads that were widened or reoriented. On the northern side of Piazza San Francesco, close to where the noisy Beehive bar and other eyesores once stood, Casa Rizzetti, a Renaissance palazzo that had once housed Lord Byron and later Ricci's own family, was refashioned in a mixed style of original (sixteenth-century) and modern elements.[54] Renamed Casa Oriani, after a nineteenth-century writer viewed as a patriotic prophet of fascism, the palace became the home of the Mussolini Library (Biblioteca Mussolini), a repository for publications pertaining to the fascist movement and regime.[55] Designed "to evoke and celebrate the figure of Dante Alighieri," the Zona Dantesca was a cultural project, not just an artistic one, and Corrado Ricci was the center holding together its disparate parts.[56] Ricci, who died on June 5, 1934, would have rejoiced knowing that nearly all the changes he advocated came to pass by the time the scaffolding was removed and the area was inaugurated on September 13, 1936, exactly 615 years after Dante's death.[57]

A vast and varied horde of fascists—male and female, young and old, professionals, artists, other workers—descended on Ravenna to attend the inauguration that Sunday. Welcomed by residents waving flags from windows, the visitors filled all the local establishments. The list of prominent fascists and other authorities gathered at the Palazzo del Governo included the vice secretary of the party (Renzo Morigi), the commander of the armed forces of Bologna, provincial officials, the Archbishop of Ravenna (Antonio Lega), Senator Luigi Rava and other senators and deputies, representatives of Florence and Rome, the president of the Società Dante Alighieri (Felice Felicioni), and scores of other civic, religious, and military leaders. Thousands of voices raised a powerful cry of "profound gratitude to their Leader, whose name was invoked in irrepressible demonstrations of faith and enthusiasm."[58] With Italy flexing its colonialist muscles following the conquest of Ethiopia four months earlier, organizers strove to highlight Dante's role as a prophet of the empire and hence of Mussolini's achievement. "By one of those coincidences that always accompanies great events," observed one journalist covering the ceremonies, the renovated area "around the Tomb of the Poet who sang of the Empire was inaugurated in the first year of the Italian empire founded by the Duce."[59]

Piazza San Francesco was "packed beyond belief" when Arrigo Solmi, Mussolini's minister of justice, arrived to inaugurate the Zona Dantesca on behalf of the fascist government.[60] Ordered to salute Mussolini as if he were there in person, the crowd responded in one loud voice: "Duce!" Giovanni Cottignola, Ravenna's mayor, introduced Minister Solmi by offering his city's gratitude to Mussolini for "creating more worthy surroundings for the tomb that holds the mortal remains of the immortal Poet, who finally has peace today after seeing Italy achieve its greatness and affirm its strength."[61] Solmi followed in the long tradition of Italian ministers with strong academic backgrounds, in his case as an accomplished historian of law and political thought whose prodigious scholarly output included essays and a book on Dante.[62] In an article on Dante's political treatise (*Monarchia*), Solmi praised him as the precursor of Mussolini, whose fascist regime—through its 1929 accords with the Vatican—achieved the poet's vision of harmony between political and ecclesiastical powers. Dante, for this scholar and minister, was "the supreme, unsurpassed, sublime initiator of the new greatness of modern Italy."[63]

Solmi showed off some of this erudition by inaugurating the renovation of Dante's burial site in the name of Mussolini's imperial enterprise: "Ravenna, the imperial city, rich in glorious memories and resplendent with eminent monuments, today consecrates a dignified area of art, science, and silence surrounding the venerable tomb of the Divine Poet. And it consecrates it in this epic moment of our history, when by the brilliance of the Duce, by the valor of the victorious Italian arms, by the harmonious will of the nation, the unshakable foundation of the new Empire—Italian and fascist—has been laid for the defense of civilization."[64] By giving "final refuge" to Dante, Ravenna enabled the "great and ill-fated singer of the Empire" to bring his "sacred poem" to completion.[65] Dante's imperial vision arose from the divisions and ruins of medieval Italy, a dire situation inspiring him to see, as Solmi put it, "in the unity of the peninsula—what he called 'the garden of the Empire'—the fulcrum needed for the universal expansion of Roman, Christian civilization."[66]

Solmi highlighted the role of his fascist government in helping Ravenna, which "held and defended Dante's precious mortal remains with jealous pride," to free the poet's gravesite of the encumbrances of urban life—the unsightly buildings and noisy traffic—that compromised its solemn function.[67] He saw it as a propitious sign that Romagna, the region of Italy that opened the way for Caesar when Justinian brought the Empire back to Italy in the sixth century, was also the birthplace of Mussolini, "the genius of the race, who raised up again the sign of the Lictors (*fasces*) and renewed human values in the virtues of struggle and sacrifice."[68] In this light, the new Mussolini Library was but the latest milestone on a historical journey stretching from the Roman Empire cherished by Dante down to the idea of empire "kindled

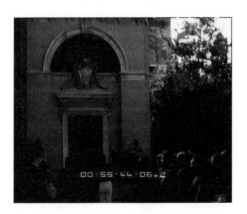

12.4. Still from newsreel footage of Minister of Justice Arrigo Solmi giving the fascist salute at Dante's tomb, September 13, 1936 (Archivio Storico Luce)

by the genius of a Son of this fertile and prodigious land—an idea that, fulfilling in its emerging lines the Dantean goal, has replenished Italy and restored its ancient power, enabling it yet again to save the treasures of the spirit and the forms of civilization."[69]

Dismissing the League of Nations' condemnation of Italy's colonial war in Ethiopia as the "hostility of fifty-two nations united against justice," the minister of justice declared that "Italy seeks peace but is ready for every challenge."[70] In peace or war, Solmi boasted, Italy "has its tutelary gods, among whom Dante has held a high place for centuries." With these words, he officially inaugurated the Zona Dantesca "by order of the Duce in the august name of His Majesty the King and Emperor," as the crowd, cheering wildly, again shouted salutes to the Duce.[71] Newsreel footage shows Minister Solmi and his entourage right after this rousing speech, their traditional black shirts set off by white pants, as they walk briskly through the renovated historic area. Giving and receiving the fascist salute along the way, Solmi passes Casa Oriani, site of the Mussolini Library, and soon arrives at Dante's mausoleum. There he again raises his right hand, this time facing the bronze doors given by Rome in 1921, a salute at once to Mussolini and to the poet who dreamed of a very different kind of earthly ruler. Soon after the inauguration of the Zona Dantesca on September 13, 1936, Italian moviegoers heard a young female voice introduce official news coverage of the event by announcing, "Fascist Italy has created by the will of the Duce a zone of silence and respect around the tomb of the prophet of the empire and divine poet."[72]

13

Dante's Roman Temple

The Building we wish to construct must not be primarily a Museum or
a Palace or a Theater but a *Temple*.

        —GIUSEPPE TERRAGNI

• Dante's contribution to fascist empire-building would have gained even
greater prominence had Giuseppe Terragni and Pietro Lingeri's architectural
plans for the Danteum—a veritable temple to the poet in Rome—come to fruition before war broke out in 1939. This homage to Dante was the brainchild
of Rino Valdameri (1889–1943), a lawyer from Milan who had marched on
Rome with other fascists in 1922. Valdameri also commissioned a deluxe edition of the *Divine Comedy* (illustrated by Amos Nattini), personally contributing four and a half million lire (about US$236,700) toward its production
and publication. Mussolini received the first volume (*Inferno*) in 1936, and Valdameri presented the second volume (*Purgatorio*) to the Duce in a private
audience on February 9, 1938, in anticipation of Hitler's visit to Italy later that
year.[1] Hoping to have copies of the Dante volumes sent also to Hitler and to
organize exhibitions of the work in Munich and Berlin, Valdameri expressed
confidence to Dino Alfieri, minister of popular culture, that he would succeed in his plans owing to "the cult of the Divine Poet, Hitler's beliefs, and
the fervent political climate in Germany."[2] Hitler soon received Nattini's illustrated edition. Returning the favor, the Führer presented his Italian
counterpart with an edition of the *Divine Comedy* in Karl Witte's acclaimed
German translation made specially for the meeting of the two leaders held
in Rome on May 3, 1938. Partially through this exchange of Dante gifts, Mussolini and Hitler marked the alliance between fascist Italy and Nazi Germany, formalized in the Pact of Steel a year later (May 22, 1939).[3]

 Valdameri used his considerable influence in the art world as director of
the prestigious Brera Academy of Fine Arts in Milan to promote fascist ideals.

Above all, he saw great potential in employing "the art of architectural propaganda" to help Mussolini stamp his imperial vision on Rome, much as Augustus Caesar had done nearly two thousand years earlier.[4] By the time Valdameri proposed the Danteum to Mussolini, he had secured the financial backing of Alessandro Poss, a Milanese industrialist who had accumulated vast wealth in the textile sector. Guaranteeing a personal contribution of two million lire (about US$105,200) to the project, Poss accompanied Valdameri to the audience with Mussolini in Palazzo Venezia at 6:30 p.m. on November 10, 1938. Also present were the two architects, Terragni and Lingeri, whose plans for the building drew a favorable response from the Duce. On the basis of the success of their drawings, they were given the green light to construct a model of the Danteum.[5]

Giuseppe Terragni (1904–1943) and Pietro Lingeri (1894–1968) were well-known exponents and practitioners of the rationalist style of architecture then in vogue. Inspired by the work of the Swiss architect Le Corbusier (pseudonym of Charles-Édouard Jeanneret), Italian rationalism in the 1920s and 1930s celebrated simple geometric forms, transparency (with ample use of glass), and functionality.[6] Mussolini famously declared on June 20, 1929, that fascism, as "a glass house in which everyone must and can see one another," had no place for corruption and opportunism among its members.[7] Terragni's Casa del Fascio in Como, built in 1932–1936, exemplified this architectural metaphor through the open spaces of its façade and the abundance of glass and other reflective materials covering surfaces of its interior. If physical transparency in Como's party headquarters and other fascist buildings bolstered the regime's claim to accountability by encouraging public access, it less benignly subjected individuals to the gaze—and therefore control—of the regime and its leader.[8]

Before taking on the Danteum, Terragni and Lingeri had collaborated on project proposals in several architectural competitions, including those for the Monument to the Fallen in Como (1925–1926) and the Palazzo del Littorio in Rome (1934 and 1937). The Italian Movement of Rationalist Architecture (Movimento Italiano Architettura Razionalista), to which both men belonged, held a major exhibition in Rome in 1931. During the inauguration on March 30, organizers presented Italy's dictator with a copy of their official manifesto. It opens with the obsequious line, "Mussolini wants an art of our time, a fascist art."[9] Rather than stating aesthetic principles and criteria of the rationalist movement, the manifesto reads like a political statement seeking to curry favor with the fascist regime as it began to reject rationalist

13.1. Model of the Danteum, front view
(Courtesy of Attilio Terragni@
Archivio Giuseppe Terragni, Como)

13.2. Model of the Danteum, top view
(Courtesy of Attilio Terragni@
Archivio Giuseppe Terragni, Como)

architecture in favor of a more monumental, neoclassical style. Signatories of the rationalist manifesto—fifty young architects in all—made their case by accusing the "old architects" of "transforming Italy into a museum of itself." Believing that fascist architecture must reflect "the Revolution's character of nationalism, power, and pride," they belittled their predecessors for embodying an unacceptable "impotence."[10]

Terragni, Lingeri, and Valdameri proposed to erect the Danteum—not "a Museum or a Palace or a Theater but a *Temple*"—at a propitious time in a highly symbolic location.[11] Camillo Morigia's *tempietto,* or "little temple," solidified Ravenna's claim to Dante's bones in 1782, while Stefano Ricci's cenotaph in 1830—joined by Enrico Pazzi's colossal statue in 1865—celebrated the poet's Italian symbolism in his native city. The Danteum now promised to transform Dante's *Divine Comedy* into an elaborate three-dimensional allegory of Mussolini's imperial aspirations. This project, like Ricci's funeral monument in Florence, was empty of bones but full of meaning. A memorial to the poet and his work, the Danteum at the same time aimed to glorify the fascist dictator in the city Dante revered as the divinely ordained center of imperial power. During the inauguration of the Zona Dantesca in Ravenna, speakers hailed Dante as the prophet of Italy's new empire with the conquest of Ethiopia in 1936. The Danteum would complete this mapping of Mussolini's fascist empire onto the medieval poet's proimperial politics.

The renovations in Ravenna left Dante's mortuary chapel intact. The Danteum likewise posed no threat to the poet's remains and their final resting place. From an aesthetic and functional point of view, however, the proposed Roman temple to Dante was "best understood as a combination of tomb and cathedral," according to the academic architect Thomas L. Schumacher.[12] Even without Dante's bones, this temple—like Ricci's cenotaph in Santa Croce—would allow pilgrims to worship the dead poet and contemplate continuity between his worldview and contemporary events, in this case Italy's pretension to an empire under Mussolini.

The Danteum was to be completed in time for the world's fair planned for Rome in 1942, the twentieth anniversary of the fascist march on the Italian capital. (The Universal Exposition—known as "E42"—was canceled because of the war.) The building would have occupied prime real estate on the Via dell'Impero (Avenue of the Empire), which had been inaugurated in 1932 to mark the tenth anniversary of the march. Placed halfway between the Colosseum and Palazzo Venezia, this temple to Dante would have linked the most conspicuous sign of the Roman Empire to the seat of the new Italian

Empire founded by Mussolini. In Valdameri's "Statute for the Danteum" in 1938, he announced plans to erect "a Temple to the greatest of Italian poets on the Via dell'Impero in this epoch, in which the will and genius of the Duce are realizing the imperial dream of Dante."[13] Terragni, for his part, believed providence had chosen the Via dell'Impero as the site of the Danteum, a location that "could not be more spiritually suitable or prophetic."[14]

Considered by 1939 "without doubt the most talented and innovative modern Italian architect," Terragni took the creative lead in designing the Danteum.[15] Arguably his most original project, it impressed Le Corbusier at a retrospective of the Italian architect's work in 1949. While touring the exhibit, the master paused to comment on only one project. "This is the work of an architect," he reportedly said upon examining Terragni's conception of the Danteum.[16] Such high praise was indicative of Le Corbusier's acceptance of Terragni as "a friend": "one of my comrades in arms in our great battle for pure art."[17] The "Relazione," or project proposal, shows how this architect "midway in the journey" of his life—Terragni turned thirty-five on April 19, 1939—sought to convert Dante's poem of the afterlife into a monument to fascist Italy's empire and its leader. Like other public buildings designed by rationalist architects, the Danteum combined modern and monumental styles in accordance with "fascist values of the intransigent, imperial, organic state."[18] In form and function, Terragni's temple to Dante sought to glorify Mussolini as the incarnation of the poet's messianic emperor.

Let us imagine Terragni's Danteum had been built and we are visiting it during the world's fair in Rome in 1942.[19] Walking along Via dell'Impero from Piazza Venezia toward the Colosseum, we enter the structure on the left-hand side of the avenue. Directly across the road stands the Basilica of Maxentius, an architectural homage to Emperor Constantine from the early fourth century celebrating the alliance of the empire and the church. Because Constantine, the first Christian emperor, had triumphed under the sign of the cross, fascists viewed the basilica as a testament to religiously sanctioned military might.[20] We proceed through a narrow passageway between a massive outer wall of the Danteum on our left and, on our right, a parallel, stand-alone wall made of one hundred marble blocks (one for each canto of the *Divine Comedy*), their size proportionate to the length of the canto. The exterior of this stand-alone wall—the side on the Via dell'Impero directly across from the Basilica of Maxentius—displays verses from the poem referring or alluding to the Roman Empire, written on blocks corresponding to the cantos in which they appear. An "immense blackboard or monumental tablet," this inscribed wall, like the facing basilica, illustrates "the lesson of the universality of the Roman Empire" exalted by Dante.[21]

Turning the corner around the outer wall on our left, we double back along a pathway to an open space evoking Dante's life before his otherworldly journey. This courtyard faces a large portico populated with one hundred thick, evenly spaced columns. Terragni's conception of the Danteum incorporated elements he had used in two tombs in the cemetery of Como and in other funeral monuments. His temple to Dante, like the earlier works, featured stone blocks and columns that "never lose their concreteness to become idealized into an abstract world."[22]

Walking through this marble forest, symbolic of the "dark wood" of sin and error in which Dante is lost at the midpoint of his life, we approach the main rooms on the lower level, beginning with a library filled with "everything that could be of use to Dante scholars."[23] After passing through a dark corridor—the antechamber of Hell—we enter the Inferno room. The space, like the entire Danteum structure, is shaped like a golden rectangle, the ratio of its long side to its short side equal to phi. This geometric figure, as popular with Le Corbusier, Terragni, and other modern architects as it was with the ancients, has the symbolic, aesthetically pleasing property of producing another golden rectangle, ad infinitum, every time a square whose sides are the length of the short side of the rectangle is removed.[24] In designing the building in whole and in part according to the golden mean ratio, Terragni sought to emulate Dante's use of symbolic numbers (principally 1, 3, 7, and 10) in the "wondrous structure of the Divine Poem."[25] He also paid homage to the Basilica of Maxentius across the road by having the long side of the Danteum equal in length to the short side of the basilica, itself proportioned according to the golden mean ratio. Constantine's basilica was therefore a golden rectangle generating Dante's (smaller) golden rectangle, Terragni's way of interweaving the "imperial theme" through "the entire fabric of the Danteum."[26]

The Inferno hall contains seven columns representing the seven deadly or capital sins, an arrangement only partially true to Dante's vision: while most if not all of these sins are somehow punished in his underworld, they are not the realm's organizing principle, as they are in Purgatory. The columns divide the room into square blocks derived from the successive division of golden rectangles, the diminishing size of the squares proportionate to the columns' diminishing thickness. The spiraling arrangement of the blocks imitates the spiraling course of "Dante's journey through the abyss of Hell

13.3. Danteum Project, Inferno Room, watercolor panel (Courtesy of Attilio Terragni@ Archivio Giuseppe Terragni, Como)

and the Mountain of Purgatory."[27] Centered on the diminishing squares, the columns support parallel blocks in the ceiling, which is perforated by slits allowing scant illumination in the infernal room. Enveloping visitors in a "spiritual atmosphere of astonishment," these features evoke "that feeling of catastrophe—of pain and of useless aspiration to gain the sun and light—that we often find in the doleful speeches of the sinners interrogated by Dante."[28]

True to Dante's conception of the afterworld, Terragni's room dedicated to Purgatory, which we reach by ascending a short staircase, mirrors the infernal space. The seven squares generated from golden rectangles are repeated on the floor of the purgatorial room but in reverse order, thus encouraging us to spiral in the other direction, just as Dante spirals up and around the Mountain of Purgatory.[29] Counterbalancing—or correcting—the dark, heavy atmosphere of the preceding space, the purgatorial room is empty of columns

13.4. Danteum Project, Purgatorio Room, watercolor panel (Courtesy of Attilio Terragni@ Archivio Giuseppe Terragni, Como)

but filled with "abundant light from the wide bands of sun that burst through the ample openings in the ceiling." The room seeks "to create around visitors a salutary feeling of comfort by directing their gaze to the sky."[30]

After climbing a set of stairs to the top floor, we traverse another corridor, this one divided into two pathways separated by a stone wall running down the middle of the length of the space. This long, narrow room represents the Terrestrial Paradise or Garden of Eden at the summit of the Mountain of Purgatory in the *Divine Comedy*. Within this idyllic place, where humankind experienced the pinnacle of earthly happiness, Beatrice prophesies the coming of the "Five Hundred Ten and Five" identified by commentators as a messianic emperor or political leader needed to contain and balance the power of the papacy—the sort of providential savior fascist students of Dante believed Mussolini to be.[31] The poet famously lamented that his world lacked an effective emperor invested with divine authority to guide humankind "to temporal happiness in conformity with the teachings of philosophy." Terragni therefore dedicated the Danteum's Earthly Paradise to the poet's "imperial conception."[32]

Walking the length of the room, we reach the far wall, where we come face-to-face with an engraved eagle inspired by Dante's glorification of righteous rulers in *Paradiso*. Performing like a marching band in the sky, these celestial spirits in the Heaven of Jupiter exhort their earthly counterparts to pursue justice by spelling, one letter at a time, the opening line of the biblical Book of Wisdom, "Diligite Iustitium Qui Iudicatis Terram" (Love justice, you who judge the earth).[33] With the movement of some souls and the addition of others, the final letter *M* morphs into an eagle, the symbol of Jupiter and the Roman Empire. The eagle in the Danteum's imperial space fulfills and evokes this sign, the first letter of *Monarchia,* the title of Dante's treatise on the empire. For Terragni and other fascists, the empire's champion in their place and time is the leader, or Duce, whose name begins with this letter. Mussolini famously initialed documents he had reviewed with a large *M,* as he did upon reading Valdameri's "Statute for the Danteum."[34] In the Danteum, a temple to Dante and to fascism, this *M* "would have served as a triumphal arch, as a monument, as the seal and signature of the fascist era."[35]

As in other fascist interpretations of Dante's work, Terragni's Danteum coupled the imperial eagle cherished by the poet and the Duce with the Christian cross. While the room representing Dante's (and Mussolini's) imperial designs culminated in the figure of the eagle, this long, tight space—the "longitudinal spine" of the building—was one of two perpendicular corridors "needed to complete the figure of the Cross" as it points "to the crystalline square of Heaven."[36] If the building functioned in part like a cathedral or church, then the imperial room was the central nave, with the Mussolini-like eagle at its end rising like a crucifix above the high altar of Dante's temple.

After contemplating the *M*-shaped eagle in honor of Dante and Mussolini, we turn around and, passing back through the room dedicated to the empire and the Earthly Paradise, arrive in the Room of Heaven, the Celestial Paradise. Here we are dazzled by light mirrored and multiplied by thirty-three glass columns, one for each canto of *Paradiso*. This modern, rationalist space exploits the resplendent nature of Dante's celestial kingdom—a realm infused with sparkling spirits, luminous spheres, and divine light—to represent the controlling transparency of fascism, the "glass house" extolled by

13.5. Danteum Project, Paradiso Room, watercolor panel (Courtesy of Attilio Terragni@
Archivio Giuseppe Terragni, Como)

Mussolini. We finally exit the building by descending the long stairway from
Heaven that deposits us smack in front of a large monolith alongside the monumental wall inscribed with Dante's imperial verses that we passed on our
way into the Danteum. This single block of stone stands for Dante's prophesied
veltro, the heroic greyhound that fascists thought their leader embodied.[37]
Our visit to the Danteum thus ends as it began, with the glorification of
Dante in the name of the Duce, and vice versa. In and around this Roman
temple to Dante, all roads lead to Mussolini.

Following Germany's invasion of Poland on September 1, 1939, Terragni
was called up for military duty. He still participated in architectural matters
through letters and articles, but the Danteum became a lower priority as the
conflict escalated and Italy joined forces with Germany, declaring war on
England and France on June 10, 1940. Valdameri and Poss continued to press
Mussolini on pursuing the project, though with diminishing likelihood of
success, while Lingeri carried more of the creative load in Terragni's absence,

as seen in the wooden model he built (on a scale of 1:50) in early 1940.[38] Terragni fought in Yugoslavia in the spring of 1941 before going to Russia as part of the Italian contribution—the CSIR, or Corpo di Spedizione Italiano in Russia (Italian expeditionary corps in Russia)—to Operation Barbarossa, Germany's ill-fated assault on the Soviet Union launched on June 22, 1941. Terragni rose through the ranks during this ferocious campaign, serving as lieutenant in an artillery unit on the front lines before being promoted to captain in the spring of 1942.

Terragni fought in the Ukraine with his Italian comrades—often alongside German soldiers—witnessing and participating in bloody battles and horrific killings. While the soldier-architect reveled in the "unforgettable days" and "supreme happiness" of military success against enemy soldiers, his letters from the front also placed him nearby or at the mass murder of Jews, Ukrainians, and Russians at the Babi-Yar ravine (seventy-two to eighty thousand shot to death) and other locations around Kyiv, Vinnitsa, and Stalino (now Donetsk). Although Terragni's friend and protégé Luigi Zuccoli wrote that the bloodbath took a heavy toll on his physical and mental state, his documented approval of the Nazi-fascist denigration of Jews, Slavs, and communists—culturally (even architecturally) as well as politically and militarily—argues against the notion that he was outraged or distressed by the systematic murder of civilians and prisoners with Italian complicity if not involvement.[39]

There is little doubt, on the other hand, that Terragni was traumatized when he returned from a reconnaissance mission to discover that a bombardment had wiped out his entire unit soon after he left them. Suffering a severe mental and physical breakdown, Terragni was hospitalized in the Ukrainian city of Voroshilovgrad (now Luhansk), and after arriving in Italy on January 20, 1943, he endured up to nine rounds of electroshock therapy at the military hospital in Cesenatico, a town just south of Ravenna on the Adriatic coast. Visiting Terragni the day after his arrival in Cesenatico, Zuccoli was shocked to find his friend convinced that he had deserted his comrades and would be shot. Back in Como, where he had lived and worked for most of his adult life, Terragni collapsed while climbing the stairs of the house where his fiancée awaited him. He died, probably from a cerebral hemorrhage, at age thirty-nine on July 19, 1943.[40]

14

Wartime Perils

I was in agony lest Dante's tomb be blown to bits.

—ANTONIO FUSCONI

• Rome was bombed the same day that Giuseppe Terragni died—July 19, 1943—for the first time in the war. Over five hundred American aircraft dropped a thousand tons of bombs, devastating the neighborhood of San Lorenzo and killing up to fifteen hundred civilians in addition to destroying airfields, railway yards, and other military targets.[1] Six days later, in the small hours of July 25, 1943, the Fascist Grand Council voted to transfer leadership of the war effort to Victor Emmanuel III. The king informed Mussolini at their afternoon meeting that Marshal Pietro Badoglio would replace him as prime minister.[2] The deposed Duce was immediately arrested and whisked from the capital, first to the island of Ponza (between Rome and Naples) then to La Maddalena (off the coast of Sardinia) and finally to the Campo Imperatore hotel and ski resort on the mountain of Gran Sasso high in the Apennines.

The fascist fantasy of a Roman temple to Dante and imperial Italy vanished with Terragni's death and Mussolini's fall from power in 1943. The Danteum therefore joined an illustrious group of unrealized architectural monuments to the poet from earlier times—the "excellent tomb" pledged by Guido Novello in 1321, the "large, magnificent, honorable" mausoleum proposed by the Florentine Council in 1396, the "lasting monument" to Dante in the Duomo sought by Cristoforo Landino in 1481—culminating in the "worthy tomb for the divine poet in an honorable place in this city" offered by Michelangelo in 1519.[3] Besides leaving Terragni's Dante temple forever stalled in the design stage, the Second World War had serious—nearly fatal—consequences for the poet's physical remains.

Even before the Badoglio government announced Italy's surrender to the Allies on September 8, 1943, German troops began streaming into the peninsula, subjecting the population of their partner-turned-foe to harsh occupation as they fought American, British, and other Allied forces.[4] After German paratroopers freed Mussolini from his prison-resort on September 12, Hitler kept Italian fascism alive and useful to the Nazi war effort when he split the nation in two by installing the Duce as head of the Repubblica Sociale Italiana (RSI) in northern Italy. Better known as the Republic of Salò, after the town on Lake Garda that was home to several of its ministries, Mussolini's rump state sought in vain to recapture the aura of the early fascist era while waging war on the growing Italian resistance movement. As the military contest for control of Italy intensified, so too did Anglo-American bombing raids on towns and cities, especially across the north-central region of the country. Bologna alone was hit over ninety times in the second half of 1944, the bombardments claiming more than two thousand lives in addition to inciting fear and inflicting heavy structural damage.[5]

Ravenna, located on the Adriatic coast about fifty miles east of Bologna, was also targeted by Allied aircraft. Under Nazi-fascist control as part of the Republic of Salò, Ravenna was bombed on December 30, 1943, the first of over thirty aerial attacks before the city was liberated nearly a year later. Planes began attacking just after one o'clock in the afternoon. One bomb hit the Basilica dello Spirito Santo, a five-minute walk from Dante's tomb. Others killed fifteen civilians and injured over forty more.[6] This initial raid rattled Dante's graveyard history without directly impacting the poet's mortal remains: Santi Muratori, the esteemed director of Ravenna's Classense Library who chronicled many episodes in the life of Dante's bones, including their exhumation in 1921, died of a heart attack at age sixty-nine after a large bomb exploded in front of his house.[7] The second major bombardment, on March 22, 1944, badly damaged buildings in the heart of Ravenna but took fewer lives.[8] This raid convinced city leaders to remove Dante's bones once more—and soon—from their original marble sarcophagus. Like the Franciscan friars in the sixteenth century who stole the bones to preserve them, custodians of the tomb during World War II took drastic measures to safeguard Dante's remains. But instead of a Florentine-papal plot to repatriate the exiled poet's bones, local authorities this time feared that American and British warplanes might pulverize them with a powerful bomb dropped on the "little temple" housing the tomb.[9] Unlike the friars who relocated Dante's remains in 1519 and the officials who exhumed them in 1921, the poet's guardians did not extract and view the individual bones in 1944. They simply took the lead-encased walnut coffin from the marble tomb and hid it, intact, in a safer place outside the building.

Antonio Fusconi, the faithful "watchman" of Dante's tomb since 1921, described the destruction wrought by the Allied bombing. "During World War II, Ravenna was blasted in air raids," he recalled. "Many bodies lay in the streets and the smoky atmosphere was haunted by the wails of the living." Fusconi renewed these memories for Walden Garratt, an American poet and English teacher who visited Ravenna after the war. "I was in agony lest Dante's tomb be blown to bits," he told Garratt, adding how he and two assistants one night "opened Dante's sarcophagus, removed his casket, and buried it in the adjoining garden."[10] Fusconi probably exaggerated his role in the removal of Dante's remains—a decision made by Ravenna's mayor, prefect, and superintendent of monuments—but his account to the American visitor is largely consistent with the documented version of events.[11]

On March 23, 1944, one day after the aerial bombardment, several men removed the heavy lid of Dante's marble tomb and lifted out the container holding his bones. Never opening the lead box, much less the enclosed walnut casket, they placed it inside another container, this one made of steel, its sides over half an inch thick all around. In the meantime, workers dug a large round hole—over eleven feet deep and six and a half feet in diameter—in the garden between Dante's mortuary chapel and the Quadrarco of Braccioforte. Protected by wood, lead, and steel cases, the poet's bones were then lowered into the hole, and a thick layer of cement was poured over the steel top. Dante's guardians took a final precaution before the rest of the hole was filled and a reinforced concrete cone was set above the provisional grave and covered with dirt and grass: they buried the relocated bones "deeply beneath a decoy coffin which bore the dust of some unknown."[12] To be precise, they placed a metal casket containing an unknown person's remains several feet above the cement slab covering Dante's well-sealed bones. They resorted to this extreme measure because a bomb dropped on the tomb by an American or British warplane was not the only nightmare scenario. They also feared that occupying German troops would raid the poet's grave and confiscate his remains. This was no idle threat as the Nazis accelerated their pillaging of Italy's artistic heritage in Tuscany in 1944 and set their sights on Ravenna.[13] Fusconi and others therefore aimed "to trick the Nazis" by burying another casket in the same hole above Dante's triple coffin. Looters who grew suspicious of the fresh mound and decided to investigate would presumably stop their search upon finding this "decoy coffin," thus leaving Dante's bones in peace.[14]

This peace was precarious, however, as Allied bombs continued to rain down on Ravenna. On March 30, 1944, one week after the removal and concealment of Dante's bones, Cardinal Luigi Maglione, the Vatican secretary of state, wrote to British and American officials on behalf of the Archiepiscopal Curia of Ravenna and the Diocesan Delegate for Sacred Art. He implored the Allied powers not to destroy churches and other historic sites in and around Ravenna, including "Dante's tomb, ancient basilicas, baptisteries, and mausoleums of inestimable value." Recognizing how difficult it would be to avoid this "irreparable disaster for history and for art" if Ravenna were subjected to repeated aerial attacks, Pope Pius XII's foreign minister asked that, "in consideration of its treasures and its negligible military importance," the entire city "be spared Allied bombardment."[15]

The papacy's plea fell on deaf ears: Allied warplanes hit Ravenna hard and often during the summer and early fall of 1944, with three "lethal nighttime bombardments" (August 25, September 4, and September 9) wreaking much of the death and destruction.[16] As feared, Ravenna's famous churches and monuments paid a high price. Many damaged buildings stood within a half-mile radius of Dante's original tomb and his temporary gravesite, including the Cathedral of Ravenna (Duomo), the Basilica of Sant'Agata Maggiore, the Church of San Domenico, the Basilica of Sant'Apollinare Nuovo, the Basilica of San Vitale, the Basilica of San Giovanni Evangelista, the Basilica of Santa Maria in Porto, and the cloisters of the Classense Library. Not even the Church of Saint Francis, located just behind Dante's gravesite, came away unscathed. In addition to these partially damaged sites, the Church of San Vittore, about a mile from Dante's tomb, was reduced to rubble—only the bell tower was left standing—during the nighttime attack of September 4, 1944.[17] As foreseen by Vatican minister Maglione in his letter to British and American officials, harm to old churches and other historic buildings packed in such close quarters was an inevitable result of bombing Ravenna from the air.

Because bombs dropped from planes during the war were notoriously inaccurate, collateral damage was most often to blame for destruction of the city's architectural treasures. By the time Allied forces began launching raids on Ravenna, "top Air Force commanders in Europe were reluctantly coming to the realization that what they had been weaned on during the 1930s, the cherished concept of precision bombing, was proving to be unattainable."[18]

The Basilica of San Giovanni Evangelista suffered the consequences of this imprecision when bombs intended for the nearby train depot instead crashed through the apse and destroyed a side chamber of the church.[19] In some instances, however, the Allies actually targeted historic buildings because the occupying Germans, indifferent to Ravenna's architectural heritage and civilian population, gathered troops and equipment in these locations to protect themselves and inflict maximum harm on their enemies. Warplanes dropped a dozen incendiary bombs and one fragmentary bomb close to the Basilica of Sant'Apollinare in Classe, just outside the city, blowing out windows and doors of the rectory and setting it ablaze. The sixth-century Byzantine church, famous for mosaics that had inspired Dante's Paradise, was itself badly damaged after the Germans drew fire from the British by placing heavy artillery all around the building.[20] Less than three miles from Dante's tomb, German soldiers took positions in and around the Basilica of Santa Maria in Porto Fuori. On November 5, 1944, a Sunday, the church "was reduced to a pile of ruins." Having sought shelter in the bell tower, nine civilians were killed in the attack, including the mother and aunt of Don Mario Mazzotti, the parish priest (he was also an archeologist) whose diary provides precious details on this and other Allied bombardments.[21]

Dante's camouflaged (temporary) gravesite escaped the bombing and looting that cast a pall over Ravenna during the war. "All turned out well," Antonio Fusconi reflected, and the poet's bones, sealed within their lead-encased walnut casket, were returned to the original marble sarcophagus in the mortuary chapel.[22] This re-entombment occurred seven months after the end of the war in Europe (May 8, 1945) and over a year after the liberation of Ravenna (December 4, 1944). Dante's remains had lain in protective exile for nearly twenty-one months. "Under this mound they rested safely," a commemorative plaque informs visitors to the location where they had been buried, "from March 23, 1944 until December 19, 1945."

If the Nazis never planned to violate Dante's tomb and desecrate his bones, the same cannot be said of hardcore Italian fascists toward the end of the war. As Dante's body fueled nationalist fervor at the advent of fascism, so his mortal remains also helped sound the regime's death knell. The man behind the final episode in this fascist chapter of Dante's physical afterlife was Alessandro Pavolini, a well-to-do Florentine intellectual and provocateur who bound himself to the fascist movement from its origins in violent *squadrismo* and the March on Rome to its grim demise at the end of World War II. Rising quickly through the fascist ranks, Pavolini became federal secretary of the

14.1. Mound under which Dante's casket was protected from bombardment and looting during World War II (Photo: Elisa Valentini, July 2016)

Florentine *fascio* in 1929 and moved to Rome in 1934 after his election to the Italian parliament. His stock soared when Galeazzo Ciano, Mussolini's son-in-law, took him under his wing during the war in Ethiopia. Back in Italy, Pavolini joined the regime's upper echelon through his association with Ciano, who was appointed Italy's foreign minister in 1936. Pavolini succeeded Dino Alfieri in 1939 as minister of popular culture, a portfolio that included oversight of media and propaganda. When the deposed Mussolini resurfaced as head of the Republic of Salò in 1943, he appointed Pavolini secretary of the Fascist Republican Party. As ruthless as he was erudite, Pavolini created the *brigate nere* (black brigades), a militia that collaborated with the Nazis to fight Italian partisans. He also led efforts to prosecute members of the Fascist Grand Council (including his benefactor, Ciano) who had betrayed the Duce on July 25, 1943. They were executed on January 11, 1944.

Part of Italy's cultural elite (he edited literary journals and wrote novels), Alessandro Pavolini—whose brother, Corrado, was an accomplished critic, poet, and playwright—had a flare for the dramatic. He combined his passions for politics and spectacle in the conception and organization of *18 BL,* an extravagant display of Mussolini's call for a "theater of masses." In a speech to the Italian Society of Authors and Editors in Rome, the Duce had called on Italian dramatists to stage huge theatrical productions, spectacles requiring "a theater able to hold 15,000 or 20,000 persons." Mussolini made this proposal in his speech right after praising the *Divine Comedy*—"the greatest poem in Italian literature"—as an expression of the "suffering of Dante," whose "every fiber quivers with human passions, with the bitterness of exile, with love and hate." While Mussolini did not invoke Dante to make the case for his "theater of masses," the *Divine Comedy,* as the dictator urged theatrical works to do, had also managed to "stir up the great collective passions, draw inspiration from the sense of living, profound humanity, and bring onstage what truly matters in spiritual and everyday life."[23]

Pavolini sought to put Mussolini's vision into practice with *18 BL,* a massive play for a massive audience. Named for its titular heroine, the model of one of Fiat's first mass-produced trucks, the play was conceived at the end of 1933 and developed over the next four months. The starring truck served as an allegorical vehicle—"the fascist everyman and everywoman, a humble and heroic soldier as well as soldier carrier"—to raise the history of fascism "to the status of myth."[24] The three-act play told the story of this patriotic truck through World War 1, the fascist rise to power (culminating in the March on Rome), and Mussolini's major land-reclamation project (draining the Pontine Marshes). The show ended with the truck's death and burial but also the prophecy of its resurrection—in three days—and future service on behalf of the nation. Directed by Alessandro Blasetti, a thirty-three-year-old film director chosen by Pavolini, three thousand actors performed the two-hour play before twenty thousand spectators on the left bank of the Arno River across from Florence's main park (the Cascine) on the evening of April 29, 1934. While Pavolini's brainchild drew some favorable reviews "for its audacity and patriotic sentiments," the overall popular and critical reception of this "theater of masses for masses" was so negative—in some cases brutally so—that the performance was not repeated.[25]

In the spring of 1945, with the war lost and the Republic of Salò on the verge of collapse, Pavolini brought his fascination with mass spectacle to bear on the fascist regime's final act. Instead of producing a colossal outdoor play for an audience of twenty thousand citizens, he was now determined to assemble a force of that many (or more) "black shirts" in the Valtellina, a mountain valley near the Swiss border less than one hundred miles northeast of Milan. Fascist leaders and soldiers would make their last stand there and "die a heroic death after a legendary battle."[26] When Mussolini convened a meeting of fascist leaders and Nazi officers on April 14, 1945—the last formal gathering of the two groups—he introduced the acronym RAR, or Ridotto Alpino Repubblicano (Republican Alpine Stronghold), and called on the plan's author to fill in the details. Pavolini enthusiastically reported on progress to transfer provisions and several hundred *squadristi* (some with their families) to the Valtellina, with the promise of many more fighters to arrive in the days to come. Seeking to ensure their legacy and inspire future generations, the fascists would leave a lasting impression by fighting to the bitter end. Valtellina, in Pavolini's poetic reflection, would be "Fascism's Thermopylae," site of the epic last stand of a small contingent of Spartan soldiers against the much larger Persian army in 480 BCE.[27] They would share these final, dramatic days with the outside world by broadcasting radio transmissions from the redoubt and having an airplane drop copies of their newspaper (produced in the stronghold) on Italian cities. Pavolini's plan included a small but significant additional detail: he proposed having Dante's bones brought from Ravenna to the Valtellina so that fascism could go out in a blaze of glory accompanied by the remains of "the greatest symbol of Italianness."[28]

Lost in a fog of delirium and denial, Mussolini seriously considered Pavolini's wish for the fascists to sacrifice themselves—along with Dante's bones—in the fortified valley. Other listeners responded coolly and skeptically to the plan. Marshal Rodolfo Graziani, Mussolini's minister of defense (and former viceroy of Ethiopia), rejected it outright, while General Heinrich von Vietinghoff, commander of the German army in Italy, snidely remarked that if the Italians were so invested in this project, they should have begun it much sooner. Undeterred, Pavolini repeated his fervent plea for a heroic finale when Mussolini and his highest-ranking officials gathered in Milan on April 25, 1945, to debate their next move. While Mussolini still may have been inclined to stage a final act of resistance in the Valtellina, Graziani and many others decided the only viable option was to negotiate terms of surrender or to plan their own escape. Upon hearing Pavolini announce that twenty-five thousand men would soon arrive in Como on their way to the stronghold, the marshal lost his cool in Mussolini's presence. Calling the plan "illusory and undoable," he accused Pavolini of "continuing to lie right up to the final moment." "It's foolish and childish to continue to deceive the Duce," he scolded his colleague.[29]

Pavolini's proposal to include Dante's bones in his grand fascist farewell was no more realistic. Even if he had convinced a band of loyal men to execute the operation, they would have faced formidable obstacles in taking possession of the poet's skeletal remains. Upon removing the cover from Dante's marble tomb, they would have found, as Florentine emissaries to Ravenna had discovered in the early sixteenth century, that someone else had already removed the bones. To recover them, the grave robbers would have had to know to break through the reinforced concrete cone (covered in dirt) in the garden outside the mortuary chapel. After discovering a metal casket holding the remains of an unknown individual and coming upon a concrete slab, they would then have had to decide to dig deeper. Only after smashing the slab would they have found the steel cage containing Dante's lead-encased walnut coffin. Even if Pavolini's men had somehow managed to get this far, they would still have had to transport the poet's bones from Ravenna, a liberated city, to the fascist stronghold near the Italian-Swiss border nearly 250 miles away. The odds of stealing Dante's remains and getting them to the redoubt would have been slim indeed.

Pavolini's far-fetched, ill-conceived proposition was arguably a logical conclusion to the fascist cult of Dante. Emblematic of the regime's delusional state in its final throes, it also underscored fascism's potent if perverse idolization of the poet from start to finish. Mussolini, we recall, inaugurated the fascist political party in Dante's name, using him to legitimate the movement's "animating principle."[30]

Whatever strategy Mussolini thought to follow when he left Milan on the evening of April 25, 1945, he ultimately abandoned plans for a "final glorious immolation" with his most devoted followers in the Valtellina.[31] Wearing a German army overcoat and helmet to disguise his identity, he sought to escape Italy by passing through the partisan-controlled area around Lake Como on the way to safety in Switzerland. The ruse did not work. Mussolini was captured on April 27 when partisans stopped his convoy outside the village of Dongo on the lake. Mussolini, then sixty-one years old, and Clara ("Claretta") Petacci, his thirty-three-year-old mistress, were executed the next day by communist fighters led by Colonel "Valerio" (Walter Audisio) and "Guido" (Aldo Lampredi) outside the lakefront Villa Belmonte at Giulino di Mezzegra.

Alessandro Pavolini, meanwhile, had departed from Milan in a separate convoy the day after Mussolini left the city. Leaving Milan along Via Dante early in the morning of April 26, Pavolini led over four thousand fascists north to Como. By the time Mussolini ran into the partisan roadblock outside Dongo, Pavolini was riding with the Duce, Claretta, and fifteen other fascists in the same armored car. After Mussolini was identified and arrested,

Pavolini staged a final act of resistance. Shouting, "I'm not a coward, I want to die well," he dove out of the car and came up shooting before jumping into the lake. While his comrades surrendered or were captured, Pavolini continued fighting—sustaining wounds to his face and thigh—until partisans fished him out of the water and took him with the other prisoners to Dongo. Soon after killing Mussolini and Claretta on April 28, Colonel "Valerio" took the remaining sixteen prisoners, Pavolini at their head, to face the firing squad. Right before the order to open fire, Pavolini—theatrical to the end—yelled, "Viva l'Italia!"[32]

Pavolini's threat to desecrate Dante bones in the name of fascism never came to fruition. Mussolini's dead body, by contrast, endured a level of abuse worthy of the poet's law of *contrapasso*—fitting punishment for sin—under Italy's new political order. After being mauled, shot repeatedly, and suspended from a steel girder like a butchered animal carcass, Mussolini's corpse was buried in Milan's Musocco cemetery. Rejoicing antifascists danced on his grave, and one woman went so far as to urinate on it. On Easter morning of 1946, two days before the anniversary of Mussolini's death, the hardcore fascist Domenico Leccisi and two accomplices dug up the body, wrapped it in canvas, and wheeled it out of the cemetery in a gravedigger's cart. Leccisi stored the decomposing cadaver in at least three different locations over the next year—first in the Valtellina, the area near the Swiss border where Pavolini had urged Mussolini to make a glorious last stand—before authorities recovered the body and brought it to Cerro Maggiore, a Franciscan convent outside Milan. Mussolini's corpse remained there for eleven years, its location known only to a few insiders. On August 30, 1957, an entourage of friars transferred the remains to the San Cassiano cemetery in Predappio, Mussolini's hometown. The day after a memorial mass attended by his widow, Rachele, and a group of neofascists, he was buried in the family crypt.[33]

Toward the end of the twentieth century, a period of historical revisionism in which fascist and partisan offenses too often received equal moral weight, Mussolini's tomb welcomed around one hundred thousand visitors a year. Robust sales of his portrait and other souvenirs showed that the Duce's body was "still selling briskly."[34] Dante's bones, meanwhile, had been resting undisturbed less than thirty miles away in the poet's original tomb after their reburial on December 19, 1945, four months before Leccisi stole Mussolini's body. But even as Dante's remains lay dormant, traces of his physical afterlife announced themselves at the end of the millennium. The world learned then of another piece of the poet's graveyard history, one even more bizarre than the thefts, concealments, discoveries, exhumations, and reburials of his bones. Excluded from the official record (for good reason), this leg of Dante's postmortem journey is less known and more difficult to navigate than previous ones. Fittingly for a poet whose majestic *Divine Comedy* looks back and builds on earlier episodes while propelling the protagonist—and readers—forward through the circles of Hell, terraces of Purgatory, and spheres of Paradise, these final chapters wind back through the national and regional campaigns of earlier pages as they elevate Dante to a one-name global icon.

Three

Relics of Return and Renewal

15

Dante Dust

Earth to earth, ashes to ashes, dust to dust.

—BURIAL SERVICE, *THE BOOK OF*
COMMON PRAYER

On July 20, 1999—a Tuesday—stories with eye-catching headlines ran on the first page of Italy's three major newspapers. "Found by chance an envelope with Dante's ashes," announced *Corriere della Sera*, while *La Repubblica* opted for the terse "Dante, his forgotten ashes." *La Stampa* took a more poetic angle by riffing on the final verse of the *Inferno* with "And Dante sees the stars again: missing ashes found."[1] The news was big enough to warrant additional coverage in separate articles inside the three papers. Wanda Lattes, writing for *Corriere*, explained what all the fuss was about: "Yesterday afternoon the director of the National Central Library, Antonia Ida Fontana, presented to the press, with great solemnity, the small envelope believed to contain a portion of Dante Alighieri's ashes."[2] Director Fontana, accompanied by a library colleague, Antonio Giardullo, had held the press conference on Monday afternoon, just a few hours after the discovery of the "noble memento" that had been missing since its display in 1929, seventy years earlier. The director was "extremely excited," Lattes observed, and she insisted on revealing right away that "the relic appeared almost by chance among the second-floor bookshelves in the area reserved for rare manuscripts, among 17th-century books containing illustrations of the world's most beautiful cities." Underscoring the impact of the discovery, Fontana acknowledged that "this was a very emotional moment for everyone, a new source of pride for the library and for Dante's native city."[3] One Italian commentator noted the beauty of finding the relic of the author of the *Divine Comedy*, perhaps the world's greatest travelogue, among books on travel. That Italy had lost the relic in the first place—and may not even have known it had gone missing—just confirmed that Italians "are a nation of poets and navigators," he wrote, "but also, let's face it, greatly disorganized people."[4]

Agenzia Giornalistica Italia (AGI), then Italy's main source for breaking news, scooped the major papers by carrying the library director's announcement on the same day that she made it. Reuters (in English, French, and Spanish), the Associated Press, the German Press Agency, and the People's Republic of China's Xinhua News Agency also reported the discovery on July 19, 1999, a news day dominated by military developments in Iraq and Afghanistan and the sorrowful reclassification of efforts to find John F. Kennedy Jr., Carolyn Bessette-Kennedy, and Lauren Bessette following their plane crash from "search and rescue" to "search and recovery." While Italy debated the significance of the discovery of Dante's ashes, wrote one of Italy's best-known journalists several days later, "in America they are scattering in the sea those ashes, for which the entire world grieves, of John John and his companions in flight and in death."[5]

Under the telegraphic title ("Dante–Florence, Found after 70 Years Portion Ashes Poet"), the AGI article gave essential information on the relic and how it was found. That morning, while conducting a routine review of the library's collection of rare books and manuscripts, two workers, Carmela Santalucia and Giuseppe Capecci, came across a large brown envelope holding something hard. Its unusual appearance and numbering prompted them to look inside. "And we saw a frame," recounted Santalucia, whose illustrious namesake—Saint Lucy—Dante revered as his patron saint of sight (her name means "light") owing to his own struggle with eyestrain and Lucy's symbolism as a purveyor of God's illuminating grace.[6] The workers immediately brought the strange object to the library's administrative offices. One can imagine the tumult of emotions everyone felt—surprise, confusion, excitement, joy—upon viewing the contents.

Within a simple black frame, like aged photographs under glass, were not one but two strange items allegedly related to the discovery of Dante's bones in 1865. Centered at the bottom was the small packet or envelope. Measuring seven by eleven and a half centimeters—smaller than a three-by-five-inch index card—the envelope contained only "a few grams of grayish material."[7] Writing on the outside stipulated that in Ravenna on June 9, 1865, "the enclosed dust was gathered from the mat on which lay the wood box and the bones of Dante Alighieri."[8] Someone evidently collected some material—here called dust (*polvere*), not ashes (*ceneri*)—from the cloth or mat (*tappeto*) on which Dante's bones and the broken box that had held them were laid out

15.1. Relics donated by Enrico Pazzi to the National Central Library of Florence in 1889
(Biblioteca Nazionale Centrale di Firenze)

after their discovery on May 27, 1865. Saturnino Malagola, the notary who certified the authenticity of the official report on that discovery, wrote this note on "the enclosed dust." He not only signed his name but, to guarantee the note's veracity, used his professional title ("notaio in Ravenna") and stamped his notarial seal—in blue ink—on the envelope.

Although Malagola does not say who collected these small particles, evidence from several related "relics" points to Enrico Pazzi, the sculptor who was riding high following the unveiling of his colossal statue of the poet in Florence less than two weeks before the discovery of Dante's bones. A native of Ravenna, Pazzi (born 1818) had lived and worked for so long in Florence that reports on the opening of Dante's tomb (June 7) and the reburial of his bones (June 26), both of which he witnessed, identify him as a current resident of the poet's native city.[9] He died and was buried in Florence in 1899. Pazzi was close not only with leading citizens of Ravenna—notably Mayor Gioacchino Rasponi and his brother Senator Achille Rasponi—but also with prominent Tuscans. He owed his commission for the Dante statue largely to the support of Luigi Paganucci, president of the Florentine committee that selected him, and he numbered Atto Vannucci and Giambattista Giuliani among his "illustrious friends." Pazzi later sculpted the monument to Vannucci displayed in the Basilica of Santa Croce's Salviati Chapel.[10]

These Tuscan representatives conspired with Pazzi as collaborators or witnesses in the gathering of relics. Most alarming, Vannucci, Paganucci, and Giuliani were part of the national commission, appointed by Minister of Education Giuseppe Natoli and headed by Giovanni Gozzadini, charged with verifying the facts of the discovery of Dante's bones. Chosen for their expertise and probity, these distinguished citizens were supposed to assure current and future generations that the investigation was conducted properly and its results accurately reported. Commission members were not supposed to join others in exploiting their position for personal gain by gathering or creating relics. For this improper if not illicit activity, Pazzi and his friends found a ready accomplice in Saturnino Malagola from Ravenna. The well-named notary ("Evil Throat") unsurprisingly agreed to vouch for the authenticity of their unauthorized relics. After all, he had picked up his own ill-gotten souvenir at the time of the discovery, though—as we saw in Chapter 10—Drs. Sergi and Frassetto doubted the bone fragment belonged to Dante when they compared it with the poet's exhumed skeleton in 1921.[11]

The other relic in the picture frame is even more unusual than the packet of grayish matter taken from the cloth on which Dante's bones and the wooden box had been placed. Set within a thin black border—a frame within the larger frame—sits a yellowed sheet of paper with writing above and below three brown streaks or blotches. These parallel markings appear about an inch wide and several inches long. The note at the top of the sheet says that on June 11, 1865, in the poet's mausoleum in Ravenna, "the patina of Dante's cranium was softened and impressed here." The three dark marks were made, we are told, from pressing the paper on Dante's skull after the patina—the brownish surface film—had been softened, most likely by wetting it. Luigi Paganucci, one of the three medical experts who examined Dante's bones in 1865, says he created these cranial impressions. The two doctors who wrote the anatomical report on the bones—Giovanni Puglioli and Claudio Bertozzi—signed as witnesses. That same day, June 11, 1865, they had examined and measured Dante's bones more accurately than they had been able to do on the day of the discovery (May 27), in part to confirm that the three phalanges found in the tomb on June 7 were indeed part of the skeleton.[12]

In the doctors' report, Puglioli and Bertozzi describe the technique Paganucci used to create the cranial impressions. After noting the varying color of Dante's bones—ranging from deep orange and dark red to an even darker shade, tending toward black—they observe that "when moistened paper was rubbed over them, it immediately picked up a rust-like color."[13] Dante's skull shares this color scheme with the other bones but with greater variation, its rust-hued foundation "covered here and there by much darker patches."[14] Paganucci must have taken the impressions while helping the doctors conduct their examination, the autumnal colors of Dante's cranium transferring onto the moistened paper. Consistent with the official report, this investigative procedure raises no red flags. Nor does careful documentation of the impressions, including a description of the work and signatures of those who performed or witnessed it, in this case Paganucci and the two doctors.

Other aspects of the cranial impressions and their fate tell a different story. Four more prominent Italians wrote their names just below the skull marks. Luigi Ciardi, a teacher of Dante's works who had Florentine roots, signed in large letters, followed by Giovanni Gozzadini, who added his title, president of the "commissione governativa," or national commission. Giambattista Giuliani and Atto Vannucci, Florentine friends of both Paganucci and Enrico Pazzi, rounded out the group. Since the commission was there to observe and report on the physical examination as part of its mandate, there was nothing wrong with having its members authenticate the sheet of impressions, as four of them did: Paganucci, Gozzadini, Giuliani, and Vannucci. Conspicuously missing, however, are the signatures of Mayor Gioacchino Rasponi and Count Alessandro Cappi, the only two commission members from Ravenna. Their absence alone may not indicate foul play by Florentine representatives and allies, but the document's disposition fuels suspicion. Other items related to the discovery and examination of Dante's bones, meticulously documented, were eventually returned to the original tomb or preserved for posterity in Ravenna's museums and archives. Paganucci and his accomplices instead transformed the cranial impressions from scientific evidence into relics for their own use.

Not by chance, they only made relics of the marks taken from Dante's skull, when the anatomical report suggests the technique had been used more generally during the examination. As the home of Dante's brain, the physical generator of his thoughts and their poetic expression, the cranium was the most precious part of his skeleton. Tangible signs of Dante's privileged skull bones were therefore also signs, however tenuous, of his mind and its glorious achievement. Given Ravenna's threats to Giovanni Gozzadini when he was entrusted with material scraped from the poet's tomb a few days earlier, the relic makers knew to keep the public from learning that the treasured item was in their hands. To maintain secrecy, they also kept their deed out of official reports. Yet they strove to guarantee its authenticity, perhaps to establish its value among a small circle of family and friends, perhaps also to demonstrate its validity to a future public less possessive of Dante's remains. So they had Saturnino Malagola, their trusty insider, exercise his notarial function by declaring "true and original" the signatures of Ciardi, Gozzadini, Giuliani, and Vannucci. He recorded the date—June 11, 1865—and stamped his official seal, again in blue ink, in three places on the document.[15]

Popular and elite audiences responded differently when library workers found the missing relics in 1999. Newspaper articles naturally hyped the story that a portion of the remains of Dante, the great poet of the afterlife who died in exile, had been found by chance—a miracle!—in the Florentine library. Conversely, renowned Italian professors—"Barons" (Baroni) as they are known to students and others within their fiefdoms—dismissed news of the discovery, doing nothing to counter the public perception of academics as tone-deaf if not arrogant. Cesare Segre, a cultural commentator and literary critic best known for contributions to the field of semiotics, declared himself wholly unmoved by the Dante relic, adding that he failed to understand "expressions of fetishism for the visible remains of a figure whose glory is the foundation of our culture, of our very soul."[16] Francesco Mazzoni, a distin-

guished Florentine philologist and the president of the Dante Society of Italy
for nearly three decades at the time of discovery, was initially more receptive. He welcomed the find as a promising sign for the Global Dante Conference planned for the following year (2000). But his mood quickly soured.
Two days after the announcement, he took issue with the library director's
characterization of the particles as *ceneri:* "Dante's ashes?" he queried, before
flatly denying that possibility: "They are only dust."[17]

Of course he was right in the narrowest sense. Dante's body had not been
cremated at his death. Nor had his bones later been burned, however much
some people would have liked, whether as punishment for heresy (Cardinal
Bertrando del Poggetto in 1329) or as a glorified symbol of Italy (Alessandro
Pavolini in 1945). And so, Professor Mazzoni and other learned commentators lectured director Fontana, "there simply could not exist ashes belonging
to him." Reminding everyone that "the remains of the Great Poet are still in
Ravenna," Mazzoni curtly dismissed the discovery and the sensation it caused
as a full-fledged "whopper" (*una bufala*).[18] But rather than clarifying a murky
semantic issue, experts sowed greater confusion and often came across as
churlish to boot.

Even a cursory review of the textual history of *cenere*—the sort of philo-
logical research at which the naysayers excelled—validates its use in describing
Dante's remains. Based on Classical writings, the *Oxford Latin Dictionary*
gives a definition of *cinis* as "ashes as the condition of the body after death
(whether cremated or not)." The application of the word to mortal remains
"whether cremated or not" persisted in later Latin usage. The Florentine humanist Giannozzo Manetti (1396–1449) urged his city to "cleanse herself of
infamy" and attain a measure of "glory and honor" by recovering Dante's *sa-
crorum cinerum,* or "holy ashes." When Latin *cinis* evolved into Italian *cenere,*
it brought along the meaning of uncremated mortal remains. Thus, Giovanni
Boccaccio, in his *Life of Dante,* described Ravenna as "like one great sepulcher of most holy bodies, and no part of her can be trodden on without passing
over ashes most reverend [*reverendissime ceneri*]." The *Vocabolario degli accademici della Crusca,* Italy's highest authority on linguistic correctness, gave its
stamp of approval, affirming that the plural form (*ceneri*) often means "the
remains of a buried human body." The term has long been used by informed
writers and speakers to refer to human remains, especially those of distinguished individuals, in an elegant and dignified (often poetic) manner. Even
Corrado Ricci, who knew more about Dante's skeletal and graveyard history
than anyone in the early twentieth century, referred to the particles collected

from the cloth on which Dante's bones had lain as *ceneri*.[19] All these people well understood that Dante's body had been buried, not cremated.

But were the particles gathered by Enrico Pazzi after the examination of Dante's bones even *ceneri* in the broader sense—physical remains of the poet—or were they "just dust," as Francesco Mazzoni and others insisted? Calling the material *polvere* (dust), notary Malagola made no such bodily claim in his description. To complicate matters further, *polvere*—like its English counterpart, *dust*—can also refer to the human body, usage supported by no less an authority than the Vulgate, the Latin translation of the Bible. The most humble, abject form of physical matter, dust is also a sign of creation and regeneration. "Quia pulvis es et in pulverem reverteris," says God to Adam in Genesis 3:19, translated in the King James Bible as "for dust thou art, and unto dust shalt thou return." From early in the Christian era, observes Cynthia Hahn, an expert in medieval relics, dust "finds its place above all as a base material that is collected and honored and then disseminated."[20] Both *ceneri* and *polvere*—"ashes" and "dust"—can therefore describe a person's mortal remains, even particles of uncremated bodies. The Church of England encapsulates the intimate relationship of these words in a memorable phrase from its burial service in *The Book of Common Prayer:* "Earth to earth, ashes to ashes, dust to dust." Lord Byron, no friend to either church, Roman or English, nonetheless appreciated the poetic beauty of their languages. The Basilica of Santa Croce in Florence, he reflected, was a place to worship great Italians of the past in hopes of a glorious future for the land and its people. As the final resting place of such luminaries as Michelangelo, Alfieri, Galileo, and Machiavelli, the church holds "ashes which make it holier, dust which is even in itself an immortality."[21]

The National Library in Florence was criticized for presenting its relic as a portion of Dante's *ceneri,* or physical remains, in the announcement of July 19, 1999, and took a more nuanced approach in displaying the item online a few weeks after the discovery. A webpage titled "Le ceneri di Dante" (Dante's ashes) anticipated the library's public exhibition of the Dante relic, along with manuscripts and printed editions of the poet's works, for the Jubilee in 2000. This year also marked the seven hundredth anniversary of the fictional date of Dante's journey to the afterlife (1300). Exhibit curators carefully framed the controversial item with commentary. While honoring Ravenna as the "indisputable guardian of the Great Poet's mortal remains [*resti mortali*]," they also imagined Dante's presence in the particles discovered in the Florentine library. The curators took on skeptics of the material's value by ambiguously labeling it "sediment from the remains of the Divine Poet (dust and bone-flakes)" that was collected from the cloth and the wood box during the assembly of the skeleton. Acknowledging that "no one has ever compared the ashes [*ceneri*] in the Florentine library with the bones in the tomb in Ravenna," they still concluded that "it is undeniable that the envelope held in the case preserves dust [*polvere*] of those bones."[22]

"Undeniable," no—though it cannot be ruled out that the "grayish material" in the envelope includes particles, however few and minute, of Dante's skeleton. At the very least, this possibility cannot be excluded without sophisticated scientific analysis, to which the "dust" has never been subjected. Offering to test the material after its discovery in 1999, an Italian geneticist, Bruno Dallapiccola, hoped that if there were traces of DNA, they would be preserved "until a gene for poetry is discovered." Director Fontana politely but firmly refused the proposal. Channeling diplomatic prowess worthy of previous protagonists in Dante's graveyard history, she argued that "to open the envelope at this stage would seem to her to denigrate the memory of the poet."[23]

Although the precise nature of these material traces—dirt, wood chips, cloth fibers, bone specks?—has never been scientifically determined, Dante's admirers treat them as objects of worship. Commentators on the Florentine packet of Dante dust and related items regularly call them "relics" (*reliquie*), often modified by other signs of piety: words like "sacred," "holy," "venerable," and "blessed" adorn the objects. For true believers, even if the mementos were tested and shown to contain "only dust"—pulverized pieces of the mat, perhaps the wood casket, but not Dante himself—they would still possess the power of sacred objects simply by virtue of having once touched him. This logic of veneration applies not only to parts of objects that once held the poet's bones—like the wood box and the cloth on examining tables (in 1865 and 1921)—but also to sheets of paper that took impressions of them. Anything that came into contact with Italy's ancestral father and prophet could qualify as a relic, its "holiness" magnified by Dante's reputation as a world-famous poet of the afterlife. Even if distinct from Dante's body, such items could be sanctified through mere contact with his venerated bones.

History has shown that faithful followers of acclaimed leaders, athletes, musicians, actors, and other celebrities often revere objects attached to their idols (clothing, equipment, anything autographed) during their lifetimes and even more so after they die. In the Christian tradition of relic veneration, "contact" or "secondary" relics hold a prominent place dating at least to the sixth century, when Pope Gregory the Great extended the meaning of *rel-iquiae* to encompass clothing and other objects that came into contact with the bodies or remains of holy persons.[24] Items believed to have touched Jesus's body were naturally the most venerable and sought-after sacred commodities. John Calvin, whose reforming theology vehemently opposed the Catholic veneration of relics, delighted in debunking a stunning assortment of these objects. Revered in one place—often in multiple places—were relics from Jesus's life and death, including all or portions of the manger, cradle, swaddling clothes, shirt, shoes, temple altar, water pots, and wine he had touched, with special devotion reserved for items from the Last Supper (table, bread, knife, plate, cup) and Crucifixion (cross, nails, spear, crown of thorns, tunic, sponge). Calvin directed his most acerbic barb at the "true cross," observing that if all its displayed pieces were gathered together, "they would form a whole ship's cargo," a cross that would take not one but over three hundred men to carry.[25] Or as William of Baskerville quips in *The Name of Rose,* Umberto Eco's novel set in the early fourteenth century, if all the fragments of the cross he had seen were authentic, "our Lord's torment could not have been on a couple of planks nailed together, but on an entire forest."[26]

To meet the increasing demand for relics—a required item for church altars—suppliers turned to the material legacy of saints. Contact relics included not only clothing and other items of daily life (rings, goblets, seats, books, cells) but also devices used for torture: "Crosses, chains, nails, iron claws, pincers, whips, stakes, gridirons, were all imbued with the merits of those who had suffered from them."[27] Martin Luther, consistent with his hostility to the church's use of indulgences, found these and other relics to be no more than cynical ploys to fleece the faithful: "One man claims to have a feather from the wing of the angel Gabriel, and the Bishop of Mainz has a flame from Moses's burning bush. And how does it happen that eighteen apostles are buried in Germany," he mocked, "when Christ had only twelve?" Calvin likewise derided saintly relics, arguing that their exhibition encouraged the faithful to venerate "bones, shifts, sashes, caps, and other similar trash" rather than the exemplary lives of "apostles, martyrs, and other saints."[28]

In some cases, worshipers collected dust from a saint's tomb through holes made solely for that purpose, while at Saint Peter's sepulcher in Rome, strips of cloth (*brandea*) lowered into the crypt became relics by virtue of having absorbed "divine power" emanating from the apostle's remains. No matter the relic's nature or source, some form of documentation was required to vouch for its authenticity. "Authorities," after all, "did not want the faithful venerating mistakes or frauds."[29] The collectors of Dante's contact relics well understood these rules. They produced a written record of the object—its quality, who gathered or created it, when and where it was taken—close in time to the event. Witnesses authenticated the document by adding their signatures (better if they were highly respected individuals) in the presence of a notary public who verified their identities with a brief statement and official seal.

Dante's singular place in the Italian imagination makes it unsurprising that he, too, served up relics—not just alleged pieces of his dead body but also objects that touched it—upon the discovery of his bones in 1865. Escaping notice in official reports, these prized items can nearly all be traced to the sculptor Enrico Pazzi and a web of accomplices present at one or more key moments during those fateful days, from the discovery on May 27 and the opening of the original tomb on June 7 to the examination of Dante's bones on June 11 and their reburial on June 26. A citizen of Ravenna residing in Florence, the sculptor of Dante's colossal statue outdid even the great Michelangelo—as well as Leonardo Bruni, Lorenzo de' Medici, Girolamo Benivieni, Pope Leo X, and other prominent Florentines—by allowing the poet's native city to retrieve traces of his mortal remains.

Florence may not have planned all along to repatriate these small traces of Dante's remains, but the poet's native city could not have devised a better long-term strategy to do so. If Vannucci, Giuliani, and others had in fact wanted to deceive the public in Ravenna, this was the way to go: gather relic materials, as Paganucci and Pazzi had done, and create documents with all the trappings of officialdom (signed witnesses, notarial seals) to establish authenticity and legitimacy, while making sure to keep this incriminating evidence out of the public record until the danger had passed.

16

Lost Treasure

Nothing prevents us from believing it may yet be found in some forgotten corner of the library itself.

—LUIGI FALLANI, LUCIA
MILANA, AND ANTONIO
GIARDULLO

Ravenna's citizens falsely accused Giovanni Gozzadini, president of the national commission, of attempting to steal residue of Dante's corpse scraped from his tomb when it was opened on June 7, 1865, but their suspicions were not entirely unfounded: Florentines and others did remove traces, however minuscule, of Dante's physical afterlife from Ravenna. Concerned citizens erred only in focusing on the tomb scrapings and in not keeping an even closer eye on the commission members and other VIPs with access to the bones and the sites of their discovery and examination. Worse, participants in the ethically dubious activity of gathering, authenticating, and removing relics were not only "foreigners" but leading citizens of Ravenna itself. What many feared most—the transfer elsewhere of even the smallest portion of Dante's remains or material intimately connected with them—turns out to have been an inside job. Several relics eventually made their way to Florence, where at least two—the packet of Dante dust and the cranial impressions—are still held today. The history of these objects, donated by Pazzi to the National Central Library of Florence, captures in miniature the wild course of Dante's physical afterlife.

The first published notice of Enrico Pazzi's relics was the library director's announcement of his "splendid donation" on August 15, 1889.[1] Desiderio Chilovi, like Pazzi, was a friend of Senator Atto Vannucci. In fact, Chilovi had the Florentine statesman to thank for his career. He worked for Vannucci at the Biblioteca Magliabechiana in 1861, becoming director of the library in

1879 before serving as head of the National Central Library of Florence from 1885 until his death in 1905.[2] Reminding readers that Pazzi was the "illustrious sculptor" responsible for the Dante statue in Piazza Santa Croce, Chilovi thanked and praised him for donating a rich assortment of items from the Dante centenary, including papers documenting work on the statue and the punch used for coining the commemorative medal designed by Pazzi himself. The "distinguished artist" would have deserved effusive gratitude even if he had given only these items, for they complemented the Dante collection that Chilovi was assembling for the library's planned new home in Florence. Recalling how the celebrations of Dante in 1865 had moved Italians "to solemnly affirm the unity of their country," he imagined the collection as the cornerstone of the library in its new location.[3]

But the Dante relics were far more precious than any documents or paraphernalia from the centenary events. Dust gathered by Pazzi and cranial impressions taken by Luigi Paganucci added a fresh if morbid dimension to the library's Dante collection. Fruit of Pazzi's "noble thought," these relics gave tangible, visual evidence of the poet's physical existence. They represented nothing less than "the image of Dante Alighieri himself," much as the holy relic of a saint—part of a body, an object that touched it—brought the venerated person's corporeal form to a worshiper's mind.[4] The impressions of Dante's skull reminded some people of a sindon, a shroud or piece of fine linen used to wrap a dead body, such as the famous Shroud of Turin alleged to bear the image of the body of Jesus of Nazareth.[5]

The cranial impressions even more closely resemble another relic of Jesus's Passion: the cloth a woman used to wipe the sweat from his face (hence *sudarium,* or "sweat cloth") on the way to Cavalry.[6] Known as the "Veronica"—after the woman (not mentioned in the Gospels) who wiped Jesus's face—the relic gets its name from the phrase *vera icona,* or "true likeness," meaning Jesus's actual features were forever impressed on the cloth. Dante refers to the Veronica several times in his work and may have seen the relic in Rome when Pope Boniface VIII had it displayed in Saint Peter's Basilica for the Jubilee in 1300. By 1450, another Jubilee year, the Veronica had become so powerful—it reduced more time in Purgatory than other relics—that pilgrims risked their lives to venerate it. A planned display of the cloth at the end of December drew massive crowds. When they learned the viewing had been canceled, they turned around on the bridge and met those still arriving from the other direction. Nearly two hundred people died in the panic, the vast majority crushed to death, others drowned in the river.[7]

Dante's cranial impressions were accorded no such influence—for good or ill—but the Florentine library recognized their potent symbolism. Far from rebuking Enrico Pazzi for keeping these and other precious mementos from the Dante centenary, Chilovi gave thanks for the "grandissimo amore"—the "great love"—that motivated the industrious sculptor. The librarian, true to his professional devotion to texts and his personal devotion to Dante, went further. Until then, the Florentine Dante collection comprised primarily manuscripts and editions of Dante's works. With these traces of Dante's body, the library now possessed something so intimate that Chilovi believed it could help compensate for what had been lost to the world: a Dante original, a manuscript written in the poet's own hand. When the relic was found by chance in 1999, 110 years after Pazzi donated it to the library and 70 years since it had gone missing, experts were still searching "among the tons of manuscripts that fill the shelves of [Italian] libraries," hoping to find "a page, a phrase, or at least a word by the author of the *Commedia*."[8] Absent the original texts, physical reminders of the man who wrote them would have to do, signs of the poet's dead body standing in for the body of his work.

An inventory of holdings published ten years later, in 1899, recorded Enrico Pazzi's donation of various items to the National Central Library of Florence. Listed among the library's artistic possessions are the plaster cast of Dante's head that Pazzi made for his colossal statue of the poet and "an envelope containing a minute portion of Dante's ashes taken from his tomb in Ravenna and authenticated by members of the Commission with their signatures." As head librarian, Desiderio Chilovi signed this inventory. Notary Saturnino Malagola's bland term for the particles (*polvere,* or "dust") has here become "ashes" (*ceneri*), a transformation—like water into wine—markedly elevating the material's value and meaning. Part of Dante's body, it has become a relic in the fullest sense of the word.[9] Precious items deserve proper vessels in which to hold and display them, especially when they are objects of veneration. Understanding this, influential Florentines with knowledge of the poet's relic lamented that the library had been unable "to care for it in a worthy manner." Dante's native city "must not preserve it so poorly."[10] The relic needed a suitable receptacle to occupy the place of honor in the library's new home in Florence.

A year after the library confirmed possession of the relic—"a minute portion of Dante's ashes [*ceneri*]"—Giuseppe Pescetti, an ambitious young Florentine deputy, took matters into his own hands. He enlisted a well-known artist to design an urn "worthy of the high honor to which it was destined."

Rinaldo Barbetti (1830–1904), a native of Siena who had lived and worked in Florence for many years, was an obvious choice. An expert engraver, silversmith, and goldsmith, Barbetti had amassed an impressive list of accomplishments by the time Pescetti asked him to design the urn in 1900. His works included embellishments to the façade of the Florentine Duomo and a silver table celebrating Apollo that King Victor Emmanuel II sent as a gift to Czarina Maria Feodorovna in Petersburg. Enrico Montecorboli (1837–1923), an Italian playwright who wrote on art for Italian and French periodicals, praised Barbetti as "the purest type of Florentine artist from earlier times." His studio brought to mind the workshops of Lorenzo Ghiberti and Filippo Brunelleschi during their famous competition to make gilded bronze doors for the Florentine Baptistery in the fifteenth century. His refined metalwork made him an heir to the Renaissance sculptor and goldsmith Benvenuto Cellini.[11]

Barbetti, Pescetti, and Chilovi exchanged letters that showed their faith in the Dante dust as a bona fide relic. Their plan for an urn to hold this relic—the object of choice for cremated remains of the deceased—did nothing to question the conflation of the dust (*polvere*) with ashes or other physical remains (*ceneri*). On the contrary, the writers never referred to *polvere* (dust), notary Malagola's description of the material in his authenticating document. They instead fashioned the collection of particles into a holy object—one worthy of a funeral urn—through language identifying it with Dante's body: "Mortal remains" (*resti mortali*), "sacred relics" (*sacre reliquie*), and "ashes" (*ceneri*) were their preferred terms. This relic was especially valuable, they pointed out, because it was the only physical trace of Dante in Florence's possession—a unique piece, however small, of the body that the poet's native city had sought from Ravenna since the late fourteenth century. Having these particles in Florence meant that, while Dante never again saw his native city after it cast him into bitter exile, at least "part of his mortal remains returned there." By bringing to fruition a "monumental receptacle for the sacred relics," Italy—Florence above all—would perform "an act of merciful reparation."[12]

Barbetti envisioned a large and lavish reliquary for Dante's dust. Made of silver or bronze—metals that lend themselves well to a colorful enamel finish—the proposed urn was over seven and a half feet tall. The marble pedestal comprised two concentric platforms with a triangular block centered on the second, smaller disk. Attached to this block, the decorated metal urn rose up in a cylindrical form punctuated by three, evenly spaced pillars. A figure representing one of Dante's minor works (*De vulgari eloquentia*,

16.1. Rinaldo Barbetti's design for the urn to hold dust collected from the cloth on which Dante's bones and the wood box had lain (Enrico Montecorboli, "L'urna della tribuna dantesca," *Il Giorno,* June 24, 1900)

Convivio, Monarchia) sat atop each pillar, with three major figures from the *Divine Comedy*—Virgil, Aristotle, and Saint Bernard of Clairvaux—occupying niches in the pillars. Panels between the pillars depicted a trio of the poet's dearest female subjects: Beatrice appearing before Dante as a figure of the contemplative life, Matelda representing the active life by singing and gathering flowers, and the Blessed Virgin Mary reigning in Heaven.

Set above this elaborate tribute to Dante's work was the receptacle itself, a circular vessel with three rectangular windows or grates through which viewers could see "the precious relics." Finally, the majestic figure of Dante, holding the *Divine Comedy* open in his hands, stood atop the reliquary, a tribute at once to the poet's body and the book for which he was worshiped. Beatrice, transported by angels, appeared beside Dante as, bending, she laid the flower of Narcissus—a flower pleasing to the dead—on top of "the case holding the ashes of the one who elevated her to such high glory."[13] Intended or not, Barbetti's scene of Beatrice paying homage to Dante recalls one of the *Divine Comedy*'s most moving moments. Just before Dante realizes Virgil has left his side upon the arrival of Beatrice at the summit of Mount Purgatory, angels sing a Latin verse from the Roman poet's *Aeneid*, "manibus date lilia plenis" (give lilies with full hands).[14] Dante's evocation of Virgil's words—spoken in the underworld by Anchises to Aeneas while foreshowing the premature death of the emperor's young nephew—honors his beloved Roman guide as he disappears from the action of the poem. By having Beatrice honor Dante's relic with a flower, the urn likewise fulfilled its memorial function by fusing intense feelings of loss and veneration.

Barbetti clearly had in mind reliquaries holding remains of holy persons—and objects that touched their bodies—in designing this urn for particles that Enrico Pazzi collected from the cloth on which Dante's bones lay in 1865. As objects used to hold and display venerated content, reliquaries are themselves "material treasures" for the artistry and precious materials with which they are made. Their aesthetic value mirrors and confirms "the spiritual value of authentic relics."[15] Reliquaries often hold material—bodily parts or other physical items—that are neither beautiful nor intrinsically valuable. The urn for the Dante dust was no exception, and that was the point: presenting in a gorgeous, finely crafted container "the stuff holy bodies had become in death" to show how such mortal matter rises to eternal life in Heaven.[16] Reliquaries transform the corruptibility of dead bodies, their putrefaction, into displays of permanence and beauty. While celebrating the earthly fame and eternal glory of their revered subjects, works like the proposed urn envision the reunion of all blessed souls with their glorified bodies at the end of time in the Catholic tradition.

Barbetti's design eschewed gold, crystal, and gemstones commonly used for reliquaries holding objects from the life and death of Jesus or other holy persons.[17] He aimed instead to celebrate his poetic subject in a more personal way. Adorned with sculpted likenesses of special characters in the *Divine Comedy*—from Aristotle, Virgil, and Bernard to Beatrice, Matelda, and

Mary—the proposed work highlighted the philosophical, theological, and literary foundations of Dante's vision of the afterlife. The urn's culminating scene, in which Beatrice honors Dante's memory by laying a flower on his relic, reciprocated the poet's homage to his beloved muse. Dante's text shaped the design of Barbetti's proposed urn—much as words inscribed on other reliquaries informed medieval literary works—through a "poetics of enshrinement."[18]

Despite pleasing Chilovi, Pescetti, and other Florentines with the thoughtful design, Barbetti apparently never made the urn. The physical object has not been found, and no photographs of it are known to exist.[19] Construction of the new library complex, including the Tribuna Dantesca, or "Dante Gallery," at the heart of it, proved more difficult than Chilovi anticipated. The gallery, in fact, was only completed in 1929 and the rest of the library in 1935. The director expended so much time and energy on the library's new home that he could not raise the funds required for Barbetti to execute his design. With Chilovi's death in 1905, hope for the urn died as well.

Public awareness of plans for Dante's reliquary also contributed to its demise. When Corrado Ricci learned of Florence's intention to create an urn to hold a portion of Dante's alleged remains, he launched a fusillade of outrage and criticism. Ricci forcefully rejected the arguments of Desiderio Chilovi and other proponents of the urn, but he directed his sharpest barbs at Enrico Pazzi, his predecessor as head of the Museo Nazionale (originally the Museo Civico Bizantino), which the sculptor directed from 1884 until Ricci's appointment in 1898. One month after Chilovi and Pescetti exchanged notes on Barbetti's design for the urn, Ricci insisted that if Pazzi once possessed a fragment of Dante's bones taken after their discovery in 1865, it must have been stolen—"whether by him or someone else hardly matters." Pazzi compounded his error by not returning the fragment to authorities in Ravenna, as others (including Ricci himself) did with alleged remains later examined in 1921. Instead of "creating new reliquaries," Florence should correct Pazzi's moral failings by returning the fragment so it can lie in peace with the rest of the poet's skeleton. A master of understatement, Ricci felt that Pazzi had "not done a good deed" and Florence would "not do well" by keeping the relic for "display in a case." If Florence failed to show "the respect owed a tomb held sacred by the entire civilized world," he hoped Ravenna would take legal action to retrieve the ill-gotten remain.[20]

Ricci's view of the matter hardly changed when he learned that Pazzi had not stolen (or received) a bone fragment but had instead distributed packets of Dante dust as if they were "powdered medicinal herbs." Ricci left it to readers to decide if they thought it right that "after so many years, vestiges of the skeleton turn up here and there, outside the tomb."[21] He vilified Pazzi for creating and distributing relics. When the bones were discovered on May 27, 1865, Pazzi was at the height of his popularity, basking in the afterglow of the unveiling of his Dante statue on the first day of the centenary festivities in Florence. Ravenna was proud of its native son for his success. But to Ricci, also a citizen of Ravenna, Pazzi was an opportunist, "an enterprising spirit, intrusive even, who had a hand in everything." Ever the operator, he "advised, proposed, did things, undid things, while others were filled with admiration." Even if Pazzi had gathered the relics "in the light of day," even if they were displayed in a beautiful urn, "I will repeat that what he did was shameful," Ricci wrote, "so long as I have breath."[22]

With or without a stunning reliquary urn, Florence looked to its precious Dante dust as the centerpiece of the city's new library. But like the bones themselves, even these smallest vestiges of the poet's physical afterlife embarked on an adventurous journey, mysteriously disappearing after 1929 before being found by accident seventy years later.

Desiderio Chilovi first announced the need to relocate the National Central Library of Florence in 1885. Holdings had grown too large for their cramped quarters in the Uffizi palace complex. A new building offered room to expand but also an opportunity for the director to impose his cultural values on a national institution in Florence. Chilovi's first priority was to house and augment the city's rich collection of manuscripts, editions, translations, and scholarly studies of Dante's *Divina Commedia* and the poet's other works. He envisioned a gallery or wing devoted to Dante, with the relics occupying the place of honor in this Tribuna Dantesca. Tangible signs of the poet's presence would transform the gallery into the library's *sanctum sanctorum,* its holy "shrine."[23] Chilovi and Pescetti had therefore turned to Barbetti to design a reliquary worthy not only of its precious contents but of its exalted location in the library. Like a saint's relic at the main altar of a church, the urn with traces of Dante's physical afterlife promised to make the gallery "one of the beautiful marvels of . . . Italy." Anyone who wonders at "this great passion for Dante that has invaded all Florence," continued Enrico Corboli in 1900, need only recall that the city "has but one maestro, one founder, one legitimate king: Dante Alighieri."[24]

When submitting Barbetti's design to Chilovi in 1900, Pescetti hoped this cult of Dante would overcome obstacles and enable the library "to rise up soon as affirmation of a great civil thought." The director joined Pescetti in urging the library's speedy construction, adding his desire for Dante's relics "to be held in its heart with artistic splendor." Chilovi expressed confidence in his note to Barbetti, telling the artist he believed "that soon we will be able to display properly these precious relics in our library's new home."[25] He initially had good reason to be optimistic. In 1900, a site for the building was selected on the north bank of the Arno between Corso dei Tintori and the cloisters of Santa Croce. Two years later, the Italian government passed legislation proposed by Pescetti to fund the project.

Expectations for timely planning and construction of the library's new home were in retrospect wishful thinking. It took three rounds of competition before architect Cesare Bazzani was awarded the commission to design the library in 1906, a year after Chilovi's death, and King Victor Emmanuel III did not lay the cornerstone until 1911. Construction proceeded at an exasperatingly slow pace after this, occurring in fits and starts according to the whims and funding priorities of the government. Visitors to the site in 1929, seeing only the "skeleton" of the planned structure, felt like tourists at the "archeological dig of some ancient building."[26] This was the state of the library when the Dante Gallery, one of the first completed parts of the new complex, was inaugurated that year.

Mussolini's government had a strong incentive to showcase the new National Central Library of Florence even before it was finished and operational: Italy was hosting the "First World Congress of Libraries and Bibliography" in 1929. By the time the congress began on June 15, only the book-storage area and the building on Corso dei Tintori (facing the Arno)—including the Dante Gallery—had been completed, or nearly so. Sponsored by the International Federation of Library Associations (IFLA) and held under the "august patronage of His Majesty, King of Italy," and the "high honorary chairmanship of His Excellency, Sir Benito Mussolini," this congress marked a watershed moment in the history of library science. Over one thousand bibliophiles from twenty-six nations on five continents (Australia was not represented) gathered to discuss and establish procedures for organizing, cataloging, and sharing the world's holdings of books, manuscripts, codices, and other documents.[27] Over two weeks, June 15–30, 1929, visiting librarians and other participants enjoyed an abundance of excursions and exhibitions when not attending conference panels and plenary assemblies. While the main business of the congress took place in Rome and Venice, respective sites of the opening and closing assemblies, Florence hosted a plenary session (June 25) in which delegates discussed and adopted the resolutions to put before the general assembly in Venice.[28]

The itinerary in Florence naturally included organized tours of the city's cultural gems, such as the Medici Riccardi Palace and the Laurentian Library, where visitors saw illuminated manuscripts and precious editions of works by Dante, Petrarch, Boccaccio, and "a hundred other witnesses to an ardent spiritual life combining glory and truly stirring beauty."[29] The book lovers could not have gathered in Florence at a better time. Workers had just put most of the final touches on the Dante Gallery, the "august temple" of the new National Library (still under construction), thus allowing librarians from around the world to attend its inauguration.[30] Desiderio Chilovi had imagined the tribute to Dante as the heart and soul of the library from the start. After the director's death in 1905, Cesare Bazzani honored his conception in designing the gallery and the rest of the library.

The Tribuna Dantesca rose at the corner of Corso dei Tintori and Via Magliabechi "like a magnificent apse," the semicircular or polygonal end of a church traditionally covering its main altar.[31] Bazzani fulfilled Chilovi's desire to join scientific and humanistic knowledge in the library by constructing a monumental staircase connecting the Galileo Gallery (holding most of the scientist's known manuscripts) on the lower floor to the Dante Gallery on the *piano nobile,* or second floor. Sharing the same dimensions as the Galileo room, the circular space devoted to Dante featured a dome supported by twelve columns of pink granite resting on octagonal bases. The columns traced the circumference like the hands of a clock under the graceful cupola. Light from five tall, rectangular windows "converged on the center of the hall."[32]

Inauguration of the Dante Gallery on June 26, 1929, allowed Italy to celebrate a major accomplishment and honor the poet before an international audience. Following brief ceremonies, participants directed their attention to the center of the room. There lay the "small portion of the poet's remains held by the National Library." The "ashes [*ceneri*] of the divine poet" were like the sun at the center of the cosmic system that Galileo proved so adept at imagining—and for which he ran afoul of the Inquisition under Pope Urban VIII, much as Dante had suffered at the hands of Pope Boniface VIII three centuries earlier.[33] Or, to adopt the medieval poet's cosmology, these relics— whether flecks of his mortal remains or just matter that had touched them— were like the earth around which revolve "the sun and the other stars," as the final verse of his 14,233-line epic so memorably sings.[34] Encircling Dante's physical traces, the Tribuna Dantesca was not the library's "most symbolic and significant part" solely for its rich collection of the poet's works. In form and content, it was truly a Florentine temple to Dante, perhaps even more so than the Basilica of Santa Croce. While the church could claim the empty tomb sculpted by Stefano Ricci and installed in 1830, the Dante Gallery of the National Central Library of Florence housed cherished relics of the poet and, for a brief time, allowed visitors from around the world to see them.[35]

Objects of worshipful admiration, the Florentine relics disappeared from view and discussion after the inauguration of the Dante Gallery in 1929. Exile, the defining theme of the poet's life and *Divine Comedy,* clung just as tightly to his physical afterlife. These vestiges of Dante's posthumous existence, like his bones in earlier times, fell prey to fickle forces that buried their tracks, banishing them from the historical record for many years. The relics' fate was still unknown in 1987, when three staff members of the National Library revealed this uncomfortable truth in a scholarly article. Their meticulous research unearthed no mention of the relics—published or unpublished— after 1929, whereas several documents implied their absence. Inaugural exhibit catalogs for the completed library (October 30, 1935) and its Renaissance Hall (May 15, 1955) contained no indication of the Dante dust and cranial impressions. Nor were they included in the library's detailed inventory (1935–1942), which did, however, list Pazzi's plaster cast of Dante's head and Barbetti's design of the urn intended to hold the dust. So, the whistleblowers surmised, the relics must have gone missing sometime between 1929, when they were displayed for the inauguration of the Dante Gallery, and 1935, when the library's vast holdings were transferred to their new home in Piazza dei Cavalleggeri.[36] But how could they have "gone missing"? And where might they be?

One plausible if mundane scenario involved furniture. While books in the original library buildings went directly to the new location, many old furnishings were instead donated to other libraries and various museums in and around Florence. The State Archives, the Laurentian Library, and the Museum of the Risorgimento were among nine destinations for tables, chairs, cabinets, bookcases, and desks from old library quarters in Palazzo de' Giudici and Palazzo degli Uffizi.[37] If, as seems likely, the director or another administrator locked the relics in a cabinet or desk drawer after the inauguration in 1929, this could explain their misadventure. Domenico Fava succeeded Angelo Bruschi as director of the library in 1933. If Fava had somehow lost track of the relics in the confusion of the massive move two years later, perhaps the item with the locked drawer—its precious contents unknown to those who were overseeing the operation—landed in a neighboring cultural institution. There, concealed in a piece of surplus furniture, the relics could have easily lain forgotten for years, lost to future generations.

Or worse. Maybe some harried custodian, coming across a yellowed packet and not even bothering to examine its contents, threw it in the trash, the dust bin of history—or, not appreciating the value of what lay inside, simply tossed "the ashes of good old Dante to the four winds."[38] Nor could one exclude a watery end to the relics. Perhaps, hidden in the basement of the National Library, they shared the tragic fate of thousands of volumes and other precious objects lost in the "great flood of Florence." On November 4, 1966, the Arno River broke its banks and rushed into the city, immediately flooding the library's basement (destroying valuable manuscripts that had been moved there for safety during World War II) and soon submerging streets, piazzas, and buildings, its floodwaters rising as high as twenty feet in some parts.[39]

The three library workers in 1987 also postulated a less dramatic theory—both more optimistic and more cynical—for the disappearance of the Dante relics donated to the Florentine library in 1889. Perhaps keepers of the treasure in 1929, fearing a resurgence of the harsh polemics that swirled around Florence's possession of the relics at the turn of the century, chose silence as their best option. Perhaps they hoped that, with time, challenges to Florentine claims on traces of Dante's body would become a thing of the past. Knowingly or not, they may have repeated an earlier chapter of Dante's graveyard history. After stealthily removing Dante's bones from their tomb in the early 1500s, Franciscan friars strove over the next three centuries to keep knowledge of the treasure held in their convent also to stay within its walls. If the Florentine strategy mirrored that of the Franciscans, so may have its unintended consequence. A secret, in the end, only matters for as long as at least one person knows it. If calculated silence ever became unintentionally permanent—a situation arising when people in the know die without leaving a record of the secret location—then the relics would be as good as lost, unless, of course, they were discovered by accident, unless someone played the part of Pio Feletti, the stone mason whose pickax miraculously freed Dante's bones from their forgotten hideout in 1865. This shaky "unless" enabled researchers who lamented the loss of the relics to hold out hope they might yet turn up "in some forgotten corner of the library itself"—a hypothesis that proved prophetic when two colleagues found the missing treasure by chance in 1999.[40]

Luigi Fallani, Lucia Milana, and Antonio Giardullo, the library personnel who documented the missing Florentine relics in 1987, anticipated publication of their scholarly article with a preview for popular consumption. They made their point by drawing up a petition with fifty-six signatures, one for each year of Dante's life. Their letter denounced the National Central Library of Florence for losing the relics acquired by Chilovi in 1889 and displayed to the world at the inauguration of the library's Dante Gallery in 1929. With a theatrical flourish, the whistleblowers enclosed the accusatory petition in a weathered yellow envelope meant to recall the one believed to hold the packet of Dante dust and the impressions of his skull. The missing relics, for the accusers, were a symptom of a larger problem with the library: its declining ability to document and preserve Italy's bibliographic patrimony, an issue exacerbated by suspending publication of the bulletin of new Italian books, a bibliographic ritual that not even World War II or the flood of 1966 had managed to halt.[41]

The press exploited this well-staged announcement to shine critical light on the sorry state of Italian libraries and cultural institutions in general, their deficiencies leading to such scandals as the missing Dante relics. One article complained of staff reductions, inadequate storage space, and delays in cataloging tens of thousands of volumes as the National Library transitioned to a computerized system.[42] Public disclosure also allowed reporters to rehearse (with inevitable inaccuracies) the entertaining if troubling history of the poet's remains, with the latest outrage cast as one of the many indignities Dante suffered after death. Commentators imagined additional scenarios to explain the missing relics. They could have been lost during the upheavals of World War II, or perhaps someone simply stole them from the library. "Anything is possible," concluded one writer.[43]

With nearly forty miles of shelves containing over four million books and pamphlets, the National Central Library of Florence also housed thousands of manuscripts and original letters by a who's who of Italian cultural giants, from Benvenuto Cellini, Niccolò Machiavelli, and Lorenzo the Magnificent to Ugo Foscolo and Giacomo Leopardi.[44] Yet no library, in Florence or elsewhere, possessed any work in Dante's own hand. Treasured traces of the poet's body at least provided partial compensation for the absence of his original body of work. But for seventy years—a lifetime in Dante's imagination—the relics shown to a global audience in 1929 had gone missing.[45] Political divisiveness, fueled by the machinations of a ruthless pope, had caused Florence to lose Dante in life; bureaucratic negligence, abetted by the relocation of a massive library—if not by war, a natural disaster, or a criminal mind—caused Florence to lose track of whatever small portion it held of Dante in death. After recovery of the relics in 1999, they were displayed once again in the Dante Gallery during the Great Jubilee of 2000 decreed by Pope John Paul II—a reminder that Dante may have viewed the Veronica, the cloth said to bear Christ's facial image, in Rome during the Jubilee in 1300.[46] By the time these smallest pieces of Dante's physical afterlife grabbed headlines, the poet's international fame was beyond question.

17

Saved by Love

It was May of 1987 and in a dusty attic room of the Senate they found a
medallion containing nothing less than a portion of Dante's ashes.

—"GIORGIA E MARCO,"

SENATORAGAZZI

• Italian cities and regions, like their counterparts around the world, rarely
miss a chance to claim superiority over other places in the nation to which
they belong. Rome, in this case, profited from Florence's loss. The director
of the Senate Library in Rome hosted an event for journalists on May 6, 1987,
the same day the public learned of the Florentine library's missing Dante
relics. On the fourth floor of Palazzo Madama, seat of the Italian Senate,
Dr. Maria Teresa Buonadonna Russo exuded "understandable pride" in displaying a relic of Dante's physical afterlife that had been kept in a "tiny
windowless room" of the library. News of Florence's scandal gave Rome a
perfect opportunity to announce that the nation's capital had its own tangible connection to the poet's body. Even better, the Roman library knew
where it was.[1]

Reporters described the reliquary as a piece of gold jewelry alleged to contain "a portion of the ashes of the 'Supreme Poet' Dante Alighieri."[2] One
observer compared it to a "round brooch resembling those that today could
be called *da tailleur* because women wear them on the lapel of their suit
jackets." At the center of the brooch sat a small crystal within a gold border.
Appearing within the crystal was the relic itself, a pinch of material "grayish
and dust-like, as one would expect." Framed by laurel leaves, an inscription
on the back of the case identified the precious contents as *polvere di Dante*—
"Dante's dust." The gold object recalled keepsakes popular in the nineteenth
century, but instead of holding a loved one's lock of hair, it displayed a poet's
sepulchral dust. In addition to showing other special items in its collection

in 1987—Camillo Cavour's inkwell, the gold pen with which King Victor Emmanuel III signed his oath of office, General Armando Diaz's bulletin announcing victory in World War I—the Senate Library presented documents explaining how it came to possess the Dante relic.[3] The library later posted these records, along with a photograph of the gold brooch, on a website accompanying an exhibition held at Palazzo Giustiniano in Rome for the Extraordinary Jubilee of Mercy decreed by Pope Francis for December 8, 2015, to November 26, 2016.[4]

Mario La Rosa, a journalist for RAI (Radiotelevisione Italiana), Italy's national public broadcasting company, had first seen this Dante relic during a private visit in 1968. He wrote an article at the time for *Il Tempo*. The Roman newspaper reprinted La Rosa's piece in its coverage of the missing Florentine relics and the Senate Library's display of its own "Dante dust" in 1987. The original version, titled "A medallion with Dante's ashes held in a room of the Senate," appeared just under a cartoon featuring two scantily clad women. Looking up at the moon, one of them comments, "I have the impression someone is watching us." The caption, "Astronauts toward the Moon," referred to the Apollo 7 mission, which was at that time transmitting the first live television images from humans in space.[5] The page layout was provocative: minuscule traces of Dante, a poet who imagined traveling through the heavens, juxtaposed with the first human sight of the planet Earth from space.

Unlike the particles and cranial impressions that Enrico Pazzi gave to Florence in 1889, the "Dante dust" held in the Senate Library in Rome lacked contemporaneous authentication. There was no document—signed, witnessed, and notarized—from the time of the relic's creation in 1865. But Senator Alessandro D'Ancona, who bequeathed the gold brooch to the library in the early twentieth century, identified Pazzi as the source of this relic as well. D'Ancona wrote that the sculptor had gathered dust and bits of laurel leaves from the poet's tomb when it was opened on June 7, 1865. This claim contradicts official reports, which state that authorities in Ravenna carefully packaged, documented, and preserved all the loose material in the tomb. Nor does it seem likely that Pazzi took or acquired any of the organic residue scraped from the tomb for chemical analysis—if nothing else, threats of bodily harm to Giovanni Gozzadini when he temporarily held these samples should have dissuaded the sculptor from attempting to keep contents of the tomb for himself. The gold brooch in Rome—like the small envelope in Florence—more plausibly contains particles that Pazzi had gathered from the

(left) 17.1. Obverse of the gold medallion said to hold dust from Dante's tomb (Photo, 2017; Biblioteca del Senato della Repubblica, Rome)
(right) 17.2. Reverse of the gold medallion with "Polvere di Dante" (Photo, 2017; Biblioteca del Senato della Repubblica, Rome)

cloth or mat on which Dante's bones and the wood box had been laid out for examination. But whether the dust came from the tomb or the cloth matters little in the end: it was relic material simply by virtue of having once been in contact with the poet's remains.

Alessandro D'Ancona had no doubt that the particles were part of Dante himself. They were dust (*polvere*), he wrote in a letter from Rome in 1911, "but what could this dust be if it were not made of molecules of flesh and bone separated from the body during the long period of time it lay in the tomb, from 1321 to 1677!" He repeated his conviction that the particles were "bits of the poet's mortal remains" in a note written in Florence three years later.[6] Although the physical nature of this Roman relic, like that of its Florentine sibling, has never been scientifically determined, later descriptions took the senator at his word. The official website of the Italian Senate, like the Florentine library website for the Great Jubilee of 2000, has kept alive the possibility that its relic carries Dante's DNA. An online description of the Senate Library's special collections lists D'Ancona's donation of "a gold medallion containing dust and fragments of laurel leaves gathered from Dante's sarcophagus" in addition to over four hundred volumes and two manuscripts.[7]

For ten years, a section of the Italian Senate website designed for school children age ten to twelve unequivocally identified the relic with Dante's remains. Among a series of cartoon skits featuring young "Marco" and "Giorgia" in the guise of Sherlock Holmes and Dr. Watson was one titled "Dante's Ashes" (Le Ceneri di Dante). Marco riffed on the opening line of the *Divine Comedy,* reciting (in his speech balloon), "in the middle of the road of the attic, we found ourselves holding a medallion inscribed with the ashes of the great Poet." Giorgia then explained that "it was May of 1987 and in a dusty attic room of the Senate they found a medallion containing nothing less than a portion of Dante's ashes." Marco, flashing a big smile, commented: "An exceptional discovery that experts continue to discuss today." "Right, that's true," said Giorgia in the final frame, with Dante's bust in profile set between Marco and her. "How did Dante's ashes wind up there?" she asked before addressing the viewer: "Do you know anything about this?"[8] Fortunately, we do. Thanks to Senator D'Ancona's documentation, combined with what we know of Enrico Pazzi's role in creating and disseminating related relics, we can reconstruct the relic's chain of custody.

This history is intimately bound up with the history of the D'Ancona family. Alessandro D'Ancona was born in Pisa in 1835 to Ester della Ripa and Giuseppe D'Ancona, who were married in 1813 in Pesaro, a city on the Adriatic coast.[9] Ester's brother Laudadio moved his family from Pesaro to Florence in 1827, when, under Pope Leo XII (1823–1829), Jewish residents of the Papal States were subjected to harsh discriminatory measures, including the reinstatement of ghettos and the renewal of prohibitions against ownership of property. Laudadio's home in Piazzetta Sant'Egidio was a gathering place for scientists, writers, and artists as well as for Italian patriots and political exiles. Seeking the freer Tuscan air, the D'Ancona family joined Laudadio in Florence when Ester, already a mother of five, was pregnant with her sixth child, Alessandrina. The family, however, had difficulty securing Florentine citizenship and was forced to move to Pisa. Alessandro, the youngest of nine children, was born there in a house on Piazza della Fonte di San Francesco, now named Piazza Alessandro D'Ancona. Giuseppe D'Ancona received Florentine citizenship just before his death in 1848, after which his wife and children settled in Florence for good, taking up residence near Ester's brother in the center of town.

Alessandro D'Ancona first distinguished himself in literature and philosophy in Pisa and Florence before pursuing legal studies in Turin, where he immersed himself in the political culture of the Piedmontese capital. After war broke out with Austria in 1859, he returned to Florence and helped facilitate the annexation of Tuscany to the realm of Victor Emmanuel II, the last king of Piedmont-Sardinia (1849–1861) and the first king of the united Italy (1861–1878). Alessandro worked as a journalist and directed the Tuscan newspaper *La Nazione* before being named, at age twenty-six, professor of literature at the University of Pisa, where he established himself as an authority on Italian literary history. He authored over twelve hundred publications during his career. In 1900, at age sixty-five, Alessandro retired from full-time teaching but continued to offer a course on Dante's works (1900–1907), one of his main areas of expertise. He was one of the founding members of the Società Dantesca Italiana in 1888. On April 3, 1904, he was nominated to the Italian Senate.[10]

Several of Alessandro D'Ancona's siblings also left their mark on Italy during the nation's formative years. Sansone (1814–1894), following in the footsteps of his uncle Laudadio, was a leader in Italian finance. A member of Italy's provisional government in 1859, he served in six legislatures of the parliament in the 1860s and 1870s and was nominated to the Senate in 1882.[11] Prospero studied law, while Salvatore and Giacomo studied medicine, the latter working as personal physician to the pasha of Egypt and later, in Paris, to the opera composer Gioachino Rossini. Vitale (Vito) was an accomplished painter, one of whose most successful works was titled *Dante's First Encounter with Beatrice*. Cesare, just three years older than Alessandro, was a renowned scientist. A founding member of the Italian Botanical Society, he had a long and distinguished career as a paleontologist and botanist, authoring influential studies and serving for three decades on the executive council of the Tuscan Horticultural Society.[12]

Senator D'Ancona initiated negotiations to give the Dante relic in his possession to the Senate Library in Rome in 1911. In a letter of March 1, he promised the library director, Fortunato Pintor, "a few pertinent details to clarify the relic's authenticity." D'Ancona felt this information was necessary because the director's silence had led him "to reasonably infer some impediment in the business [they] were discussing."[13] Pintor, who knew D'Ancona from his university days in Pisa, moved in 1903 from the National Central Library of Florence to the Senate Library in Rome, which he directed for the next twenty-five years. In the letter, D'Ancona weighed pros and cons about donating the relic. On the one hand, he hoped that depositing the precious item with the Senate would "remove it from the vicissitudes of private possession." On the other hand, he feared the negative repercussions of placing the relic in public hands. What if questions were raised about its history or if the relic's very existence—owing to Enrico Pazzi's actions in 1865—triggered accusations of desecration? What if the press were to treat the esteemed senator's donation of the relic with derision or ridicule? Perhaps worst of all, what if Ravenna should seize on publicity of the relic to demand its restitution, as Corrado Ricci had encouraged when he learned of the Florentine library relic in 1900? If his donation were likely to produce "one or another of these unpleasant scenarios," D'Ancona concluded, then "let's not go through with it."[14]

Despite these worries, D'Ancona brought the medallion to Rome and delivered it to the Senate on March 30, 1911. The library committee decided at this point to accept the relic not as a permanent gift but—concerned that it might "give rise to controversy"—as an item in "fiduciary deposit."[15] An official document drawn up at the time confirms that Senator D'Ancona "deposits with the Senate of the Kingdom a small box containing a precious relic of a great Italian." The statement records that D'Ancona consigns the relic "with the understanding that it would be preserved for now in the Senate Library and would be moved to a more worthy location at a later date," according to the senator's written wishes. The library committee, for its part, "accepts the deposit and, recognizing their esteemed colleague's trust, places it in the care of the librarian, who will set the box among the library's most precious objects." Alessandro D'Ancona and the five members of the library committee—including Senator Giorgio Sonnino, father of Sidney, prime minister in 1906 and 1909–1910—approved and signed this acknowledgment of the relic's transfer to Rome.[16]

Three years later, on March 14, 1914, D'Ancona expressed his intention to grant the Senate Library permanent possession of the relic upon his death. He died eight months later, on November 8, 1914. Couching his wishes in the language of a last will and testament, the senator stipulated that the relic, deposited with the library according to the statement signed by him and the committee in 1911, "pass into full and everlasting ownership by the Senate itself."[17] That D'Ancona took time to convey these wishes when his health was already in decline shows how strongly he believed in the Dante relic as a national treasure. On November 18, 1914, just ten days after Senator D'Ancona's death in Florence, his eldest son, a respected agronomist, wrote to the Senate. Giuseppe D'Ancona's letter cited his father's will, which reconfirmed the bequest: "I also leave to the Senate—and it is already in the care of Director Pintor—a brooch containing Dante's ashes."[18]

Although the Italian Senate respected Alessandro D'Ancona's final wishes, the Dante relic kept a conspicuously low profile through most of the twentieth century. An inventory dated November 10, 1932, nearly two decades after the Senate Library took permanent possession of it, describes the relic: "The small cardboard box (61 by 43 millimeters, with the name of the jeweler Leopoldo Settepassi, Pontevecchio 6 Florence) . . . contains a round gold object 38 millimeters in diameter, in which—as it says inside—'dust from Dante' is enclosed." The inventory states that Annibale Alberti, secretary general of the Senate, received the gold brooch and the jewelry box, along with the letter Alessandro D'Ancona had written to Fortunato Pintor in 1911, "in which he explained the provenance of these 'ashes of Dante.'" Secretary General Alberti, who signed this inventory himself, reports that he then stored these items in a safe.[19] Since Alberti became secretary general of the Senate in 1929, it may well be the case that Dante's dust was locked away in Rome the very year in which another portion of his dust was displayed to librarians from around the world during the inauguration of the Dante Gallery in Florence.

Luigi Federzoni, president of the Senate, wrote to Giuseppe D'Ancona in Florence the day the inventory was taken in 1932. Federzoni assured him that the Senate would "always jealously preserve [his] father's precious gift to the assembly."[20] The well-preserved relic's complicated history undoubtedly contributed to whatever other reasons dissuaded authorities from displaying or otherwise publicizing it over the years. D'Ancona wrote in 1911 that Enrico Pazzi took some of the Dante dust he had gathered in 1865 and put it inside the small gold medallion or brooch. This reliquary, according to writing on the jewelry box that held it, was the work of Leopoldo Settepassi, a legendary Florentine goldsmith and jeweler whose creations included a sixteen-row pearl necklace given to Queen Margherita of Savoy by her husband, King Umberto I. Settepassi, whose family business in Florence dated to the fourteenth century, opened his shop on the Ponte Vecchio in 1850.[21] Pazzi gave the gold brooch to a woman whose identity has never been revealed. The relic later passed from her to Cesare D'Ancona, the esteemed Florentine horticulturalist, who gave it to Senator Alessandro D'Ancona, his Dante-loving brother.

Alessandro withholds the name of the mystery woman to whom Pazzi gave the dust-filled brooch, but he clearly knew her. From the moment Pazzi gave the bejeweled relic to this *signora,* the senator told Fortunato Pintor in 1911, "it was always under my watchful eye."[22] We can only imagine his delight when his brother Cesare gained possession of the cherished object. Alessandro D'Ancona's refusal to "out" the female recipient of Pazzi's unusual gift—no doubt a chivalrous omission—has not stopped others from trying to solve the puzzle. Assailing Pazzi for having created and disseminated relics, Corrado Ricci provided a tantalizing clue to the woman's identity in 1900. He claimed the sculptor "gave a pinch" of his Dante dust to a "Wallachian Princess," the only known female recipient of Pazzi's largesse.[23] Although the woman's name remains hidden, the geographic marker of her royal heritage— Wallachia being a Romanian principality bordered by the lower Danube River, the Transylvanian Alps, and the Seret River—narrowed the field of contenders. Santi Muratori, Ricci's friend and colleague from Ravenna, pondered the identity of this Wallachian princess in 1928, wondering if she were "perhaps Princess Costanza Ghika, wife of Count Gioacchino Rasponi?"[24]

The director of Ravenna's Classense Library betrayed a lack of conviction by beginning his thought with "perhaps" and ending with a question mark. But he had good reason for positing the wife of Ravenna's mayor as the princess in question. Costanza Ghika (1835–1895)—daughter of Costantino Ghika (hospodar, or prince, of Wallachia) and Maria Vacarescu Ghika—was wed to Gioacchino Rasponi in 1858. Her sister Pulcheria (1837–1895) married Gioacchino's brother Achille in 1862. As sons of Count Giulio Rasponi and Princess Luisa Murat, the Rasponi brothers also had royal blood. Achille Rasponi (1835–1896) was elected to the Italian House of Deputies in 1865 and to the Senate in 1876. Gioacchino Rasponi (1829–1877) served for many years in the House of Deputies (beginning in 1860) and was the mayor of Ravenna in 1863–1865 and again in 1873.[25]

Enrico Pazzi's memoir attests to his close relations with the Rasponi brothers and Ghika sisters over many years. Gioacchino Rasponi "always honored me with his welcome and enviable friendship," Pazzi reflected, "of which I will keep a lasting memory."[26] Artistic commissions reflected and strengthened bonds of friendship between the sculptor and the Rasponi-Ghika families. Pazzi made several works for Princess Costanza Ghika Rasponi, including a "statuette" of Dante in 1862. Her son Giulio (1863–1916) was a favorite subject. For Costanza in 1871, Pazzi sculpted a statue of the boy playing with a dog. That same year, her sister, Pulcheria, and her brother-in-law, Pietro Rasponi, each commissioned Pazzi to sculpt a bust of Giulio. In 1875, Pazzi replicated the scene of Giulio with the dog for Alessandrina (1840–1903), another Ghika sister, and sent it to her residence in Paris. Over the next two years, he completed two allegorical representations of Amore for Pulcheria. After Gioacchino Rasponi died in 1877, Costanza had Pazzi carve the monument honoring her deceased husband for the family chapel in Ravenna.[27]

Costanza Ghika may well have been the unnamed Wallachian princess whom Pazzi honored with a portion of the Dante dust he had collected after the discovery of the poet's bones in 1865. She would have appreciated this gift, no less than the statues, as a tangible sign of the sculptor's esteem and affection for her and her family. If Pazzi gave the relic to Costanza, he must have waited a number of years before doing so. Although the princess was a citizen of Ravenna, other residents would have looked no more kindly on Pazzi's distribution of relics to her than on the mayor's temporary consignment of tomb scrapings to "foreign" members (including Tuscans) of the national commission. Only after the dust had settled, so to speak, would Pazzi have risked publicizing the relic by having a renowned jeweler like Leopoldo Settepassi encase it in a gold brooch as a gift for the first lady of Ravenna. How Cesare D'Ancona obtained the bejeweled Dante dust from Princess Costanza Ghika remains unknown. Alessandro D'Ancona reports only that he kept a close watch on the relic from the time Pazzi gave it "to a woman": "from whom it passed to my brother, Prof. Cesare, and from him to me."[28]

Dora D'Istria, who had praised Dante's Beatrice as a harbinger of female emancipation when she spoke in Ravenna in 1865, presents an intriguing possibility as an intermediary between Costanza Ghika and Cesare D'Ancona—if she herself was not the direct recipient of Pazzi's gift. Dora was a cousin of Costanza and Pulcheria Ghika. Born Elena Ghika, she was the daughter of Mihail Ghika (1792–1850), minister of internal affairs of Wallachia and older brother of Alexander and Costantino, the father of Costanza and Pulcheria.[29] As the widow of a Russian prince, Alexander Koltzoff-Massalsky, Dora was a princess twice over. A fixture of Florentine high society after Italian unification, she frequented the same Tuscan circles as Enrico Pazzi and Alessandro D'Ancona, and their paths crossed in Ravenna as distinguished guests at commemorative events following the discovery of Dante's bones.[30]

Dora's speech at the banquet on June 24, 1865, received ample coverage in Ravenna's local papers, which also noted the presence of Alessandro D'Ancona from Tuscany. When Dora wrote of her pilgrimage that year to Dante's tomb, she showed familiarity with D'Ancona's scholarly work by drawing on his authority to refute those who believed Beatrice was a fictive or philosophical ideal rather than a real-life example for future generations of strong, intelligent women.[31] Both Dora and Alessandro were guests of Willard Fiske (1831–1904), an eminent American professor, librarian, and editor who in 1883 resigned his position at Cornell University in Ithaca, New York, and moved to Italy, where he first rented the historic Villa Forini in Florence (near Porta alla Croce) and later purchased the Villa Landor (named for the English poet William Savage Landor) just outside the city in Fiesole. While in Italy, Fiske assembled one of the world's finest Dante collections, including many early printed editions of the poet's *Divine Comedy,* which he left to Cornell.[32] In a letter to Charles ("Charley") Dudley Warner, his lifelong friend, on April 10, 1884, Fiske wrote that "the much traveled Princess Dora D'Istria, whose house and garden here are very pretty," and "Professor D'Ancona of Pisa, the foremost of Italian critics," were among the writers, artists, and aristocrats who had visited him at Villa Forini that winter.[33]

Dora D'Istria's attractive Villa D'Istria on Via Leonardo da Vinci, "known to many American friends and admirers who have been welcome guests there," was undoubtedly also familiar to members of the prominent D'Ancona clan as well as to Enrico Pazzi and other artists and writers living in and around Florence. Putting Dora "in contact with the fervent intellectual and political society of the post-unification period," her residence in Florence enhanced her reputation as "one of Europe's most distinguished women."[34] Dora and Enrico would have certainly been among the influential visitors to Palazzina D'Ancona in the elegant Piazza Massimo D'Azeglio. Built in 1869–1871 for Sansone D'Ancona and his siblings, this palace was the site of one of Florence's most fashionable political and literary salons. Cesare D'Ancona, to whom the "Wallachian princess" gave the Dante dust collected by Enrico Pazzi in 1865, occupied one floor of the house.[35] Pazzi was himself close with the entire D'Ancona family. As he had for the Rasponi-Ghika families in Ravenna, he applied his artistic talents to honoring his Florentine friends, sculpting busts of Ester, the family matriarch, and Sansone D'Ancona. He gave a signed photograph of his famous Dante statue to Dr. Giacomo D'Ancona.[36] This web of Florentine social relations helps explain how Alessandro D'Ancona kept tabs on the Dante dust after Pazzi gave it to the unnamed princess until it came—via his brother Cesare—into his own possession.

The medallion remained nearly forgotten after D'Ancona's donation to the Senate Library in 1911 until Mario La Rosa's newspaper article in 1968. Writing again about the Roman relic in 1987, La Rosa recalled the emotion of his visit to the Senate Library nearly twenty years earlier. He came upon the Dante dust by chance when he was granted permission to browse the "tiny and forgotten" museum in Rome, located at that time in a small, windowless room of the Senate Library. He was amazed when, while perusing such curiosities as Cavour's inkwell and Verdi's walking stick, his eyes fell upon "a round case, made of gold, as small as a box of matches, with these words inscribed on it: '*Ceneri di Dante*.'" Perhaps La Rosa substituted "ashes" (*ceneri*) for "dust" (*polvere*), the actual word on the medallion, because time played tricks on his memory, but the mistake was consistent with his classification of the material as "a small portion of the remains of the Great Poet."[37]

Whether this dust came from Dante's bones or had merely touched them, Mario La Rosa considered it sacred. "Before such a Relic," he recalled, "I lowered myself, bending my knee," as if he were worshiping the remains of a saint in a church. The library clerk who was supervising the visit was "stunned" by the journalist's spontaneous act of reverence. Considering it his duty to bear witness, the clerk "reported to his superiors what he had seen." Impressed by the presence of this Dante relic in Rome, La Rosa thought to inform the public not only through the press but, as a RAI journalist, through television. To that end, he taped a segment that he himself wrote, directed, and presented but that, he lamented, "for some odd reason, never aired."[38]

Absent this publicity, the next opportunity to shine light on the Dante dust held in Italy's Senate Library came with news of the missing Florentine relics in 1987. The Roman relic did not appear again until the Jubilee of 2015–2016, nearly thirty years later. By this time, the library had for twelve years occupied Palazzo della Minerva near the Pantheon, less than a quarter mile from its original location in Palazzo Madama. The medallion was stored in a locked safe, where it remains today.[39] This Dante relic never received the lasting, widespread veneration that its display in a prominent location, as urged by Alessandro D'Ancona and Mario La Rosa, would have afforded. Still, Senator D'Ancona's vigilance ensured that the gold-encased dust would not be lost to posterity, and it has known a single, stable home since its arrival in the nation's capital in 1911. The relic may well owe its survival, moreover, to Enrico Pazzi's whimsical decision to transform traces of Dante's physical afterlife into a unique if morbid gift for an unspecified woman.

The Dante dust and cranial impressions Pazzi donated to the Florentine library in 1889 went missing for seventy years, as we saw, before being found by chance in 1999, while other relics he collected and disseminated—including items once belonging to Father Giambattista Giuliani and Minister of Education Giuseppe Natoli—briefly surfaced in the early twentieth century before completely disappearing from the historical record.[40] Unlike those relics, the bejeweled dust may have been forgotten for a time, but it was never lost. Perhaps the creator of Dante's most famous statue sought to romance "a mysterious lover" with a gold ornament holding not diamonds or other gemstones but physical traces of Italy's greatest poet, the lover of Beatrice. Or maybe Pazzi simply meant to show his deep affection for an aristocratic female patron. Either way, it was love that saved this portion of Dante dust from oblivion.[41]

18

Dante's Global Face

Langdon closed the case and stood a moment, gazing at Dante's pale
visage, a ghostly presence in the darkened room. *Home at last.*
— DAN BROWN

• While almost the entirety of Dante's graveyard history has taken place
in Italy, mostly in Ravenna and Florence, one small piece—actually fragments
of the wood chest discovered in 1865—crossed the Atlantic to the United
States, entering the home of the poet Henry Wadsworth Longfellow in Cambridge, Massachusetts, in 1872. This relic's complicated chain of custody
began with Pio Feletti's discovery of the pine box containing Dante's bones
on May 27, 1865.[1] The next day Fedele Spada, a master mason working under
Feletti at the site, avowed that he had taken possession of "four broken pieces"
of the chest. In his statement of authenticity, signed by three witnesses in addition to Spada, the mason explains that he gave the fragments to his friend
Luigi Casamenti, a local bookseller and antiquarian.[2]

Colonel T. Bigelow Lawrence, heir to his family's fortune from New
England textile manufacturing, lived in Florence as the US consul general to
Italy during this period. His wife, Elizabeth, recalled "the flurry" that "then
was all over Italy at the discovery" of Dante's bones.[3] An assiduous collector
of medieval weapons and armor and other historical objects, Colonel Lawrence acquired the relic from Casamenti in 1868. After Lawrence's untimely
death the following year, his thirty-nine-year-old widow inherited the bulk
of his wealth and possessions, including the fragments, which she loaned with
other items to the Boston Athenæum. Elizabeth's "small piece of Dante's
coffin" lay in a case in the museum's art room until 1872, when she offered it
to Longfellow to reciprocate for the gift of "a volume of [his] latest poems."[4]
While Longfellow waited to transfer the relic from the Athenæum to his
home, he showed his appreciation by giving Elizabeth Lawrence one of only

18.1. Decorative casket with coffin fragments and related items in Longfellow's study
(Courtesy of the National Park Service, Longfellow House–Washington's Headquarters
National Historic Site, March 2010; photo: David Daly)

ten privately printed copies of his translation of the *Divine Comedy*.[5] He was
deeply gratified to hear of her joy in having this rare three-volume set but insisted that her pleasure "cannot be half so great" as that she had given him
"by the very precious Dante relic." Promising to "always keep it and guard it
with reverential care," Longfellow preserved the coffin fragments—along
with Fedele Spada's statement, a photo of the mason, and a pamphlet on
the discovery of Dante's bones—in a small decorative casket on a table in
his study.[6]

The location matters. The stately house in Cambridge that held the relic
of Italy's prophetic father had once been occupied by America's founding
father. George Washington not only slept in this house, but—as commander
in chief of the Continental Army—he used it as his headquarters for nine
months during the Siege of Boston in 1775–1776. Soon after completing the
first American translation of the whole *Divine Comedy,* Longfellow guarded

Dante's relic with "reverential care" in the room in which General Washington had met with the likes of John Adams and Benjamin Franklin and had consulted with military officers to advance the cause of American freedom a century earlier. Living and working in Washington's former quarters, Longfellow set Dante on course to a long and healthy life in the New World at a time when the medieval poet was viewed as a beacon of liberty on both sides of the Atlantic.

Dante's impact on American life and culture first took literary, artistic, scholarly, and educational forms, even when his writings served political ends. By the end of the nineteenth century, the United States had become "the new Ravenna of the great poet," wrote the eminent Dante scholar Giovanni Andrea Scartazzini. Ravenna had welcomed and cared for Dante at the end of his life. America now nurtured and expanded his legacy with major contributions to the study of his works—including Longfellow's annotated translation (1867) and Edward Allen Fay's concordance (1888)—and the acquisition and preservation of the poet's "children" (manuscripts, books, "bibliographical curiosities") by US libraries, archives, and museums.[7]

Longfellow and his American contemporaries followed in a long tradition of English-language writers, from Chaucer and Milton to Byron and Tennyson, whose work drew deeply from the *Divine Comedy*. Dante's well-documented influence on Anglophone literature has continued to grow since the end of the nineteenth century, with notable contributions by James Joyce, Samuel Beckett, T. S. Eliot, Ralph Ellison, Louise Glück, Seamus Heaney, Gloria Naylor, Robert Pinsky, Toni Morrison, and Clive James, among many distinguished voices. Karen Russell's *Swamplandia!* (2011) and Nicole Krauss's *In a Forest Dark* (2017) are lauded Dante-inflected novels of the past decade, while Matthew Pearl's *The Dante Club* (2003) and *The Dante Chamber* (2018) are historical thrillers centered on the poet's nineteenth-century legacy.[8]

A multinational cast of Dante-inspired Nobel laureates points to the poet's broad and diverse appeal over the past one hundred years. Eliot, Beckett, Heaney, and Morrison join the Italians Luigi Pirandello and Eugenio Montale in this select group, as do writers from Guatemala (Miguel Àngel Asturias), the West Indies (Derek Walcott), Japan (Kenzaburo Oe), and Turkey (Orhan Pamuk). The Argentinian author Jorge Luis Borges never won a Nobel Prize, but his critically acclaimed oeuvre also drew deeply from the *Divine Comedy,* as did works by the Russian writers Osip Mandelstam and Alexsandr Solzhenitsyn. The medieval poem has likewise inspired creative minds in music and the visual and performance arts. Verses that captured the imagination of Renaissance painters like Botticelli, Michelangelo, and Raphael have found new life in the politically coded pop art of Robert Rauschenberg, the gritty cityscapes of Sandow Birk, and the vivid illustrations of Monika Beisner. Dantean notes by classical composers like Liszt, Tchaikovsky, and Puccini now share aural space with the electronic sounds of Tangerine Dream, the heavy metal of Iced Earth, and the rapid-fire smackdowns of the Italian rapper Caparezza.[9]

Dante's pervasive influence across genre and media highlights his success as the consummate "crossover artist."[10] He enjoys immense posthumous popularity—commercially and politically as well as academically and artistically—because he is a canonical figure with broad-based appeal, a magnet for elite and mainstream audiences alike. Peter Hawkins, an astute observer of Dante's modern reincarnations, pinned the crossover label on the poet for his influence on cinema. From the landmark silent *Inferno* (1911) and a Hollywood *Inferno* starring Spencer Tracy (1935) to an animated puppet *Inferno* voiced by Dermot Mulroney and James Cromwell (2007) and an adaptation of Dan Brown's *Inferno* novel (2016), filmmakers have mined the poet's vision of the afterlife—overwhelmingly the underworld—to produce popular entertainment.[11] Films like these, as well as many that call on Dante in limited yet powerful ways, pay tribute to a writer who famously sought a larger audience by composing his great poem in Italian rather than Latin.

The Italian comedian and movie star Roberto Benigni, whose *Life Is Beautiful* won the Oscar in 1999 for best foreign-language film and earned him the award for best actor (he also directed the film), has become one of Dante's best ambassadors—surely his most impassioned one—throughout Italy and to the rest of the world. After Sophia Loren shouted "Roberto!" at the Academy Awards ceremony, the exuberant winner climbed over several rows of seats (Steven Spielberg lent a helping hand) and hopped onto the stage to gather the Oscar statuette and deliver his speech. He ended by summoning the final verse of the *Divine Comedy*. "Dante said, 'L'amor che move 'l sole e l'altre stelle"—'love who move the sun and the other star'—love is a divinity, and sometimes if you have faith, like all the divinities, it can appears," Benigni declaimed in his beautifully imperfect English to tens of millions of viewers. "That's why I want to dedicate this prize to Nicoletta Braschi," his costar and wife.[12]

Benigni's heartfelt shout-out to Dante previewed *TuttoDante*—"All Dante"—the one-man show he created in homage to his Tuscan ancestor. Beginning in June 2006, he electrified audiences in Italian piazzas and theaters with his riveting recitation of Dante's poetry from memory—a canto of the *Divine Comedy* in each show—often prefaced by humorous but trenchant political commentary. Having entertained over a million spectators in Italy, Benigni took Dante on an international tour in 2009, packing houses in Paris, London, Munich, Athens, San Francisco, New York, Montreal, Boston, Toronto, Chicago, Buenos Aires, and other cities. The show's popularity brought Benigni back to Italian stages for a curtain call in 2012–2013. Millions of fans also enjoyed his tour-de-force performances on television and DVD.[13]

Dante's physical afterlife has continued to respond to his cultural legacy while also helping to shape it. As Roberto Benigni committed Dante's verses to memory and began reciting them in the piazza, a team of Italian scientists gave the poet a long-overdue makeover in the laboratory. Dante looks serious and grim in traditional representations. Famous portraits and busts fleshed out Boccaccio's fourteenth-century description, even if—as the art historian Maria Monica Donato maintains—neither this verbal sketch nor any known visual depiction can be trusted to give an accurate idea of Dante's physical appearance.[14] "His face was long, his nose aquiline," wrote Boccaccio, "and his eyes rather large than small; his jaw big, and the underlip protruding beyond the upper. . . . His expression was ever melancholy and thoughtful." A more comely Dante surfaced in the middle of the nineteenth century when Dante Gabriel Rossetti and other pre-Raphaelite artists were inspired by a fresco—discovered in 1840 and attributed at the time to Giotto—allegedly depicting the young poet-lover of the *Vita nuova*. But the "hatchet"-faced Dante—as seen in the profile painted by Raphael in 1509–1510—has dominated the poet's facial iconography over the centuries. Raphael's version was stamped on the two-euro coin in 2002.[15]

In 2006, a multidisciplinary research group gave Dante a new look in keeping with the more affable poet of recent vintage. Building on Fabio Frassetto's measurements, photographs, and casts of Dante's skull from the early twentieth century, scientists worked in the Virtual Reality Lab of the University of Bologna's Aerospace Engineering Department to create the most plausible representation of how he looked. The reproduction proceeded in several stages, each employing a different technique requiring its own disciplinary expertise and highly specialized equipment. The scientists used reverse-engineering software to generate a 3-D virtual replica of Frassetto's plaster cast of Dante's cranium. Since Dante's skull—hence Frassetto's cast—lacked the lower jawbone, they selected a mandible from the anthropology

18.2. Raphael (Raffaello Sanzio) (1483–1520) *Disputa* (Disputation over the Blessed Sacrament)—detail (head of Dante) (Stanza della Segnatura. Scala/Art Resource, NY)

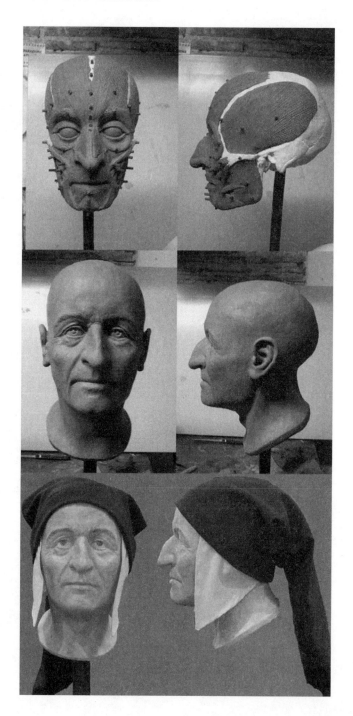

18.3. Reconstruction of
Dante's face by Francesco
Mallegni, Gabriele Mallegni,
Giorgio Gruppioni, et al.
(2006) (Image courtesy of
Giorgio Gruppioni)

museum's collection that was morphologically compatible with the skull. They then followed the same optical scanning procedure to build a virtual model of this jawbone. After virtually attaching the 3-D cranium and mandible, they used rapid prototyping—an additive, layer-by-layer method—to model Dante's complete skull. Finally, the scientists and reconstruction artists applied techniques of forensic anthropology—work typically used to reconstruct faces of unidentified persons from skeletal remains—to add soft tissues and put a face on this head.[16]

While this reconstructed face conformed "most faithfully to the anatomical traits of Dante's skull," the scientists acknowledged "a certain amount of subjectivity in a practice that mixes science, technology, and art." Apart from the problem of the missing mandible, there were too many variables involved in modeling the shape of Dante's eyes, nose, and mouth to conclude that he looked exactly this way. A documentary on the facial reconstruction nonetheless ends with the narrator highlighting its innovative consequences. "Today, thanks to scientific progress and to modern technology," he announces, "Dante has finally regained his own aspect: warm and human."[17]

Interviewed for articles in popular media outlets, the scientists spoke about how Dante's new face altered perceptions of his temperament and character. The paleoanthropologist Francesco Mallegni, like the experts who examined Dante's bones in 1865 and 1921, sees his subjects' skeletal remains as a sign of "what kind of people they were and what they did in life." Dante's new face "looks worn-out" to the scientist. Appearing "perplexed" and "less pointy" than he does in traditional representations, this Dante confirms the simple fact that "he's human." The anthropologist Giorgio Gruppioni, another lead investigator, had a similar reaction to the final product of their scientific reconstruction. "We all had our ideas of what Dante looked like," he told Reuters, "but if this is right, it shows his face was different. He looks more like a common man, a man on the street."[18] Dante's full, fleshy face contrasts with the sharp, harsh profile conventionally imposed on the author of the *Divine Comedy*. "Warm and human," this kinder and gentler Dante is not for Italians only. Nor is he just for the spiritually, intellectually, or literarily inclined. The media-savvy poet plays to diverse audiences within the global community.

Scientifically and culturally refashioned, Dante's new face appears more attractive, at times downright sexy. An outdoor shower scene by the French American actor Gilles Marini in the film *Sex and the City* (2008) gave Dante an erotic charge that made more than a few viewers go weak at the knees.

When Carrie Bradshaw (played by Sarah Jessica Parker) wanted to convey her friend's struggle to remain faithful after meeting this gorgeous neighbor, she only had to say, "from the minute she met Dante, Samantha was in Hell." The *Inferno* video game by Electronic Arts (2010) recast the poet as a muscular crusader battling the monsters of Hell and his own demons to rescue Beatrice, a troubling reversal pairing Dante's hypermasculinity with the demotion of the strong woman who saved him to "the prototypical damsel in distress."[19] Sylvain Reynard's best-selling romance trilogy—*Gabriel's Inferno* (2011), *Gabriel's Rapture* (2012), *Gabriel's Redemption* (2013)—transferred the poet's sex appeal to Professor Gabriel Emerson, a Dante scholar whose "notorious good looks and sophisticated charm" made him a "magnet for sin," as the first book's back cover informed readers. Matthew Weiner's television series *Mad Men* spectacularly exploited this contemporary embellishment of Dante by introducing a seductive character, played by Jon Hamm, living and creating his own Hell on earth. Don Draper's Dantean journey came into focus when we saw and heard him reading the first lines of John Ciardi's popular *Inferno* translation on a Hawaiian beach to open season 6 in 2013.

Global Dante received his most popular makeover to date in Dan Brown's *Inferno* and its cinematic adaptation. While Brown's *Inferno* hardly enjoyed the commercial success of his wildly popular *The Da Vinci Code*, it still sold well over a million copies in the United States alone and was the best-selling

18.4. Don Draper (Jon Hamm) reading Dante's *Inferno* (Still from *Mad Men*, season 6, episode 1 ["The Doorway," part 1], written by Matthew Weiner, directed by Scott Hornbacher, Lionsgate Television and AMC, April 7, 2013, DVD by Lionsgate Home Entertainment, 2013)

book of 2013. Three years later, revenues from Ron Howard's film likewise lagged behind those of his adaptations of Brown's earlier novels, but the movie's lackluster domestic performance—with US sales less than half the film's estimated $75 million budget—was more than offset by international box-office success. *Inferno* earned over $100 million in overseas markets even before its US release, eventually taking in nearly double that amount in ticket sales abroad.[20] This literary and cinematic blockbuster introduced readers and viewers around the world to Dante's various faces while showcasing yet another artifact from his physical afterlife.

Hell on earth in Brown's thriller combines the devastating consequences of global overpopulation with a draconian plan to prevent them from happening. Robert Langdon, the novel's sleuthing Harvard professor specializing in symbols, and his brilliant sidekick, Sienna Brooks, must decipher clues to locate a world-altering virus (called Inferno) hatched by Bertrand Zobrist, a Dante-obsessed scientific genius. While Zobrist personifies Dante as a grim prophet of humankind's self-destructive behavior, Langdon—the urbane, amiable Dante expert—embodies the poet's more appealing modern look. The professor "goes through his own day of personal hell," Dan Brown tells viewers of the film adaptation on DVD; "it is his Inferno."[21]

An actual rendering of Dante's face binds these two characters, each identified with the poet and his vision, closely together. Zobrist owns the poet's so-called death mask housed in the Museum of the Palazzo Vecchio in Florence. Marta Alvarez, an administrator at the palazzo, reports that the wealthy scientist paid a "small fortune" to the museum for the mask but agreed to leave it there on permanent display. Zobrist is "a genuine scholar of Dante," she adds, "and yet a bit . . . how do you say . . . *fanatico*?" The novel gives a romantic spin to the story of how the mask originally came to Florence. Dante was buried in Ravenna, Marta explains, "but because his true love, Beatrice, was buried in Florence, and because Dante so loved Florence, bringing his death mask here seemed like a kindhearted tribute to the man." With the mask in the Palazzo Vecchio, she adds, "we feel like Dante has finally been allowed to come home."[22]

The mask's historical journey to the Palazzo Vecchio was not completely divorced from the novel's romanticized account. No billionaire Dantophile intent on saving the world ever owned this object, but the man who donated it to Florence over a century ago was a Dante scholar deeply committed to his nation's health and prosperity. Senator Alessandro D'Ancona, the Italian patriot who bequeathed the gold locket of Dante dust to the Senate Library in Rome, also couched his gift of the mask as an act of devotion to Italy, to Florence above all. On March 31, 1911, the day after he delivered the poet's bejeweled dust to Rome, D'Ancona offered, in a letter to Florence's mayor, to fulfill an earlier promise to donate his Dante mask to the city.

D'Ancona valued the mask, no less than the dust, as a "venerated relic." Calling the funerary portrait an "ancient and authoritative likeness of our greatest citizen, the most Italian of Italians," the senator described his gift to Florence as if it brought the poet back to the city and granted him "everlasting refuge among us." How appropriate, D'Ancona observed, for Dante's likeness to grace the Palazzo Vecchio: in those very halls, over six hundred years earlier, the poet had voted (in the minority) against Pope Boniface VIII's request for Florentine troops—a decision that set in motion events leading to Dante's exile from Florence and, consequently, to his creation of the *Divine Comedy*.[23]

Senator Alessandro D'Ancona had received the mask in 1901 from the widow of Seymour Kirkup, the Englishman who in 1840 had discovered Dante's portrait in a Florentine fresco once attributed to Giotto. This mask is one of several nearly identical copies that have been traced back to a marble or terracotta head of Dante presumably displayed on or near the poet's tomb in the 1500s. Tullio Lombardo, who had assisted his father, Pietro, with renovations to Dante's chapel in 1481–1483, probably sculpted this funerary head. The novel's Marta Alvarez reports that first-time viewers of the mask in the Palazzo Vecchio were often "repulsed" by "Dante's eerily crinkled visage, hooked nose, and closed eyes"—the hatchet-faced poet seen in a photograph of another mask copied from Lombardo's lost original and also once belonging to Seymour Kirkup.[24]

"The truth can be glimpsed only through the eyes of death." These mysterious words, placed by Bertrand Zobrist on an altered copy of Sandro Botticelli's map of Dante's Hell, direct Robert Langdon to the poet's death mask. Langdon and Sienna Brooks—played by Tom Hanks and Felicity Jones in the film—later find the mask in the Florentine baptistry, where Dante had fantasized he might one day return to receive the laurel crown. Arranged on the back of the mask—"through the eyes of death"—is a swirl of clues, its nine spiraling revolutions matching the circles of Hell, that Langdon must decipher to find the world-changing Inferno virus. Along the way, he checks the mask in a locker at the Venice train station. Dante's face emerges again only after the usual series of twists and turns of a Dan Brown novel, when Langdon receives a package with the mask back in Florence. In the novel's

18.5. Funerary mask of Dante, once belonging to Baron Kirkup (Photograph, ca. 1915–1920; Alinari/Art Resource, NY)

last chapter—the film's final scene—the Dante-loving professor surreptitiously returns the poet's likeness to its rightful place in the Palazzo Vecchio. After setting the object back in its display case, Langdon "stood a moment, gazing at Dante's pale visage, a ghostly presence in the darkened room." As Senator Alessandro D'Ancona had felt when he gave the mask to Florence in 1911, Langdon thought that the poet's face—and so the exiled Florentine himself—was *"home at last."*[25]

But Dante is not "home at last," at least not physically, except for whatever minuscule particles of his bones might be contained in the dust collected by Enrico Pazzi in 1865 and now held in the National Central Library of Florence. So far authorities have not permitted scientific testing that could confirm or refute this possibility. Even as Dante's dead body lives in exile, however, his persona and imagination find ever more hospitable homes throughout the world. For the poet's 750th birthday in 2015, over 180 events took place in Italy, with Italian Cultural Centers sponsoring nearly as

18.6. Robert Langdon (Tom Hanks) and Sienna Brooks (Felicity Jones) examining Dante's death mask (Still from *Inferno*, directed by Ron Howard, Columbia Pictures and Imagine Entertainment, US release on October 28, 2016, DVD by Sony Pictures Home Entertainment, 2017)

many in other countries. Marking the occasion were exhibits, conferences, concerts, and shows—including Roberto Benigni's performance before the Italian Senate—along with biographies, translations, memoirs, and other publications.[26]

Two birthday gifts gave new meaning to Dante's bold claim that his "sacred poem" was created by "heaven and earth." Pope Francis, the first pontiff to take the name of the saint most dear to Dante, sent a message praising the poet as a "prophet of hope" for his vision of a "new condition" of humankind "marked by harmony, peace and happiness." The second gift originated out of this world. Viewing the globe from the heavens, as Dante imagined doing from his birth sign (Gemini) in the *Divine Comedy,* the Italian astronaut Samantha Cristoforetti honored the poet by reciting the opening verses of his *Paradiso* while orbiting the Earth in the International Space Station. A live feed transmitted her voice and image to a rapt audience in Dante's native city.[27]

If history is any guide, the seven hundredth anniversary of the poet's death in 2021 will bring new discoveries about his physical afterlife and add new chapters to his legacy in Italy and throughout the world. The most astonishing tribute by far would be the transfer of Dante's physical remains from Ravenna to Florence, the repatriation inevitably sought—and inevitably thwarted—during previous milestone anniversaries and at other propitious times. A serious proposal to do just that is in the news as I write these words in the summer of 2019.

This proposal, unlike earlier requests, calls only for temporary repatriation. Like a priceless work of art, Dante's body would be on loan to Florence for the centenary before returning to its permanent home in Ravenna. To succeed where previous efforts to reclaim the poet's bones have failed, the limited-time transfer must overcome several obstacles. Moving Dante from Ravenna to Florence requires permission to circumvent legal prohibitions against the exhumation and transportation of human remains. Even if temporary, moreover, the repatriation already faces opposition by critics insisting that, because the exiled poet rejected Florentine offers of amnesty, it is disrespectful to bring him home now. Most daunting of all, the loan presumes an agreement between the two principal cities. "This would obviously be a historic achievement, something extraordinary," said Mayor Dario Nardella of Florence, before cautiously adding, "it could happen only in complete accord with the city of Ravenna." Reaching this accord, he knows, will not be easy: "It's no coincidence that," as we have seen, "no one has been able to do it in seven hundred years."[28]

Repatriating Dante in 2021 would have major economic and cultural consequences for both cities. Several hundred thousand people visit his tomb in Ravenna each year. Many more Italians and foreigners would relish the unprecedented opportunity to be in the company of the poet's mortal remains in his native city—Florence hosts millions of tourists each year.[29] Dante's physical presence there would expose even more people to the poet and his great work.

Whether Dante finally returns to Florence, even provisionally, or stays where he is in Ravenna, we can be sure of this: the poet's bones and his *Divine Comedy*—his physical and spiritual afterlives, his two bodies—will continue to spark creative fires that keep the man and his achievement alive across time and place. And new works forged in those fires will continue, in turn, to encourage readers (as I hope this book does) to meet for the first time or renew their acquaintance with the poetic masterpiece that lifts us to the stars but begins "in a forest dark," in Longfellow's translation, "midway upon the journey of our life."

Note on Texts and Translations

References to Dante's works are taken from the following editions and translations:

La divina commedia. Edited by Giorgio Petrocchi. Turin: Einaudi, 1975. Translated by Robert Hollander and Jean Hollander. New York: Doubleday, 2000–2007.

Vita nuova. Edited and translated by Dino S. Cervigni and Edward Vasta. Notre Dame, IN: University of Notre Dame Press, 1995.

Convivio. Edited by Piero Cudini. 6th ed. Milan: Garzanti, 2005. Translated by Richard Lansing. New York: Garland, 1990.

Monarchia. Edited by Pier Giorgio Ricci. Verona: Mondadori, 1965. Translated by Prue Shaw. Cambridge: Cambridge University Press, 1996.

De vulgari eloquentia. Edited and translated by Steven Botterill. Cambridge: Cambridge University Press, 1996.

Epistole. Edited Angelo Jacomuzzi. Vol. 2 of *Opere minori di Dante Alighieri*. Turin: Unione Tipografico-Editrice Torinese, 1986. Translated by Paget Toynbee. Oxford: Oxford University Press, 1920.

Ecloge. Edited by Giorgio Bárberi Squarotti, Sergio Cecchin, Angelo Jacomuzzi, and Maria Gabriella Stassi. Vol. 1 of *Opere minori di Dante Alighieri*. Turin: Unione Tipografico-Editrice Torinese, 1983.

Unless otherwise indicated, all other translations are my own. I occasionally modify translations for American English spelling.

Notes

PROLOGUE

Epigraph: Henry Clark Barlow, *The Sixth Centenary Festivals of Dante Allighieri in Florence and Ravenna* (London: Williams and Norgate, 1866), 67. I keep "Allighieri," an older form of Dante's surname ("Alighieri"), when it is used in titles and quotations.

1   Agnellus of Ravenna, a ninth-century abbot, tells this story in *The Book of Pontiffs of the Church of Ravenna,* trans. Deborah Mauskopf Deliyannis (Washington, DC: Catholic University of America Press, 2004), 128–133.

2   Filippo Lanciani to the Prefecture of Ravenna on October 27, 1864, quoted in Maria Carmela Maiuri, "Filippo Lanciani e il restauro dei monumenti ravennati nella seconda metà dell'Ottocento," *Ravenna studi e ricerche* 7, no. 2 (2000): 77–113, at 79.

3   Filippo Lanciani's reports on the excavations are contained in letters from his father, Pietro, to the editor of *L'Osservatore Romano* (the newspaper of the Holy See), published on June 1 and June 14, 1865.

4   Dante, *Par.* 22.106–117. A passage in Giovanni Boccaccio's commentary on the *Divine Comedy* suggests the end of May (Boccaccio, commentary on Dante, *Inf.* 1.1–3, in the Dartmouth Dante Project database, https://dante.dartmouth.edu); Robert M. Durling and Ronald L. Martinez, in *Time and the Crystal: Studies in Dante's Rime Petrose* (Berkeley: University of California Press, 1990), "incline toward May 27," the day of the discovery, "as the date Dante knew or supposed to be his birthday" (85).

5   For Fedele Spada's participation, I rely on his personal statement, signed and witnessed on May 28, 1865. I examined this document at Longfellow House–Washington's Headquarters National Historic Site (LONG 27930, box 4, folder 68), Cambridge, MA.

6   Later that day, Angelo Dradi, identified as an "illiterate laborer," signed the official report with an *x* (*Della scoperta delle ossa di Dante: Relazione con documenti per cura del Municipio di Ravenna* [Ravenna: Angeletti, 1870], xlix–liv, at liv). In the census of 1871, 62 percent of Italian males and 76 percent of Italian females over the age of six were illiterate, with an illiteracy rate of 72 percent (male and female combined) in the Emilia-Romagna region, where Ravenna is located (Martin Clark, *Modern Italy, 1871–1982* [Longman: London, 1984], 35–36).

7   The official report of May 27 contains the results of this preliminary examination of the bones (*Della scoperta,* li–lii). The doctors' full, more detailed anatomical-physiological report includes information from a later examination (*Della scoperta,* i–xv).

8   Giovanni Boccaccio, *Trattatello in laude di Dante,* first redaction, ed. Pier Giorgio Ricci, in *Tutte le opere di Giovanni Boccaccio,* ed. Vittore Branca, 10 vols. (Milan: Mondadori, 1964–1983), 3:437–496, at 465, translated by Philip H. Wicksteed, rev. William Chamberlain, as *Life of Dante* (Richmond, UK: Oneworld Classics, 2009).

9   *L'Osservatore Romano,* June 1, 1865.

10   Romolo Conti, *La scoperta delle ossa di Dante* (Ravenna: Angeletti, 1865), 25.

11   The official report of May 27, 1865, lists the measurements of the pine box as 77 centimeters long by 28.4 centimeters wide by 30 centimeters high (*Della scoperta,* l). The report of the National Commission, on June 12, 1865, specifies the length of one side of the box as 77.5 centimeters and the length of the other side as 74.8 centimeters (Ludovico Frati and Corrado Ricci, eds., *Il sepolcro di Dante: Documenti raccolti* [Bologna: Monti, 1889], 105–132, at 116).

12   Primo Uccellini, *Relazione storica sulla avventurosa scoperta delle ossa di Dante Alighieri* (Ravenna: Angeletti, 1865), 13.

13   At first the inscribed board was mistakenly believed to form part of the top or cover of the wood box. See Conti, *La scoperta,* 42–43; and Corrado Ricci, *L'ultimo rifugio di Dante Alighieri* (Milan: Hoepli, 1891), 348–349.

14   The repackaging of the bones is described in the May 27 report (*Della scoperta,* lii–liii) and in Lanciani's eyewitness account (*L'Osservatore Romano,* June 1, 1865).

15   James Bentley, *Restless Bones: The Story of Relics* (London: Constable, 1985), 29.

16   Barlow, *Sixth Centenary Festivals,* 67–68.

INTRODUCTION

Epigraph: Giambattista Vico, *New Science,* trans. David Marsh (London: Penguin, 2001), 8.

1   Corrado Ricci, *L'ultimo rifugio di Dante Alighieri* (Milan: Hoepli, 1891), 174.

2   Catherine Mary Phillimore, who cribs Ricci's study in her account of Dante's graveyard history, identifies the sacristan by name as Angelo Grillo (*Dante at Ravenna: A Study* [London: Elliot Stock, 1898], 215). Ricci's statement that he was called or known as "Grillo"—"detto *Grillo*"—suggests that the word, even if it was the sacristan's surname, served as his nickname.

3   Dante, *Vita nuova* 3.15.

4   The "scandals of his corpus and corpse," as Sherry Roush puts it in the title of her chapter on narratives of Dante's ghost, including these two dream sequences (*Speaking Spirits: Ventriloquizing the Dead in Renaissance Italy* [Toronto: University of Toronto Press, 2015], 69–107). For Saint Catherine of Siena (1347–1380), Jane Tylus likewise notes that "to a certain extent, there is a parallel between collecting Catherine's works and

gathering the relics of her physical body" (*Reclaiming Catherine of Siena: Literacy, Literature, and the Signs of Others* [Chicago: University of Chicago Press, 2009], 104).

5 Boccaccio may have visited Ravenna on four or five occasions. Ricci (*L'ultimo rifugio,* 213–217) believes he was definitely there twice, in 1346 and 1353. Boccaccio would have met Piero Giardino in 1346.

6 Giovanni Boccaccio, *Trattatello in laude di Dante,* first redaction, ed. Pier Giorgio Ricci, in *Tutte le opere di Giovanni Boccaccio,* ed. Vittore Branca, 10 vols. (Milan: Mondadori, 1964–1983), 3:437–496, at 485, translated by Philip H. Wicksteed, rev. William Chamberlain, as *Life of Dante* (Richmond, UK: Oneworld Classics, 2009).

7 Boccaccio, *Trattatello,* 3:485.

8 Dante affirms the veracity of early-morning dreams in *Inf.* 26.7 and *Purg.* 9.13–18.

9 Boccaccio, *Trattatello,* 3:485–486. Jacopo probably sent the transcribed cantos not to Cangrande, as Boccaccio says, but to Guido Novello da Polenta. Dante's host in Ravenna, Guido had gone to Bologna in 1322 to serve as Capitano del Popolo (Ricci, *L'ultimo rifugio,* 175–177). Jacopo probably sent the entire *Commedia*—the first complete version—to Guido, accompanied by his canto-length summary of the poem, his commentary on the *Inferno,* and the sonnet in which he calls the epic poem his "sister." Jacopo's canto and sonnet are included in *Poesie di mille autori intorno a Dante Alighieri,* ed. Carlo del Balzo, 15 vols. (Rome: Forzani, 1889–1909), 1:317–326.

10 Giannozzo Manetti, "Life of Dante," in *Biographical Writings,* ed. and trans. Stefano U. Baldassarri and Rolf Bagemihl (Cambridge, MA: Harvard University Press, 2003), 8–61, at 53.

11 Gabriella Pomaro, "*Commedia:* Manuscript Tradition," in *Dante Encyclopedia,* ed. Richard Lansing (New York: Garland, 2000), 198–201; Umberto Bosco, ed., *Enciclopedia dantesca,* 6 vols. (Rome: Istituto della Enciclopedia Italiana, 1970–1975), 2:83–86.

12 Felice Mazzeo, *Dante e Ravenna* (Bologna: Cappelli, 1987), summarizes theories about the "lost" manuscript of the *Divine Comedy* and attempts to locate it (59–64). Bishop Giovanni Fallani announced the search for Dante's original manuscript in the archives of the Vatican Library in 1985 ("Dante in Vaticano," *La Repubblica,* May 29, 1985).

13 Paul Klopsch, *Pseudo-Ovidius De Vetula: Untersuchungen und Text* (Leiden: E. J. Brill, 1967), 281, translated by J. B. Trapp in "Ovid's Tomb: The Growth of a Legend from Eusebius to Laurence Sterne, Chateaubriand and George Richmond," *Journal of the Warburg and Courtauld Institutes* 36 (1973): 35–76, at 41–42. See also Seth Lerer, *Chaucer and His Readers: Imagining the Author in Late-Medieval England* (Princeton, NJ: Princeton University Press, 1993), 153; and Thomas A. Prendergast, *Poetical Dust: Poets' Corner and the Making of Britain* (Philadelphia: University of Pennsylvania Press, 2015), 11.

14 Boccaccio crafts a dream episode in his *Decameron* that more closely resembles the sacristan's dream: Lisabetta da Messina is visited in her sleep by the ghost of her lover Lorenzo, who tells her he has been killed by her brothers and indicates the location of his buried corpse (Day 4, novella 5).

15 Romolo Conti, *La scoperta delle ossa di Dante* (Ravenna: Angeletti, 1865); Filippo Lanciani, in letters from his father, Pietro, to *L'Osservatore Romano,* June 1 and June 14, 1865; Henry Clark Barlow, *The Sixth Centenary Festivals of Dante Allighieri in Florence and Ravenna* (London: Williams and Norgate, 1866); Ricci, *L'ultimo rifugio;* Santi Muratori, Corrado Ricci, Giuseppe Sergi, and Fabio Frassetto, eds., *Ricognizione delle ossa di Dante fatta nei giorni 28–31 ottobre 1921* (Rome: Reale Accademia Nazionale dei Lincei, 1923).

16 Umberto Eco, "Abduction in Uqbar," in *The Limits of Interpretation* (Bloomington: Indiana University Press, 1990), 152–162. *Abduction,* Eco's preferred term for this investigative procedure, is an inferential process applied to strange events that cannot be explained satisfactorily by given rules (deduction) or carefully executed experiments (induction).

17 Bess Lovejoy includes short entries on several of these bodies and many others—Dante among them—in *Rest in Pieces: The Curious Fates of Famous Corpses* (New York: Simon and Schuster, 2013).

18 Patrick J. Geary, *Living with the Dead in the Middle Ages* (Ithaca, NY: Cornell University Press, 1994); Geary, *Furta Sacra: Thefts of Relics in the Central Middle Ages* (1978; rev. ed., Princeton, NJ: Princeton University Press, 1990); Peter Brown, *The Cult of Saints: Its Rise and Function in Latin Christianity* (Chicago: University of Chicago Press, 1981); Benjamin Brand, *Holy Treasure and Sacred Song: Relic Cults and Their Liturgies in Medieval Tuscany* (Oxford: Oxford University Press, 2014); James Bentley, *Restless Bones: The Story of Relics* (London: Constable, 1985); Caroline Walker Bynum, *Christian Materiality: An Essay on Religion in Late Medieval Europe* (New York: Zone Books, 2011); Alison Knowles Frazier, *Possible Lives: Authors and Saints in Renaissance Italy* (New York: Columbia University Press, 2005); Charles Freeman, *Holy Bones, Holy Dust: How Relics Shaped the History of Medieval Europe* (New Haven, CT: Yale University Press, 2011); Seeta Chaganti, *The Medieval Poetics of the Reliquary: Enshrinement, Inscription, Performance* (New York: Palgrave, 2008); Cynthia Hahn, *Strange Beauty: Issues in the Making and Meaning of Reliquaries, 400–circa 1204* (University Park: Pennsylvania State University Press, 2012); Hahn, *The Reliquary Effect: Enshrining the Sacred Object* (London: Reaktion Books, 2017).

19 Giambattista Vico, *New Science,* trans. David Marsh (London: Penguin, 2001), 8; Robert Pogue Harrison, *The Dominion of the Dead* (Chicago: University of Chicago Press, 2003), xi.

20 Ugo Foscolo, "Dei sepolcri," in *Opere,* ed. Franco Gavazzeni, 4 vols. (Milan: Ricciardi, 1995–1996), 1:291–327 (lines 151–154), translated by J. G. Nichols in *Last Letters of Jacopo Ortis; and Of Tombs* (London: Hesperus, 2002); Giacomo Leopardi, "Sopra il monumento di Dante che si preparava in Firenze," in *Canti,* ed. and trans. Jonathan Galassi (New York: Farrar, Straus and Giroux, 2010), 12–27 (lines 24–29).

21 Here, as elsewhere in the *Divine Comedy,* Dante bends or extends church doctrine of the time: he not only allows for intercessory prayers of the living for purgatorial souls

but also believes, against the view of Thomas Aquinas (*Summa theologiae,* Blackfriars edition, 61 vols. [New York: McGraw-Hill, 1964–1981], 39:77–81 [2a2ae.83.11]), in the efficacy of purgatorial prayers for the living (Dante, *Purg.* 11.22–36).

22 Dante, *Purg.* 3.103–145.

23 Guelphs and Ghibellines—terms originating with the rival German houses of Welf and Waiblingen—came to be known, roughly speaking, for their allegiance to the papacy (Guelphs) or to the empire (Ghibellines). Italian cities, especially in northern and central regions, were typically dominated by one or the other party.

24 Dante, *Purg.* 5.85–129, lines 100–102: "Quivi perdei la vista e la parola; / nel nome di Maria fini', e quivi / caddi, e rimase la mia carne sola" (my translation).

25 Giovanni Papini, *Dante vivo* (Florence: Libreria Editrice Fiorentina, 1933), translated by Eleanor Hammond Broadus and Anna Benedetti (New York: Macmillan, 1935), 259. Written under the fascist regime, which Papini supported, *Dante vivo* won the Premio Mussolini in 1933. Roush, *Speaking Spirits,* 13, 170–171. Matelda appears in Dante, *Purg.* 28–29 and 31–33, and the eagle speaks in Dante, *Par.* 19–20. Roush also excludes Fra Alberigo from the list because, as one who betrayed guests, his body (possessed by a demon) still lives on earth while his soul speaks with Dante in Hell (Dante, *Inf.* 33.109–157).

26 Papini, *Dante vivo,* 259.

27 Dante, *Inf.* 11.10–12.

28 Dante, *Inf.* 3.64–69 (cowards), 7.112–114 and 8.58–63 (wrathful), 12.100–139 (murderers), 19.7–24 (simonists), 28.7–42 (sowers of discord), 29.46–51 (falsifiers), 32.16–39 (traitors), 34.128 (Lucifer's "tomba"), 9.112–133 and 10.1–15 (heretics), at 15: "che l'anima col corpo morta fanno."

29 The glutton is Ciacco (Dante, *Inf.* 6.37–93), the musician is Belacqua (Dante, *Purg.* 4.97–135), the ex-nun is Piccarda Donati (Dante, *Par.* 3.34–123).

30 Cicero, *Pro archia poeta,* trans. N. H. Watts (Cambridge, MA: Harvard University Press, 1979), 6–41, at 33.

31 Teodolinda Barolini, "Dante and Francesca da Rimini: Realpolitik, Romance, Gender," *Speculum* 75, no. 1 (2000), 1–28, at 1.

32 Dante, *Inf.* 19.52–57, 76–87; Dante, *Par.* 30.133–148. Boniface died in 1303, Clement in 1314, and Henry in 1313.

33 Voltaire, "Lettre XXII, Sur M. Pope et quelques autres poëtes fameux," in *Oeuvres complètes de Voltaire,* ed. Louis Moland, 52 vols. (Paris: Garnier Frères, 1877–1885), 22:168–179, at 174; Joseph Luzzi, *Romantic Europe and the Ghost of Italy* (New Haven, CT: Yale University Press, 2008), 104–123, at 122–123. For signs of Dante's vitality in the Age of Enlightenment, see Aldo Vallone, ed., *Storia della critica dantesca dal XIV al XX secolo,* 2 vols. (Padua: La Nuova Libraria, 1981), 1:519–610, 2:611–652; and Domenico Pietropaolo, *Dante Studies in the Age of Vico* (Ottawa: Dovehouse, 1989).

I. DEATH AND BURIAL IN RAVENNA

Epigraph: Giovanni Boccaccio, *Trattatello in laude di Dante,* first redaction, ed. Pier Giorgio Ricci, in *Tutte le opere di Giovanni Boccaccio,* ed. Vittore Branca, 10 vols. (Milan: Mondadori, 1964–1983), 3:437–496, at 458: "del mese di settembre negli anni di Cristo MCCCXXI . . . al suo Creatore rendé il faticato spirito; il quale non dubito che ricevuto non fosse nelle braccia della sua nobilissima Beatrice"; translated by Philip H. Wicksteed, rev. William Chamberlain, as *Life of Dante* (Richmond, UK: Oneworld Classics, 2009).

1   Dante, *Inf.* 17.85–87: "Qual è colui che sí presso ha 'l riprezzo / de la quartana, c'ha già l'unghie smorte, / e triema tutto pur guardando 'l rezzo."

2   Michele Barbi, *Life of Dante,* ed. and trans. Paul G. Ruggiers (Berkeley: University of California Press, 1954), 10, 28; Giuseppe Mazzotta, "Life of Dante," in *The Cambridge Companion to Dante,* ed. Rachel Jacoff, 2nd ed. (Cambridge: Cambridge University Press, 2007), 1–13, at 6, 12; Stephen Bemrose, *A New Life of Dante* (Exeter, UK: University of Exeter Press, 2000), 208; Marco Santagata, *Dante: The Story of His Life* [*Dante: Il romanzo della sua vita*], trans. Richard Dixon (Cambridge, MA: Harvard University Press, 2016), 53–54, 209–210, 256–257, 316.

3   Boccaccio, *Trattatello,* 3:457; Boccaccio, *Trattatello,* second redaction, in *Tutte le opere,* 3:497–538, at 510 (my translation).

4   Boccaccio, *Esposizioni sopra la Comedia di Dante,* ed. Giorgio Padoan, in *Tutte le opere,* 6:449 (Canto 8, Esposizione litterale, par. 12–13), translated by Michael Papio as *Boccaccio's Expositions on Dante's "Comedy"* (Toronto: University of Toronto Press, 2009).

5   Santagata, *Dante,* 325; Corrado Ricci, *L'ultimo rifugio di Dante Alighieri* (Milan: Hoepli, 1891), 102.

6   Ricci, *L'ultimo rifugio,* 209–216; Boccaccio, *Esposizioni,* 20 (Canto 1, Esposizione litterale, par. 5).

7   A digital facsimile of HRC 45 is available at http://norman.hrc.utexas.edu /pubmnem/details.cfm?id=45.

8   Dante's letter (now lost) is cited by Leonardo Bruni, "Vita di Dante," in *Opere letterarie e politiche,* ed. Paolo Viti (Turin: UTET, 1996), 539–552, at 542, translated by Philip H. Wicksteed, rev. William Chamberlain (Richmond, UK: Oneworld Classics, 2009), 87–99.

9   Morris L. Ghezzi, ed., *Il processo di Dante celebrato il 16 aprile 1966 nella Basilica di S. Francesco in Arezzo* (Milan: Mimesis, 2011), 200.

10   Dante, *Convivio* 1.3.4–5.

11   Ghezzi, *Il processo di Dante,* 212, 214; Santagata, *Dante,* 300–301.

12   Dante, *Epistola* 13.1.

13   Dante, *Par.* 17.58–59; Dante, *Epistola* 12.9 (I have slightly modified Toynbee's translation).

14   Ricci, *L'ultimo rifugio,* 74–78; Santagata, *Dante,* 319–323; Felice Mazzeo, *Dante e Ravenna* (Bologna: Cappelli, 1987), 24–27.

15 Boccaccio, *Trattatello,* 3:464; Oscar Wilde, "Ravenna," in *The Complete Works of Oscar Wilde,* vol. 1, ed. Bobby Fong and Karl Beckson (Oxford: Oxford University Press, 2000), 46–54, at 47 and 53; Mazzotta, "Life of Dante," 11.

16 Filippo Villani, *De origine civitatis Florentiae et de eiusdem famosis civibus,* ed. Giuliano Tanturli (Padua: Antenore, 1997), 22.63, translated by Philip H. Wicksteed, rev. William Chamberlain (Richmond, UK: Oneworld Classics, 2009), 103–104; Ricci, *L'ultimo rifugio,* 417–420.

17 Ricci, *L'ultimo rifugio,* 145–154.

18 Villani, *De origine,* 22.65, 22.67; Giannozzo Manetti, "Life of Dante," in *Biographical Writings,* ed. and trans. Stefano U. Baldassarri and Rolf Bagemihl (Cambridge, MA: Harvard University Press, 2003), 8–61, at 61.

19 Gerald Weissmann, "Gore's Fever and Dante's *Inferno:* Chikungunya Reaches Ravenna," *FASEB Journal* 22, no. 3 (2008): 635–638, http://www.fasebj.org/content/22/3 /635.full.

20 Ricci, *L'ultimo rifugio,* 154. Villani reported that Dante was already ill in Venice (*De origine,* 22.66), while Manetti identified the return journey as the proximate cause of the fever ("Life of Dante," 61). Dante, *Purg.* 28.2: "la divina foresta spessa e viva" (my translation).

21 Boccaccio, *Trattatello,* 3:458.

22 Denis Renevey describes the "ideal medieval funeral" in "Looking for a Context: Rolle, Anchoritic Culture, and the Office of the Dead," in *Medieval Texts in Context,* ed. Graham D. Cale and Denis Renevey (New York: Routledge, 2008), 192–210, at 193.

23 Boccaccio, *Trattatello,* 3:458.

24 Giovanni Villani, *Nuova cronica,* ed. Giuseppe Porta, 3 vols., 2nd ed. (Parma: Fondazione Pietro Bembo, 2007), 2:335 (10.136), translated by Philip H. Wicksteed, rev. William Chamberlain (Richmond, UK: Oneworld Classics, 2009), 101–102; L'Ottimo Commento, commentary on Dante, *Par.* 17.94–99, in the Dartmouth Dante Project database, https://dante.dartmouth.edu; Boccaccio, *Trattatello,* 3:458–459; Manetti, "Life of Dante," 61.

25 Jason M. Houston, *Building a Monument to Dante: Boccaccio as Dantista* (Toronto: University of Toronto Press, 2010); Boccaccio, *Trattatello,* 3:459.

26 Giuseppe Verdi, *I copialettere di Giuseppe Verdi,* ed. Gaetano Cesari and Alessandro Luzio (Milan: Stucchi Ceretti, 1913), 372; Henry James, *Italian Hours,* ed. John Auchard (University Park: Pennsylvania State University Press, 1992), 301.

2. A MARKED GRAVE

Epigraph: Giuseppe Indizio, "Saggio per un dizionario dantesco delle fonti minori: Gli epitafi danteschi: 1321–1483," *Studi danteschi* 75 (2010): 269–323, at 271: "Hic claudor Dantes patriis extorris ab oris / Quem genuit parvi Florentia mater amoris."

1 Giovanni Boccaccio, *Trattatello in laude di Dante,* first redaction, ed. Pier Giorgio Ricci, in *Tutte le opere di Giovanni Boccaccio,* ed. Vittore Branca, 10 vols. (Milan: Mondadori,

1964–1983), 3:437–496, at 460, translated by Philip H. Wicksteed, rev. William Chamberlain, as *Life of Dante* (Richmond, UK: Oneworld Classics, 2009).

2   On Dante's exchange with del Virgilio, see Jonathan Combs-Schilling, "Tityrus in Limbo: Figures of the Author in Dante's Eclogues," *Dante Studies* 133 (2015): 1–26; and Marco Santagata, *Dante: The Story of His Life* [*Dante: Il romanzo della sua vita*], trans. Richard Dixon (Cambridge, MA: Harvard University Press, 2016), 316–317, 324–329.

3   Dante, *Ecloga* 1.51, 1.18, 1.21. I cite the compositions from *Ecloge,* in *Opere minori di Dante Alighieri,* ed. Giorgio Bárberi Squarotti, Sergio Cecchin, Angelo Jacomuzzi, and Maria Gabriella Stassi, 2 vols. (Turin: Unione Tipografico-Editrice Torinese, 1983), 1:550–589.

4   Dante, *Ecloga* 3.38; Dante, *Purg.* 14.63: "molti di vita e sé di pregio priva" (my translation); Dante, *Ecloga* 4.47.

5   Boccaccio, *Trattatello,* 3:460: "vulgo gratissimus auctor"; "Antropos heu letum livida rupit opus"; "Huic ingrata tulit tristem Florentia fructum, / exilium, vati patria cruda suo. / Quem pia Guidonis gremio Ravenna Novelli / gaudet honorati continuisse ducis" (my translations).

6   Giovanni Quirini, *Rime,* ed. Elena Maria Duso (Rome: Antenora, 2002), 82–83, at 82; Dante, *De vulgari eloquentia* 2.2.9; Dante, *Epistola* 3; Cino da Pistoia in *Poeti del Duecento,* ed. Gianfranco Contini, 2 vols. (Milan: Riccardo Ricciardi, 1960), 1:689–690, at 689. Elisabetta Cavallari, *La fortuna di Dante nel Trecento* (Florence: Società anonima editrice Francesco Perrella, 1921), discusses these poems by Giovanni Quirini and Cino da Pistoia along with four other Italian poems written on the occasion of Dante's death (35–38).

7   Quirini, *Rime,* 82; Cavallari, *La fortuna di Dante,* 37–38; Cino, *Poeti del Duecento,* 1:690.

8   Cecco d'Ascoli, *L'Acerba* 4.9.4401–4402. I cite the edition of Achille Crespi (1927; repr., Milan: La Vita Felice, 2011). Seth Boniface Fabian, "Cecco vs. Dante: Correcting the *Comedy* with Applied Astrology" (PhD diss., Columbia University, 2014), 67, 145.

9   Dante, *Inf.* 7.73–96, at 89; d'Ascoli, *L'Acerba* 2.1.719–736; Teodolinda Barolini, "Contemporaries Who Found Heterodoxy in Dante, Featuring (but Not Exclusively) Cecco d'Ascoli," in *Dante and Heterodoxy: The Temptations of 13th Century Radical Thought,* ed. Maria Luisa Ardizzone (Newcastle upon Tyne, UK: Cambridge Scholars, 2014), 259–275, at 269–270.

10   The *Journal of Church and State* is a quarterly journal issued by the J. M. Dawson Institute of Church-State Studies of Baylor University.

11   Anthony K. Cassell, *The "Monarchia" Controversy: An Historical Study with Accompanying Translations of Dante Alighieri's "Monarchia," Guido Vernani's "Refutation of the 'Monarchia' Composed by Dante," and Pope John XXII's Bull "Si fratrum"* (Washington, DC: Catholic University of America Press, 2004), 34–41.

12   Dante, *Inf.* 19.31–87.

13   Guido Vernani, "De reprobatione Monarchiae compositae a Dante," in *Il più antico oppositore politico di Dante: Guido Vernani da Rimini,* ed. Nevio Matteini (Padua: CEDAM,

1958), 91–118, at 93, translated by Cassell in *"Monarchia" Controversy,* 174–197. On Vernani and Dante, see also Zane D. R. Mackin, "Dante *Praedicator:* Sermons and Preaching Culture in the *Commedia*" (PhD diss., Columbia University, 2013), 1–5, 235–236, 240, 244.

14 Boccaccio, *Trattatello,* 3:487–488, at 488.

15 Dante, *Par.* 18.130–136, 27.55–60, at 55: "In vesta di pastor lupi rapaci."

16 Boccaccio, *Trattatello,* 3:488. Boccaccio mentions Bertrando's prohibition against studying the *Monarchia* only in the second redaction, in *Tutte le opere,* 3:497–538, at 530.

17 Pio Tommaso Masetti, *Monumenta et antiquitates veteris disciplinae ordinis praedicatorum ab anno 1216 A.D. 1348,* 2 vols. (Rome: Typographia Rev. Cam. Apostolicae, 1864), 1:128; Cassell, *"Monarchia" Controversy,* 38.

18 Giannozzo Manetti, "Life of Dante," in *Biographical Writings,* ed. and trans. Stefano U. Baldassarri and Rolf Bagemihl (Cambridge, MA: Harvard University Press, 2003), 8–61, at 59; Oddone Zenatti, *Dante e Firenze: Prose antiche con note illustrative ed appendici,* ed. Franco Cardini (Florence: Sansoni, 1984), 521–523.

19 Boccaccio, *Trattatello,* 3:488.

20 Ibid., 3:453–454.

21 Ibid., 3:460–462.

22 Ibid., 3:462.

23 Ibid., 3:462–464.

24 Ibid., 3:464.

25 Ibid.; Dante, *Inf.* 26.49–63.

26 Boccaccio, *Trattatello,* 3:464.

27 For dates and attributions of the epitaphs, I rely most on Saverio Bellomo, "Prime vicende del sepolcro di Dante," *Letture classensi* 28 (1999): 55–71; and Giuseppe Indizio, "Saggio per un dizionario dantesco delle fonti minori: Gli epitafi danteschi: 1321–1483," *Studi danteschi* 75 (2010): 269–323.

28 Though Bellomo prefers Guglielmo Maramauro, a Dante commentator from Naples ("Prime vicende," 71).

29 Indizio, "Saggio," 272:

> Inclita fama cuius universum penetrat orbem
> Dantes Aligherii florenti genitus urbe,
> Conditor eloquii, lumen decusque musarum,
> Vulnere seve nescis stratus ad sidera tendens
> Dominicis annis ter septem mille tercenis
> Setenbris ydibus presenti clauditur aula.

30 Ibid., 271:

> Iura Monarchie superos Phlegetonta lacusque
> Lustrando cecini voluerunt fata quosque;
> Sed quia pars cessit melioribus hospita castris
> Actoremque sum petit felicior astris
> Hic claudor Dantes patriis extorris ab oris
> Quem genuit parvi Florentia mater amoris.

3. FLORENTINE REMORSE

Epigraph: Marsilio Ficino, in Cristoforo Landino, *Comento sopra la Comedia,* ed. Paolo Procaccioli, 4 vols. (Rome: Salerno, 2001), 1:268–270, at 268: "Florentia iam diu mesta, sed tandem leta, Danthi suo Aligherio, post duo ferme secula iam redivivo, et in patriam restituto, ac denique coronato, congratulatur"; translated in *Images of Quattrocento Florence: Selected Writings in Literature, History, and Art,* ed. Stefano Ugo Baldassarri and Arielle Saiber (New Haven, CT: Yale University Press, 2000), 180.

1 Giannozzo Manetti, "Life of Dante," in *Biographical Writings,* ed. and trans. Stefano U. Baldassarri and Rolf Bagemihl (Cambridge, MA: Harvard University Press, 2003), 8–61, at 33.

2 Corrado Ricci, *L'ultimo rifugio di Dante,* 2nd ed. (Milan: Hoepli, 1921), 411–412; Vittorio Rossi, "Ravenna e il 'sepolcro,'" in *Per l'inaugurazione della zona dantesca,* ed. Province and Commune of Ravenna (Ravenna: Società Tipo-Editrice Ravennate Mutilati, 1936), 20–21, at 20. I cite the letter from Giuseppe Biadego, *Per la storia della cultura veronese del XIV secolo: Antonio da Legnago e Rinaldo da Villafranca* (Venice: C. Ferrari, 1903), 583–621, at 588–589.

3 Dante, *Inf.* 15.106–110, at 107: "litterati grandi e di gran fama."

4 Gasparo Martinetti Cardoni, *Dante in Ravenna: Memorie storiche con documenti* (Ravenna: Angeletti, 1864), 108; Romolo Conti, "Relazione storica," in *Della scoperta delle ossa di Dante: Relazione con documenti per cura del Municipio di Ravenna* (Ravenna: Angeletti, 1870), 1–30, at 25; Corrado Ricci, *L'ultimo rifugio di Dante Alighieri* (Milan: Hoepli, 1891), 329–330. I cite the 1396 proposal from Isidoro del Lungo, *Dell'esilio di Dante: Discorso e documenti* (Florence: Le Monnier, 1881), 170–175.

5 Del Lungo, *Dell'esilio di Dante,* 176–177.

6 Simon Gilson, *Dante and Renaissance Florence* (Cambridge: Cambridge University Press, 2005), 113–114.

7 "Dante's Hell," in "Renaissance Dante in Print (1472–1629)," ed. Theodore J. Cachey Jr., Louis E. Jordan, and Christian Y. Dupont, https://www3.nd.edu/-italnet /dante/text/Hell.html.

8 Del Lungo, *Dell'esilio di Dante,* 21–22, 178–179, at 179; Sherry Roush, "Dante Ravennate and Boccaccio Ferrarese? Post-Mortem Residency and the Attack on Florentine Literary Hegemony, 1480–1520," *Viator* 35 (2004): 543–562, at 546.

9 Gilson, *Dante and Renaissance Florence,* 8.

10 Ibid., 9.

11 Deborah Parker, *Commentary and Ideology: Dante in the Renaissance* (Durham, NC: Duke University Press, 1993), 76–85, 136–138, at 76.

12 Gilson, *Dante and Renaissance Florence,* 163.

13 Cristoforo Landino, "Orazione alla Signoria," in *Comento,* 1:108–112, at 111.

14 Landino, *Comento,* 1:245.

15 Ibid., 1:246.

16 Dante, *Inf.* 27.36–54, at 38: "guerra ne' cuor" (my translation); Landino, *Comento,* 2:908.

17 Dante, *Par.* 25.1–12, at 1–3: "'l poema sacro / al quale ha posto mano e cielo e terra, / sí che m'ha fatto per molti anni macro."

18 Landino, *Comento,* 1:268–270, at 268. I cite the translation of Ficino's text from Baldassarri and Saiber, *Images of Quattrocento Florence,* 180.

19 Conti, "Relazione storica," 2–9; Ricci, *L'ultimo rifugio* (1891), 261–270; Giovanni Mesini, *La tomba e le ossa di Dante* (Ravenna: Longo, 1965), 6–7.

20 Debra Pincus, "The Humanist and the Poet: Bernardo Bembo's Portrait of Dante," in *Patronage and Italian Renaissance Sculpture,* ed. Kathleen Wren Christian and David J. Drogin (Farnham, UK: Ashgate, 2010), 61–94, at 79–80, 85.

21 Ricci, *L'ultimo rifugio* (1891), 275–276; Maria Giulia Benini, *Luoghi danteschi: La Basilica di S. Francesco e la Zona Dantesca a Ravenna* (Ravenna: Longo, 2003), 65.

22 Mary D. Garrard, "Who Was Ginevra de' Benci? Leonardo's Portrait and Its Sitter Recontextualized," *Artibus et historiae* 27, no. 53 (2006): 23–56, http://www.jstor.org /stable/20067109. Belonging to the National Gallery of Art in Washington, DC, Leonardo's painting *Ginevra de' Benci* (front and back) can be viewed online at https://www.nga.gov/collection/art-object-page.50724.html.

23 Garrard, "Who Was Ginevra de' Benci?," 27–28, 41, 44–45.

24 Wendy Stedman Sheard, "Bernardo e Pietro Bembo, Pietro, Tullio e Antonio Lombardo: Metamorfosi delle tematiche cortigiane nelle tendenze classicistiche della scultura veneziana," in *Tiziano: Amor sacro e amor profano,* ed. Maria Grazia Bernardini (Milan: Electa, 1995), 118–132, at 124; Garrard, "Who Was Ginevra de' Benci?," 41.

25 I cite the epitaph from Ludovico Frati and Corrado Ricci, eds., *Il sepolcro di Dante: Documenti raccolti* (Bologna: Monti, 1889), 6: "Exigua tumuli Dantes hic sorte iacebas / squallenti nulli cognite pene situ / at nunc marmoreo subnixus conderis arcu / omnibus et cultu splendidiore nites / nimirum Bembus musis incensus ethr-uscis / hoc tibi quem in primis hae coluere dedit."

26 Conti, "Relazione storica," 9.

27 Ricci, *L'ultimo rifugio* (1891), 333.

28 Cristoforo Landino, *Poems,* trans. Mary P. Chatfield (Cambridge, MA: Harvard University Press, 2008), 276–303, at 276–277, 294–295; Landino, *Scritti critici e teorici,* ed. Roberto Cardini (Rome: Bulzoni, 1974), 167–169, at 169; Landino, "Lettera e epigramma a Bernardo Bembo," in *Comento,* 1:113–114, at 113.

29 Landino, "Lettera e epigramma," 1:114:

> Fecerat egregia constructum ex arte sepulcrum
> Tyrrheno Danti Prisca Ravenna novum;
> invida sed sacris obsunt quoque fata sepulcris,
> et turpi obducunt omnia pulchra situ.
> At tu, delitiae Veneti, Bernarde, senatus,
> tutela et sacri maxima, Bembe, chori,

livida mordaci quod triverat ante vetustas
dente, novum niveo marmore restituis.

30 E.-G. Ledos, "Lettre inédite de Cristoforo Landino a Bernardo Bembo," *Bibliothèque de l'École des Chartes* 54 (1893): 721–724, at 721; Pincus, "Humanist and the Poet," 65; Bibliothèque Nationale de France, Réserve des livres rares, RES-YD-17, https://www.bnf.fr/fr/mediatheque/dante-alighieri-la-commedia.

4. HOLY GRAVE ROBBERS

Epigraph: Carlo Maria Nardi, "Vita di Iacopo Nardi," in *Istorie della città di Firenze di Iacopo Nardi, ridotte alla lezione de' codici originali, con l'aggiunta del decimo libro e con annotazioni,* ed. Lelio Arbib, vol. 1 (Florence: Società e Editrice delle Storie del Nardi e del Varchi, 1842), xxiii–xciii, at lxxxii: "e fu creduto che, com'egli in vita avea ed in corpo ed in anima peregrinato per l'Inferno, Purgatorio e Paradiso, così in morte ed in anima ed in corpo avesse dovuto essere stato in alcun di quei ricettacoli ricevuto ed accolto."

1   Gianandrea Piccioli, "Le ossa di Dante e la sacra accademia medicea," in *Annali dell'Istituto di Studi Danteschi,* vol. 1 (Milan: Vita e Pensiero, 1967), 453–465, at 464; Ludovico Frati and Corrado Ricci, eds., *Il sepolcro di Dante: Documenti raccolti* (Bologna: Monti, 1889), 45, 49. See Paul Oskar Kristeller, "Francesco da Diacceto and Florentine Platonism in the Sixteenth Century," in *Studies in Renaissance Thought and Letters* (Rome: Edizioni di Storia e Letteratura, 1956), 287–336, at 301–303, 323–325, 328–336; Anthony M. Cummings, "The Sacred Academy of the Medici," in *The Maecenas and the Madrigalist: Patrons, Patronage, and the Origins of the Italian Madrigal* (Philadelphia: American Philosophical Society, 2004), 79–97; Sherry Roush, "Dante Ravennate and Boccaccio Ferrarese? Post-Mortem Residency and the Attack on Florentine Literary Hegemony, 1480–1520," *Viator* 35 (2004): 543–562, at 548–550; Simon Gilson, *Reading Dante in Renaissance Italy: Florence, Venice, and the "Divine Poet"* (Cambridge: Cambridge University Press, 2018), 94, 287.

2   Kristeller, "Francesco da Diacceto," 324, 328–329. I cite the text of the letter from Lucrezia de' Medici Salviati to Pope Leo X, *Il veltro* 9 (1965): 678–679. Adjusting for the Florentine calendar, in which the new year began on March 25 (conventional date of the Incarnation), March 15, 1514, indicates the year 1515.

3   Lucrezia de' Medici Salviati to Pope Leo X, 678.

4   Ibid., 679.

5   I cite the letters of the Sacred Academy of the Medici from Frati and Ricci, *Il sepolcro,* 43–57, at 43.

6   Giannozzo Manetti, "Life of Dante," in *Biographical Writings,* ed. and trans. Stefano U. Baldassarri and Rolf Bagemihl (Cambridge, MA: Harvard University Press, 2003), 8–61, at 33; Patrick J. Geary, *Furta Sacra: Thefts of Relics in the Central Middle Ages* (1978; rev. ed., Princeton, NJ: Princeton University Press, 1990), 88–107.

7   Frati and Ricci, *Il sepolcro,* 44.

8   Ibid., 45–46.

9   Ibid., 47–48.

10   Ibid., 48; Roush, "Dante Ravennate," 549.

11   Frati and Ricci, *Il sepolcro,* 50–57, at 51. On identifications of the signatories, see Kristeller, "Francesco da Diacceto," 323–324; and Cummings, "Sacred Academy," 80–82.

12   Frati and Ricci, *Il sepolcro,* 56; Howard Hibbard, *Michelangelo* (New York: Harper and Row, 1974), 161–167, 177–202, 209–219.

13   Melissa Nicole Demos discusses Michelangelo's familiarity with Dante's poem and its influence on his artwork, the *Last Judgment* in particular, in "Time and the Experience of Narrative in Italian Renaissance Art" (PhD diss., University of Texas at Austin, 2015), 207–282.

14   Christopher Ryan, introduction to *The Poems,* by Michelangelo (London: J. M. Dent, 1996), xix.

15   I cite Michelangelo's poems from Michelangelo, *Poems,* 200–203.

16   Marco Ruffini, *Art without an Author: Vasari's Lives and Michelangelo's Death* (New York: Fordham University Press, 2011), 11–38, at 12, 15.

17   Pier Desiderio Pasolini, *Ravenna e le sue grandi memorie* (Rome: Ermanno Loescher, 1912), 155; Corrado Ricci, preface to *Cronache e documenti per la storia ravennate del secolo XVI,* ed. Corrado Ricci (Bologna: Gaetano Romagnoli, 1882), v–cxxxi, at xxxiv–xxxvii; Agostino Ruboli, "Cronaca di Agostino Ruboli," in Ricci, *Cronache e documenti,* 1–36, at 5–6; Ricci, *L'ultimo rifugio di Dante Alighieri* (Milan: Hoepli, 1891), 337.

18   Nardi, "Vita di Iacopo Nardi," lxxxii.

19   Dante, *Par.* 11.37–39: "L'un fu tutto serafico in ardore; / l'altro per sapïenza in terra fue / di cherubica luce uno splendore." Francis sits just below John the Baptist—and immediately above Saints Benedict and Augustine—in the celestial rose (*Par.* 32.34–35). Dante, *Convivio* 2.12.7; Nick Havely, *Dante and the Franciscans: Poverty and the Papacy in the "Commedia"* (Cambridge: Cambridge University Press, 2004), 31–43.

20   For the reconstruction of this crime scene, I am indebted to the accounts of Corrado Ricci in *L'ultimo rifugio,* 341–343, and "L'arca lapidea," in *Ricognizione delle ossa di Dante fatta nei giorni 28–31 ottobre 1921,* ed. Santi Muratori, Corrado Ricci, Giuseppe Sergi, and Fabio Frassetto (Rome: Reale Accademia Nazionale dei Lincei, 1923), 13–18.

21   Ricci, *L'ultimo rifugio,* 341–342.

22   I cite the sonnet from Frati and Ricci, *Il sepolcro,* 20.

5. AN EMPTY TOMB

Epigraph: George Gordon (Lord) Byron, *The Prophecy of Dante,* in *The Complete Poetical Works,* ed. Jerome J. McGann, 7 vols. (Oxford, UK: Clarendon, 1980–1993), 4:213–239, at 218 (canto 1, lines 83–84).

1   Corrado Ricci, "Codicillo a *L'ultimo rifugio di Dante,*" in *Cogliendo biada o loglio: Scritti danteschi* (Florence: Le Monnier, 1924), 171–182, at 176–178; Ricci, *L'ultimo rifugio di Dante Alighieri* (Milan: Hoepli, 1891), 292–294, 303–304, 465–469, at 467.

2 "Perizia calligrafica sopra le epigrafi scritte sulla cassetta contenente le ossa di Dante," in *Della scoperta delle ossa di Dante: Relazione con documenti per cura del municipio di Ravenna* (Ravenna: Angeletti, 1870), xvii–xxxiii; Ricci, *L'ultimo rifugio,* 348–351.

3 Santi Muratori, "Il sepolcro e le ossa di Dante," in *Dante: La vita, le opere, le grandi città dantesche, Dante e l'Europa* (Milan: Fratelli Treves, 1921), 239–249, at 243; Ludovico Frati and Corrado Ricci, eds., *Il sepolcro di Dante: Documenti raccolti* (Bologna: Monti, 1889), 62–63, at 63; Dante, *Inf.* 11.60: "simile lordura."

4 Frati and Ricci, *Il sepolcro,* 58–62; Ricci, *L'ultimo rifugio,* 303.

5 Frati and Ricci, *Il sepolcro,* 68–69; Ricci, *L'ultimo rifugio,* 298.

6 Frati and Ricci, *Il sepolcro,* 66–70, at 70; Camillo Spreti, *Memorie intorno i domini e governi della città di Ravenna* (1822; repr., Bologna: Arnaldo Forni, 1975), 185; Ricci, *L'ultimo rifugio,* 299; Giovanni Mesini, *La tomba e le ossa di Dante* (Ravenna: Longo, 1965), 11.

7 Ricci, *L'ultimo rifugio,* 299–301.

8 Ibid., 302.

9 Ibid., 301, 308.

10 Ibid., 306–307.

11 Ibid., 307.

12 Ibid., 313–314.

13 Felice Mazzeo, *Dante e Ravenna* (Bologna: Cappelli, 1987), 96; "Deliberazione del Comune di Ravenna pel restauro del Card. Valenti Gonzaga," in Frati and Ricci, *Il sepolcro,* 90–91, at 90.

14 In addition to visual observation, I rely on Mazzeo, *Dante e Ravenna,* 96–97, for this description of the chapel.

15 Ricci, *L'ultimo rifugio,* 315–317, at 316.

16 Romolo Conti, "Relazione storica," in *Della scoperta,* 1–30, at 13.

17 Spreti, *Memorie,* 186.

18 Andrea Ciccarelli, "Dante and the Culture of Risorgimento: Literary, Political or Ideological Icon?," in *Making and Remaking Italy: The Cultivation of National Identity around the Risorgimento,* ed. Albert Russell Ascoli and Krystyna Von Henneberg (Oxford, UK: Berg, 2001), 77–102, at 80–81.

19 Vittorio Alfieri, *Vita,* ed. Vittore Branca (Milan: Mursia, 1983), 220; Alfieri, *Opere,* ed. Francesco Maggini, 2 vols. (Milan: Rizzoli, 1940), 1:664. In the periphery of Hell, through the gate but before the river Acheron, Virgil tells Dante not to speak of the wretched cowards but only to "look and pass by" (Dante, *Inf.* 3.51: "guarda e passa").

20 Cristoforo Landino, *Comento sopra la Comedia,* ed. Paolo Procaccioli, 4 vols. (Rome: Salerno, 2001), 1:246; Joseph Luzzi, *Romantic Europe and the Ghost of Italy* (New Haven, CT: Yale University Press, 2008), 138; Giuseppe Parini, "Dell'origine, de' progressi, della natura, dell'uso, e del presente sistema della lingua Italiana," in *Prose,* ed. Silvia Morgana and Paolo Bartesaghi, 2 vols. (Milan: Edizioni Universitarie di Lettere Economia Diritto, 2003), 1:198–221, at 206; Antonio Bruers, "Dante nel pensiero del Risorgimento italiano," in *Dante e la guerra,* ed. Maria del Vasto Celano (Rome: Nuovo Convito, 1917), 53–59, at 54–55.

21 Ugo Foscolo, *Ultime lettere di Jacopo Ortis,* in *Opere,* ed. Franco Gavazzeni, 4 vols. (1974–1981; repr., Milan: Ricciardi, 1995–1996), 2:557–703, at 674. I cite the translation by J. G. Nichols (*Last Letters of Jacopo Ortis; and, Of Tombs* [London: Hesperus, 2002]), with occasional modifications.

22 Ricci, *L'ultimo rifugio,* 318–319, at 319.

23 Leone Vichi, *Vincenzo Monti: Le lettere e la politica in Italia dal 1750 al 1830,* vol. 4 (Fusignano: Edoardo Morandi, 1887), 544–553, at 544–545, 551.

24 Ibid., 546–553.

25 Ricci, *L'ultimo rifugio,* 320.

26 Ugo Foscolo, "Dei sepolcri," in *Opere,* 1:291–327, at 315 (line 281) and 314 (line 174). I cite the translation by J. G. Nichols (*Of Tombs*). Luzzi, *Romantic Europe,* shows how Foscolo was read primarily as a political poet who conceived a necessary nexus between the text and the nation in his literature (3–11, 36–40).

27 Muratori, "Il sepolcro," 247.

28 I cite measurements from Ravenna's official, notarized report on May 27, 1865 (*Della scoperta,* xlix–liv, at l); Ricci, *L'ultimo rifugio,* 351–357, at 357.

29 George Gordon (Lord) Byron, *Childe Harold's Pilgrimage,* in *Complete Poetical Works,* 2:135–142 (canto 4, lines 307–315, 352–355, 478–488).

30 Byron to John Murray, Foligno, April 26, 1817, in *Byron's Letters and Journals,* ed. Leslie A. Marchand, 12 vols. (Cambridge, MA: Harvard University Press, 1973–1982), 5:218, 256–257; Byron, *Childe,* Notes, 235–236; Madame de Staël, *Corinne, or Italy,* ed. and trans. Sylvia Raphael (Oxford: Oxford University Press, 1998), 353.

31 Byron, *Childe,* 142–144 (canto 4, lines 496–529).

32 Iris Origo, *The Last Attachment: The Story of Byron and Teresa Guiccioli as Told in Their Unpublished Letters and Other Family Papers* (New York: Charles Scribner's Sons, 1949), 493; Teresa Guiccioli, unpublished manuscript, quoted in Thomas Moore, ed., *Letters and Journals of Lord Byron: With Notices of His Life,* 2 vols. (New York: J. and J. Harper, 1830–1831), 2:153–154; Byron to Teresa Guiccioli, Ravenna, June 11, 1819, in *Byron's Letters,* 6:153–154.

33 John Cam Hobhouse, *Italy: Remarks Made in Several Visits from the Year 1816 to 1854,* rev. ed., 2 vols. (London: John Murray, 1861), 1:232.

34 Byron to Hobhouse, Ravenna, July 30, 1819, in *Byron's Letters,* 6:189; Guiccioli, unpublished manuscript, quoted in Moore, *Letters,* 2:154; Filippo Mordani, *Elogio storico di Giorgio Lord Byron* (Ravenna: Roveri, 1841), 15.

35 Pier Desiderio Pasolini, *Ravenna e le sue grandi memorie* (Rome: Ermanno Loescher, 1912), 279–280. Pasolini cited Sabbatini's recollection from notes by Frances Elliot for a historical novel (never published) on Byron's stay in Ravenna. McGann, Commentary, in Byron, *Complete Poetical Works,* 4:499.

36 Byron, *Prophecy,* 4:213–239, at 214; Guiccioli, unpublished manuscript, quoted in Moore, *Letters,* 2:158; Thomas Medwin, *Medwin's Conversations of Lord Byron,* ed. Ernest J. Lovell Jr. (Princeton, NJ: Princeton University Press, 1966), 158; Dante, *Inf.* 5.127–138.

37 Byron to John Murray, Ravenna, March 23, 1820, in *Byron's Letters*, 7:59; Byron, *Prophecy*, 214–215.

38 Byron, *Prophecy*, 218 (canto 1, lines 74–84).

39 Ibid., 220 (canto 1, lines 149–157).

40 George Gordon (Lord) Byron, *Don Juan*, in *Complete Poetical Works*, 5:235–236 (canto 4, lines 825–832).

6. PROPHET OF ITALY

Epigraph: Giuseppe Mazzini, "Dante," *Apostolato popolare* 3 (September 15, 1841): 21–24, at 22: "Dante ha fatto più per l'Italia, per la gloria e per l'avvenire del nostro Popolo, che non dieci generazioni d'altri scrittori o d'uomini di stato."

1 *New Monthly Magazine* 10, no. 58 (November 1, 1818): 354.

2 George Gordon (Lord) Byron, *The Prophecy of Dante*, in *The Complete Poetical Works*, ed. Jerome J. McGann, 7 vols. (Oxford, UK: Clarendon, 1980–1993), 4:213–239, at 238 (canto 4, lines 137–140) and 239 (canto 4, lines 153–154).

3 Ibid., 221 (canto 1, line 178) and 226 (canto 2, lines 142–145).

4 Giacomo Leopardi, "Sopra il monumento di Dante che si preparava in Firenze," in *Canti*, ed. and trans. Jonathan Galassi (New York: Farrar, Straus and Giroux, 2010), 12–27 (lines 27, 36, 70, 74, 196–200); Dante, *Purg.* 6.76–151, at 113: "vedova e sola" (widowed and bereft).

5 I cite the manifesto from Melchior Missirini, *Delle memorie di Dante in Firenze, e della gratitudine de' Fiorentini verso il divino poeta*, 2nd ed. (Florence: Tipografia Calasanziana, 1830), 47–50, at 47–48.

6 Pio Rajna, "I centenarii danteschi passati e il centenario presente," *Nuova antologia di lettere, scienze ed arti*, 6th ser., 296 (May–June 1921): 3–23, 297–319, at 4.

7 Missirini, *Delle memorie*, 47.

8 Ibid., 51.

9 Ibid., 51, 44.

10 Ibid., 45.

11 Ibid., 40.

12 Rajna, "I centenarii," 8–9.

13 Christopher M. S. Johns, *Antonio Canova and the Politics of Patronage in Revolutionary and Napoleonic Europe* (Berkeley: University of California Press, 1998), 46; Missirini, *Delle memorie*, 53.

14 Mazzini, "Dante," 21.

15 Ibid., 22.

16 Ibid., 23.

17 Giuseppe Mazzini ("Un'Italiano"), "Prefazione all'edizione," in *La Commedia di Dante Allighieri, illustrata da Ugo Foscolo*, 4 vols. (London: Pietro Rolandi, 1842–1843), 1:iii–xx, at xviii; Gabriele Rossetti, "L'ombra di Dante" (1830), in *Poesie di mille autori intorno a Dante Alighieri*, ed. Carlo del Balzo, 15 vols. (Rome: Forzani, 1889–1909),

9:107–113, at 110; Rossetti, ed., *La Divina Commedia di Dante Alighieri con comento analitico di Gabriele Rossetti,* 2 vols. (London: John Murray, 1826–1827), 2:353–354; Giuseppe Mazzini, "Note autobiografiche," in *Scritti editi ed inediti,* 94 vols. (Imola: Paolo Galeati, 1906–1943), 77:9; Mazzini, "Dell'amore patrio di Dante," in *Scritti,* 1:1–23, at 4–5, 22–23. On Mazzini's political reading of Dante, see Sidney M. Brown, *Mazzini and Dante* (New York: Academy of Political Science, 1927); and Mario Scotti, "Dante nel pensiero di Mazzini," in *Mazzini e il mazzinianesimo* (Rome: Istituto per la Storia del Risorgimento Italiano, 1974), 563–578.

18 Adrian Lyttelton, "Creating a National Past: History, Myth and Image in the Risorgimento," in *Making and Remaking Italy: The Cultivation of National Identity around the Risorgimento,* ed. Albert Russell Ascoli and Krystyna Von Henneberg (Oxford, UK: Berg, 2001), 27–74, at 29; Benedict Anderson, *Imagined Communities: Reflections on the Origin and Spread of Nationalism* (1983; rev. ed., London: Verso, 1991), 37–46.

19 Dante, *Purg.* 6.76; Cesare Balbo, *Vita di Dante* (Naples: Tramater, 1839), 15; Vincenzo Gioberti, *Del primato morale e civile degli italiani,* 3rd ed., 2 vols. (Brussels: Meline, Cans e Compagnia, 1844), 2:143. See Charles T. Davis, "Dante and Italian Nationalism," in *A Dante Symposium in Commemoration of the 700th Anniversary of the Poet's Birth (1265–1965),* ed. William De Sua and Gino Rizzo (Chapel Hill: University of North Carolina Press, 1965), 199–213, at 205–208.

20 Dante, *Purg.* 6.77: "nave sanza nocchiere in gran tempesta"; Adolfo Borgognoni, "L'albo dei visitatori del sepolcro di Dante," *Fanfulla della Domenica* 4, no. 14 (April 2, 1882): 2–3, at 2.

21 Dante, *Purg.* 11.100–102: "Non è il mondan romore altro ch'un fiato / di vento . . . / e muta nome perché muta lato"; Borgognoni, "L'albo dei visitatori," 2; Bernardino Zendrini, *Per il centenario di Dante: Ghirlanda di canti* (Milan: Biblioteca utile, 1865), 18.

22 Giannina Milli, "Dante e l'unità d'Italia," in del Balzo, *Poesie,* 11:510.

7. SAINT DANTE

Epigraph: "Relazione della Commissione incaricata di verificare il fatto del ritrovamento delle ossa di Dante in Ravenna," in *Il sepolcro di Dante: Documenti raccolti,* ed. Ludovico Frati and Corrado Ricci (Bologna: Monti, 1889), 105–132, at 132: "la Commissione si congratula colla città di Ravenna, cui i cieli riservavano la lieta ventura di mostrare alla risorta Italia le sacre ossa di Dante, ed augura che siano custodite come tesoro della nazione, la quale nel nome di Dante affermò di nuovo la propria unità."

1 David I. Kertzer, *Prisoner of the Vatican: The Popes' Secret Plot to Capture Rome from the New Italian State* (Boston: Houghton Mifflin, 2004), 14–15.

2 Pio Rajna, "I centenarii danteschi passati e il centenario presente," *Nuova antologia di lettere, scienze ed arti,* 6th ser., 296 (May–June 1921): 3–23, 297–319, at 18–21, 297–299; Henry Clark Barlow, *The Sixth Centenary Festivals of Dante Allighieri in Florence and Ravenna* (London: Williams and Norgate, 1866), 5–6; Mahnaz Yousefzadeh, *City and Nation in the Italian Unification: The National Festivals of Dante Alighieri* (New York:

Palgrave Macmillan, 2011), 3–4, 31, 204–205. I discuss Florence's final serious attempt at repatriation at greater length in "Bones of Contention: Ravenna's and Florence's Claims to Dante's Remains," *Italica* 92, no. 3 (2015): 565–581. Harald Hendrix notes the "remarkable mix of religious and profane attitudes" informing interpretation of Dante's and Petrarch's physical afterlives ("Framing the Bones of Dante and Petrarch: Literary Cults and Scientific Discourses," in *Great Immortality: Studies on European Cultural Sainthood*, ed. Marijan Dović and Jón Karl Helgason [Leiden: Brill, 2019], 28–55, at 38).

3 Giovanni Folchi, "Proposte per la celebrazione del centenario di Dante," in *Giornale del Centenario di Dante Allighieri celebrato in Firenze nei giorni 14, 15 e 16 maggio 1865* (Florence: Cellini, 1864–1865), 78; Nicola Gaetani Tamburini, "Proposte," in *Giornale del Centenario,* 77–78, at 78; Dante, *Par.* 25.1–9; Dante, *Inf.* 19.17: "bel San Giovanni"; Julius Braun, "Proposte," in *Giornale del Centenario,* 91–92; Giacomo Baratta, "Proposte," in *Giornale del Centenario,* 79.

4 Atto Vannucci, "Lettera del Prof. Atto Vannucci al Presidente della Commissione Fiorentina per il Centenario di Dante," in *Giornale del Centenario,* 85–86.

5 "Deliberazione del Consiglio Municipale di Firenze de' 4 maggio 1864," in Isidoro del Lungo, *Dell'esilio di Dante: Discorso e documenti* (Florence: Le Monnier, 1881), 196–197, at 197; "Il Gonfaloniere di Firenze al Sindaco di Ravenna," ibid., 195–196.

6 "Il Sindaco di Ravenna al Gonfaloniere di Firenze," ibid., 197–198, at 198; "Deliberazione del Consiglio Municipale di Ravenna," ibid., 200.

7 Barlow, *Sixth Centenary,* 7. Yousefzadeh estimates that the centenary drew fifty thousand Italians to Florence (*City and Nation,* 1, 95), while Barlow puts the number of visitors (including foreigners) at nearly one hundred thousand (*Sixth Centenary,* 8).

8 Barlow, *Sixth Centenary,* 7; Gabriele Fantoni, "Il gran rifiuto di Ravenna a Firenze e il Sesto Centenario," in *Poesie di mille autori intorno a Dante Alighieri,* ed. Carlo del Balzo, 15 vols. (Rome: Forzani, 1889–1909), 13:156–157; Dante, *Inf.* 3.59–60: "colui / che fece per viltade il gran rifiuto."

9 Barlow, *Sixth Centenary,* 26–27; *Guida officiale per le feste del Centenario di Dante Alighieri nei giorni 14, 15 e 16 maggio 1865 in Firenze* (Florence: M. Cellini, 1865), 10.

10 *La Nazione,* May 15, 1865; *La Nazione,* May 16, 1865; Barlow, *Sixth Centenary,* 27–29, 34–36.

11 Dante, *Inf.* 4.80: "Onorate l'altissimo poeta" (my translation); Barlow, *Sixth Centenary,* 29. Barlow states that Giuliani spoke after the statue was revealed, but contemporary newspaper accounts put his speech before the unveiling (May 21, 1865 issue of *La festa di Dante: Letture domenicali del popolo italiano* [Florence: M. Cellini, 1865], 221).

12 Francesco Mazzoni, "Le celebrazioni dantesche in Italia," in *Contributi di filologia dantesca* (Florence: Sansoni, 1966), 280–292, at 282–283.

13 "Monumento di Dante in Firenze," *La festa di Dante,* May 21, 1865, 223; Barlow, *Sixth Centenary,* 32–34; *Guida officiale,* 7–9, at 7.

14 Barlow, *Sixth Centenary,* 60–66; Yousefzadeh, *City and Nation,* 125.

15 Barlow, *Sixth Centenary,* 62; John Carbutt and Joseph Meredith, *Biographical Sketches of the Leading Men of Chicago* (Chicago: Wilson and St. Clair, 1868), 73–80, at 79.

16 Henry Wadsworth Longfellow to Mary Appleton, December 10, 1837, in *The Letters of Henry Wadsworth Longfellow,* ed. Andrew Hilen, 6 vols. (Cambridge, MA: Harvard University Press, 1966–1982), 2:50–51, at 51.

17 "Longfellow and Dante" is the special topic of the 2010 volume of *Dante Studies,* edited by Arielle Saiber and Giuseppe Mazzotta. It contains valuable contributions by Christian Y. Dupont, Joan Nordell, Kathleen Verduin, Christoph Irmscher, and others.

18 Henry Wadsworth Longfellow, journal entry, April 16, 1863, in *Life of Henry Wadsworth Longfellow: With Extracts from His Journals and Correspondence,* ed. Samuel Longfellow, 3 vols. (Boston: Houghton Mifflin, 1891), 3:21–22.

19 Henry Wadsworth Longfellow, "O Star of Morning and of Liberty," in *The Complete Writings of Henry Wadsworth Longfellow,* 11 vols. (Boston: Houghton Mifflin, 1904–1917), 3:150–151; Dennis Looney, *Freedom Readers: The African American Reception of Dante Alighieri and the "Divine Comedy"* (Notre Dame, IN: University of Notre Dame Press, 2011), 54–63, at 63.

20 Barlow, *Sixth Centenary,* 63–66, at 63. On Mamiani's vexed relationship with Pope Pius IX, see David I. Kertzer, *The Pope Who Would Be King: The Exile of Pius IX and the Emergence of Modern Europe* (New York: Random House, 2018), 79–91, 131–132.

21 *La Nazione,* May 19, 1865.

22 Ibid.; Victor Hugo, *La Nazione,* May 16, 1865, reprinted as "Le centenaire de Dante," in *Oeuvres complètes,* 48 vols. (Paris: J. Hetzel, 1880–1889), 25:353–358, at 354–355.

23 "Ultime notizie," *La Nazione,* May 28, 1865.

24 Official report of May 27, 1865, in *Della scoperta delle ossa di Dante: Relazione con documenti per cura del Municipio di Ravenna* (Ravenna: Angeletti, 1870), xlix–liv, at li; Filippo Lanciani quoted in Pietro Lanciani, letter to the editor, *L'Osservatore Romano,* June 1, 1865.

25 Luigi Fallani, Lucia Milana, and Antonio Giardullo, "Le ceneri dantesche della Biblioteca nazionale di Firenze," *Rassegna storica toscana* 33, no. 1 (1987): 89–104, at 92; official report of May 27, 1865, liii–liv.

26 The Florentine newspaper *La Nazione* reprinted the article on June 9, 1865.

27 Official report of May 27, 1865, liii; "Relazione della Commissione," 113–114; Lanciani, letter to the editor, June 1, 1865; Pietro Lanciani, letter to the editor, *L'Osservatore Romano,* June 14, 1865.

28 Santi Muratori, "Per il centenario dantesco: Una ignota esplorazione dell'urna di Dante," in *Scritti danteschi,* ed. Giovanna Bosi Maramotti (Ravenna: Longo, 1991), 97–103, at 101.

29 Official report of June 7, 1865, in *Della scoperta,* lv–lxii, at lv; Primo Uccellini, *Relazione storica sulla avventurosa scoperta delle ossa di Dante Alighieri* (Ravenna: Angeletti, 1865), 14; Lanciani, letter to the editor, June 14, 1865.

30 Official report of June 7, 1865, lvii–lviii.

31 Ibid., lviii; Uccellini, *Relazione storica*, 14–15; Barlow, *Sixth Centenary*, 72.

32 Romolo Conti, "Relazione storico-critica," in *La scoperta delle ossa di Dante* (Ravenna: Angeletti, 1865), 3–30, at 22. I cite Pasolini's letter of June 24, 1865, from Romolo Comandini, "Alessandro Cappi e la scoperta delle ossa dell'Alighieri: Con documenti inediti," *L'Alighieri: Rassegna bibliografica dantesca* 6, no. 1 (1965): 61–75, at 70; Barlow, *Sixth Centenary*, 72.

33 Conti, "Relazione storico-critica," 33; Melchior Missirini, *Vita di Dante Alighieri* (Florence: Fabris, 1840), 181; Filippo Mordani, *Della vita privata di Dionigi Strocchi: Memorie estratte dalle effemeridi dell'autore*, in *Operette*, 3 vols. (Florence: Barbèra, 1874), 3:193–255, at 232. Antonio Codronchi was Archbishop of Ravenna from 1785 until his death in 1826.

34 Corrado Ricci, *L'ultimo rifugio di Dante Alighieri* (Milan: Hoepli, 1891), 370; Medardo Morici, "Una visita clandestina alla tomba di Dante," *Giornale dantesco* 14 (1906): 279–281; Muratori, "Per il centenario dantesco," 99–100.

35 Official report of June 7, 1865, lviii–lx; Giovanni Puglioli and Claudio Bertozzi, "Relazione anatomico-fisiologica," in *Della scoperta*, i–xv, at xv.

36 Puglioli and Bertozzi, "Relazione," xiv–xv, at xv; official report of June 7, 1865, lviii–lx. See also Uccellini, *Relazione storica*, 14–15.

37 Lanciani, letter to the editor, June 14, 1865.

38 Ricci, *L'ultimo rifugio*, 333.

39 Lanciani, letter to the editor, June 14, 1865; Ricci, *L'ultimo rifugio*, 333.

40 Luigi Paganucci, *Dell'anatomia umana: Discorso del prof. Luigi Paganucci letto il dì 8 marzo 1874 nella inaugurazione degli studi superiori pratici e di perfezionamento in Firenze* (Florence: Tipografia Bencini, 1874), 3. The official report of June 7, 1865, lists Paganucci as a professor of anatomy from Monte Laterone, in the Province of Siena (lvi).

41 Fabbri was born in Ravenna in 1835 and died in Rome in 1912. After serving in the Piedmontese army during the Risorgimento, he held various administrative posts in Ravenna and other northern Italian cities before turning full-time to political journalism. He was editor in chief of *Tribuna* from 1884 to 1900.

42 "Per le ossa di Dante," *Corriere della Sera*, July 22–23, 1900.

43 Ibid.

44 Lanciani, letter to the editor, June 14, 1865.

45 Puglioli and Bertozzi, "Relazione," xii, xv.

46 Ibid., xi; "Relazione della Commissione," 121, 128–129. Similarly, Andrea Drusini and Maurizio Rippa Bonati argue, scientific analysis of Petrarch's cranium in 1873 "still shows traces of the influence of phrenology" ("Le fragili ossa del poeta: Lo studio antropologico dei resti di Petrarca," in *Petrarca: Canoni, esemplarità*, ed. Valeria Finucci [Rome: Bulzoni, 2006], 327–346, at 340).

47 "Relazione della Commissione," 130, 132.

48 Barlow, *Sixth Centenary,* 74–75.

49 Official report of June 26, 1865, in *Della scoperta,* xliii–lxxii, at lxix; "Le Feste di Dante in Ravenna: Il 24, 25, 26 giugno 1865," ibid., xxxv–xlvii, at xxxv–xxxvii; Claudio Zirardini, *Giubileo per la scoperta delle ossa di Dante Alighieri e sottoscrizione mondiale per erigere a lui un mausoleo a Ravenna: Frammenti di cronaca* (Ravenna: Unione Tipografica Editrice Cooperativa, 1894), 17.

50 "Feste di Dante," xxxvii–xli, at xxxviii, xl.

51 Ibid., xlii–xliv, at xlii; Barlow, *Sixth Centenary* 76–77.

52 G[iovanni] A[ndrea] Scartazzini, *A Companion to Dante,* trans. Arthur John Butler (London: Macmillan, 1893), 171; Barlow, *Sixth Centenary,* 77; Ricci, *L'ultimo rifugio,* 371; Zirardini, *Giubileo,* 56–57.

53 Dora D'Istria, "Les fêtes dantesque, a Ravenne," *L'illustration, journal universel* 46, no. 1168 (July 15, 1865): 35–38, at 36.

54 Ibid., 38. Altina Hoti discusses Dora D'Istria's promotion of women's emancipation within national struggles—Italian and other—in "Nationalism, Cosmopolitanism, and Female Intellectuality: The Paradoxes of Dora D'Istria and the Gendering of Risorgimento Italy" (PhD diss., University of Texas at Austin, 2019).

55 Pier Desiderio Pasolini, letter of June 24, 1865, in Comandini, "Alessandro Cappi," 70.

56 Giambattista Giuliani, *Nella solenne deposizione delle ritrovate ossa di Dante nell'antico loro sepolcro: Discorso recitato il 26 giugno 1865* (Ravenna: Gaetano Angeletti, 1865), 3–6.

57 Official report of June 26, 1865, lxvii–lxx, at lxviii.

58 Zirardini, *Giubileo,* 28.

8. THE REDEEMER

Epigraph: Giosuè Carducci, "Per il monumento di Dante a Trento," in *Poesie di Giosuè Carducci, MDCCCL–MCM,* 5th ed. (Bologna: Zanichelli, 1906), 1007–1008: "Ed or s'è fermo, e par ch'aspetti, a Trento."

1 Dante, *Purg.* 6.112–114: "Vieni a veder la tua Roma che piagne / vedova e sola, e dí e notte chiama: / 'Cesare mio, perché non m'accompagne?'" Henry Clark Barlow, *The Sixth Centenary Festivals of Dante Allighieri in Florence and at Ravenna* (London: Williams and Norgate, 1866), 8–9.

2 Barlow, *Sixth Centenary,* 27, 35; *La Nazione,* May 16, 1865.

3 Barlow, *Sixth Centenary,* 36; *La Nazione,* May 16, 1865.

4 Barlow, *Sixth Centenary,* 21, 33.

5 "L'Italia irredenta alla tomba di Dante: Il Trentino, la Venezia Giulia e la Dalmazia alla Tomba di Dante," in *Il Secentenario della morte di Dante, MCCCXXI–MCMXXI: Celebrazioni e memorie monumentali per cura delle tre città Ravenna-Firenze-Roma* (Rome: Bestetti and Tumminelli, n.d. [1924?]), 405–419, at 408.

6 "L'Alighieri e l'odierna rivoluzione italiana," *L'Osservatore Romano,* May 18, 1865.

7 "Cose italiane," *Civiltà Cattolica,* 6th ser., 2 (April–June, 1865): 619–634, at 633.

8 "L'Italia irredenta," 407. Antonio Bruers writes that Dante is not only Mazzini's prophet of Italy but the "Redeemer of the Nation" ("Dante nel pensiero del Risorgimento italiano," *Dante e la guerra,* ed. Maria del Vasto Celano [Rome: Nuovo Convito, 1917], 53–59, at 59).

9 Theodore J. Cachey Jr., "La mappa d'Italia in Dante, Petrarca e Boccaccio," *Tre corone: Rivista internazionale di studi su Dante, Petrarca e Boccaccio* 5 (2018): 11–38, at 13.

10 Dante, *Inf.* 10.15: "l'anima col corpo morta fanno"; Dante, *Inf.* 9.112–114: "Sí come ad Arli, ove Rodano stagna, / sí com' a Pola, presso del Carnaro / ch'Italia chiude e suoi termini bagna."

11 Dante, *Inf.* 20.61–63: "Suso in Italia bella giace un laco / a piè de l'Alpe che serra Lamagna / sovra Tiralli, c'ha nome Benaco" ("High in fair Italy lies a lake at the foot of the Alps locking in Germany above Tyrol, its name Benaco") (my translation).

12 Dante, *De vulgari eloquentia* 1.15.7.

13 "Annunzi bibliografici," *Bullettino della Società Dantesca Italiana* 4, nos. 1–2 (1896): 19–32, at 19.

14 "A Dante, al Padre, il Trentino col plauso e l'aiuto della Nazione."

15 Carducci, "Per il monumento di Dante a Trento," 1007–1008.

16 I cite the poem from Emanuele Sella, "Dante e i poeti delle terre irredente," in del Vasto Celano, *Dante e la guerra,* 105–106.

17 R. J. B. Bosworth, *Italy, the Least of the Great Powers: Italian Foreign Policy before the First World War* (London: Cambridge University Press, 1979), 49–50. Sarah Finn gives a detailed account of the Società Dante Alighieri in her PhD dissertation, "'Padre della nazione italiana': Dante Alighieri and the Construction of the Italian Nation, 1800–1945" (University of Western Australia, 2010), 145–164.

18 "Manifesto della fondazione della Società Dante Alighieri," Società Dante Alighieri, accessed November 18, 2019, https://ladante.it/images/attualita/2016/07-lug /ManifestoFondazioneSDA.pdf.

19 Ibid.

20 Ibid.

21 Isidoro del Lungo, *Il priorato di Dante e il palazzo del popolo fiorentino nel Sesto Centenario: Discorso letto nel Salone dei Cinquecento il 17 giugno 1900* (Rome: Comune di Firenze, 1900), 13.

22 Ibid., 23. Del Lungo cites Dante, *Convivio* 1.3.4.

23 Del Lungo, *Il priorato di Dante,* 24.

24 Charles T. Davis, "Dante and Italian Nationalism," in *A Dante Symposium in Commemoration of the 700th Anniversary of the Poet's Birth (1265–1965),* ed. William De Sua and Gino Rizzo (Chapel Hill: University of North Carolina Press, 1965), 199–213, at 201.

25 Christopher Duggan, *The Force of Destiny: A History of Italy since 1796* (Boston: Houghton Mifflin, 2008), 336–337, 345–347, at 347.

26 The lamp made for the 1908 occasion was later replaced in the chapel by the eighteenth-century lamp used today (Felice Mazzeo, *Dante e Ravenna* [Bologna: Cappelli, 1987], 100).

27 Pietro Stromboli, "Onoranze dantesche a Ravenna nel settembre 1908," *Società Dantesca Italiana: Atti e notizie* 2 (1907–1908): 73–86, at 76.

28 Ibid., 80.

29 Ibid., 83.

30 Ibid., 84.

31 "Doxologia Minor: Glory Be," Thesaurus Precum Latinarum, accessed November 18, 2019, http://www.preces-latinae.org/thesaurus/Basics/GloriaPatri.html; Adrian Fortescue, "Doxology," in *The Catholic Encyclopedia,* vol. 5 (New York: Robert Appleton, 1909), accessed November 18, 2019, http://www.newadvent.org/cathen/05150a .htm.

32 Stromboli, "Onoranze dantesche," 84.

33 Ibid., 85.

34 Thies Schulze, *Dante Alighieri als nationales Symbol Italiens (1793–1915)* (Tübingen: Max Niemeyer, 2005), 222. No Dante statues were erected in piazzas of Italian cities after 1874, and the statue of Dante in Trent (1896) was the last major nineteenth-century monument to the poet (Schulze, "Dante nel Risorgimento," *Rassegna storica del Risorgimento* 88, no. 4, supp. [2001]: 97–108, at 104, 106).

35 Emanuele Sella, "La religione di Dante negli anni di guerra," in del Vasto Celano, *Dante e la guerra,* 95–124, at 109–112.

36 Matthew 5:3–10; Gabriele D'Annunzio, "Orazione per la Sagra dei Mille (V maggio MDCCCLX–V maggio MCMXV)," in *Per la più grande Italia: Orazioni e messaggi* (Rome: L'Oleandro, 1933), 13–30, at 29–30.

37 *Corriere della Sera,* May 5, 1915; "Garibaldi Day Passes Peacefully," *New York Times,* May 6, 1915; Anthony Rhodes, *The Poet as Superman: A Life of Gabriele D'Annunzio* (London: Weidenfeld and Nicolson, 1959), 147.

38 "Discorso di Paolo Boselli alla Camera dei deputati, 20 maggio 1915," Studi Risorgimentali, accessed November 18, 2019, http://www.studirisorgimentali.org /L'ORA%20FATIDICA.htm. Boselli became prime minister after the fall of Antonio Salandra's government in June 1916 and was himself replaced following the disaster at Caporetto in October 1917.

39 Paolo Boselli, "Proclama agli Italiani," in del Vasto Celano, *Dante e la guerra,* 19.

40 Sella, "La religione," 113.

41 "Il Re in Romagna," *Gazzetta Ufficiale del Regno d'Italia,* May 20, 1918, accessed November 18, 2019, http://augusto.agid.gov.it/gazzette/index/download/id/1918118_PM.

42 Corrado Ricci, *Il sepolcro e le ossa di Dante* (Ravenna: Longo, 1977), 74.

43 Santi Muratori, "Le cerimonie inaugurali e commemorative," in *Secentenario,* 40–78, at 71.

44 Dante, *Purg.* 6.76; Mazzeo, *Dante e Ravenna,* 116.

45 Gabriele D'Annunzio, "Vittoria nostra, non sarai mutilata," *Corriere della Sera,* October 24, 1918.

46 Gabriele D'Annunzio, *La penultima ventura: Scritti e discorsi fiumani,* ed. Renzo De Felice (Milan: Mondadori, 1974), 149–150.

47 Ibid., 471.

48 Dante, *Par.* 17.68–69: "a te fia bello / averti fatta parte per te stesso" (my translation); D'Annunzio, *La penultima ventura,* 508.

49 D'Annunzio, *La penultima ventura,* 511.

50 "In Praeclara Summarum: Encyclical of Pope Benedict XV on Dante," in *The Papal Encyclicals 1903–1939,* ed. Claudia Carlen, vol. 5 (Ann Arbor, MI: Pierian, 1990), 213–216, at 213. Benedict viewed Dante's condemnation of contemporary popes such as Boniface VIII as an intemperate reaction to political differences, and he used the example of the *Divine Comedy* as a reason to teach Christian doctrine in public schools (215–216).

51 Barlow, *Sixth Centenary,* 37; Mahnaz Yousefzadeh, *City and Nation in the Italian Unification: The National Festivals of Dante Alighieri* (New York: Palgrave Macmillan, 2011), 125.

52 "Il messaggio di Gabriele D'Annunzio," in *Secentenario,* 105–106, at 105.

53 Ibid., 106.

54 Ibid.

55 Michael Scott, *Delphi: A History of the Center of the Ancient World* (Princeton, NJ: Princeton University Press, 2014), 119.

9. TOMB OF THE POET-SOLDIER

Epigraph: Speech of General Ugo Sani in *Il Secentenario della morte di Dante, MCCCXXI–MCMXXI: Celebrazioni e memoriali monumentali per cura delle tre città Ravenna-Firenze-Roma* (Rome: Bestetti and Tumminelli, n.d. [1924?]), 107–112, at 109: "E voi, gente di Romagna e cittadini di Ravenna, come bene avete compreso che sulla tomba del divino Poeta deve trovarsi la più solenne affermazione del pensiero italico!"

1 "Le feste per il VI centenario dantesco a Firenze," *L'illustrazione italiana* 49, no. 39 (September 25, 1921): 354.

2 "La colonna di Campaldino," in *Secentenario,* 317–318, at 318.

3 Fulvio Conti, "1921: Il sesto centenario della morte di Dante," in *Dante vittorioso: Il mito di Dante nell'Ottocento,* ed. Eugenia Querci (Turin: Umberto Allemandi, 2011), 91–97, at 91.

4 Santi Muratori, "Le cerimonie inaugurali e commemorative," in *Secentenario,* 40–78, at 46.

5 Ibid., 47.

6 General Sani's speech is reprinted in full in *Secentenario,* 107–112, with related details in Muratori's account ("Le cerimonie inaugurali," 48).

7 *Secentenario,* 107–109.

8 Ibid., 109–110.

9 Ibid., 111–112.

10 Ibid., 112.

11 Muratori, "Le cerimonie inaugurali," 48. General Sani quoted a stanza of Carducci's "Bicocca di San Giacomo" (composed in 1891), a poem memorializing Italian resistance against Napoleon's military campaign in 1796: "Hold high, O brothers, your hearts! Hold high your banners / and memories! Onward, onward, O Italy, / new and ancient."

12 Muratori, "Le cerimonie inaugurali," 48.

13 Ibid., 49.

14 Ibid.

15 Ibid., 54.

16 Ibid.

17 Dante, *Par.* 1.28–29: "Sí rade volte, padre, se ne coglie / per trïunfare o cesare o poeta."

18 Muratori, "Le cerimonie inaugurali," 54.

19 Ibid.

20 "Le feste per il VI centenario," 325.

21 Dante, *Purg.* 8.1–6:

> Era già l'ora che volge il disio
> ai navicanti e 'ntenerisce il core
> lo dí c'han detto ai dolci amici addio;
> e che lo novo peregrin d'amore
> punge, se ode squilla di lontano
> che paia il giorno pianger che si more.

22 Corrado Ricci, "La campana di Dante," in *Cogliendo biada o loglio: Scritti danteschi* (Florence: Le Monnier, 1924), 151–159.

23 Ibid., 155.

24 Muratori, "Le cerimonie inaugurali," 57.

25 Muratori, true to his vocation as a librarian and Dantophile, adds that "there would be no more poetry" (ibid., 57–58).

26 Ibid., 58; Felice Mazzeo, *Dante e Ravenna* (Bologna: Cappelli, 1987), 173–176.

27 Quoted in Ben Downing, *The Queen Bee of Tuscany: The Redoubtable Janet Ross* (New York: Farrar, Straus and Giroux, 2013), 257.

28 *Secentenario,* 79–82.

29 "Il pellegrinaggio americano," *Bollettino del Comitato Cattolico per l'omaggio a Dante Alighieri* 8, no. 5 (1921): 113–115, at 113.

30 "L'inaugurazione trionfale del Monumento a Dante," *Il Progresso Italo-Americano,* November 6, 1921; "Dante Dedication Today," *Washington Post,* December 1, 1921.

31 "Le feste per il VI centenario," 325; *Il Progresso Italo-Americano,* September 14, 1921. A journalist for *Il Carroccio,* a self-styled review of "Italian culture, propaganda, and defense in America," attended the ceremonies in Ravenna and took one leaf from each of the three sacks. He sent them to the director of the publication, Agostino de Biasi, back in New York (*Il Carroccio* 14, no. 4 [October 1921]: 386).

32 Muratori, "Le cerimonie inaugurali," 68.

33 Ibid., 68.

34 Ibid., 69.

35 *Secentenario,* 113–114.

36 Ibid., 114.

37 Ibid.

38 "Il messaggio di Gabriele D'Annunzio," in *Secentenario,* 105–106, at 105.

39 Ibid., 106.

40 Muratori, "Le cerimonie inaugurali," 69; "La commemorazione civile del centenario," *Bollettino del Comitato Cattolico per l'omaggio a Dante Alighieri* 8, no. 5 (1921): 128–129.

41 Muratori, "Le cerimonie inaugurali," 69.

42 Antonello Capurso, *Le frasi celebri nella storia d'Italia: Da Vittorio Emanuele II a Silvio Berlusconi* (Milan: Mondadori, 2011), 138–140.

43 Muratori, "Le cerimonie inaugurali," 69–70.

44 "Discorso di S. E. Luigi Rava," in *Secentenario,* 115–117, at 116–117.

45 "Political Songs of Modern Italy," trans. G. Cresciani, *Teaching History* 12, no. 1 (1978), 30–43, at 38. See also R. J. B. Bosworth, *Mussolini's Italy: Life under the Fascist Dictatorship, 1915–1945* (New York: Penguin, 2006), 197–199.

46 Grandi later opposed Italy's entry in World War II and orchestrated events leading to Mussolini's arrest in 1943. Balbo died in World War II when his plane was accidentally shot down by Italian anti-aircraft guns.

47 Muratori, "Le cerimonie inaugurali," 64.

48 For a description of these fascist assaults in Ravenna, see "Le cooperative obiettivo dello squadrismo fascista: 12 settembre 1921," Fondazione Memorie Cooperative, September 9, 2013, http://www.memoriecooperative.it/calendario/le-cooperative -obiettivo-dello-squadrismo-fascista/.

49 Lucy Hughes-Hallett, *Gabriele d'Annunzio: Poet, Seducer, and Preacher of War* (New York: Knopf, 2013), 491–492; Muratori, "Le cerimonie inaugurali," 68.

50 "Le feste centenarie di Dante e le gazzarre dei sovversivi in Italia," *Civiltà Cattolica* 72, no. 4 (1921): 3–11, at 6.

51 "Le feste per la commemorazione del centenario dantesco a Ravenna," *Civiltà Cattolica* 72, no. 4 (1921): 79–84, at 81.

52 "La celebrazione del Centenario Dantesco in Ravenna," *Bollettino del Comitato Cattolico per l'omaggio a Dante Alighieri* 8, no. 5 (1921): 113–124; "Le feste per la commemorazione," 79. These and other Catholic tributes to Dante for the centenary are summarized in Conti, "1921," 91–92; and listed in the "Tavola cronologica dell'anno dantesco," in *Secentenario,* 29–39.

53 "La dimostrazione fascista," *Bollettino del Comitato Cattolico per l'omaggio a Dante Alighieri* 8, no. 5 (1921): 128.

54 Giuseppe Frignani, "Auspici e presagi presso la tomba di Dante," in *Per l'inaugurazione della zona dantesca,* ed. Province and Commune of Ravenna (Ravenna: Società Tipo-Editrice Ravennate Mutilati, 1936), 3–11, at 9.

55 Ibid.

10. ILL-GOTTEN REMAINS

Epigraph: Corrado Ricci, "Le ossa di Dante," *Il Marzocco* 5, no. 29 (1900): 1–2, at 2: "se tutti furono raccolti, non tutti furono restituiti."

1 Victricius of Rouen, *Praising the Saints [De laude sanctorum],* trans. Gillian Clark, "Victricius of Rouen *Praising the Saints," Journal of Early Christian Studies* 7, no. 3 (1999): 365–399, at 390–393. Robyn Malo wonders whether Victricius "addresses an undocumented complaint that possessing such fragments was not as impressive as having the entire body, or a bigger part of it" (*Relics and Writing in Late Medieval England* [Toronto: University of Toronto Press, 2013], 13).

2 James Bentley, *Restless Bones: The Story of Relics* (London: Constable, 1985), 51.

3 Peter Brown, *The Cult of Saints: Its Rise and Function in Latin Christianity* (Chicago: University of Chicago Press, 1981), 11.

4 Charles Freeman, *Holy Bones, Holy Dust: How Relics Shaped the History of Medieval Europe* (New Haven, CT: Yale University Press, 2011), 4.

5 Benedict of Peterborough in *The Lives of Thomas Becket,* trans. and ed. Michael Staunton (Manchester, UK: Manchester University Press, 2001), 204.

6 The Met, "Reliquary Casket with Scenes from the Martyrdom of Saint Thomas Becket, ca. 1173–80," accessed November 13, 2019, http://www.metmuseum.org/art /collection/search/464490. A reliquary pendant (ca. 1174–1177) says that once on display under a crystal were not only the saint's blood but parts of his cloak, shirt, hood, belt, and shoes stained with it (The Met, "Reliquary Pendant with Queen Margaret of Sicily Blessed by Bishop Reginald of Bath, 1174–77," accessed November 13, 2019, http://www .metmuseum.org/art/collection/search/468600).

7 Caroline Walker Bynum, *Christian Materiality: An Essay on Religion in Late Medieval Europe* (New York: Zone Books, 2011), 192–193.

8 Ibid., 193.

9 Corrado Ricci, *L'ultimo rifugio di Dante Alighieri* (Milan: Hoepli, 1891), 348–370.

10 Santi Muratori, "Verbale," in *Ricognizione delle ossa di Dante fatta nei giorni 28–31 ottobre 1921,* ed. Santi Muratori, Corrado Ricci, Giuseppe Sergi, and Fabio Frassetto (Rome: Reale Accademia Nazionale dei Lincei, 1923), 3–12, at 3.

11 Corrado Ricci to Antenore Cancellieri, in *Per l'inaugurazione della zona dantesca,* ed. Province and Commune of Ravenna (Ravenna: Società Tipo-Editrice Ravennate Mutilati, 1936), 28–32.

12 Ibid., 30.

13 Ibid.

14 Whereas Drs. Puglioli and Bertozzi in their report described the rust-like coloration as a sort of "soapy varnish from residual animal substances that remained on the bones during the cadaver's decomposition" ("Relazione anatomico-fisiologica sulle ossa di Dante," in *Della scoperta delle ossa di Dante: Relazione con documenti per cura del Municipio di Ravenna* [Ravenna: Angeletti, 1870], i–xv, at iii).

15 Ricci to Cancellieri, 30.

16 Ibid.

17 Maria Giulia Benini, *Luoghi danteschi: La Basilica di S. Francesco e la Zona Dantesca a Ravenna* (Ravenna: Longo, 2003), 14.

18 Ricci, *L'ultimo rifugio,* 359.

19 The photograph appears ibid., after page 368, with explanatory notes on pages 372 and 516.

20 Ibid., 372; Claudio Cornazzani, "Dante Alighieri e la fotografia delle sue ossa (nel centocinquantesimo del loro rinvenimento)," *Bollettino dantesco* 4 (2015): 165–170, at 170.

21 *Annuario della Reale Accademia Nazionale dei Lincei* (Rome: Reale Accademia Nazionale dei Lincei, 1921), 52.

22 Ricci to Cancellieri, 31.

23 Photographs of Dante's bones are reproduced in the official report of the examination (Muratori et al., *Ricognizione*) and in the even more lavishly illustrated book published ten years later by one of the two examining scientists: Fabio Frassetto, *Dantis ossa: La forma corporea di Dante, scheletro, ritratti, maschere e busti* (Bologna: Università di Bologna, 1933).

24 Muratori, "Verbale," 3.

25 Frank Spencer, ed., *History of Physical Anthropology,* 2 vols. (New York: Garland, 1997), 1:408–409, 2:922–924.

26 Giuseppe Sergi and Fabio Frassetto, "Le ossa di Dante nel VI Centenario della sua morte," in Muratori et al., *Ricognizione,* 18–26, at 18.

27 Ricci, "Le ossa di Dante," 2.

28 Muratori, "Verbale," 8.

29 Ricci, "Le ossa di Dante," 2. This punishment may have been due as much to the professor's radical political affiliations as to his ethical lapse, with the delayed restitution merely providing a convenient pretext. Friendship with the influential poet Giosuè Carducci enabled Borgognoni to regain his position at the institute two years later. He was eventually awarded the chair in Italian literature in Pavia, where he died in 1893 (Luigi Fallani, Lucia Milana, and Antonio Giardullo, "Le ceneri dantesche della Biblioteca nazionale di Firenze," *Rassegna storica toscana* 33, no. 1 [1987]: 89–104, at 97).

30 Muratori, "Verbale," 8.

31 Corrado Ricci, *L'ultimo rifugio di Dante,* 2nd ed. (Milan: Hoepli, 1921), 462.

32 Muratori, "Verbale," 9; Ricci, "Le ossa di Dante," 2.

33 Muratori, "Verbale," 9.

34 Ibid., 9; Sergi and Frassetto, "Le ossa di Dante," 19.

35 Muratori, "Verbale," 7.

36 Ibid.

37 Filippo Mordani, *Vita di Filippo Mordani scritta da lui stesso,* in *Operette di Filippo Mordani da Ravenna,* 3 vols. (Florence: G. Barbéra, 1874), 2:329–388, at 374.

38 Mordani, *Iscrizioni originali italiane,* in *Operette,* 3:291–407, at 373.

39 Muratori, "Verbale," 9.

40 Ricci, "Le ossa di Dante," 2; Ricci, *L'ultimo rifugio* (1921), 463; Fallani, Milana, and Giardullo, "Le ceneri dantesche," 95.

41 *Della scoperta,* liv, lxi, lxxi.

42 Following medieval thinking on Purgatory, Dante emphasizes the efficacy of intercessory prayer (*Purg.* 3.142–145, 11.31–36, 23.85–93, 26.127–132) and "works of satisfaction," as they are called in Catholic tradition (Edward Hanna, "Purgatory," in *The Catholic Encyclopedia,* vol. 12 [New York: Robert Appleton, 1911], accessed November 13, 2019, http://www.newadvent.org/cathen/12575a.htm). Dante is moved by the penitents' prayers for the living to wonder what words and deeds the living can offer in return (*Purg.* 11.31–33), and he is told that his own works could reduce the amount of time (already over one hundred years) spent by his great-grandfather in Purgatory on the Terrace of Pride (*Par.* 15.91–96), a place where the proud poet foresees serving considerable time in his own afterlife (*Purg.* 13.136–138).

43 Muratori, "Verbale," 10.

44 V[ittorio] N[ivellini], "Notizie," *Giornale dantesco* 35 (1934): 237–240, at 239; Felice Mazzeo, *Dante e Ravenna* (Bologna: Cappelli, 1987), 171. I calculate the dollar amount using the 1921 exchange rate at MeasuringWorth.com and the Department of Labor's CPI Inflation Calculator for 1921 to 2019.

45 Frassetto, *Dantis ossa,* 13–14.

46 Sergi and Frassetto, "Le ossa di Dante," 19; Santi Muratori, "Il ricupero di una reliquia dantesca," in *Scritti danteschi,* ed. Giovanna Bosi Maramotti (Ravenna: Longo, 1991), 110–111; Muratori, "Verbale," 9–10.

47 Muratori, "Il ricupero di una reliquia dantesca," 111.

48 Muratori, "Verbale," 10.

49 Muratori, "Il ricupero di una reliquia dantesca," 111.

50 Frassetto, *Dantis ossa,* 7–10.

II. MANLY MEDITERRANEAN BONES

Epigraph: Giuseppe Sergi and Fabio Frassetto, "Le ossa di Dante nel VI Centenario della sua morte: Esame antropologico," in *Ricognizione delle ossa di Dante fatta nei giorni 28–31 ottobre 1921,* ed. Santi Muratori, Corrado Ricci, Giuseppe Sergi, and Fabio Frassetto (Rome: Reale Accademia Nazionale dei Lincei, 1923), 18–26, at 26: "Dante quindi è il rappresentante più glorioso e più autentico della stirpe mediterranea."

1 Laura Wittman, *The Tomb of the Unknown Soldier, Modern Mourning, and the Reinvention of the Mystical Body* (Toronto: University of Toronto Press, 2011), discusses the modern rituals and expressions of public mourning inaugurated by monuments to the Unknown Soldier in France, England, and especially Italy in the early twentieth century.

2 Ibid., 57–58.

3 Ibid., 37–39, 43, 66, 218.

4 Dante, *Inf.* 4.80–81: "Onorate l'altissimo poeta; / l'ombra sua torna, ch'era dipartita" (my translation).

5 Dante, *Inf.* 4.42: "sanza speme vivemo in disio."

6 Wittman argues that the context of Dante's verse questions the "traditional symbolic vocabulary" of religious and patriotic ritual (*Tomb of the Unknown Soldier,* 90).

7 I draw on Muratori's official report for details of the exhumation: Santi Muratori, "Verbale," in Muratori et al., *Ricognizione,* 3–12.

8 This room, inaugurated as a repository of Dante mementos on September 11, 1921, has been expanded into the Museo Dantesco, or Dante Museum, housed today in the Centro Dantesco dei Frati Minori in Ravenna.

9 Muratori, "Verbale," 4.

10 Ibid., 6.

11 Stefano Albertini, "Dante in camicia nera: Uso e abuso del divino poeta nell'Italia fascista," *Italianist* 16 (1996): 117–142, at 117. Albertini cites this inspection as the first in a series of steps toward the "lay canonization of Dante" under fascism (132–137).

12 Muratori, "Verbale," 6–7. On the viewing of Francis's remains in 1818–1819 (they were exhumed again in 1978), see Rosalind B. Brooke, *The Image of St Francis: Responses to Sainthood in the Thirteenth Century* (Cambridge: Cambridge University Press, 2006), 454–471.

13 Though the examiners noted a discrepancy, due to transcription errors, between the report of May 27, 1865, and the version published in 1870; allowing for this error, the 1921 report confirmed the 1865 data (Muratori, "Verbale," 6).

14 Ibid., 4–6; Sergi and Frassetto, "Le ossa di Dante," 18–19. Frassetto provides the most detailed list and description of the bones in *Dantis ossa: La forma corporea di Dante, scheletro, ritratti, maschere e busti* (Bologna: Università di Bologna, 1933), 7–10.

15 For Antonio Fusconi's guardianship of Dante's tomb, I draw on accounts by Muratori, "Verbale," 11–12; Felice Mazzeo, *Dante e Ravenna* (Bologna: Cappelli, 1987), 173–176; Giovanni Mesini, *La tomba e le ossa di Dante* (Ravenna: Longo, 1965), 35; Giovanni Lugaresi, "Il personaggio: Antonio Fusconi, la 'sentinella' di Dante," *Bollettino dantesco: Per il settimo centenario* 2 (2013): 103–105; and Walden Garratt, "Dante's Friend," *Ball State University Forum* 12, no. 4 (1971): 47–50.

16 Garratt, "Dante's Friend," 48.

17 Muratori, "Verbale," 11.

18 Mazzeo, *Dante e Ravenna,* 174.

19 Lugaresi, "Il personaggio," 104; Mazzeo, *Dante e Ravenna,* 175.

20 Lugaresi, "Il personaggio," 104.

21 Mesini, *La tomba e le ossa di Dante,* 35; Mazzeo, *Dante e Ravenna,* 174. Fusconi died in 1976 at age eighty-seven.

22 Muratori, "Verbale," 11; Franco Gabici, "Vittorio Guaccimanni, pittore e incisore dallo stile inconfondibile," *Il Resto del Carlino,* March 15, 2009, http://www .ilrestodelcarlino.it/ravenna/2009/03/15/158273-vittorio_guaccimanni_pittore_incisore _dallo_stile_inconfondibile_nasceva.shtml.

23 Muratori, "Verbale," 6, 11.

24 I was perplexed by Frassetto's association of Dante's skull with "east" until I looked closely at the photograph of Dante's bones in the coffin (ibid., 5): there we see that the skull sits at the top end of the rectangular coffin, which, placed in the marble tomb at the back of the chapel (along an east-west axis), means Dante would indeed face north toward the doorway.

25 Ibid., 12. Although Verdi mistakenly believed that Dante was the author of an Italian "Ave Maria" when he set it to music in 1879, the composer later wrote a choral work, *Laudi alla Vergine Maria,* based on Dante's prayer to Mary in the final canto of the *Divine Comedy* (*Par.* 33.1–39).

26 Sergi and Frassetto, "Le ossa di Dante," 20.

27 Frassetto, *Dantis ossa,* 40–44.

28 Ibid., 134.

29 Barbara Spackman, *Fascist Virilities: Rhetoric, Ideology, and Social Fantasy in Italy* (Minneapolis: University of Minnesota Press, 1996), xii. Spackman concludes that Mussolini's body "became the single most compelling binding mechanism of the fascist regime. Its 'unity' stood in the place of all divisions and heterogeneities, ideological, political, sexual, and racial, that fascism sought to deny" (155). Ruth Ben-Ghiat, *Fascist Modernities: Italy, 1922–1945* (Berkeley: University of California Press, 2001), notes Mussolini's belief that authoritarian measures were needed to "toughen and discipline" Italians "'feminized' and 'disarmed' by centuries of foreign occupation" (6). John Champagne, *Aesthetic Modernism and Masculinity in Fascist Italy* (London: Routledge, 2013), complicates the narrative of fascist virility (and homofascism) by discussing nuanced representations of masculinity in art, literature, and music while the regime was in power as products of the tension between fascist ideology and modernist aesthetics.

30 Fabio Frassetto, "How Dante Really Looked," *Research and Progress* 5, no. 3 (1939): 169–172, at 172.

31 Fabio Frassetto, "Il volto del divino poeta: Devozione di uno scienziato," *L'illustrazione italiana* 65, no. 6 (February 6, 1938): 178. In this article, Frassetto reproduces two of the photographs Ricci allowed (front and side views of the skull) along with front and side views of the bust made by him and Alfonso Borghesani.

32 See John van Wyhe's valuable resource, *History of Phrenology on the Web,* accessed November 20, 2019, http://www.historyofphrenology.org.uk.

33 Frassetto, *Dantis ossa*, 83.

34 Alfredo Cottignoli and Giorgio Gruppioni, *Fabio Frassetto e l'enigma del volto di Dante* (Ravenna: Longo, 2012), 36.

35 Frassetto, "How Dante Really Looked," 170.

36 Sergi and Frassetto, "Le ossa di Dante," 24.

37 Frassetto, *Dantis ossa*, 14–15, 31–35.

38 Sergi and Frassetto, "Le ossa di Dante," 26. Frassetto confirmed this view in the lecture he gave in Berlin in 1938: "Contrary to all foregoing assertions concerning Dante's belonging to the one or the other race is our anthropological argument, from which Dante must be viewed finally as belonging to the Mediterranean race, whose most glorious representative was he himself" ("How Dante Really Looked," 170).

39 Aaron Gillette, *Racial Theories in Fascist Italy* (London: Routledge, 2002), 24–34, at 32. A believer in the notion of a "superior race"—albeit Mediterranean rather than Aryan or Nordic—Sergi was also a proponent of eugenics (ibid., 194n65). Jeffrey David Feldman, "The X-Ray and the Relic: Anthropology, Bones, and Bodies in Modern Italy," in *In Corpore: Bodies in Post-Unification Italy,* ed. Loredana Polezzi and Charlotte Ross (Madison, NJ: Fairleigh Dickinson University Press, 2007), 107–126.

40 Giuseppe Sergi, *The Mediterranean Race: A Study of the Origin of European Peoples* (London: Walter Scott, 1901), v–vi.

41 Giuseppe Sergi, *Le prime e le più antiche civiltà* (Turin: Fratelli Bocca, 1926), 310.

42 Gillette, *Racial Theories,* 26; Sergi, *Le prime e le più antiche civiltà,* 310: "it is a human variety with special, superior physical and psychological qualities, with artistic instincts it has developed everywhere it has moved or migrated."

43 Giorgio Gruppioni, *"Dantis ossa:* Una ricognizione delle ricognizioni dei resti di Dante," in *Dante e la fabbrica della "Commedia,"* ed. Alfredo Cottignoli, Donatino Domini, and Giorgio Gruppioni (Ravenna: Longo, 2008), 255–267, at 267.

44 Cottignoli and Gruppioni, *Fabio Frassetto,* includes two previously unedited scripts of the film and an appendix with related documents (47–77).

45 Ibid., 41.

46 Gruppioni, *"Dantis ossa,"* 255–256; Nella Doria Cambon, *Il convegno celeste* (Turin: Fratelli Bocca Editori, 1933), 155–161.

47 Frassetto, *Dantis ossa,* 73; Cottignoli and Gruppioni, *Fabio Frassetto,* 33–34, 42–45.

48 Cottignoli and Gruppioni, *Fabio Frassetto,* 53.

49 Ibid., 54; Frassetto, *Dantis ossa,* 44; Giovanni Boccaccio, *Trattatello in laude di Dante,* first redaction, ed. Pier Giorgio Ricci, in *Tutte le opere di Giovanni Boccaccio,* ed. Vittore Branca, 10 vols. (Milan: Mondadori, 1964–1983), 3:437–496, at 480, translated by Philip H. Wicksteed, rev. William Chamberlain, as *Life of Dante* (Richmond, UK: Oneworld Classics, 2009).

50 Dante, *Purg.* 27.49–51: "Sí com' fui dentro, in un bogliente vetro / gittato mi sarei per rinfrescarmi, / tant' era ivi lo 'ncendio sanza metro." Cottignoli and Gruppioni, *Fabio Frassetto,* 54.

51 Cottignoli and Gruppioni, *Fabio Frassetto,* 64, 70, 74.

52 Ibid., 18, 27, 32, 54.

12. DANTE'S DUCE, MUSSOLINI'S DANTE

. Epigraph: Arrigo Solmi, "Notizie," *Giornale dantesco* 38 (1937): 197–202, at 198: "Ravenna, la città imperiale, ricca di memorie gloriose e splendente di insigni monumenti, consacra oggi una zona austera d'arte, di scienza e di silenzio, intorno al sepolcro venerato del Divino Poeta."

1 Benito Mussolini, "Dio non esiste," in *L'uomo e la divinità,* in *Opera omnia di Benito Mussolini,* ed. Edoardo Susmel and Duilio Susmel, 44 vols. (Florence: La Fenice, 1951–1980), 33:5–25, at 11.

2 On racist and anti-Semitic policies under fascism, see Ruth Ben-Ghiat, *Fascist Modernities: Italy, 1922–1945* (Berkeley: University of California Press, 2001), 122–170; Aaron Gillette, *Racial Theories in Fascist Italy* (London: Routledge, 2002), 50–99; and Mario Avagliano and Marco Palmieri, *Di pura razza italiana: L'Italia "ariana" di fronte alle leggi raziali* (Milan: Baldini and Castoldi, 2013).

3 Benito Mussolini, preface to *Regresso delle nascite: Morte dei popoli,* by Richard Korherr (Rome: Libreria del Littorio, 1928), 7–23.

4 Ibid., 19, 25.

5 Ibid., 23. Mussolini went on to denounce the growing percentage of African Americans in the United States, with areas like Harlem in New York "exclusively populated by blacks," whom he blamed for bloody confrontations with police (10–11).

6 Dante, *Par.* 11.63: "di dí in dí l'amò piú forte." Mussolini, "Il programma fascista," in *Opera omnia,* 17:216–223, at 221–222.

7 Benito Mussolini, *My Autobiography* (New York: Charles Scribner's Sons, 1928), 7–8.

8 Ibid., 204.

9 Ibid., 36, 55.

10 Ibid., 129–132.

11 "Italian Premier Takes Up Foreign Policies—Dante Bust for Each Embassy," *New York Times,* November 29, 1922.

12 Giordano Bruno Guerri, *Galeazzo Ciano: Una vita, 1903/1944* (Milan: Bompiani, 1979), 173.

13 Francesco Giunta, *Un po' di fascismo* (Milan: Consalvo, 1935), 52–53.

14 Dante, *Inf.* 1.95: "non lasciar altrui passar per la sua via"; 1.60: "mi ripigneva là dove 'l sol tace"; 1.15: "ove uderai le disperate strida"; 1.104: "sapïenza, amore e virtute."

15 Anthony K. Cassell, *Inferno I* (Philadelphia: University of Pennsylvania Press, 1989), 94–113.

16 These and other "propagandistic" interpretations are noted by Charles T. Davis, "Il problema del Veltro nell'*Inferno* di Dante," in *Enciclopedia dantesca,* ed. Umberto Bosco, 6 vols. (Istituto della Enciclopedia Italiana, 1970–1978), 5:908–912.

17 Dante, *Inf.* 1.106: "umile Italia" (my translation).

18 Giovanni Giuriati, *La parabola di Mussolini nei ricordi di un gerarca,* ed. Emilio Gentile (Bari: Laterza, 1981), xxviii.

19 Ibid., 39. The cross appears in the sphere of Mars (Dante, *Par.* 14–18) and the eagle in the sphere of Jupiter (*Par.* 18–20).

20 Luigi Valli, *Il segreto della croce e dell'aquila nella "Divina Commedia"* (Bologna: Zanichelli, 1922), xi.

21 Domenico Venturini, *Dante Alighieri e Benito Mussolini,* 2nd ed. (Rome: Nuova Italia, 1932), 187–202, at 194. Dante lays out his doctrine of Rome's "two suns"—pope and emperor—in *Purg.* 16.106–129 and *Monarchia* 3.15. In the former, he laments the harm done from the church's arrogation of both powers.

22 Venturini, *Dante Alighieri e Benito Mussolini,* 246.

23 Ibid., 109–122, at 120.

24 Dante, *Purg.* 33.50: "enigma forte" (my translation).

25 Dante, *Purg.* 32.124–160.

26 Dante, *Purg.* 33.37–45:

> Non sarà tutto tempo sanza reda
> l'aguglia che lasciò le penne al carro
> per che divenne mostro e poscia preda;
> ch'io veggio certamente, e però il narro,
> a darne tempo già stelle propinque,
> sicure d'ogn' intoppo e d'ogne sbarro,
> nel quale un cinquecento diece e cinque,
> messo di Dio, anciderà la fuia
> con quel gigante che con lei delinque.

27 I discuss these and other interpretations in "Five Hundred Ten and Five," in *The Dante Encyclopedia,* ed. Richard Lansing (New York: Garland, 2000), 381–383.

28 Venturini, *Dante Alighieri e Benito Mussolini,* 299.

29 Ibid.

30 Pope Pius XI, "Vogliamo anzitutto," February 13, 1929, https://w2.vatican.va /content/pius-xi/it/speeches/documents/hf_p-xi_spe_19290213_vogliamo-anzitutto .html.

31 David I. Kertzer, *The Pope and Mussolini: The Secret History of Pius XI and the Rise of Fascism in Europe* (New York: Random House, 2014), 110–113, at 111.

32 Venturini, *Dante Alighieri e Benito Mussolini,* 299.

33 Ibid., 115.

34 Peter Bondanella, *The Eternal City: Roman Images in the Modern World* (Chapel Hill: University of North Carolina Press, 1987), 172–206.

35 Mussolini, "Il discorso della mobilitazione," in *Opera omnia,* 27:158–159, at 159.

36 Christopher Duggan, *The Force of Destiny: A History of Italy since 1796* (Boston: Houghton Mifflin, 2008), 502–505.

37 Mussolini, "La proclamazione dell'Impero," in *Opera omnia,* 27:268–269.

38 Ibid.

39 Dante, *Monarchia* 1.15.8–10, 3.10.14–17, 3.15.10 (3.16.10 in Prue Shaw's translation).

40 Giuseppe Frignani, "Auspici e presagi presso la tomba di Dante," in *Per l'inaugurazione della zona dantesca,* ed. Province and Commune of Ravenna (Ravenna: Società Tipo-Editrice Ravennate Mutilati, 1936), 3–11, at 9.

41 For sources documenting the fascist-era planning and execution of renovations to the area around Dante's tomb, I am indebted to Maria Giulia Benini, *Luoghi danteschi: La Basilica di S. Francesco e la Zona Dantesca a Ravenna* (Ravenna: Longo, 2003).

42 Among the over 250 individuals who declared their allegiance to the document—either as signatories or through letters—were a number of well-known writers and artists, including Filippo Tommaso Marinetti, Giuseppe Ungaretti, Ardengo Soffici, and Luigi Pirandello.

43 Benini, *Luoghi danteschi,* 49.

44 Ibid., 50.

45 The photographs are shown in a short video created by Fausto Fiasconaro and Gabriele Pezzi from collections of the Classense Library, "Ravenna in foto: La zona Dantesca nei fondi fotografici della Biblioteca Classense," March 10, 2016, https://m .youtube.com/watch?v=hMqWlPT_l4M.

46 Benini, *Luoghi danteschi,* 58.

47 Ibid., 76.

48 Ibid., 77.

49 Ibid., 71–72.

50 Ibid., 78. I calculate the 1933 exchange rate from MeasuringWorth.com. According to the Department of Labor's CPI Inflation Calculator, $268,000 in 1933 had the buying power of over $5.2 million in 2019.

51 Ibid, 80.

52 Ibid.

53 Ibid., 80–81.

54 Ricci's father, Luigi, lived in an apartment above the café in Casa Rizzetti, where Corrado spent his childhood (ibid., 71).

55 Today called the Biblioteca di Storia Contemporanea "Alfredo Oriani," the library holds about 170,000 nineteenth- and twentieth-century works of Italian history, political science, economics, and sociology.

56 Benini, *Luoghi danteschi,* 95.

57 Luigi Federzoni, president of the Italian Senate, eulogized his colleague as a "loyal militant of Fascism" who was among the first senators to "welcome the regenerating movement of the spirit and life of the Nation in the Revolution of the Black Shirts." Prime Minister Mussolini then demanded the floor to express the government's endorsement of these "moving words" and offer a special tribute to the memory of Corrado Ricci for his "faithful service to the State" (Senato della Repubbica, *Atti*

parlamentari, discussioni, December 3, 1934). An obituary in the *New York Times* (June 6, 1934) remembered Ricci primarily for his archeological projects in Rome, including "the draining of Lake Nemi to disclose the sunken galleys of Caligula, which had been hidden for more than 1,800 years."

58 "Notizie," *Giornale dantesco* 38 (1937): 197–202, at 197.

59 From *Il Resto del Carlino,* reprinted ibid., 197.

60 Ibid., 198.

61 Ibid.

62 Arrigo Solmi, *Il pensiero politico di Dante: Studi storici* (Florence: "La Voce," 1922). For showing how not only propagandists but Solmi and other reputable scholars reinforced politicized readings of Dante in sync with fascist ideology, I am indebted to Stefano Albertini, "Dante in camicia nera: Uso e abuso del divino poeta nell'Italia fascista," *Italianist* 16 (1996): 117–142; Luigi Scorrano, "Il Dante 'fascista,'" in *Il Dante "fascista": Saggi, letture, note dantesche* (Ravenna: Longo, 2001), 89–125; and Martino Marazzi, *Danteum: Studi sul Dante imperiale del Novecento* (Florence: Franco Cesati, 2015), 40–64. Stéphanie Lanfranchi discusses the fascist appropriation of other canonical Italian authors (Petrarch, Alfieri, Leopardi, and Foscolo) in addition to Dante, in "'Verrà un dì l'Italia vera . . .': Poesia e profezia dell'Italia futura nel giudizio fascista," *California Italian Studies* 2, no. 1 (2011), http://escholarship.org/uc/item/2m5817bv.

63 Arrigo Solmi, "La 'Monarchia' di Dante," *Nuova antologia,* 7th ser., 378 (1935): 321–331, at 331.

64 "Notizie," 198.

65 Ibid.

66 Ibid., 199.

67 Ibid., 198.

68 Ibid., 199.

69 Ibid.

70 Ibid., 199–200.

71 Ibid., 200.

72 The short film, lasting just over one minute, was produced on September 16, 1936, three days after the inauguration, by Giornale Luce, part of the fascist propaganda machine. These news reports were shown in theaters before the main features. The film (Giornale Luce, B0955) is available online through the Archivio Storico Luce (http://archivioluce.com) and on YouTube (https://www.youtube.com/watch?v=-KwTk7bFdK0).

13. DANTE'S ROMAN TEMPLE

Epigraph: Giuseppe Terragni, "Relazione sul Danteum," in *Terragni e il Danteum, 1938,* by Thomas L. Schumacher, 2nd ed. (Rome: Officina Edizioni, 1983), 135–144, at 142: "Quindi, non Museo, non Palazzo, non Teatro, ma *Tempio* dovrà essere principalmente l'Edificio che vogliamo costruire."

1   Thomas L. Schumacher, *Terragni's Danteum: Architecture, Poetics, and Politics under Italian Fascism,* 2nd ed. (New York: Princeton Architectural Press, 2004), 58. I calculate the 1938 exchange rate from MeasuringWorth.com. According to the Department of Labor's CPI Inflation Calculator, $236,700 in 1938 had the buying power of over $4.2 million in 2019.

2   Rino Valdameri to Dino Alfieri, November 5, 1937, quoted in Martino Marazzi, *Danteum: Studi sul Dante imperiale del Novecento* (Florence: Franco Cesati, 2015), 33.

3   Ibid., 64–85, at 62.

4   Peter Bondanella, *The Eternal City: Roman Images in the Modern World* (Chapel Hill: University of North Carolina Press, 1987), 203.

5   Schumacher, *Terragni's Danteum,* 36, 58. I calculate the 1938 exchange rate from MeasuringWorth.com. According to the Department of Labor's CPI Inflation Calculator, $105,200 in 1938 had the buying power of over $1.8 million in 2019.

6   Schumacher, *Terragni's Danteum,* 65; Bondanella, *Eternal City,* 192, 205.

7   Benito Mussolini, "Ai gerarchi milanesi," June 20, 1929, in *Opera omnia di Benito Mussolini,* ed. Edoardo Susmel and Duilio Susmel, 44 vols. (Florence: La Fenice, 1951–1980), 24:123–125, at 124.

8   Simona Storchi, "'Il fascismo è una casa di vetro': Giuseppe Terragni and the Politics of Space in Fascist Italy," *Italian Studies* 62, no. 2 (2007): 231–245, at 240–241. Fascism's "glass house," in Jeremy Tambling words, was "not so much for people to look in as for those inside to look out" ("Terragni, Fascism, and Allegory: Reading the Danteum," *Italianist* 17 [1997]: 123–144, at 130).

9   I cite the manifesto from *Materiali per l'analisi dell'architettura moderna. Il M.I.A.R.,* ed. Michele Cennamo (Naples: Società Editrice Napoletana, 1976), 103–104, at 103.

10   Ibid.

11   I cite Giuseppe Terragni's "Relazione sul Danteum" from Schumacher, *Terragni e il Danteum,* 142.

12   Thomas L. Schumacher, *Surface and Symbol: Giuseppe Terragni and the Architecture of Italian Rationalism* (New York: Princeton Architectural Press, 1991), 204.

13   I cite Rino Valdameri's "Statuto del Danteum" from Schumacher, *Terragni e il Danteum,* 145.

14   Terragni, "Relazione," 140.

15   Antonino Saggio, *Giuseppe Terragni: Vita e opere* (Rome-Bari: Laterza, 1995), 83. Although uncertainty remains over how to apportion credit for the Danteum, Schumacher believes "Terragni conceived the project virtually alone," with Lingeri and others helping to draw up and model the plans (*Terragni's Danteum,* 59).

16   Schumacher, *Surface,* 206.

17   "Testi e selezioni critiche," ed. Renato Pedio, *L'architettura: Cronache e storia* 14, no. 3 (July 1968): 146.

18   Richard A. Etlin, *Modernism in Italian Architecture, 1880–1940* (Cambridge, MA: MIT Press, 1991), 392; Schumacher, *Terragni's Danteum,* 62.

19 Visitors can take a virtual tour of Lorenzo Russo's 3-D reconstructions of the Danteum made from the plans and models of architects Terragni and Lingeri. The videos are available at: https://www.youtube.com/channel/UCKcH-jhEyrBCev MQal62WKw.

20 Etlin, *Modernism,* 549.

21 Terragni, "Relazione," 140.

22 Schumacher, *Surface,* 204.

23 Valdameri, "Statuto," 145.

24 The golden rectangle is expressed mathematically as a:b::a+b:a, where *a* is the short side and *a+b* is the long side of the rectangle.

25 Terragni, "Relazione,"136.

26 Etlin, *Modernism,* 557.

27 Terragni, "Relazione," 142.

28 Ibid., 142–143.

29 Dante and Virgil spiral to the left in their infernal descent but walk to the right as they climb the Mountain of Purgatory.

30 Terragni, "Relazione," 144.

31 Dante, *Purg.* 33.40–45.

32 Dante, *Monarchia* 3.15.10 (3.16.10 in Prue Shaw's translation); Terragni, "Relazione," 139.

33 Dante, *Par.* 18.91–93.

34 Schumacher, *Terragni's Danteum,* 152, fig. 114. Mussolini similarly initialed the frontispiece of the *Paradiso* illustrated by Amos Nattini in 1941 with a gigantic letter *M* (Marazzi, *Danteum,* 73).

35 Jeffrey Schnapp, "Un tempio moderno," in *Giuseppe Terragni: Opera completa,* ed. Giorgio Ciucci (Milan: Electa, 1996), 267–279, at 272.

36 Terragni, "Relazione," 139; Etlin, *Modernism,* 547, 557.

37 Terragni, "Relazione," 140.

38 Marazzi, *Danteum,* 69–70.

39 Ibid., 81–83, at 81. Marazzi debunks the postwar Italian mythology of "good Italians"—the "italiani brava gente" in the famous film of that title by Giuseppe De Sanctis (1965)—in contrast with "bad Germans." On the massacres of Jews and others in the Ukraine, see the "Online Guide of Murder Sites of Jews in the Former USSR," published by Yad Vashem, accessed November 20, 2019, http://www.yadvashem.org /research/research-projects/killing-sites/killing-sites-catalog; Luigi Zuccoli, *Quindici anni di vita e di lavoro con l'amico e maestro architetto Giuseppe Terragni,* ed. Luca Lanini (Melfi: Libria, 2015), 60.

40 Saggio, *Giuseppe Terragni,* 86–87; Marazzi, *Danteum,* 84; Zuccoli, *Quindici anni,* 60–61.

14. WARTIME PERILS

Epigraph: Antonio Fusconi, quoted in Walden Garratt, "Dante's Friend," *Ball State University Forum* 12, no. 4 (1971): 47–50, at 48.

1 Stephen Harvey, "The Italian War Effort and the Strategic Bombing of Italy," *History* 70, no. 228 (1985): 32–45, at 40–41.

2 R. J. B. Bosworth, *Mussolini's Italy: Life under the Fascist Dictatorship, 1915–1945* (New York: Penguin, 2006), 491–497.

3 Giovanni Boccaccio, *Trattatello in laude di Dante,* first redaction, ed. Pier Giorgio Ricci, in *Tutte le opere di Giovanni Boccaccio,* ed. Vittore Branca, 10 vols. (Milan: Mondadori, 1964–1983), 3:437–496, at 458–459, translated by Philip H. Wicksteed, rev. William Chamberlain, as *Life of Dante* (Richmond, UK: Oneworld Classics, 2009); Isidoro del Lungo, *Dell'esilio di Dante: Discorso e documenti* (Florence: Le Monnier, 1881), 172–173; Cristoforo Landino, *Comento sopra la Comedia,* ed. Paolo Procaccioli, 4 vols. (Rome: Salerno, 2001), 1:246; Ludovico Frati and Corrado Ricci, eds., *Il sepolcro di Dante: Documenti raccolti* (Bologna: Monti, 1889), 56.

4 Bosworth, *Mussolini's Italy,* 502–504.

5 Centre for the Study of War, State and Society, University of Exeter, "Bombing Italy: Allied Strategies, 1940–1945," accessed November 13, 2019, http://humanities .exeter.ac.uk/media/universityofexeter/collegeofhumanities/history/researchcentres/cen treforthestudyofwarstateandsociety/bombing/THE_BOMBING_OF_ITALY.pdf.

6 Dino Guerrino Molesi, *Ravenna nella seconda guerra mondiale* (Ravenna: Longo, 1974), 332–333.

7 Ibid., 61.

8 Ibid., 334.

9 The Boeing B-17 ("Flying Fortress") and the Consolidated B-24 ("Liberator") flown by the US Air Force and Britain's Royal Air Force carried bombs weighing up to two thousand pounds, with five-hundred- and one-thousand-pound bombs being the most popular ones (Stewart Halsey Ross, *Strategic Bombing by the United States in World War II: The Myths and the Facts* [Jefferson, NC: McFarland, 2003], 89–93, 105–106).

10 Garratt, "Dante's Friend," 48.

11 Felice Mazzeo, *Dante e Ravenna* (Bologna: Cappelli, 1987), 176–177.

12 Garratt, "Dante's Friend," 48.

13 Marta Nezzo, "The Defence of Works of Art from Bombing in Italy during the Second World War," in *Bombing, States and Peoples in Western Europe, 1940–1945,* ed. Claudia Baldoli, Andrew Knapp, and Richard Overy (London: Continuum, 2011), 101–120, at 112. An annotated catalog of Italian artwork and other precious objects stolen by the Nazis, including items taken from Ravenna, is contained in *Treasures Untraced: An Inventory of the Italian Art Treasures Lost during the Second World War,* ed. Luisa Morozzi and Rita Paris (Rome: Istituto Poligrafico e Zecca dello Stato, 1995), 71, 78–79, 193–196.

14 Garratt, "Dante's Friend," 48.

15　The letter is published in Arrigo Boldrini, "Il patrimonio artistico di Ravenna e la guerra," *Il movimento di liberazione in Italia* 70, no. 1 (1963): 46–62, at 48. Maglione served as secretary of state under Pius XII from March 10, 1939, until his death on August 23, 1944.

16　Molesi, *Ravenna*, 65.

17　Ibid., 34, 336.

18　Ross, *Strategic Bombing*, 108.

19　Janet Charlotte Smith, "The Side Chambers of San Giovanni Evangelista in Ravenna: Church Libraries of the Fifth Century," *Gesta* 29, no. 1 (1990): 86–97, at 86–87.

20　Molesi, *Ravenna*, 25, 59–60, 118–120.

21　Ibid., 309–344, at 309.

22　Garratt, "Dante's Friend," 48.

23　Benito Mussolini, "Discorso per il cinquantenario della società italiana degli autori ed editori," April 28, 1933, in *Opera omnia di Benito Mussolini,* ed. Edoardo Susmel and Duilio Susmel, 44 vols. (Florence: La Fenice, 1951–1980), 44:49–51, at 50.

24　Jeffrey T. Schnapp, *Staging Fascism: "18 BL" and the Theater of Masses for Masses* (Stanford, CA: Stanford University Press, 1996), 55, 77.

25　Ibid., 57, 59, 68–76, 79.

26　Arrigo Petacco, *Pavolini: L'ultima raffica di Salò* (Milan: Mondadori, 1982), 223; Bosworth, *Mussolini's Italy,* 529; Giordano Bruno Guerri, *Galeazzo Ciano: Una vita, 1903/1944* (Milan: Bompiani, 1979), 637; Gian Franco Vené, "Alessandro Pavolini: Il letterato feroce," in *I gerarchi di Mussolini,* ed. Mario Nilo (Novara: Istituto Geografico De Agostini, 1973), 137–147, at 146.

27　Petacco, *Pavolini,* 213.

28　Ibid.

29　Ibid., 213–214, 221–223, at 223.

30　Mussolini, "Il programma fascista," in *Opera omnia,* 17:216–223, at 221–222.

31　Bosworth, *Mussolini's Italy,* 529.

32　Vené, "Alessandro Pavolini," 139–140, at 140; Petacco, *Pavolini,* 233–241, at 240; Sergio Luzzatto, *The Body of Il Duce: Mussolini's Corpse and the Fortunes of Italy,* trans. Frederika Randall (New York: Metropolitan, 2005), 46–49.

33　Luzzatto, *Body,* 62–70, 82, 99–118, 202–218.

34　Ibid., 229. The recent success of populist, nationalist campaigns in Italian politics has coincided with a significant uptick in the tomb's popularity, with estimates as high as two hundred thousand visitors a year by 2018 (Cristina Verdi, "Il 28 ottobre riapre la cripta del Duce, ma è polemica con l'Anpi," *il Giornale.it,* October 17, 2018, http://www.ilgiornale .it/news/cronache/28-ottobre-riapre-cripta-duce-polemica-lanpi-1589233.html).

15. DANTE DUST

Epigraph: Church of England, "The Order for the Burial of the Dead," in *The Book of Common Prayer,* accessed November 22, 2019, https://www.churchofengland.org/prayer -and-worship/worship-texts-and-resources/book-common-prayer/burial-dead.

1   Paolo Di Stefano, "Trovata per caso una busta con le ceneri di Dante," *Corriere della Sera,* July 20, 1999; Nello Ajello, "Dante, le ceneri dimenticate," *La Repubblica,* July 20, 1999; Nico Orengo, "E Dante rivede le stelle: trovate le ceneri scomparse," *La Stampa,* July 20, 1999; Dante, *Inf.* 34.139: "E quindi uscimmo a riveder le stelle" (Then we came forth, to see again the stars).

2   Wanda Lattes, "Dante Alighieri, le ceneri ritrovate dopo 70 anni," *Corriere della Sera,* July 20, 1999.

3   Ibid.

4   Orengo, "E Dante rivede le stelle."

5   "Dante–Firenze, Ritrovata Dopo 70 Anni Parte Ceneri Poeta," Agenzia Giornalistica Italia, July 19, 1999; "Dante's Lost Ashes Found in Florentine Library," Reuters News, July 19, 1999; "Les cendres de Dante découvertes sur une étagère à Florence," Reuters: Les actualités en français, July 19, 1999; "Encuentran cenizas de Dante en biblioteca de Florencia," Reuters: Noticias Latinoamericanas, July 19, 1999; "After 70 Years, Library Finds Ashes Taken from Dante's Tomb," Associated Press Newswires, July 19, 1999; "After 70 Years, Part of Dante's Ashes Are Rediscovered," Deutsche Presse-Agentur, July 19, 1999; "Italy's Florence Library Rediscovers Dante's Ashes," Xinhua News Agency, July 19, 1999; Indro Montanelli, "Somme ceneri, polveri italiane," *Corriere della Sera,* July 23, 1999.

6   Lorenza Pampaloni, "Dante, ritrovate le ceneri perdute," *La Repubblica,* July 20, 1999. Dante reports his strained eyesight in *Convivio* 3.9.15–16. Saint Lucy is one of the "three blessed women"—with the Virgin Mary and Beatrice—who set in motion Dante's journey (*Inf.* 2.94–126). She also intervenes at crucial moments in his purgatorial ascent and appears in Heaven, seated next to John the Baptist and across from Adam in the Celestial Rose (*Purg.* 9.52–63, 19.25–30; *Par.* 32.28–33, 136–138).

7   Lattes, "Dante Alighieri."

8   Biblioteca Nazionale Centrale di Firenze, Banco Rari 399. I am grateful to the manuscripts division of the library for providing images of the relics.

9   *Della scoperta delle ossa di Dante: Relazione con documenti per cura del Municipio di Ravenna* (Ravenna: Angeletti, 1870), lv, lxiv.

10   Enrico Pazzi, *Ricordi d'arte di Enrico Pazzi statuario* (Florence: Tipografia Cooperativa, 1887), 204.

11   Santi Muratori, "Verbale," in *Ricognizione delle ossa di Dante fatta nei giorni 28–31 ottobre 1921,* ed. Santi Muratori, Corrado Ricci, Giuseppe Sergi, and Fabio Frassetto (Rome: Reale Accademia Nazionale dei Lincei, 1923), 7, 9.

12   Romolo Conti writes that Paganucci, a professor of anatomy, helped Drs. Puglioli and Bertozzi ascertain the authenticity of the three phalanges found in the tomb on June 7, 1865 (*La scoperta delle ossa di Dante* [Ravenna: Angeletti, 1865], 36).

13   Giovanni Puglioli and Claudio Bertozzi, "Relazione anatomico-fisiologica," in *Della scoperta,* i–xv, at iii.

14   Ibid., vi.

15   Just below Malagola's verification of the signatures ("vere ed autografe") is another statement, this one in darker, thinner script, by Enrico Pazzi, who says that on June 10,

1865, he arranged Dante's bones within the crystal urn. Pazzi may very well have helped reconstruct Dante's skeleton for display, but official reports suggest this work took place on June 24 and attribute it solely to Drs. Puglioli and Bertozzi. Antonio Giardullo believes Pazzi added this note at a later date (the ink is less faded here than in the other writing) to inflate his importance and the value of the relic ("Le ricorrenti polemiche intorno alle ceneri di Dante," *Rivista di studi politici internazionali* 67, no. 2 [2000]: 314–317, at 318).

16 Lattes, "Dante Alighieri."

17 Ibid.; Giulia Borgese, "Mazzoni: 'Le ceneri di Dante? Sono solo polvere,'" *Corriere della Sera,* July 21, 1999.

18 Giulia Borgese, "Merini: Non ridete delle ceneri di Dante," *Corriere della Sera,* July 27, 1999; Montanelli, "Somme ceneri."

19 *Oxford Latin Dictionary,* ed. P. G. W. Glare (Oxford: Oxford University Press, 1982), 316; Giannozzo Manetti, "Life of Dante," in *Biographical Writings,* ed. and trans. Stefano U. Baldassarri and Rolf Bagemihl (Cambridge, MA: Harvard University Press, 2003), 8–61, at 33; Giovanni Boccaccio, *Trattatello in laude di Dante,* first redaction, ed. Pier Giorgio Ricci, in *Tutte le opere di Giovanni Boccaccio,* ed. Vittore Branca, 10 vols. (Milan: Mondadori, 1964–1983), 3:437–496, at 464, translated by Philip H. Wicksteed, rev. William Chamberlain, as *Life of Dante* (Richmond, UK: Oneworld Classics, 2009); *Vocabolario degli accademici della Crusca,* vol. 2, pt. 1 (Florence: Successori Le Monnier, 1881), 747; Corrado Ricci, "A proposito delle ossa di Dante," *Corriere della Sera,* July 17, 1900.

20 Cynthia Hahn, *The Reliquary Effect: Enshrining the Sacred Object* (London: Reaktion Books, 2017), 20.

21 Church of England, "Order for the Burial of the Dead"; George Gordon (Lord) Byron, *Childe Harold's Pilgrimage,* in *The Complete Poetical Works,* ed. Jerome J. McGann, 7 vols. (Oxford, UK: Clarendon, 1980–1993), 2:4.478–480.

22 Biblioteca Nazionale Centrale di Firenze, "Le ceneri di Dante," August 7, 1999, http://www.bncf.firenze.sbn.it/notizie/testi/dante.html.

23 Pampaloni, "Dante"; Borgese, "Mazzoni."

24 Charles Freeman, *Holy Bones, Holy Dust: How Relics Shaped the History of Medieval Europe* (New Haven, CT: Yale University Press, 2011), 7–8.

25 John Calvin, *A Treatise on Relics,* trans. Valerian Krasinski (Edinburgh: Johnstone and Hunter, 1854), 227–243, at 233. Calvin also mentions the tail of the ass that carried Jesus into Jerusalem, the towel Jesus used to wipe the apostles' feet (one example bearing the imprint of Judas's foot), silver pieces paid to Judas, steps of Pilate's tribunal, the column of flagellation, the kerchief used to wipe Jesus's face, and the shroud in which he was buried.

26 Umberto Eco, *Il nome della rosa* (1980; repr., Milan: Bompiani, 2014), translated by William Weaver as *The Name of the Rose* (1983; repr., San Diego: Harcourt, 1994), 425.

27 James Bentley, *Restless Bones: The Story of Relics* (London: Constable, 1985), 42–43; see also Patrick J. Geary, *Living with the Dead in the Middle Ages* (Ithaca, NY: Cornell

University Press, 1994), 202; Caroline Walker Bynum, *Christian Materiality: An Essay on Religion in Late Medieval Europe* (New York: Zone Books, 2011), 136–139; Alison Knowles Frazier, *Possible Lives: Authors and Saints in Renaissance Italy* (New York: Columbia University Press, 2005), 2–6; and Marika Räsänen, *Thomas Aquinas's Relics as Focus for Conflict and Cult in the Late Middle Ages: The Restless Corpse* (Amsterdam: Amsterdam University Press, 2017), 253–254.

28 From Luther's *Table Talk,* quoted in Roland H. Bainton, *Here I Stand: A Life of Martin Luther* (New York: Abingdon-Cokesbury, 1950), 296; Calvin, *Treatise on Relics,* 218.

29 Peter Brown, *The Cult of Saints: Its Rise and Function in Latin Christianity* (Chicago: University of Chicago Press, 1981), 87–88; Freeman, *Holy Bones,* figs. 6 and 7; Bynum, *Christian Materiality,* 136, 212.

16. LOST TREASURE

Epigraph: Luigi Fallani, Lucia Milana, and Antonio Giardullo, "Le ceneri dantesche della Biblioteca nazionale di Firenze," *Rassegna storica toscana* 33, no. 1 (1987): 89–104, at 101: "nulla ci vieta di credere che possa ancora trovarsi in qualche angolo dimenticato della Biblioteca stessa."

1 Desiderio Chilovi, "Per la collezione dantesca," *Bollettino delle pubblicazioni italiane ricevute per diritto di stampa* 87 (August 15, 1889): lviii.

2 Fallani, Milana, and Giardullo, "Le ceneri dantesche," 90.

3 Chilovi, "Per la collezione dantesca."

4 Ibid.

5 Nello Ajello, "Dante, le ceneri dimenticate," *La Repubblica,* July 20, 1999.

6 Sandro Bertuccelli, "Per un pugno di ceneri del Divino Alighieri," *La Repubblica,* May 3, 1987, describes the Dante relic as "a sort of sudarium."

7 Dante, *Vita nuova* 40.1; Dante, *Par.* 31.103–108; Charles Freeman, *Holy Bones, Holy Dust: How Relics Shaped the History of Medieval Europe* (New Haven, CT: Yale University Press, 2011), 204.

8 Paolo Di Stefano, "Trovata per caso una busta con le ceneri di Dante," *Corriere della Sera,* July 20, 1999.

9 *Notizie sulla Biblioteca Nazionale Centrale di Firenze, 1898* (Florence: I Principali Librai, 1899), 20.

10 "L'urna per la tribuna dantesca," *Bollettino delle pubblicazioni ricevute italiane per diritto di stampa* 348 (June 30, 1900): xlvi; Enrico Montecorboli, "L'urna della tribuna dantesca," *Il Giorno,* June 24, 1900.

11 Montecorboli, "L'urna."

12 The letters, exchanged on June 15–16, 1900, are published in *Bollettino delle pubblicazioni italiane ricevute per diritto di stampa* 348 (June 30, 1900): 209.

13 Montecorboli, "L'urna."

14 Dante, *Purg.* 30.21.

15 Robyn Malo, *Relics and Writing in Late Medieval England* (Toronto: University of Toronto Press, 2013), 7.

16 Caroline Walker Bynum, *Christian Materiality: An Essay on Religion in Late Medieval Europe* (New York: Zone Books, 2011), 132, 184.

17 Cynthia Hahn, *Strange Beauty: Issues in the Making and Meaning of Reliquaries, 400–circa 1204* (University Park: Pennsylvania State University Press, 2012), 26.

18 Seeta Chaganti, *The Medieval Poetics of the Reliquary: Enshrinement, Inscription, Performance* (New York: Palgrave, 2008).

19 Silvia Alessandri, "La Tribuna Dantesca della Biblioteca Nazionale Centrale di Firenze," in *Dante vittorioso: Il mito di Dante nell'Ottocento,* ed. Eugenia Querci (Turin: Umberto Allemandi, 2011), 187–191, at 190.

20 Corrado Ricci, "Le ossa di Dante," *Corriere della Sera,* July 15–16, 1900.

21 Corrado Ricci, "A proposito delle ossa di Dante," *Corriere della Sera,* July 17–18, 1900.

22 Corrado Ricci, "Le ossa di Dante," *Il Marzocco* 5, no. 29 (July 22, 1900): 1–2, at 2.

23 Cipriano Giachetti, "La 'Tribuna' d'oggi e la Biblioteca di domani," *L'illustrazione toscana: Rassegna di ogni energia* 7, no. 7 (July 1929): 5–8, at 7.

24 Montecorboli, "L'urna."

25 *Bollettino delle pubblicazioni* 348 (June 30, 1900), 209.

26 Giachetti, "La 'Tribuna' d'oggi," 5–6.

27 Program, "First World Congress of Libraries and Bibliography," accessed November 22, 2019, https://www.ifla.org/files/assets/hq/history/1929_rome_congress _programme.pdf; Marcel Godet, *Le Congrès Mondial des Bibliothequès: Rome–Venise, 15–30 juin 1929* (Bern: Musée Gutenberg Suisse, 1929).

28 Johanna L. de Vries, "The History of the International Federation of Library Associations, from Its Creation to the Second World War: 1927–1940" (master's thesis, Loughborough University of Technology, 1976), 20.

29 Godet, *Le Congrès Mondial,* 5.

30 Giachetti, "La 'Tribuna' d'oggi," 6.

31 Mario Malan, "La Tribuna Dantesca di Claudio Bazzani inaugurata nella nuova Biblioteca di Firenze," *Il Giornale d'Italia,* June 26, 1929.

32 Alessandri, "La Tribuna Dantesca," 189.

33 "La 'Tribuna Dantesca' inaugurata nella Biblioteca Nazionale a Firenze," *Corriere della Sera,* June 27, 1929; Giachetti, "La 'Tribuna' d'oggi," 7.

34 Dante, *Par.* 33.145: "il sole e l'altre stelle" (my translation).

35 Malan, "La Tribuna Dantesca."

36 Fallani, Milana, and Giardullo, "Le ceneri dantesche," 100.

37 Mario La Rosa, "Si cercano in nove musei le 'ceneri di Alighieri,'" *Il Tempo,* May 6, 1987.

38 Fallani, Milana, and Giardullo, "Le ceneri dantesche," 101.

39 Daniela Pasti, "Dante? È in una spilla," *La Repubblica,* May 7, 1987; Eileen Horne, "The Great Flood of Florence, 50 Years On," *Guardian,* November 5, 2016, https://www .theguardian.com/artanddesign/2016/nov/05/the-great-flood-of-florence-50-years-on.

40 Fallani, Milana, and Giardullo, "Le ceneri dantesche," 101.

41 "Caccia al tesoro per le ceneri di Dante," *La Repubblica,* May 6, 1987.

42 Ibid.

43 Bertuccelli, "Per un pugno di ceneri."

44 "Caccia al tesoro."

45 Dante views a lifespan as an arc, with its peak at age thirty-five, the midpoint of the biblical lifespan of seventy years (*Convivio* 4.23.9; Psalm 90.10).

46 Biblioteca Nazionale Centrale di Firenze, "Le ceneri di Dante," August 7, 1999, http://www.bncf.firenze.sbn.it/notizie/testi/dante.html; Pope John Paul II, "Bull of Indiction of the Great Jubilee of the Year 2000," November 29, 1998, http://www.vatican.va/jubilee_2000/docs/documents/hf_jp-ii_doc_30111998_bolla-jubilee_en.html.

17. SAVED BY LOVE

Epigraph: "Giorgia e Marco," "Gioca con noi," Senatoragazzi, http://www.senatoperiragazzi.it/flash/Giorgia_e_Marco/index.htm: "Era il maggio 1987 e in una soffitta polverosa del Senato veniva trovato un medaglione contenente nientemeno che una parte delle ceneri di Dante." The Internet Archive Wayback Machine (https://web.archive.org) indicates the online presence of this feature between January 6, 2010 and February 6, 2019. I took screenshots of the animated cartoon on June 5, 2017.

 1 Daniela Pasti, "Dante? È in una spilla," *La Repubblica,* May 7, 1987; Mario La Rosa, "Si cercano in nove musei le 'ceneri di Alighieri,'" *Il Tempo,* May 6, 1987.

 2 Mario La Rosa, "Il lungo tragitto delle ceneri di Dante da Ravenna a Roma," *Il Tempo,* May 7, 1987.

 3 Pasti, "Dante? È in una spilla."

 4 Senato della Repubblica, "Aniquorum habet," accessed November 23, 2019, http://antiquorum-habet.senato.it/en/character-witness/alighieri-dante-en/.

 5 Mario La Rosa, "Un medaglione con le ceneri di Dante custodito in una stanza del senato," *Il Tempo,* October 17, 1968. Apollo 7 orbited the Earth 163 times during nearly eleven full days in space, October 7–22, 1968 (Smithsonian Air and Space Museum, "Apollo 7 (AS-205)," accessed November 23, 2019, https://airandspace.si.edu/explore-and-learn/topics/apollo/apollo-program/orbital-missions/apollo7.cfm.

 6 Alessandro D'Ancona, *Lettera autografa,* Rome, March 1, 1911, quoted in La Rosa, "Un medaglione"; D'Ancona, *Biglietto autografo con il quale stabilisce il lascito al Senato del medaglione contentente le ceneri di Dante,* Florence, March 14, 1914, http://antiquorum-habet.senato.it/en/character-witness/alighieri-dante-en/: "È evidente che furono avanzi delle spoglie mortali del poeta" (my transcription).

 7 Senato della Repubblica, "Biblioteca: Edizioni antiche e fondi speciali," accessed November 23, 2019, http://www.senato.it/4442?voce_sommario=195&testo_generico=1172.

 8 "Giorgia e Marco," "Gioca con noi."

9   For information on the D'Ancona family, see Flora Aghib Levi D'Ancona, *La giovinezza dei fratelli D'Ancona* (Rome: De Luca, 1982).

10 Senato della Repubblica, "Alessandro D'Ancona," accessed November 23, 2019, http://notes9.senato.it/Web/senregno.NSF/c1544f301fd4af96c125785d00598476/b4f8ba2 0dd043fea4125646f005aaabd?OpenDocument.

11 Senato della Repubblica, "Sansone D'Ancona," accessed November 23, 2019, http://notes9.senato.it/web/senregno.nsf/4c1a0e70e29a1d74c12571140059a394/39c8f367d 6e1a4974125646f005aabaa?OpenDocument.

12 Levi D'Ancona, *La giovinezza*, 48, 67; Emily Braun, "From the Risorgimento to the Resistance: One Hundred Years of Jewish Artists in Italy," in *Gardens and Ghettos: The Art of Jewish Life in Italy*, ed. Vivian B. Mann (New York: Jewish Museum, 1989), 137–190, at 184–185; Pasquale Baccarini, "Cesare D'Ancona," *Bullettino della R. Società Toscana di Orticultura* 33, no. 5 (May 1908): 129–131.

13 Alessandro D'Ancona, *Lettera autografa*, Rome, March 1, 1911, http://antiquorum -habet.senato.it/en/character-witness/alighieri-dante-en/: "qualche particolare oppor- tuno a chiarire l'autenticità della reliquia"; "mi pare dover ragionevolmente arguire che c'è qualche incaglio negli affari di cui trattavamo" (my transcription).

14 Ibid.: "sottrarla alle vicissitudini di un privato possesso"; "se, insomma, si veri- ficasse l'uno o l'altro di tali inconvenienti, non facciamone altro" (my transcription).

15 Emilia Campochiaro, *Gli archivi del Senato (1848–1948)*, 37, accessed November 13, 2019, https://www.senato.it/documenti/repository/relazioni/archiviostorico/02.pdf.

16 La Rosa, "Un medaglione." The other committee members were Pasquale Villari, Filippo Mariotti, Oreste Tommasini, and Fabrizio Colonna.

17 Ibid.

18 Levi D'Ancona, *La giovinezza*, 126; Campochiaro, *Gli archivi*, 38.

19 La Rosa, "Un medaglione." The jewelry box measures 2.4 by 1.7 inches, while the gold brooch is about 1.5 inches in diameter.

20 Ibid.

21 Olga Mugnaini, "Settepassi in Europa volta pagina: Rilancia i marchi di una secolare dinastia orafa," *Il Giorno*, July 9, 2009, http://www.ilgiorno.it/milano/2009/07 /09/203286-settepassi_europa_volta_pagina.shtml.

22 D'Ancona, *Lettera autografa*, quoted in La Rosa, "Un medaglione."

23 Corrado Ricci, "Le ossa di Dante," *Il Marzocco* 5, no. 29 (July 22, 1900): 1–2, at 2.

24 Santi Muratori, "Tesori intatti," in *Scritti danteschi*, ed. Giovanna Bosi Maramotti (Ravenna: Longo, 1991), 216–220, at 218.

25 Senato della Repubblica, "Achille Rasponi," accessed November 23, 2019, http:// notes9.senato.it/web/senregno.nsf/317f3dc642f7f5e5c125711400599b3a/8203c0b87326a811 4125646f005ee07e?OpenDocument; Angelo Varni, "Gioacchino Rasponi," in *Dizionario biografico degli italiani* (2016), Treccani, http://www.treccani.it/enciclopedia/gioacchino -rasponi_%28Dizionario-Biografico%29/.

26 Enrico Pazzi, *Ricordi d'arte di Enrico Pazzi statuario* (Florence: Tipografia Coopera- tiva, 1887), 136.

27 Ibid., 95, 134, 162–163.

28 D'Ancona, *Biglietto autografo:* "ad una Signora, donde passò a mio fratello prof. Cesare, e da lui a me" (my transcription).

29 Anatolio di Demidoff, *Viaggio nella Russa meridionale e nella Crimea per l'Ungheria, la Moldavia, e la Valachia* (Turin: Fontana, 1841), 71–72.

30 *Giornale del Centenario di Dante Allighieri celebrato in Firenze nei giorni 14, 15 e 16 maggio 1865* (Florence: Cellini, 1864–1865), 403–404.

31 Dora D'Istria, "Pellegrinaggio alla tomba di Dante," trans. Augusto Negri, *Rivista sicula di scienze, letteratura ed arte* 1, no. 2 (September 1869): 212–235, at 226.

32 Cornell University Library, "The Passionate Collector: Willard Fiske and His Libraries," accessed November 23, 2019, http://rmc.library.cornell.edu/collector/index.html.

33 Horatio S. White, *Willard Fiske, Life and Correspondence: A Biographical Study* (New York: Oxford University Press, 1925), 385.

34 Grace A. Ellis, "Dora D'Istria," *Scribner's Monthly, an Illustrated Magazine for the People* 17, no. 2 (December 1878): 225–233, at 231; Marta Questa, "Dora D'Istria: Storia di una principessa rumena a Firenze," Paolopianigiani: Scritti e immagini dalla terra d'Empoli, March 13, 2014, https://paolopianigiani.wordpress.com/tag/marta-questa/; Zenepe Dibra, "Elena Gjika (Dora D'Istria)," trans. Aurora Elezi, in *Biographical Dictionary of Women's Movements and Feminisms in Central, Eastern, and South Eastern Europe: 19th and 20th Centuries,* ed. Francisca de Haan, Krasimira Daskalova, and Anna Loutfi (New York: Central European University Press, 2006), 158–161, at 160.

35 Levi D'Ancona, *La giovinezza,* 125; Palazzo Spinelli Firenze, "Palazzina D'Ancona," in *Repertorio delle architetture civili di Firenze,* ed. Claudio Paolini, accessed November 23, 2019, http://www.palazzospinelli.org/architetture/scheda.asp?denominazione =&ubicazione=&button=&proprieta=D%27Ancona&architetti_ingegneri=&pittori _scultori=&note_storiche=&uomini_illustri=&ID=282.

36 Levi D'Ancona, *La giovinezza,* 65, 84–85.

37 Mario La Rosa, "Una piccola urna si trova al Senato," *Il Tempo,* May 6, 1987.

38 Ibid.

39 I thank Alessandra Casamassima, director of special collections for the Senate Library, for this information on the relic's current disposition.

40 Ricci, "Le ossa di Dante," 2; Muratori, "Tesori intatti," 216–219; Ludovico Perroni-Grande, "Per una reliquia: Delle ceneri di Dante a Messina," in *Letterine dantesche* (Messina: A. Trimarchi, 1900), 81–89.

41 Pasti, "Dante? È in una spilla."

18. DANTE'S GLOBAL FACE

Epigraph: Dan Brown, *Inferno* (New York: Doubleday, 2013), 460.

1 I document the history of this relic in "Fragments of Freedom: Dante's Relic in the Re-United States," *California Italian Studies* 6, no. 1 (2016), http://escholarship.org/uc /item/1ps8s9kd.

2   Fedele Spada, Statement Vouching for the Authenticity of the Coffin Fragments, LONG 27930, box 4, folder 68, Longfellow House–Washington's Headquarters National Historic Site, Cambridge, MA.

3   Elizabeth Lawrence to Henry Wadsworth Longfellow, July 26, 1872, ibid., box 1, folder 35.

4   Elizabeth Lawrence to Henry Wadsworth Longfellow, June 3, 1872, MS Am 1340.2, folder 3345, Houghton Library, Harvard University, Cambridge, MA.

5   Joan Nordell, "Search for the Ten Privately Printed Copies of Longfellow's Translation of the *Divine Comedy* 'In Commemorazione del secentesimo Anniversario della Nascita di Dante Alighieri,'" *Dante Studies* 128 (2010): 71–101, at 88.

6   Henry Wadsworth Longfellow to Elizabeth Lawrence, July 20, 1872, in *The Letters of Henry Wadsworth Longfellow,* ed. Andrew Hilen, 6 vols. (Cambridge, MA: Harvard University Press, 1966–1982), 5:568. Longfellow's decorative casket performs the traditional function of miniature tomb reliquaries, "the obvious expression of an appropriate container for a body no longer living" (Cynthia Hahn, *Strange Beauty: Issues in the Making and Meaning of Reliquaries, 400–circa 1204* [University Park: Pennsylvania State University Press, 2012], 70).

7   G[iovanni] A[ndrea] Scartazzini, *A Companion to Dante,* trans. Arthur John Butler (London: Macmillan, 1893), 477.

8   Recent additions to scholarship on Dante and Anglophone literature include Eric Griffiths and Matthew Reynolds, eds., *Dante in English* (London: Penguin, 2005); David Wallace, "Dante in English," in *The Cambridge Companion to Dante,* ed. Rachel Jacoff, 2nd ed. (Cambridge: Cambridge University Press, 2007), 281–304; Aida Audeh and Nick Havely, eds., *Dante in the Long Nineteenth Century: Nationality, Identity, and Appropriation* (Oxford: Oxford University Press, 2012); and Deborah Parker and Mark Parker, *Inferno Revealed: From Dante to Dan Brown* (New York: Palgrave Macmillan, 2013), 139–198.

9   Franz Liszt (*Dante Symphony,* 1856), Pyotr Ilyich Tchaikovsky (*Francesca da Rimini,* 1876), and Giacomo Puccini (*Gianni Schicchi,* 1918); Tangerine Dream (*Inferno,* 2002; *Purgatorio,* 2004; *Paradiso,* 2006), Iced Earth ("Dante's Inferno," 1995), Caparezza ("Argenti vive," 2015).

10   Peter S. Hawkins, *Dante: A Brief History* (Malden, MA: Blackwell, 2006), 131–166, at 150.

11   Dante Today, a crowd-sourced website curated by Arielle Saiber and Elizabeth Coggeshall, contains an extensive bibliography of scholarship on Dante in art, cinema, music, theater, and popular culture (https://research.bowdoin.edu/dante-today /bibliography).

12   Roberto Benigni, acceptance speech, 71st Academy Awards Ceremony (March 21, 1999), available on YouTube, http://www.youtube.com/watch?v=8cTR6fk8frs.

13   Ben Sisario, "Funnyman Takes on Dante's *Comedy,*" *New York Times,* May 23, 2009.

14   Maria Monica Donato, "Il primo ritratto documentato di Dante e il problema dell'iconografia trecentesca: Conferme, novità e anticipazione dopo due restauri," in

Dante e la fabbrica della "Commedia," ed. Alfredo Cottignoli, Donatino Domini, and Giorgio Gruppioni (Ravenna: Longo, 2008), 355–380, at 378–379.

15 Giovanni Boccaccio, *Trattatello in laude di Dante,* first redaction, ed. Pier Giorgio Ricci, in *Tutte le opere di Giovanni Boccaccio,* ed. Vittore Branca, 10 vols. (Milan: Mondadori, 1964–1983), 3:437–496, at 465, translated by Philip H. Wicksteed, rev. William Chamberlain, as *Life of Dante* (Richmond, UK: Oneworld Classics, 2009); Joshua Reid, "Textual Physiognomy: A New Theory and Brief History of Dantean Portraiture," *California Italian Studies* 6, no. 1 (2016), http://escholarship.org/uc/item/2519foxw; David Piper, *The Image of the Poet: British Poets and Their Portraits* (Oxford, UK: Clarendon, 1982), 110: "that hatchet profile that cleaves its way through the centuries with such authority."

16 Stefano Benazzi, Giorgio Gruppioni, Massimiliano Fantini, Francesca De Crescenzio, Franco Persiani, Francesco Mallegni, and Gabriele Mallegni, "From the History of the Recognitions of the Remains to the Reconstruction of the Face of Dante Alighieri by Means of Techniques of Virtual Reality and Forensic Anthropology," *Conservation Science in Cultural Heritage* 7 (2007): 379–409, https://doi.org/10.6092/issn .1973-9494/1262; "The Face of the Poet Dante Alighieri Reconstructed by Virtual Modelling and Forensic Anthropology Techniques," *Journal of Archaeological Science* 36 (2009): 278–283.

17 Benazzi et al., "Face of the Poet," 282–283. Maria Martinelli directed the documentary, *Dante: The Unrevealed Poet* (Zeeva Production, 2007). The trailer is available on YouTube, https://www.youtube.com/watch?v=83A7rW_xpD8.

18 Marta Falconi (Associated Press), "Dante's New Look," *Live Science,* January 13, 2007, https://www.livescience.com/1220-dante.html; Philip Pullella, "Dante Gets Posthumous Nose Job—700 Years On," Reuters, January 21, 2007, https://www .reuters.com/article/us-italy-dante/dante-gets-posthumous-nose-job-700-years-on -idUSL1171092320070111.

19 Teodolinda Barolini, "An Ivy League Professor Weighs In," *Entertainment Weekly,* February 26, 2010.

20 "Dan Brown," *Forbes,* accessed November 15, 2019, https://www.forbes.com/profile /dan-brown; Bob Minzesheimer and Christopher Schnaars, "Dan Brown's 'Inferno' Tops All Book Sales in 2013," *USA Today,* January 15, 2014, https://www.usatoday.com/story /life/books/2014/01/15/usa-today-best-selling-books-of-2013/4451561; "Inferno (2016)," IMDb (Internet Movie Database), https://www.imdb.com/title/tt3062096; Zak Wojnar, "Was Inferno a Box Office Success?," *Screenrant,* November 17, 2016, https://screenrant .com/inferno-2016-box-office-success-bomb.

21 "Visions of Hell," special feature, *Inferno,* dir. Ron Howard, DVD (Sony Pictures Home Entertainment, 2017).

22 Dan Brown, *Inferno* (New York: Doubleday, 2013), 176, 166–167.

23 Alessandro D'Ancona, *La "Maschera di Dante" donata al Comune di Firenze dal Senatore Alessandro D'Ancona* (Florence: Barbèra, 1911), 11, 18–19.

24 Brown, *Inferno,* 169; Corrado Ricci, *L'ultimo rifugio di Dante Alighieri* (Milan: Hoepli, 1891), 278–285; "Portraits of Dante," *Bodleian Quarterly Record* 2, no. 14 (1917): 53–57.

25 Brown, *Inferno,* 66, 255, 460.

26 "Pope Francis Leads Celebration for Dante," *ANSA,* May 5, 2015, http://www.ansa .it/english/news/lifestyle/arts/2015/05/04/benigni-reads-dante-in-senate_2a2f6c95-b785 -4f8a-9084-d5519bb6598e.html.

27 Dante looks back at the Earth in *Paradiso* 22.133–153 and 27.79–87. Junno Arocho Esteves, "Pope Commemorates the 750th Anniversary of Dante Alighieri's Birth," *Zenit,* May 4, 2015, https://zenit.org/articles/pope-commemorates-the-750th-anniversary-of -dante-alighieri-s-birth/; Eugenio Giani, "Samantha Cristoforetti legge Dante dallo spazio," YouTube, April 24, 2015, https://www.youtube.com/watch?v=_KgqC_WWFa4.

28 Ilaria Ulivelli, "Sette secoli di guerre, ora le reliquie di Dante tornano a Firenze," *La Nazione,* July 30, 2019, https://www.lanazione.it/firenze/cronaca/resti-dante-1 .4717073.

29 Over five million tourists arrived in Florence in 2018: "Number of Tourist Arrivals in the Italian City of Florence from 2012 to 2018," Statista, November 18, 2019, https://www.statista.com/statistics/722438/tourist-arrivals-in-florence-italy/.

Acknowledgments

I am pleased to recognize the individuals and institutions that supported the creation of this book. Fellowships from the National Endowment for the Humanities, the American Council of Learned Societies, and the University of Texas (UT) at Austin provided essential research and writing time. A Humanities Research Award and a Special Research Grant from UT helped cover research expenses.

A project of this scope is unthinkable without the participation of many interlocutors. Colleagues and friends at UT and other institutions pushed me to discover, develop, and present my ideas for the book. I greatly appreciate the feedback and encouragement I received from Thomas Mussio, Daniela Bini, Antonella Del Fattore-Olson, Douglas Biow, Paola Bonifazio, Cinzia Russi, David Birdsong, Carl Blyth, Alexandra Wettlaufer, Michael Johnson, Hervé Picherit, Marc Bizer, Karen Pagani, Barbara Bullock, Marjorie Woods, Alison Frazier, Hannah Wojciehowski, Joseph Luzzi, Akash Kumar, Kristina Olson, Elizabeth Coggeshall, Teodolinda Barolini, Jeffrey Schnapp, Peter Hawkins, Giuseppe Mazzotta, Theodore Cachey Jr., Nancy Vickers, Albert Ascoli, Regina Psaki, Karen Christianson, Maria Cecire, Christian Dupont, Simone Marchesi, Dennis Looney, Deborah Parker, Scott Mendel, Christopher Kleinhenz, John Ayanian, Virginia Jewiss, and the late María Rosa Menocal and Peter Bondanella. I owe a special debt of gratitude to Arielle Saiber for helping me see the shape and significance of this project from proposal to publication.

I am fortunate to teach courses on Dante's *Divine Comedy* and its cultural afterlife each year at the University of Texas at Austin. Discussing the poem and related works with bright, inquisitive students at all levels—from first-year Longhorns to dissertating doctoral students—helped me figure out what I had to say and, just as important, how best to say it.

Two world-class library systems, at Columbia University and the University of Texas at Austin, provided the overwhelming majority of published sources required for my research, and when an item was not part of their collections, the interlibrary loan folks at UT-Austin astounded me with their ability to put works from other libraries in the United States and other nations before my eyes. I hope readers benefit as much as I have from visual documentation of Dante's graveyard history. For assistance in obtaining images, I thank Elisa Valentini, Stephanie Vyce, Anita Israel, Chris Wirth, Giorgio Gruppioni, Susanna Pelle, Alessandra Casamassima, Robbi Siegel, Alessandra Altomare, Floriana Amicucci, Attilio Terragni, Elizabeth Garver, Chris Bryce, Emily Watson, Vickie Kight, and Ishtiak Rahman.

I am grateful to the professionals at Harvard University Press for using their special skills and resources to transform my obsession with Dante's afterlife into this book. The editorial journey began with John Kulka's warm reception of my cold pitch at the 2016 gathering of the Modern Language Association in Austin, Texas, and continued with Sharmila Sen and Heather Hughes's exemplary combination of know-how, determination, and kindness in preparing my work to go out into the world. I am also profoundly grateful to two expert readers for giving detailed suggestions to improve the manuscript and for catching more than a few errors and infelicities. I thank Andrew Katz for copyediting the manuscript and Cheryl Hirsch for seeing the work through production. I alone am responsible for all flaws in the book.

As I began to read and write about Dante's graveyard history, I enjoyed musing on the topic while ambling through the Pinetum in New York City's Central Park. Cypress may be the traditional evergreen of cemeteries, but pine has been my totem tree for this book. The poet's imagining of the "ancient forest" at the summit of Mount Purgatory—modeled on the pine forest outside Ravenna—consoled me when my father was laid to rest in Pinelawn Cemetery on eastern Long Island, not far from my childhood home. Dante's trees inevitably transport me back to this home, where I remember spending countless hours romping in the surrounding pine woodland. Once upon a time, my sister, Grace—to whom I dedicate this book—bravely climbed one of those trees, badly gashing her leg in the process, to rescue her kitten. I thank her and the rest of my New York and Florida families for keeping me mindful of where I've come from and where I'm going.

For wise counsel, fierce support, and the brilliant example of her own work, I am most deeply indebted to Helene Meyers, the woman who made my heart sing when I first laid eyes on her and heard her voice thirty-three years ago. I believed in *beshert* before I learned the meaning of that word (from her, I'm sure) and am ever grateful for having found mine. Her loving companionship affirms the logo printed on my favorite T-shirts: *Life Is Good!*

Index